ITALIAN FASCISTS ON TRIAL,

1943-1948

ITALIAN FASCISTS ON 1943 TRIAL 1948

ROY PALMER DOMENICO

THE UNIVERSITY OF NORTH CAROLINA PRESS

CHAPEL HILL & LONDON

Library of Congress Cataloging-in-
Publication Data
Domenico, Roy Palmer.
   Italian fascists on trial, 1943–1948 / by
Roy Palmer Domenico.
      p.   cm.
Includes bibliographical references and
index.
ISBN 0-8078-2006-7 (alk. paper)
   1. Italy—Politics and government—
1943–1947.   2. Italy—Politics and
government—1945–   3. Fascism—
Italy—History—20th century.   4. Anti-
fascist movements—Italy—History—
20th century.   I. Title.
DG572.D56   1991
945.091—dc20   91-50251
                              CIP

CONTENTS

A section of illustrations follows p. xii.

ACKNOWLEDGMENTS

So much of historical investigation is a collaborative effort. The historian owes debts to those who came before, and to his or her contemporaries. Teachers, colleagues, archivists, librarians, and friends have all contributed here. I must and, more important, I want to thank them for all their help. If the reader uncovers errors in this work, they represent my own failings, and they occur in spite of the best efforts of these good people. At Rutgers University, Victoria de Grazia has never failed to be an invaluable guide through this endeavor. John Gillis, Harold Poor, Michael Curtis, and Norman Markowitz read and reread the text and were always helpful. I also benefited from a Rutgers University History Department fellowship that allowed me a year's study in Europe.

Other scholars have added valuable insights and have corrected so many of my mistakes. Charles F. Delzell, Alexander DeGrand, and Maurice Neufeld, and Lewis Bateman, Sandra Eisdorfer, and Suzanne Bell of the University of North Carolina Press, deserve special thanks and much more praise than I can ever express. I must make special mention, furthermore, of Lamberto Mercuri. His assistance and the hospitality that he and his wife, Vera, showed to me in Rome will be forever appreciated. Many archivists and librarians also donated their time and attention to aid in my research. I want to thank, in particular, Mario Missori and Gianni Paone at the Archivio Centrale dello Stato in Rome, Gaetano Grassi at Milan's Istituto Nazionale per la Storia del Movimento di Liberazione in Italia, John Taylor at the National Archives and Records Service in Washington, D.C., and the many unsung heroes at Rutgers University's Alexander Library and the Upsala College Library. I am also grateful to the National Italian American Foundation, which generously provided financial assistance toward the publication of this book.

Eternal thanks, moreover, to the many colleagues and friends who have cheerfully shouldered too much of my burden: David Barry, Lynn Berrettoni, Kelly Boyd, Mario Caruso, Jim Donado, Jim Fisher, Chris

Jespersen, Andy Koczon, Moses Matai, Jonathan Nashel, Gerry Noske, Arthur Paulson, Sallie Pisani, John Rossi, George Sirgiovanni, Laura Tabili, and Susanna Treesh. To my dear friends Lil and Gene Minogue, and the whole Minogue clan, to my sister, Linda, my brothers, Tom and Tony, and their families, and above all, to my wife, Robin, who has put up with so much and endured this so well, eternal gratitude and love. Finally, my most profound debt, which can never be adequately repaid, is reserved for my parents, Barbara and Palmer Domenico.

CHRONOLOGY OF EVENTS

October 22, 1922. The Fascist "March on Rome": the first formal step in the establishment of Mussolini's regime.

January 3, 1925. Mussolini announces the establishment of his dictatorship.

February 11, 1929. The signing of the Lateran Pacts between Italy and the church.

May 9, 1936. Mussolini announces the foundation of the Italian Empire after the conquest of Ethiopia by forces under the command of Pietro Badoglio.

June 10, 1940. Italy declares war on Great Britain and France.

December 11, 1941. Italy declares war on the United States.

July 10, 1943. Allied forces land in Sicily.

July 25–26, 1943. After the Fascist Grand Council votes him out of power, Mussolini is arrested by order of King Victor Emmanuel III. The Italian government is placed in the hands of Pietro Badoglio, who immediately outlaws the Fascist party.

September 8–9, 1943. Flight of the king and Badoglio to Brindisi, creating the so-called Kingdom of the South (Regno del Sud) and leaving most of Italy to Hitler's armies. The Allies land at Salerno.

September 23–28, 1943. A liberated Mussolini creates a northern Italian collaborationist regime under German control, the Italian Social Republic (Repubblica Sociale Italiana [RSI], otherwise known as the Salò Republic).

January 28–29, 1944. Congress of anti-Fascist parties at Bari calls for the immediate abdication of Victor Emmanuel.

March 13, 1944. The Soviet Union recognizes the Italian government. The United States and Great Britain immediately follow suit. The Communist leader Palmiro Togliatti calls for a government of national unity and suggests that the issue of the monarchy, "the institutional question," be postponed until the end of the war.

April 12, 1944. Persuaded by Liberals Benedetto Croce and Enrico De Nicola, Victor Emmanuel decides to surrender his powers, but not the crown itself, to his son, Umberto, upon the liberation of the city of Rome.

April 22, 1944. Badoglio forms Italy's first "political" ministry since 1922 by including in it representatives of anti-Fascist parties.

May 26, 1944. Administrative machinery is enacted to activate RDL 29/B. On June 2, Carlo Sforza is placed in charge of the "Zaniboni Commission."

June 1, 1944. Provisions of RDL 29/B and the May 26 decree are applied to all the Kingdom of the South. They are essentially invalidated with the liberation of Rome.

June 4–10, 1944. Rome is liberated by the Allies. Badoglio's ministry is replaced by one composed exclusively of the six parties of the Comitato di Liberazione Nazionale. Ivanoe Bonomi, of the minuscule Labor Democrats, becomes prime minister. Included in the cabinet are Alcide De Gasperi, head of the Christian Democrats, Togliatti, the Socialist Giuseppe Saragat, Croce, Guido De Ruggiero of the Action party, the Liberal Marcello Soleri, and Admiral Raffaele De Courten.

June 26, 1944. Charles Poletti, the Allied military governor of Rome, issues Administrative Order Number 1, which begins a purge of the capital.

July 27, 1944. Publication of Decreto legislativo luogotenenziale number 159, the centerpiece of anti-Fascist punishment, which creates the High Commission for Sanctions against Fascism. Under Carlo Sforza, four commissions are established to punish Fascists: one concerned with property confiscated from the party; another to sequester Fascist profits; a third to prosecute Fascists, under Mario Berlinguer; and a fourth, under Mauro Scoccimarro, to purge Fascists from the government.

September 18, 1944. The first High Court trial, of Pietro Caruso, erupts into a riot that ends in the death of Donato Carretta, former governor of Regina Coeli Prison.

September 22, 1944. Caruso is executed.

November–December 1944. Sforza and Scoccimarro are under increasing attack in the Bonomi cabinet.

November 10, 1944. Scoccimarro's interview in *Avanti!* publicizes interministerial conflicts over the purge.

November 17, 1944. General Mario Roatta is arrested.

December 6, 1944. Fearful of his impending arrest, Badoglio requests sanction at the British embassy.

December 12, 1944. Creation of the second Bonomi ministry.

December 14–23, 1944. Trial of Generals Riccardo Pentimalli and Ettore Del Tetto.

December 20–23, 1944. Trial of Cornelia Tanzi.

December 27, 1944. First issue of Guglielmo Giannini's popular right-wing newspaper, *L'Uomo Qualunque*. Sforza resigns as high commissioner.

January 1945. Bonomi becomes de jure head of the High Commission. He chooses Renato Boeri as his first assistant and replaces Scoccimarro with Ruggiero Grieco. Berlinguer retains his position.

January 15, 1945. Ambush and death of neo-Fascist provocateur Giuseppe "Gobbo" Albani.

March 4, 1945. Mario Roatta escapes from prison.

March 7, 1945. Demonstration and riot in Rome over the Roatta affair.

April 9–14, 1945. Allies launch the ultimate offensive against Germans in the north.

April 16–May 11, 1945. Trial of Umberto Salvarezza.

April 19, 1945. German military collapse in northern Italy begins.

April 25–May 1, 1945. Popular uprising against the Germans and Mussolini throughout the north. People's courts to try Fascists are soon replaced by the government's Special Assize Courts (the Corti straordinarie di Assise), established under DLL number 142 of April 22, 1945. Organization of CLN Azienda factory purge committees.

April 28, 1945. Mussolini, former Fascist party secretary Achille Starace, and other Fascist leaders (*gerarchi*) are shot.

May 2, 1945. Anglo-American administrators enter Milan.

May 11, 1945. First group of Roman politicians are permitted to travel to Milan.

June 19, 1945. Ferruccio Parri of the Action party assumes the prime minister's office from Bonomi. Pietro Nenni is chosen to head the High Commission. Grieco is replaced at the purge subcommission by Domenico Peretti Griva. Berlinguer retains his position.

July 14–22, 1945. Guido Donegani affair.

July 17, 1945. Massacre of fifty-five Fascists in Schio Prison.

August 1945. Trials of Marshal Philippe Pétain in France and Vidkung Quisling in Norway.

October 5, 1945. DLL 625 leads to the end of the Corti straordinarie di Assise.

October 31, 1945. Coltano Prison is closed.

November 4, 1945. Guido Gonella's article "Il mito dell'epurazione" in *Il Popolo* attacks the purge.

November 9, 1945. DLL 702, the "Nenni Law," threatens a broader purge at the higher ranks.

December 11, 1945. The Parri ministry falls and is replaced by one headed by Alcide De Gasperi.

1946–48. Continued anti-Fascist violence in the north.

January 1, 1946. The Allied Commission is formally concluded throughout most of Italy.

March 31, 1946. The High Commission for Sanctions against Fascism is replaced by a "mopping-up" office under Domenico Carugno. Most remaining purge activities are entrusted to the respective ministries.

April 1946. Neo-Fascists sieze control of a Rome radio station to broadcast the blackshirt hymn "Giovinezza"; others rob Mussolini's corpse from its resting place.

May 9, 1946. Victor Emmanuel abdicates and is succeeded by his son, Umberto II.

June 2, 1946. The referendum ends the Italian monarchy. Huge Christian Democratic electoral victory: 35.2 percent against 20.7 percent for the Socialists and 19 percent for the PCI.

June 22, 1946. The Togliatti amnesty is issued.

December 26, 1946. Establishment of Neo-Fascist Movimento Sociale Italiano (MSI) in Rome.

January 1947. De Gasperi travels to the United States.

May 31, 1947. De Gasperi's fourth ministry, formed without the parties of the political Left.

October 1947. MSI participates in Rome municipal elections.

December 22, 1947. The Italian Constitution is ratified.

April 18, 1948. National elections yield absolute majority for the Christian Democrats. With 2 percent of the vote, the MSI receives six deputies and one senator.

November 25, 1948. Carabinieri commander Caruso reports to Rome that the Emilian insurrection has been crushed.

*Pietro Caruso, on crutches, is led into the High Court during his trial,
September 1944. Charles Poletti is seated in the first row at left. Also visible,
behind Caruso's shoulder, is Mario Berlinguer. (Charles Poletti Papers,
Herbert H. Lehman Suite, Rare Book and Manuscript Library, Columbia
University)*

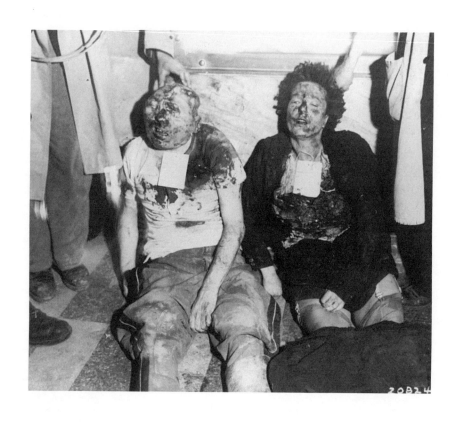

The bloodied and disfigured corpses of Benito Mussolini and Claretta Petacci are displayed in liberated Milan, April 1945. (Andrew Koczon)

A Fascist captured by partisans in newly liberated Milan. (Fernando Etnasi,
Cronache col mitra *[Milan, 1965])*

*The Socialist leader Pietro Nenni assumed the direction of the High
Commission for Sanctions against Fascism in Prime Minister Ferruccio
Parri's government. (Maria Francesca Occhipinti,* Signori D'Italia nei
fotoritratti di Ghitta Carell *[Milan, 1978]), courtesy Longanesi and Co.*

Rodolfo Graziani enters the courtroom for his first trial in the Special Section of the Assize Court, October 1948. He was charged under the terms of Article 51 of the Military War Code. (Paolo Gasparri, ed., Graziani *[Rome, 1962])*

ITALIAN
FASCISTS
ON
TRIAL,
1943-1948

CHAPTER ONE

INTRODUCTION: FASCISM AND REGIME CHANGE

Between 1943 and 1945 Fascists, National Socialists, and collaborators were forced to come to terms with the unstoppable rush of Allied troops, Resistance fighters, and popular violence that has been collectively labeled the liberation of Europe. The leaders and functionaries of crumbling empires feared, waited, and prepared for whatever might come—fates that neither they, nor anyone else, could clearly forecast. What indeed would the war's end bring for the adherents and opportunists of the fallen regimes?

We know, almost fifty years later, many of their destinies. Adolf Hitler, Josef Goebbels, and others took their own lives deep below the streets where raged the hellish battle of Berlin. A good number vanished. But many more lived to face their accusers. Punishments and retribution against them, against members of the old governments, appear to us random and uneven: at once violent and mild. Benito Mussolini's smashed and bloodied corpse, hung upside down from a gas station beam, is seared forever into our images of the Italian dictator. In France jury members shouted "swine" at Pierre Laval before he was propped up, half dead, before his firing squad.[1] Insanely, maniacally defiant to the end, Germany's Julius Streicher hurled invectives at his executioners as a rope was being adjusted around his neck.[2]

Conversely, anti-Fascists all over Europe insisted that not enough

1

had been done to eradicate old tormentors and enemies. Established government programs that dealt with members of the old regimes appeared ineffective to them. For example, anti-Nazis were outraged at the continued presence during the 1950s, within Konrad Adenauer's inner circle, of Hans Globke, a key formulator of the Nuremberg laws and one of Hitler's chief agents in occupied Poland. This dilemma has recently resurfaced in the election of Austria's President Kurt Waldheim.

The problem of punishment, or the lack thereof, against members and supporters of the fascist governments posed a vexing dilemma for the new administrators after World War II and served, in a broader sense, among the most important factors in the dynamics of regime change.[3] In western Europe, the postwar transition from dictatorship to liberal democracy presented the problem of how to deal with fascism and with that Fascist element which still existed within the bureaucratic structure of the new states or among the broader population.

Ideologically inspired mass politics, a feature of twentieth-century life in Europe and America, complicated the issue in that party politics represent large numbers of people. Defeated factions in the modern age are not merely kings or a few politicians but sizable numbers of people on the government payroll and in party ranks who cannot, and should not, be perfunctorily eliminated by firing squad or silenced in prison. Although a good number of the defeated adapt to the new regime and change their spots, many others do not or will not alter their opinions. Napoleon's government fell with his military defeat, but Bonapartism did not die at Waterloo.

That the vanquished persevere presents serious dilemmas to the new rulers: How does one deal with the defeated, the ousted, and the deposed? Solutions can take myriad forms, such as financial punishment, ostracism and exile, popular violence, selective or mass executions, prison sentences, purges, amnesty, or accommodation of the old by the new. Most actions taken against members of defeated regimes are intricate combinations of those options and are often collectively termed sanctions.[4]

The French Revolution has served Europeans for two hundred years and, as the standard by which to judge sanctions after a regime change, has particularly frightened conservatives and traditionalists. From Brienne to Robespierre to Bonaparte, that turbulent era introduced and applied revolutionary ideology to regime change. As such, it also inaugurated the Terror, in which forty thousand leaders, functionaries, and hangers-on of the *ancien régime* systematically met their deaths. The Terror cast an image of ruthless and almost wanton slaughter onto conceptions of regime change. Karl Marx's subsequent warning of a proletarian specter haunting Europe and the experience of the Paris Commune both contributed to that fear and reinforced conservatives' beliefs that the Left would adopt severe and brutal recriminations, should it ever come to power. But the French Revolution and the Commune represented those rare moments in western Europe when the Left took, or could take, retribution against the Right. Some of the irony in the postwar western European experience was that anti-Fascist sanctions were devised and applied for the most part by moderate and conservative governments with, at most, some Left representation in a coalition. Sanctions would be enforced not by Robespierres but by Talleyrands.[5]

Italy's government chose to deal with members of the old Fascist regime mainly between 1943 and 1948, that is, between the first "coup" against Benito Mussolini and the consolidation of the Italian Republic under Alcide De Gasperi. The Duce's dictatorship had collapsed in stages, commencing with the Fascist Grand Council meeting that removed him from power in July 1943 and concluding with the final Axis defeat in April–May 1945. It was ultimately replaced by an anti-Fascist coalition government. A popular referendum in June 1946 abolished the monarchy and ushered in a republic. The transition was completed by Italy's firm inclusion in the American-led Western bloc against the Soviet Union and by the expulsion of Socialists and Communists from De Gasperi's government. In his seminal work on political justice, Otto Kirchheimer wrote that "prosecutions take place at the strategic juncture when the old regime has been replaced and the incoming one prepares to sit in judgment over it." It was during precisely this period, 1943 to 1948, that sanctions and punishments against Fascists were formulated, applied, and abandoned.[6]

This work is foremost an investigation of anti-Fascist sanctions as represented within the dynamics of regime change. How did the progression from a Fascist dictatorship to a transitional regime with civil liberties and, eventually, to a republic affect the course of anti-Fascist sanctions? What were the goals of those who advocated punishment? Who were the targets of such measures, and why were they targeted? What means were used to punish or deal with leaders and functionaries of the old regime, and what reactions did this project elicit?

My aim is not to write a political history of postwar Italy, or to study neofascism or antifascism, although those tasks help us to understand the nature of punishments. Nor is this a history of the dismantling of Fascist institutions. My study instead uses these and other phenomena to examine the tensions between Italian government approaches to sanctions, whether these approaches were sincerely motivated or not, and conservatives' attempts to resist and circumvent them and remain ensconced in their positions of influence, authority, and power. Italian conservatives led the fight against punishments through pressure and argument as well as through reliance on centrist allies and the Anglo-American occupying forces—although the latter occasionally surprised the conservatives by advocating determined retributive justice.

Those who undertook sanctions against Fascists were immediately bewildered by the enormity of their task. The first problem concerned the offense itself. What was fascism, and why should it constitute a crime?[7] After the 1943 coup, many Italians, although far from all of them, wanted to define and label a crime of fascism, or at least a crime of which Fascists had been guilty. Belief in the ideology or even party membership had never been a felony; laws would thus have to be enacted in order to chastise people for something that had never been a crime. A second dilemma to haunt prosanctionists concerned those actually guilty. If fascism was now a crime, or if something Fascists did now constituted a wrong, who, then, would be targeted for punishment?

The search for answers was illustrated in debates between those who considered fascism as a class-based phenomenon and those who saw it as an individual condition. Had the dictatorship been an enslavement of forty million Italians by a narrow camarilla or by a ruling class? It was authoritarian, to be sure. But as a modern government, maintained in an advanced society for twenty years, it received at least the tacit endorsement of a large number of Italians. Through sophisticated propaganda efforts, leisure activities, and other policies to either regiment or persuade the people, Mussolini attempted to elicit the consensus of all segments of the population.[8] Renzo De Felice has written that the Duce practically achieved that consensus in 1936 with the conquest of Ethiopia.[9] Even Italy's Christian Democratic prime minister Giulio Andreotti has conceded that if the Duce had died on the day of that victory, he might have gone down in history as one of the nation's most popular leaders.[10] Before 1943 some brave souls declared their opposition to the regime. But most Italians did not follow these determined anti-Fascists, who left the country or joined clandestine subversive organizations. Some even resented the self-imposed exiles, the *fuorusciti*, as either pampered intellectuals who could afford to while away their time on the Riviera (which was, of course, rarely true) or, even worse, who treasonously worked in international conspiracies against Italy's well-being. Most Italians, rather, stayed and lived and worked and even voted during the dictatorship. When one is secure as head of state, as was the Duce for most of the dictatorship, he commands a ready-made constituency that supports and obeys the leader, as a statement of patriotism. Mussolini created such a situation where acquiescence and endorsement in the 1930s became guilt in the 1940s, which could conceivably engulf millions.

Approached as a class-based phenomenon, all ranks of Italian society had maintained their own ambivalent relations with the regime. The working class was tainted the least; but even here fascism worked its attempt at consensus. Beyond certain renegades and mavericks like Nicola Bombacci, older Socialists or Communists who had participated in the struggles of the first postwar era did not abandon their Marxism to join the blackshirts. Other workers, nevertheless, did not owe their first allegiance to the Left, and by the late 1930s, the Partito Nazionale Fascista (PNF) had made inroads among many young laborers who took out party cards if for no other reason than to get or keep their jobs.[11]

Italy's middle class remains the most problematic group in the consensus story. Much of fascism's promise was directed toward the *ceto medio*, but little is known of its adherence to the regime. Many historians such as Edward Tannenbaum have agreed with Wolfgang Sauer's conception that fascism appealed primarily to beleaguered peasants, small businessmen, white-collar workers, artisans, and craftsmen, and it was toward them that the party directed its most sophisticated propaganda.[12] They were told that to live one day as a lion was better than a thousand years as a sheep. Women donated wedding rings at the *altare della patria* to bring victory over the Ethiopians. Boys trained as soldiers with sticks instead of guns at the Campi Dux. At the movies, action stories like "Lo Squadrone Bianco" or "Scipio L'Africano" glorified expansion into Africa, while pastiches such as "Signor Max" took the rough edges off a totalitarian society. And whether the message was painted on a wall, printed on a poster, or carved in marble, Italians everywhere were told to "Believe! Obey! Fight!"

Beyond the working and middle classes, it is usually assumed that the ruling class sustained Mussolini's regime. Yet, although its support was essential for the dictatorship's continued existence, relations between the two were complex.[13] Each major segment within it—the crown,[14] the military,[15] the church,[16] the aristocracy,[17] the magistracy,[18] and big business,[19]—maintained its own particular stance on fascism. No ruling class is ever completely united, but Italy's possessed a strong traditionalist current, desirous of popular order, socially conservative, and anti-Communist. Materially and ideologically, traditionalists within the ruling class feared an antifascism that they characterized as Marxist. The worst excess of that antifascism was a demand for purges and trials to cleanse the nation and ensure the growth of democracy. Conservatives naturally questioned such serious measures, which they felt would weaken Italy's social structure and their own positions within it. By defeating a purge, conservatives could adapt to the post-Fascist political situation on their own terms. In keeping with Robert Michels's "iron law of oligarchy," members of the new anti-Fascist political, and occasionally economic, elite then successfully merged with the older, traditionalist group to form the country's leadership for the postwar era.[20]

The center of battle over sanctions lay in what has been termed the political class. Most ideological positions on the issue rested on interpretations over the size of this class, its connections to others, and the validity of focusing on it. The Italian conservative philosopher Gaetano Mosca and others, such as T. S. Bottomore, have written that an elite does not govern from a lofty position above society but rather is intimately connected to it through this peculiar sub-elite. Mosca considered this much larger group of civil servants, managers, white-collar workers, scientists, engineers, scholars, and intellectuals to be "an organized minority within the masses themselves to discharge the functions of the ruling class."[21] The very complex relationships between this sub-elite and that sector of the ruling class that had been pro-Fascist during the *ventennio*, the twenty-year regime, illustrate the problem in identifying the guilty of fascism. It was exactly this spider's web connecting ideology, party, state, and society that plagued the application of anti-Fascist sanctions. Punishments, whether formal or popular, were such that they concentrated on that political rank below the ruling class —those bureaucrats, police officials, soldiers, and others who, for many reasons, bore the Fascist stigma.

The problem of determining the guilt of Mussolini and his followers was further complicated by the rather unique formal and legal connections between state and party. After twenty years of starts and stops, thrusts and parries, the Duce had created a confusing dual system of two bureaucracies, state and Fascist, that paralleled, overlapped, and conflicted. In Rome, many ministerial offices were mirrored in party agencies. In the provinces, the nuances of power directed inquiries either to the prefectural office or to the local *fascio*, the party headquarters. Those whose goal was to find the truly guilty of the regime, therefore, approached a puzzle of many scattered pieces. Those whose aim was to prevent an effective sanctions program could only benefit from that confusion.[22]

Conscious resistance to sanctions provided the first crucial dynamic in the history of anti-Fascist measures, but other factors were also at work. Virtually the entire program, for example, was devised and applied in a world of extreme deprivation. Writing over forty years later, it is easy to forget that Italy in the mid-1940s suffered as one of the key battlefields of World War II. To carry out any government program at all in the midst of such chaos and scarcity was an exercise in frustration and failure. A politically charged endeavor, like sanctions, was burdened by these extra handicaps.

Further, while not wholly adopting Pareto's dictum that "the greater part of human actions have their origin not in logical reasoning but sentiment," I would argue that contravention to sanctions was not based exclusively on class or material interest.[23] Cultural, legal, and socio-psychological phenomena, while manipulated by antisanctionists, also stood on their own to hamper application of punishments. For example, important themes in traditional Italian and Western culture worked against sanctions. Italy's Christian and juridical heritages counseled forgiveness over retribution and abhorred notions of criminality based on laws passed ex post facto.

These cultural and religious elements tended to modify or soften the harshly political edges of punishments. Purges and prosecutions taken against members of a fallen regime leave a bitter taste. They smack of revenge and vendetta against the defeated. Whether or not the Fascists were defenseless and abused victims in Italy from 1943 until 1948 was immaterial, since it was the perception of vindictiveness, not the reality, that tempered events.[24] In the wake of the horrible barbarity of World War II, such matters of punishment confused even the wisest judges.[25] Even in Germany, despite the enormity of the crimes involved, considerable discussion and doubt plagued the Nuremberg Trials. Later, in her *Eichmann in Jerusalem*, Hannah Arendt wondered whether any type of punishment could equal the terrible pain of those who suffered at the hands of Hitler's henchmen. Such indecision, on another scale, plagued the application of punishments against Italian Fascists, an indecision that haunted the political Left as well as the Right.[26]

To support the culture or appearance of magnanimity, a network of juridical principles has been constructed over the centuries—guidelines that acted as breaks on sanctions against Italian Fascists. In Italy, the phrase *nullem crimen sine legge* was employed by countless lawyers and jurists who were doubtful of the validity of purges and trials. Applied here, it meant that no one should be prosecuted in 1945 for something done, say, in 1925, when no law had prohibited it. One should not be tried, for example, for holding a high-ranking position in the Duce's regime when, during the accused's tenure, it had not been illegal to do so. *Nullem crimen sine legge* implied that the blackshirts had become victims of a politicized and vengeful Italian government with no respect for fairness and legal tradition.

Juridical arguments against punishments were reinforced by moral ones. The political vehicle in Italy for the propagation of traditional morality was the Christian Democratic party (DC). Many of its adherents used Catholic discourse in twofold arguments against stringent sanctions. Forgiveness, among the most powerful and noble virtues in the Western/Christian tradition, should figure prominently in the ideology of such a party—particularly in a discussion of sanctions against Fascists.[27] Forgiveness might have also been used as part of the DC's tacit commitment to protect segments of its electoral base. The breadth and depth of Christian Democratic strength rested on a predominantly centrist or conservative middle class. Rallying to their interests must have complemented the party's stance on sanctions.

Along with the juridical and cultural/religious factors, sanctions were hampered by what might be loosely termed sociopsychological motives. The events of 1943–48 were clearly motivated by a reluctance to grapple with the fascism of the *ventennio*, that is, Mussolini's dictatorship of 1922(5)–43, and to focus instead on the collaborationist regime at Salò. The earlier, more profound, chapter of Italian history was ignored to concentrate on a brief government that could be better targeted under the more facile concept of treason.

The focus on collaborationists paralleled another tendency: directing blame at certain Fascist "types." Those prosecuted were often fascism's most notorious symbols and not necessarily those who bore responsibility for the regime. They were the ones most easily identified as Fascists—Mussolini and the rest of the *gerarchi* seen by all in the newsreels, or local figures like policemen so prominent in the neighborhood. Also important were those icons of corrupt and decaying regimes, such as plainclothes henchmen and girlfriends. The phenomenon of "notoriety" relates to Weberian concepts of "charisma" and helps to understand the history of sanctions. Using Max Weber's framework, the charismatic, as opposed to bureaucratic, nature of Mussolini's dictatorship made it at least appear as "the very opposite of the institutionally permanent." Fascism's quick initial "collapse" in July 1943 seemed to confirm its image as an imposition or a false construction on top of Italy's society and political body. Italians chose the narrow option to direct sanctions against collaborationists and "types," illustrating a motivation to evade the painful and difficult trauma of a national self-evaluation and extensive punishments. Beyond not inaugurating sanctions at all, aiming at the obnoxious blackshirt became the best choice for those who doubted or feared the premise of the whole notion of sanctions.

Other social scientists, such as Edward Shils, Clifford Geertz, and Suzanne Keller, have investigated the problem of elites, symbols, and class. Keller, for example, has clarified the issue for us by blending charisma and "visibility" with our conceptions of political class, labeling a critical segment of national administrators the "strategic elite."

9

These are people so closely associated with the government that they come to symbolize it.[28] For our concerns, the most visible targets were Mussolini himself and his coterie of officials, the *gerarchi*. It is still impossible to envision the *ventennio* without thinking of Benito Mussolini. Carlo Scorza's famous words, "Fascism is you, oh Duce!" illustrate the persistent conception of the regime as merely "Mussolinism" writ large. As the "originator" of fascism, its very symbol, and the *capo del governo*, the Duce more than anyone embodied the strategic elite. Any purge naturally would be obsessed with him and might, thus, limit itself to the prosecution of a few politicians and lower-level personnel like policemen. Its focus could then shift away from any profound analysis of fascism in society.[29]

Events of 1943–48 reveal that serious attempts to craft sanctions against political criminals were doomed to failure because many Italians could not or would not consider fascism per se an offense. And if ideology were not on trial, then what purpose did sanctions serve? Juridical, cultural/religious, and sociopsychological factors, then, in combination with the trouble encountered from the Italian Center-Right, the Allies, and from the logistical pressures of war, lead us to insist that the nation's main organization for sanctions, the High Commission for Sanctions against Fascism, was misnamed. These were sanctions against Fascists, not fascism.

CHAPTER TWO

THE OLD ORDER PASSES?

In the early hours of September 9, 1943, Victor Emmanuel III, king of Italy and Albania and emperor of Ethiopia, used the cover of night to sneak out of his capital, Rome. The king's entourage included his prime minister, Marshal Pietro Badoglio, and an assortment of functionaries and officers: tired men who constituted a vague nucleus of the Italian government. Their obscured escape formed part of a dramatic and very risky "about face" in which Italy dissolved its ties to Hitler's Germany and joined the Allied cause in World War II. The scenario, however, was complicated by crossed wires and deceit between the Italians and the Anglo-Americans, confusion that forced Victor Emmanuel to abandon Rome and all of northern Italy to the vengeful Nazis. In this, the blackest hour of his ancient dynasty, the monarch left military commands to their fates: some surrendered, others fought desperate yet doomed battles against the German invaders. Still others disbanded their units and went into hiding. Many joined nascent partisan efforts against the Nazis and Fascists. A large number simply chose to go home.

German reaction was more deliberate. Hitler's troops occupied the central and northern parts of the country, rescued Mussolini from a mountaintop prison, and installed him as the puppet ruler of the Italian Social Republic (Repubblica Sociale Italiana [RSI]), or, as it has come to be known, the Salò Republic.

The king abdicated military and political leadership at the moment when it was most needed, seeking to escape the chaos in the north for what was hoped would be a haven in the south, the Mezzogiorno. From Rome the sorry lot headed for the Adriatic port of Pescara and boarded the southbound Royal Italian Navy corvette *Baionetta*. They correctly reasoned that, since the Anglo-Americans were effecting landings at Salerno and in Calabria, the Germans would not bother with the defense of distant regions like Apulia. From there, then, the shreds of government could be patched together, and royalist Italy could join the United Nations in the crusade against Hitler. The last act in the drama took place on October 13, when Italy formally declared war on Germany.[1]

On Friday, September 10, the *Baionetta* reached Brindisi, famous among tourists as the main port for the Greek ferry. In 1943, however, Victor Emmanuel's presence there distinguished the city as the first capital of "liberated Italy," or at least the king's part of it, the Regno del Sud. It was Apulia, the "heel" of the boot, a dry, poor place that embraced Brindisi, Bari, Lecce, and Taranto provinces. Allied forces took the rest of southern Italy; but in this corner of the peninsula the Royal government maintained a veneer of jurisdiction. Everything else below Naples, including Sicily and Sardinia, fell under Anglo-American Military Government of Occupied Territory (AMGOT or later, AMG) and, a few months later, the Allied Control Commission (ACC or later, Allied Commission [AC]), which operated indirectly through local Italian officials.

The flight of the Royal House to Apulia and the Allied military landings in the south created the circumstances for the first chapter in the history of sanctions against fascism. Had the Anglo-Americans opted for Prime Minister Winston Churchill's earlier idea, to invade at the northern end of the Adriatic, and had the king fled north instead of south, events might have played differently. Both fascism and antifascism had left more important legacies in the north. There, the king and the Allies would have discovered a more profound anti-Fascist atmosphere, at least among urban industrial workers and politicized farm workers in the Po Valley. Instead, the testing ground for defascistization would be the Mezzogiorno, with its more traditionalist, patron-client heritage, in an atmosphere where Fascist and conservative demarcations blurred and where attempts to pinpoint groups for punishment would be more difficult.

The figures of the king and his new prime minister further complicated the problem. Had the coup of July 25, 1943, which deposed Mussolini, been a truly popular revolution, then Victor Emmanuel and Badoglio would probably have been replaced by leaders more broadly representative of the Italian political spectrum. But July 25 was not a popular revolution. It had been a palace coup against Mussolini, and the people served only to witness that spectacle. This was no real revolt against fascism; hence, the very first defascistization would be piloted by men who came from sectors most associated with the Fascist regime—the crown and the military. In Rome between July 25 and September 8, and then in Brindisi, the old king's accomplice was Marshal Pietro Badoglio, a leading member of the same military that had served Mussolini by crushing unrest, whether it was in Libya in the 1920s, Ethiopia in the 1930s, or Turin during the 1943 riots.

THE FORTY-FIVE DAYS AND THE REGNO DEL SUD: FASCIST ANTIFASCISM?

Italians have dubbed the period between the July 25 coup and September 8 the "Forty-five Days." It was an exciting time in Italy but a very fluid one, a transition bright with hopes but darkened by fear, doubt, and bloodshed. The sudden demise of the Duce's regime had launched an unexpected but largely inconsequential popular euphoria. With Mussolini gone, many hundreds of anti-Fascists resumed the active, public roles that, because of imprisonment, exile, or intimidation, had been denied to them for two decades. Propaganda sheets and manifestos were ceremoniously burned; many people took their turn to swing a sledgehammer at Mussolini's bust; and fasces were ripped from the sides of buildings. Some of the most vivid photographs of those days display truckloads of Romans waving Italian tricolors as they drove through streets filled with cheering bystanders. Those flags, however, continued to be adorned with the Savoy cross and were often displayed alongside portraits of Victor Emmanuel and Badoglio.

Beyond the first domestic complications generated by Mussolini's downfall, however, Italy remained caught in a desperate international nightmare. Anglo-American troops continued their advance through Sicily. An anxious Germany kept a close watch while Marshal Badoglio declared, in words reminiscent of Kerensky, that "the war continues." German suspicions were well founded, of course, as the prime minister was quietly negotiating with the Allies for an armistice.

The problems of the Forty-five Days were further aggravated by what did remain of Mussolini's dictatorship. The Duce and the notable *gerarchi* may have vanished from public view, but many of them waited in the wings for a chance to resume command. They depended on their National Socialist allies and government functionaries whose lesser ranks afforded them cover from the first ministerial shuffles. Pietro Badoglio understood this, and his attitudes toward Fascists were forged in the context of consolidating his own position. The new prime minister formally dissolved the Duce's PNF and related organizations—like the Fascist Militia and the *federali* network, which had regulated party activity throughout the nation—and he spoke vaguely of a commission to confiscate war profits.

Marshal Badoglio's dismantling of fascism, however, was little more than a reorganization. The Blackshirt Militia, for example, was simply reconstituted into the Italian army, a disastrous move since at one stroke the royalist ground forces received a strong dose of ideological authoritarianism. Many officers found few political problems in immediately switching their allegiance to the new government. Mussolini himself wrote, from confinement, to offer his services. Badoglio took little further action, however, to grapple with defascistization. Beyond the replacement of most cabinet ministers and dismantling of the regime's lower house, the Chamber of Fasces and Corporations, he conceived of no real government purge. Indeed, until late August, Mussolini had been included among only a few Fascists to be arrested.[2]

Despite certain freedoms of expression that it granted to organized political parties, Badoglio's Forty-five Days maintained, rather than dismantled, most of Mussolini's terror state. The secret and brutal OVRA police was not disbanded, and when demonstrators petitioned Rome for peace and bread, they were often met with bullets. No less a figure than the Fascist general Mario Roatta was entrusted with crushing those disturbances. And no words better characterize the Forty-five Days than two of his chilling orders to the troops: "March against the people as if they were the enemy," and "Aiming in the air is not permitted. Always aim to kill as in combat."[3]

By August 18 the minister to the Royal House, Duke Pietro Acquarone, confided that he carried a revolver for his own protection. He had grown alarmed over recent rumors that a group of blackshirts, with Hitler's support, had decided to retake power. Some days later, Badoglio was alerted by General Carboni of military intelligence of such a plot and, on August 25, acted to crush it. The subsequent roundup netted many of the highest *gerarchi*, including Giuseppe Bottai, Achille Starace, and Head of the General Staff Ugo Cavallero. It also resulted in the death of former party secretary Ettore Muti, who, it was said, was shot while attempting to escape after a raid on his beach house at Fregene.[4]

The marshal's vague plans for a purge before September 8 existed largely on paper. Paranoid fear of neo-Fascist *revanche* rather than faith in democratization prompted Badoglio to consider a "defascistization commission," a purge office in embryo for a bifurcated attack, separate assaults against the high and the low bureaucracy. The campaign against the high bureaucracy was the more important and perplexing of the two. Every upper-level government official, from grade 6 (assistant prefect) and up was to be screened by the relevant minister. Lower-ranking bureaucrats would be vetted by a separate commission working in liaison with the ministries and chaired by the esteemed professor and rector of the University of Naples, Adolfo Omodeo. The chaos of September 8, however, guaranteed that this early idea would never be implemented. Whatever had constituted the Omodeo defascistization commission, and whether or not it existed at all, remains unclear. It was dissolved, and its nascent activities were melded into a broader commission under the more important purge measure to come, Decreto legislativo luogotenenziale (DLL), July 27, 1944, number 159.

September 8 should have ended any Italian postures or masquerades as an Axis partner. But even after the Armistice and in its early phase as a cobelligerent in the war against fascism, the Royal government remained embarrassingly close to being staffed by Fascists. It chose to ignore the pasts of several internationally infamous characters and, indeed, admitted them into the ruling structure.

At its highest levels, Badoglio's post–September 8 cabinet contained three men who had served the Fascist regime as ministers or as undersecretaries of state. The minister of war, Antonio Sorice, had held the number two chair in that same office under the Duce. Badoglio's chief of war production, Carlo Favagrossa, occupied the same position under the Fascists, as well as the undersecretariat of state in Mussolini's own office, the Presidenza del Consiglio dei Ministri. Another veteran was Badoglio's minister of finance and foreign exchange (Cambio e delle Valute), Guido Jung, who had played a kind of Hjalmar Schacht role as Mussolini's minister of finance from 1932 until 1935.

Appointments like these soon aroused Anglo-American suspicion. The Allied intelligence unit, the Psychological Warfare Branch (PWB), was particularly concerned with Jung. It believed (incorrectly) that he had been among the original Fascist organizers on Sicily and had apparently hid his Jewish background to support the German alliance. He foolishly lambasted the Sicilian democrats in public for not opposing the liberation of the island, and the Allies promptly threw him in jail. Nevertheless, the Anglo-Americans later released him, and Guido Jung found himself a minister in Badoglio's government.[5]

Jung was joined by many others. General Gastone Gambara, a veteran of the Spanish civil war, was another important Fascist who surfaced at Brindisi. The PWB nervously reported to Washington and London that Badoglio's new police boss (questore) of Bari, Tommaso Penetta, had been an operative of the Fascist secret police, the OVRA.[6]

The most controversial appointment was the army chief of staff, General Mario Roatta. He had headed Mussolini's military secret service and an international terrorist network in the 1930s, commanded Italians in Spain with Gambara, and was accused of war crimes against the Yugoslavs. An early British intelligence report confessed incredulity that anyone with as notorious a past as General Roatta's could be free to walk the streets of Brindisi, much less be entrusted with high rank. Another Political Warfare section memo wondered when Badoglio's regime would adopt a democratic posture in keeping with the anti-Fascist goals of the United Nations. "What of this broad-based Italian Government?" it stated. "Roatta has left my boys speechless." With such characters, the Regno del Sud could not command any true popular support. Its personnel had merely found themselves in the right spot at the right time and had been either asked or coerced into service.[7]

Ties between Mussolini's old cabinets and Badoglio's new ones sank deeper than the minister level. Until a more democratically balanced cabinet was formed in April 1944, virtually all of Badoglio's major underlings had maintained positions in preceding Fascist governments. For instance, although Sorice's successor, General Taddeo Orlando, had not served Mussolini as a minister, he had been a career officer whose past activities were suspect by the Allies. Renato Prunas was another who had matured in Mussolini's Foreign Ministry and now served in it as Badoglio's secretary general. The new minister of the navy, Admiral Raffaele De Courten, saw a long career as one of the most powerful men in that service, both Fascist and "Badogliana."

The presence of men like Orlando, Prunas, and De Courten in Badoglio's government revealed a real and, soon, a persistent problem for defascistization: a problem of degree. On one hand their respective positions—a general, a diplomat, and an admiral—had not been invented by Fascists, nor did they inherently have anything to do with Fascist ideology. For example, as a diplomat, per se, was Prunas a Fascist? Were they and others in like situations liable to purge and prosecutions? Were they truly culpable Fascists, and did that fact really matter for the future of Italy? Where did such descriptive terms as "traditionalist," "conservative," "monarchist," or "rightist" end, and "Fascist" begin? Was Prunas a diplomat or a Fascist diplomat? Mussolini's dictatorship had embraced, among others, a political class of Fascist partisans—ideologues, "reformers," and politicians like Roberto Farinacci, Giuseppe Bottai, and Achille Starace. It also included bureaucrats, military personnel, police, and innumerable other types who held positions of authority closely associated with the regime but who were not necessarily fascist in its ideological or philosophical sense.[8]

The case perhaps most emblematic of the dilemma was that of the prime minister himself, Marshal Pietro Badoglio. Tall and sturdy, he often reminded observers of a stoic and hearty peasant. Yet behind the front there existed one of the most cunning and resourceful minds in Italy. Born in 1871, he rose to prominence as a lieutenant general during World War I. Although Badoglio was among the commanders most at fault for the Caporetto disaster in October 1917, he avoided recriminations and, the next year, had formed, with Armando Diaz and Ugo Cavallero, a military triumvirate that virtually controlled Italy. More devoted to king and country than to fascism, he opposed Mussolini's 1922 March on Rome and recommended use of a whiff of grapeshot to disperse it. However, the Duce recognized talent when he saw it and, instead of holding a grudge, chose to retain Badoglio through the *ventennio* as ambassador to Brazil, army chief of staff, and governor of Cyrenaica and Tripolitania.

Nevertheless, it was Badoglio's conquest of Ethiopia in 1936 that earned him an international reputation. Entering the city of Addis Ababa astride a white horse, the newly created duke was welcomed with Fascist honors and riches. With no more worlds to conquer, Badoglio retired to private life. He opposed the war in Spain and Italy's entrance into World War II but never broadcast his objections in public. His career was resurrected briefly in 1940 as chief of the Commando Supremo, but the miserable show against the British and Greeks ended that. Badoglio spent the balance of the war years mending fences with the House of Savoy and the church.

Badoglio could not be classified as ideologically Fascist. He was not a believer. The *tessera*, or party card, had been pressed on him in the late 1930s, but he never belonged to, nor did he influence, the party's decision-making circle. By 1942 his relations with the PNF had become so strained that no *gerarca* appeared at his wife's funeral, and the pro-Fascist Mondadori publishing house refused to print some of his writings. Rather, the marshal was a soldier of the old school, sworn to serve the monarchy in spite of the company it kept. By 1943 the crown had accepted the marshal's break with Mussolini and chose him to succeed the Duce. Badoglio may not have been a Fascist, but over the years he had profited handsomely from his relation to the regime. Italy was full of lesser Badoglios, and questions over their status would confuse the concept of the punishment of Fascists.[9]

Prefects, many of those lesser Badoglios, also presented a particularly troublesome problem. Under Mussolini, Rome had sent two representatives to each province: the prefect who came from the government and the *federale* from the Fascist party. The latter position was eliminated after the July coup, while the prefects, minions of the king, stayed. Representatives of Royal authority in the provinces, their roles in the purges and prosecution of the Fascists would be crucial. Badoglio and his successors would rely heavily on their networks and local power. However, as the most important officials at the provincial level before, during, and after the dictatorship, the prefects' Fascist connections could not be ignored.

Badoglio was reluctant to challenge that prefectural structure. During the Forty-five Days, from July 25 until September 8, that network remained unharmed. In the eighty-four provinces outside of Sicily, twenty-seven prefects were untouched, and composition of the rest of the force changed hardly at all. Two were substituted with either former Carabinieri or regular military officers. Fifty-five others were replaced in one of three ways: simple rotation to a different post, promotion of an assistant prefect, or replacement by prefects brought out of retirement. Between the Armistice and the liberation of Rome, from September 1943 to June 1944, Badoglio replaced seven more prefects, in Bari, Brindisi, Cagliari, Caltanisetta (twice), Campobasso, Catania, and Catanzaro. Some had been around for a fairly long time, such as Brindisi's Giovan Battista Pontiglione, who held his position from June 7, 1941, until March 10, 1944. It was soon obvious that none of Badoglio's methods changed in any real way the tenor of the prefectural group.[10]

It was often necessary to bring Anglo-American pressure to bear on the marshal for the removal of old prefects. Naples's Domenico Soprano, for example, was fired only after Allied prodding a full month after the city's liberation. The dismissal of the prefect of Taranto on November 15, 1943, was also accomplished after Allied insistence. And in October 1943 they forced out the prefect of Foggia as overly hostile to the new democratic ideals of antifascism. By November 15 that same official, Giuseppe Pieche, resurfaced in the Carabinieri.[11]

Thus, from the start, the Italian government was presented with a vexing problem: how to treat bureaucrats and government officials who, for twenty years, had been loyal to their Duce. Did their presence in the new government create a dilemma for the Allied cause and for Italy's democratic prospects? Whether he wanted to or not, Badoglio would soon be obliged to identify Fascists in his administration and take action against them. Despite the embarrassing presence of Pieche, Roatta, Jung, and others, the marshal began to entertain ideas to cleanse his government of Fascists.

Two months after the Forty-five Days Badoglio launched another half-hearted preliminary purge. A November 4, 1943, circular to the prefects of Taranto, Brindisi, Lecce, and Bari laid the foundations for this attempt at defascistization, but, like the Omodeo commission during the Forty-five Days, nothing concrete would come of it.

Subsequent November directives displayed the uncertainty that would continually plague Italy's treatment of Fascists. For example, the two fundamental purge principles in these guidelines were ambiguous and, indeed, contradictory. The first of them stated that, outside of the RSI, "the Fascist regime . . . is decidedly dead in the minds of Italians." The second principle, however, found that "it is indispensable to eradicate every last vestige of Fascism." Further on, Badoglio's circulars defined the political criteria that seemed designed to exclude more people than it did include in a classification of "Fascist."

Realizing that not every Fascist could be purged or prosecuted and that distinctions had to be made, Badoglio's November notes enumerated four categories in a hierarchy of political crime. But by drawing a line between fascism and more traditional, nonpolitical crime, the marshal appeared to be less interested in prosecuting political figures than in chasing embezzlers, extortionists, and thieves. There was little logic in the marshal's classifications, which betrayed his hasty, slapdash approach. The first class included those who merely had held the party card but did not use it for illicit gains. These were, *"rara avis,"* disillusioned but honest folk. Badoglio would probably have included himself here. The second group included Fascists who not only occupied government positions but also had a hand in the graft or violence that so discredited the regime. "They must be arrested and denounced before the military authorities," Badoglio declared. The third somewhat vague category included street fighters (*squadristi*) and propagandists. The fourth embraced those who did not necessarily take part in politics but who, through illicit methods, obtained the support of the *gerarchi* for protection and favors. Badoglio labeled these last "the most lurid vermin" and demanded that they be discovered and inflexibly prosecuted. He likely emphasized this because the fraud and payoffs of those "lurid vermin" had pushed Italy's, and his, armed forces into a swamp of corruption during the late 1930s. The faulty equipment and false numbers engineered as a result rendered Italy's defenses ineffective in the 1940s.

The prime minister's November circular concluded with cryptic advice: friendships must not get in the way. The purge must be ruthless and total. But friendships and connections, impossible to see on paper, naturally persisted and would always exist in the Italian government, as they do in all governments. Such friendships and connections would contribute to the purge's ruin.[12]

Reaction to Badoglio's instructions immediately indicated that his measures were not as ruthless as envisaged. Within a few days the prefect of Brindisi inquired whether or not those *ex-gerarchi, squadristi,* and *fascisti* who had been stopped by the police should lose their salaries during their absences from office. Badoglio's office replied on December 10 that a suspension was "only a cautionary police measure" that did not call for the loss of a stipend.[13] Furthermore, an unsigned directive to the police stated that the mere possession of a *tessera* meant nothing, and that the government was not interested in "a sterile persecution of a very extensive part of the substantially healthy middle class." Holding a party card signified only "a guarantee or at least a hope for a peaceful existence."[14] This distinction amounted to virtual absolution for simple membership in the PNF. The Badoglio government, in this early decision, had cleared practically everyone from the political crime of being a Fascist, affirming an important approach toward sanctions.

Little serious activity was undertaken by Badoglio and his prefects during the fall and winter of 1943–44. Many, if not most, of the highest-ranking Fascist politicians were either incognito, like Giovanni Papini, who hid out in a monastery; or had fled north to collaborate with Salò, like Renato Ricci and Giovanni Gentile; or languished in Fascist prisons, like Galeazzo Ciano and Emilio De Bono, whose crimes had been to vote against the Duce at the last Grand Council meeting. Many of the smaller fish also seemed to have vanished, a pattern since the first Sicilian towns fell to the Anglo-Americans. When the Allies entered a locality, they usually faced a power vacuum created by Fascist officials who had vacated their offices and had fled with the Germans. And it would be the Anglo-Americans who pushed for and indeed inaugurated most of the initial machinery with which to apply sanctions against fascism.[15]

THE ANGLO-AMERICANS

The power of governance in southern Italy was not monopolized by the Regno del Sud. In fact, even in Apulia itself, Victor Emmanuel's state maintained only the slimmest independence beyond the firm hold of the Anglo-Americans. Italy was the first Axis nation to fall, and each attempt to purge or prosecute Fascists tested not only the Regno's but the Allies' ability to deal with a defeated regime. Unfortunately, the Allies never came up with any strategem to test.

Franklin Roosevelt and Winston Churchill had issued declarations of lofty principles and had endorsed defascistization and democratization at both the conferences in Casablanca and Quebec in 1943. These goals were included in article 30 of the Long Armistice terms and further emphasized in October 1943, after a meeting of the Allied foreign ministers in Moscow. The Long Armistice was signed by General Dwight D. Eisenhower and Badoglio aboard a warship on September 29. Its draconian measures were based on the belief that Italy was a worthless, defeated enemy whose only option was to obey the Allies. Article 30 of the Armistice specified that "the Italian Government will carry out all directives which the United Nations may call for, including the abolition of Fascist institutions, the dismissal and internment of Fascist personnel, the control of Fascist funds, the suppression of Fascist ideologies and teaching." At Moscow, Joseph Stalin and his foreign minister, Vyacheslav Molotov, with Britain's Anthony Eden and America's Cordell Hull, called for a freer Italian government, meaning one without Fascists, and for the release of all anti-Fascists still held in Badoglio's prisons. The consensus among members of the United Nations was thus elaborated, but it remained just that: opinion. While the theory was endorsed, the Allies, at least in their overseas capitals, were never sure of the practice. The Italians were to cleanse their own house of fascism.[16]

Italo-Allied opinions on how to run the peninsula, never really smoothly and cordially coordinated, were complicated by sanctions, that is, by the nagging idea that many leaders in Brindisi should themselves be purged or put on trial. On September 13, for instance, the Allies appointed Major Robert Gorman to investigate charges against Fascists. Gorman's first and chief task was devoted to a study of Mussolini.[17] But, in late 1943, among the next personalities mentioned for sanctions were Badoglio and the king. As with many other issues, however, the Allies parted company and could never present to the Italians a concerted opinion on what to do with Fascists. Nicola Gallerano has observed that until the liberation of Rome, the Americans approached the regime from a different angle than did the British, who supported the Savoy monarchy as the key to any post-Fascist government. Prime Minister Winston Churchill would always make it his personal business to endorse and sustain the monarch, often against the wishes of his advisors, Roosevelt, and many Italians. But not even the British were in total concert over the continued tenure of Victor Emmanuel. Two of London's Foreign Office notes, for example, in December 1943 and January 1944, urged that while the crown should be preserved, London should "openly advise the removal of the King."[18] This ambivalence was not found in Washington, however, and the Americans rarely displayed any faith at all in the monarchy.[19]

Many in President Roosevelt's administration had long sympathized with the plight of the *fuorusciti*, those anti-Fascists who chose to leave Italy in the 1920s and 1930s rather than remain quiet or risk prison. They included people like Gaetano Salvemini, Arturo Toscanini, Carlo Sforza, and the martyred Carlo Rosselli. On the international level they exerted a great moral force against Mussolini. Their publicity campaigns and their actions, like the formation of the anti-Fascist Garibaldi Brigade in the Spanish civil war, had been constant irritants for Rome. In America many, like Salvemini at Harvard University, formed part of an international consciousness of the New Deal, which claimed the attention of high officials like Adolf Berle and Roosevelt himself.[20]

Influenced by the *fuorusciti*, many in the Roosevelt wing became sensitive to questions suggesting that, because they implicitly supported the Brindisi dyarchy, they were also sustaining the forces of conservatism. Washington was not anxious to see Badoglio portrayed as another warlord propped up by the Anglo-Americans. They already had made that mistake in French North Africa by playing the leader of the anti-Fascist movement, General Charles de Gaulle, off against a "reformed" Vichyite, Admiral Jean Darlan. Washington and London stood back while Darlan postured as a French maypole, until his assassination amidst a swirl of embarrassing crypto-Fascist politics. The North African experience was a nightmare for the Anglo-Americans, and they were afraid that a similar situation might arise in Italy.[21]

Some Allied officials, however, had mixed feelings on Brindisi and preferred to distinguish between Badoglio and the king. The commander in chief of the Mediterranean Theater, General Dwight Eisenhower, took a definite liking to the marshal and treated him with an old soldier comradeship, a friendly situation that must have pleased the Italian military. On September 30, 1943, the supreme commander wrote, "There is no question in the minds of any of us that Badoglio hates Fascism and the Germans intensely."[22] On the British side, London's highest-placed political administrator in Italy, Harold Macmillan, depicted Badoglio as "honest, broad minded, humorous." He considered it his duty to justify Badoglio before a British public that generally assumed him to be heavily tainted with fascism.[23]

On the other hand, the chief American civilian representative in Italy, Robert Murphy, considered the "grab bag assortment of military officers, diplomats, and members of the King's palace staff . . . far from impressive." He was echoed by Britain's General Noel Mason-Macfarlane, another important figure in the administration who, from the moment he arrived, claimed to loathe everyone and labeled the Italians and the king "gaga."[24] Beyond personal relations, the Anglo-Americans were never enthusiastic about the Badoglio regime; but, like it or not, the king and the general seemed to be the only men of government caliber available. General Kenyon Joyce commented to an American political observer that "we paraded the local string of hacks around the ring, the conclusion being that the only thoroughbred was Badoglio."[25]

Although they may have discussed domestic politics and occasionally intervened in them, the chief concern of the Anglo-Americans in Italy was the war and not the new Italian government or defascistization. And, many mused, who better to keep Italy on an even keel, at least for the time being, than its warrior king and the old marshal? As this state of affairs was reinforced by Churchill's royalist sympathies, Victor Emmanuel and Badoglio, for the present, remained safe. They would keep Italy docile and thus free the Allies to devote all of their attention to the defeat of Germany. Eisenhower said as much to Mason-Macfarlane on November 2 and emphasized his conviction that no Italian government would be allowed to rock the boat and sway the Allies from the task of beating the Nazis. When queried about the nascent political opposition to Badoglio then forming around Benedetto Croce and Carlo Sforza, Eisenhower wrote that "we will not recognize or cooperate with any Italian Government unless it is prepared to accept loyally to the terms of the Armistice and all that these imply."[26] The Regno del Sud and, by extension, its defascistization measures could rely on an Anglo-American guarantee.[27] The hard fact of war would both strengthen the king's position and hurt sanctions application.

Outside of Victor Emmanuel's Apulia, the administration of liberated Italy was entrusted to two organizations: AMGOT (later, AMG) and the ACC (later, AC). Forward areas were governed directly by the British general Sir Harold Alexander's AMG, while pacified regions to the rear came under indirect rule by the AC. AMG and AC relations were impossibly complex, and distinctions between the two often blurred. The Allied Control Commission did not operate until November 1943, and everything was administered by Military Government. But ultimately the Allies needed their own men for war jobs, and more of Italy came to be administered indirectly by the AC.[28]

Eventually, each province was governed through control commissions in miniature, every one subordinate, in turn, to regional commissions. Both the local and the regional commissions were further divided into bureaus responsible for particular tasks. These subcommissions looked after public safety, transportation, antiquities, and so forth. The Allies did not specifically commit any one subcommission to defascistization.

To train their civil affairs officers (CAOs) the Americans and British established schools at Charlottesville, Virginia, and at Wimbledon. The recruits tended to be older men. Many of the British were veteran colonial officers; some had served in the occupation of Libya or Italian East Africa. Although composed of both American and British contingents, the Allied Commission functioned as one unit, with both groups equal in numbers and status. While, as a general rule, U.S. combat forces fought in western Italy and Commonwealth forces saw action in the east, American and British civil affairs officers were pooled and randomly sprinkled over the occupation zones.[29]

Above the bureaucratic flow charts stood the most important Allied political figure in Italy, Harold Macmillan, the Allied commissioner. The middle-aged heir to a British publishing fortune, he stayed in close contact with his fellow Tory, Winston Churchill, and together they took a keen interest in peninsular events. His Majesty's representative enjoyed a senior position over the Americans Robert Murphy and, later, Samuel Reber and Ambassador Alexander Kirk. Under Macmillan in rank, the chief administrators of the Allied Commission were Kenyon

Joyce for a brief time, General Noel Mason-Macfarlane, and Commodore Ellery Stone. They coordinated and issued orders to the regional officers who carried on the day-to-day work of the occupation. The senior British CAO in the AMG was Air Commodore C. E. Benson, and his American counterpart was Colonel E. E. Hume.

On a lower level, among the CAOs who executed, and occasionally improvised, Allied policy, certainly the most important and innovative was the American colonel Charles Poletti. Poletti initially served as the supreme CAO (SCAO), or governor, of the First AMG Region, Sicily. His later administrative domains followed the advance of the Allies up the peninsula, as governor of Calabria and Lucania, then of Latium and Umbria, and finally, of Lombardy. Poletti brought with him a typically American gung ho attitude to the Allied Commission. He took an energetic, indefatigable, and idealistic approach to his task. Among the first Americans to land in Sicily, Poletti once found himself the only Allied soldier in a town that had just been evacuated by the Germans. The *New York Herald Tribune* reported that the indomitable Poletti "merely made a speech. They cheered and everything was fine."[30] The *Herald Tribune* and other New York Democratic papers lionized Poletti, who had briefly served as governor of New York in 1942. His forty-two-day tenure in Albany resulted from the resignation of his superior, Governor Herbert Lehman, called to Washington for war work under Roosevelt. Some other papers were less enthusiastic. Colonel Robert McCormick's *Chicago Tribune* labeled Poletti as "the Governor of New York whose three week term is remembered for the number of convicted labor sluggers and goons he turned out of the state's prisons thru executive writ."[31]

Despite the energetic leadership, the Anglo-Americans soon found their defascistization efforts caught in an Italian quagmire. CAOs counted on little or no help from their superiors, who themselves had little notion of what to do. As late as March 14, 1944, the highest-ranking American political officer in Italy, Samuel Reber, confessed to Harold Macmillan that he had no instructions nor any ideas on defascistization.[32] Colonel Poletti also frequently moaned of bureaucratic overlaps that obscured chains of command, while any subcommission, from transportation to local government, could carry on purging as it wished with little coordination from above. Furthermore, haphazard applications revealed administrative contradictions that descended through the regional level even into the communal level. For example, regional civil affairs officers (RCAOS) in Regions I and II were ordered to "eliminate officials" who had been "a) Fascist and Nazi sympathizers, b) those who have actively helped the enemy, c) those potentially dangerous to the security of the Allied Armed Forces or to the Allied Government Administration; or d) Passive resisters." A few weeks later, CAOS in Region III of the AMG were ordered to remove "all *squadristi*, *Marcia su Roma*, *Sciarpa Littorio*, *Gerarchi*, and other Fascists guilty of attacks against personal liberties."[33] Such bewildering instructions certainly confused or disheartened the most determined Allied official.

More indication of the confusion was that the Allies adopted the Latinate term "epuration" to describe their work instead of "purge." Perhaps they merely adopted the Italian term *epurazione* for their own use. A precedent might also be discovered in the French, who had been using "epuration" in North Africa. But the Anglo-American choice of "epuration" over "purge" indicates a certain uneasiness, a certain inability to grasp the business at hand.

Serious and dedicated AC officers would leave Italy disappointed. Maurice Neufeld, Poletti's right hand, later labeled Allied administration a failure. He considered the lackluster defascistization measures to be a consequence of a fundamentally flawed AMG.[34] Like Poletti, Neufeld went to Italy with lofty ideals about bringing democracy back there. Those ideals, he later wrote, were real in 1944, when the forces of freedom and their tanks controlled the country. But from the vantage of 1946, Neufeld could reexamine all the missed opportunities and conclude that the appearance of neofascism indicated a right-wing vitality the Allies could have destroyed but did not.

Neufeld, like Poletti, feared that the AMG's cumbersome chain of command worked against it. Despite the creation of G-5, a distinct civil affairs division within the military, its separation from the army was only a paper one. The bureaucracy of occupation dictated that the army provide nearly everything, from typewriters to formal authorizations, and this dependence required that decisions, both mundane and major, meandered along a tortuous highway of red tape stretching from the lowly CAO to the Allied Commission headquarters, to G-5 at Allied Forces Headquarters in Caserta, and occasionally even to the office of the Joint Chiefs of Staff in Washington, where Roosevelt or Secretary of State Cordell Hull would consult with Churchill or Foreign Minister Anthony Eden. Neufeld wrote that the problem was worsened by a heavy layer of higher brass: stodgy military men set in their ways or incompetent in the face of AMG plans. Many of these men probably criticized defascistization in the same ways and for the same reasons as their Italian counterparts did.[35] Neufeld added that the AMG needed a larger staff with proper training, a notion reinforced by an October 1943 report counting only one CAO for every twenty communes.[36] According to Neufeld, the American news media was woefully limited in their understanding of the occupation, and the State Department played a "passive and perhaps unavoidably negative [role]."

Cultural considerations combined with the war and bureaucratic lethargy to hamper Anglo-American application of stringent sanctions. Whether in Washington, in London, or among the forces in Italy, a coordinated plan of defascistization was never implemented, since, in the absence of a clear and present danger of sabotage, the task seemed to lack a sense of urgency. The Fascists were not Nazis; the Italians were not Germans. Particularly in the United States, Italian Fascists were rarely regarded as evil or menacing. Mussolini's soldiers were hardly even depicted in Allied propaganda, and when they were, in such films as "Sahara" or "Hotel Cairo," they appeared as simple-minded but lovable lackies, guitar strummers, and lovers. Even the Duce came to be depicted in cartoons and films as a rotund, henpecked, buffoon: whether as Jack Oakie's wonderful portrayal of Benzino Napaloni in "The Great Dictator" or complaining to Bob Hope in "My Favorite Spy." Frank Capra's film series "Why We Fight" labeled Mussolini as Hitler's mere "stooge." Even while Italy and America were at war, in October 1942, Attorney General Nicholas Biddle told a gathering that, unlike the Germans and Japanese, Italian aliens in the United States would not be treated as enemies.

The tendency to "go easy" on the Italians extended to the troops at the front. Harold Alexander's assistant in AMGOT, Lord Rennell Rodd, forecast little British vindictiveness or retribution against Italians. Rather, he felt obliged to advise his officers to "prevent immediate fraternization and treatment of the local population as domestic pets."[37]

Churchill himself had long been an Italophile, he held happy memories of trips to Italy in better times, and he found it difficult to hold the Italians in contempt. But there were limits to loving one's enemies.

If Italians as a group were to be spared his derision, someone else had to represent Fascist evil. In a speech for world broadcast on November 29, 1942, Churchill solved that problem by exonerating the population of Fascist guilt and blaming all of Italy's woes on the Duce.

"It is for the Italian people," he claimed, "forty million of them, to say whether they want this [prolonged, scientific, and shattering air attack] to happen to their country or not. One man, and one man alone, has brought them to this pass. . . . One man and the regime he has created have brought these measureless calamities upon the hard-working, gifted, and once happy Italian people, with whom, until the days of Mussolini, the English speaking world had so many sympathies and never a quarrel."[38] The symbolic or "strategic" significance of the Duce contributed toward a softened stand by the Anglo-Americans on the issue of Italians. For many like Churchill, when that "one man, one man alone" fell from power in July 1943, the problem of fascism had been solved.

Blaming the Duce for most, if not all, Fascist excess was a convenient simplification that facilitated the task of identifying the culpable as targets for sanctions. Beyond Mussolini's immediate camarilla of *gerarchi*, the inner circle such as Starace and Farinacci, application of the narrow parameters associated with Churchill's ideas for defascistization would not affect many Italians. Every gangster has his gang, but the Duce's coterie seemed to shrink every day. As important a figure as Foreign Minister Dino Grandi had worked his way into Churchill's, and Badoglio's, good graces. He was chief of staff to the Quadrumviri who marched on Rome in 1922 and certainly counted himself among the top five *gerarchi* throughout the regime's entire existence. From his sanctuary in Lisbon, the deposed Fascist wrote to the British prime minister and to Roosevelt's secretary of war, Henry Stimson. The retired *gerarca* lamented that his efforts to oust the Duce had been unappreciated by the United Nations, and he urged their help in resurrecting his reputation as a freedom-loving Italian.

The Americans did not make much of Grandi and his overtures, but others took them quite seriously. Marshal Badoglio, for example, was open to the Fascist's return. In late September of 1943, in fact, he even endorsed the prospect of a Grandi government in a letter to General Eisenhower. Churchill was another who placed stock in Grandi. After leaving office in 1945, the prime minister offered to go to Italy and testify on behalf of Mussolini's foreign minister. That someone of Dino Grandi's notoriety could expect, and partially receive, such help signaled that other Italian Fascists might secure the same.[39]

Nonmilitary objectives in wartime Italy, like sanctions against fascism, proved difficult to justify in the grand strategy of world war. The effect of the purge and other sanctions depended on haphazard, local circumstances and perceptions of individual administrators. Mason-Macfarlane's successor, Commodore Ellery Stone, mused that Allied treatment of Fascists was a "somewhat rough and ready operation" with few set rules.[40]

On the local level, as well as on the national, the pressures of the fighting created other factors that inhibited the development of a working strategy of defascistization. Upon entering liberated zones, Allied forces faced more immediate problems of refugees, transportation, food, and communication. One CAO recorded that his first task was not to hunt down Fascists but "to bury the dead and to feed the living."[41] When that initial, at once gruesome and pressing, job was finished, and the lights restored, and the water turned back on, military government was established in a somewhat regular fashion. Another CAO, a Charlottesville graduate, moved his court into a palatial room of an old hotel. His recollections betray a certain naive attitude to the tasks at hand: "I arranged it like a throne, with chairs surrounding a beautiful marble topped table, and me sitting back in a high backed luxurious chair." Drenching wet, he removed his leggings, put on a tie, and "sat down in my chair of state, interpreter on my right hand, and got ready for the interviews."[42]

CAOs from Poletti down acted on foggy AMG suggestions to reconstruct local government along pre-Fascist lines as quickly as possible. It was essential therefore to isolate Italians whom the CAO could trust and work with. Those chosen were generally community leaders. The head of the church, whether the archbishop of Palermo or a small-town priest, was almost always in this group. He was usually joined by a lawyer or business leader who represented some kind of establishment attitude. But their views were not coordinated, and none could be considered indicative of the whole. Even if one assumes that the churchmen held more concerted opinions than the rest, the others could have been remnants from the old, Liberal, regime; they might have been sincere anti-Fascists of any number of political persuasions; they might even have been Fascists who slipped through the net. Certainly most community leaders had possessed *tessere* before July 1943, and the Allies often saw no way out except to hire some of them. By the spring of 1944 some observers had already discerned this problem. An OSS observer noted that the "failure" of Allied Military Government in Sicily could be accounted for in the attempt to collaborate "with elements in place in the country."[43]

Language was another factor. Fluency in English was a big plus for an Italian who would secure the ear of a CAO. The AMG always needed bilingual help, and those locals who possessed this talent were gobbled up. Of course trusting bilingual Italians could also present problems to the administration. An Italian who spoke English often did so because either he or she had business or personal contacts in America, Canada, or Britain or simply represented a better-educated class. Many of them could easily have been Fascists or something less savory. An embarrassed Charles Poletti, for instance, discovered that one of his CAOs had unwittingly hired the Italo-American underworld figure Vito Genovese as an interpreter.[44]

If Vito Genovese could surface, so too could many blackshirts; yet many conservatives within the occupation staff chose to overlook the Fascist backgrounds of their friends. One CAO recognized the implications of the problem in his tale of an Allied resident general in Naples who maintained a notorious Fascist as a member of his staff as well as his constant social companion. When questioned on the wisdom of the relationship, the general conceded that his pal was a scoundrel, "but he's my scoundrel, and he's going to stay."[45]

Efficiency or technical competence were other qualifications accepted by the Allies, who knowingly retained important people at their old Fascist posts. Primarily concerned with the war effort, the AMG saw that certain concessions, like functioning utilities, were necessary for a docile population and the Allied war machine. For the Anglo-Americans, these services could not be provided without the help of certain technocrats who were known to have been important before 1943. Poletti, for one, lamented the dearth of democratic worthies with which to replace Fascists in jobs that demanded expertise.[46] For example, the head of the southern Italian communications network, Count Pellegrini, was kept on by the AMG. Despite his thoroughly Fascist past, the Allies deemed him too competent to let go. The same occurred in the Allied administration of Naples. Many with blatant Fascist pasts were maintained in positions of power.[47]

Certainly not every indication pointed against serious sanctions. The Allies could not and probably did not wish to ignore defascistization. Indeed, CAOs on the spot occasionally took matters into their own hands and carried defascistization far beyond what had been envisioned by their superiors.

The most sustained voice within the Allied Commission for concrete defascistization measures came from the American CAO, Charles Poletti. Poletti, as well as many other Americans, viewed Italy as their own laboratories where goodly doses of American-style democracy could be applied. He felt that the cure to fascism would be to catapult Italy back to a vague Giolittian paradise, a political *status quo ante Mussolini*, and his first memorandum in Sicily expressed the wish "to restore provincial and municipal administration to a pre-fascist level."[48] But as an American politician and a keen judge of popular opinion, Poletti also knew that the majority of Italians would never tolerate a return to Liberal Italy if that included Victor Emmanuel. On December 10, 1943, he wrote to Roosevelt's political envoy in Italy, Robert Murphy, and to John J. McCloy that the king-Badoglio option was unacceptable to most Sicilians. Nor should Crown Prince Umberto assume the throne. In fact, Poletti felt, the Sicilians favored an end to the monarchy altogether. It was clear to him from the start that the Royal House was too colored with fascism and that it could not remain unless drastic changes were made.[49]

There is also no doubt that the criticisms of Poletti and other regional CAOs extended beyond the crown. Mussolini's *ventennio*, a regime of twenty years, required the adherence and the active participation of more than a Royal court, and many knew it. With this in mind, however, Poletti opted for simplistic answers heavily influenced by American scientific management notions, solutions that surfaced in other areas of civil affairs government. In Sicily, for example, he developed a bureaucratic weeding-out system for civilians who came into headquarters with complaints. Forcing the islanders to pass through a number of rooms and guards, he likened his filtering method to sewage techniques. "A sifting system, based on the successive filter principle of modern sewage disposal, has worked very effectively."[50] Poletti advocated similar cost-effective methods to identify and punish Fascist culprits. Toward this end he participated with Allied political intelligence and some Italians in the creation of the first Allied framework to identify Fascists, a scientific methodology that took form soon after the initial landings in Sicily and was refined in the following months.

The finished product was the *scheda personale*, which appeared in many incarnations before the final format was agreed upon in mid-1944 and employed in both the AMG and Royal Italy. Throughout the course of the war it served as the basic "Were you a Fascist?" questionnaire and embodied the principles found in subsequent anti-Fascist legislation.

But behind official acceptance, many Italians considered the document as a joke. Just as the Germans would later make a mockery of its cousin, the *Fragebogen*, many lied, fabricated, and generally used the *scheda* to suit their own ends, regarding the document as a monument to silly American notions of scientific precision. The jurist Mario Bracci noted that such a questionnaire was utterly foreign to Italians. In the journal *Il Ponte* he predicted that "Colonel Poletti's *scheda* . . . will remain in the museums of Italy as a singular document of historic incomprehension . . . and of total ignorance of things Italian."[51]

In its final form, the *scheda* theoretically ascertained, through forty-three categories of questions, one's connection to the Fascist regime. Eventually all Italian government and parastate employees were ordered to fill them out. As if it mattered, a warning at the top of the *scheda* indicated "very severe penalties and fines" for lying. After the inevitable questions of whether or not the person had been enrolled in the PNF, the *scheda* got down to specifics. Was the person a veteran *sansepolcrista*, *squadrista*, a "Fascist of the First Hour?" Did he or she participate in the March on Rome, or in the *sciarpa littorio*? Did the person hold any party offices or a position in the Balilla, the University Youth, the Fascist Militia, the Duce's bodyguard, the secret police, the political office of the Public Security forces? Was the person a volunteer in Africa or Spain? Did he or she receive any honoraria or participate in political conferences or discourses over the radio?

By charting the framework to identify Fascists, the *scheda* itself added fire of its own to the sanctions debate. It created legal distinctions between two types of Fascists, distinctions based on a person's decision of

September 8: those who loyally followed their king south and those who loyally followed their Duce north. Conduct after September 1943 became considerably distinct from what happened during the 1922–43 *ventennio*. Categories 32 to 38 of the *scheda* pertained to Mussolini's Social Republic. If someone professed loyalty to Salò, then (increasingly in Allied eyes, as well as in Badoglio's) he or she was guilty of very serious crimes, specifically treason. The concept here was not original. Rather, the *scheda* accentuated Badoglio's notion of two fascisms that he had included in his November circulars: on the one hand was the fascism under which all Italians had lived, the amorphous, all-encompassing regime of the PNF, the Balilla, and Dopolavoro; on the other was the subsequent fascism, that of the Repubblica Sociale Italiana, the illegal Italy of traitors and collaborationists. This duality elaborated in the *scheda* came to be accepted by both the Italians and the United Nations. It tempered all subsequent debates and government action.

EARLY PURGE ATTEMPTS: OCCUPIED NAPLES AND THE REGNO DEL SUD

Naples, the first great city to be liberated after September 8, presented the Allies and the Royal government with fresh challenges on defascistization. But the city rapidly became a glaring example of the problems incurred in devising and applying sanctions. Although Naples remained under Allied military occupation, the Regno del Sud was granted permission to locate some of its administration there. Badoglio's quick transfer of certain offices and bureaucrats from Brindisi fostered Royal meddling into Neapolitan sanctions. An Allied informant reported that regardless of Anglo-Americans' high-minded notions, a purge was being effectively sabotaged by members of Badoglio's cabinet and, in particular, by his ministers of the interior, Vito Reale, and of public works, Raffaele De Caro. These two officials insisted on the retention of all Fascists, including *gerarchi*, "in the absence of positive proof from the commission of criminal acts."[52]

Two examples—those of Domenico Soprano and Giuseppe Frignani—illustrate the perplexity of the problem. Soprano, the prefect of Naples, still held office when the Allies arrived. Vividly remembered for roundups of Neapolitans to serve in Nazi labor battalions, his Fascist and collaborationist past was profound. The first scao in Naples, Colonel Erskine Hume, recognized that Soprano was "intensely unpopular" and recommended his immediate removal. The case, however, was more complicated than that, revealing a bureaucratic Byzantium that would plague defascistization: as a prefect, Soprano was technically responsible to Victor Emmanuel. Although Naples was AMG territory, much of the quotidian urban administration was the job of Royal officials like Soprano. Encumbered by protocol, the Allies were obliged to "suggest" to the kingdom that the Fascist be removed. This was negotiated in October 1943 through Leopoldo Piccardi, Badoglio's minister of labor, commerce, and industry and liaison to the Allies in Naples. Soprano was removed but only after a tenure as prefect in AMG Naples.[53]

Colonel Hume wrote to headquarters about another controversial Neapolitan, Giuseppe Frignani. The director general of the Bank of Naples, Frignani disappeared upon Allied arrival but surfaced after a few days and was accorded cordial treatment. Hume considered him to be, at worst, a moderate Fascist. The scao reported that, although Frignani had been a prominent member of the PNF, he had withdrawn from politics in recent years to devote himself exclusively to banking. What was more, Frignani was a technocrat who, Hume felt, "was without a doubt the most capable banker in the region, cooperated 100%, and was of considerable help to the Division." It was recommended that Frignani be allowed to remain at his post. On the other hand, the British intelligence officer, Raymond Klibansky, saw Frignani in another light. He described the banker as a very dangerous Fascist. Named director general in 1927, Frignani was a personal friend of party secretary Achille Starace and a financier for the Ciano family. He was also one of the ten founding members of the Italo-German Friendship League. In September Frignani had been aware that the retreating Germans planned the destruction of much of the city, so he made a deal with them to save the bank. Consequently, "the Bank of Naples is one of the few public buildings in the commercial quarter of Naples which was neither blown up nor mined."[54]

The cases, among others, of Jung and Pieche in Brindisi and Soprano and Frignani in Naples illustrate that, although

the Allies may have been uncoordinated and uneven in their treatment of Fascists, there were at least those in the AMG, like Poletti, who
took defascistization seriously. No Italian equivalent of Poletti, however, could be found in Badoglio's regime. As badly as things were
going for the AMG, it was worse among the Royal administrators. The
Anglo-Americans believed, or claimed to believe, that despite problems, their defascistization was at least progressing forward. In reports
back to headquarters, Poletti, for one, was keenly proud of his scientific
approach to the issue. From Naples he boasted that popular esteem
for the AMG had risen considerably due to his vigorous actions against
Fascists.[55]

Conversely, the Allies considered Badoglio's attempts to be, at best,
uninspired and ineffectual. And their opinion hardened every day. As
the war zone inched further north, and more of southern Italy was
safe from German attack, the Allies handed as much administration as
possible to the king and Badoglio. Brindisi would be given more rein
in devising sanctions, and, if necessary, the Anglo-Americans would
retain veto power for themselves. Many in the AMG worried, however,
that relinquishing defascistization to the Regno del Sud would sacrifice
any hopes to inferior methods and motives.

An official AC investigation concluded flatly that purges in the Regno
del Sud "were found to be no where near the Commission's minimum
standards."[56] At an Allied Control Commission Conference on April
14, 1944, Mason-Macfarlane stressed the need for a harder-hitting
purge under AMG auspices. If the Allies waited until effective control
of Italian territory had been handed back to the king, then, he claimed,
the exercise would be far more difficult to effect.[57]

The Royal government's inability was most apparent in Sardinia,
which the Nazis had abandoned in September 1943. Although its administration was entrusted to the king's high commissioner under Allied supervision, it soon was clear that, perhaps due to its isolation
from the mainland and its access to Salò, a large number of sincere
Fascists remained on the island. The situation was aggravated by the
continued presence of most of a very Fascist division, the Nembo. An
inspector general for the *pubblica sicurezza* forces (PS), Doctor Dino
Fabris, was dispatched by the Ministry of the Interior to investigate.
On December 26, 1943, he reported that the Nembo clearly remained
loyal to the Duce, had displayed hostility toward the new administra-

tion, and, with about 100,000 men, constituted a real danger to Allied and Royal presence.[58]

Even more threatening was the Martini affair, the discovery of a plot among high-ranking officers to maintain contacts between Sardinia and the RSI. Immediately after the Allies landed on the island, Badoglio's police arrested a General Martini who was caught boarding a small craft that would take him to the mainland under cover of night. It was apparent that the general had been scheming with the RSI. He was heavily incriminated, along with a number of other officers, by damning notes stuffed into the pockets of his mackintosh and instructions rolled up into an iron tube he carried. But the events of the investigation proved to be as interesting as the case itself. Badoglio placed the investigation in the hands of General Giovanni Messe, the man who had replaced Roatta in Brindisi as head of the High Command. Messe asked to examine the evidence, most of which was to be carried to the mainland by the investigating officer, Captain Lopane. Unfortunately, the airplane that carried Lopane and the evidence crashed into the Tyrrhenian Sea.[59]

Despite the sorry state of Sardinian defascistization, other signs indicated that Badoglio was attempting some half-hearted measures to clean up the island. But the results were not impressive, and it was obvious that in Sardinia, as on the mainland, the Regno del Sud had not committed itself to a serious purge, particularly of the military. In fact, despite the perilous occupation of the island, Fascist troops were simply merged into the king's army as the MVSN soldiers had been in 1943. Dr. Fabris warned the minister of the interior of the continued threat of Fascist military presence and pointed to the commander of the disbanded Ninety-sixth Blackshirt Legion. Fabris wrote that, "as ordered," the commander was reintegrated into the Royal army with the rank of major. However, he continued, someone had blundered, and "instead of being assigned to some office or under some command, he was nominated *comandante autonomo* of a machine gun battalion where he did not have to answer directly to anyone." In the same letter, Fabris mentioned another man, the last Fascist *federale* of Livorno and the "natural son" of the communications magnate Costanzo Ciano (and thus the bastard brother of Foreign Minister Galeazzo Ciano, Mussolini's son-in-law). The man had been appointed captain of aviation with the Fifth Bombing Wing, a unit attached to the Allies.[60]

37

Perhaps because responsibility for Sardinia was transferred from the Allied Forces Headquarters to the Allied Commission, by spring 1944 the Anglo-Americans became more aware of the problems. Lieutenant Colonel Donald D. Hoover, the AC's chief of communication and censorship, complained that in Sardinia, as well as in Sicily and the south, there was a noticeable and growing loss of faith in the "feeble" and "confused" Allied government. He was sorry to report that corruption was endemic and that a Fascist old *camerata* network persisted.[61] The Soviet representative to the Allied Advisory Commission, Alexander Bogomolov, complained that in Sardinia most of the Fascists were still at their posts and that nothing even approaching a purge had begun.[62] General Mason-Macfarlane evidently felt obliged to answer Bogomolov's complaint and on May 4 sent him an aide-memoire entitled "Epuration of Fascists and Prison Conditions in Sardinia." This explained that Allied pressure had forced Badoglio to remove 68 Fascists and that 25 others were still under scrutiny. Included in this list were 5 OVRA operatives, 7 militia officers, and, ironically, Dr. Fabris. However, Mason-Macfarlane admitted that tainted technicians, at least, were still being retained. To ensure efficiency, the head of the mines at Carnoia was kept on despite the knowledge that he had been a known and unpopular Fascist. He also acknowledged that two OVRA officers were maintained in police ranks in spite of requests for their dismissals. Perhaps due to this Allied pressure, the Badoglio regime stepped up its own investigation of the aforementioned Militia commander and the *federale* of Livorno. Both were transferred to jobs under close supervision.[63] The controversy over the Nembo also subsided. A later report noted that the mood of the men had changed from dangerously Fascist to merely monarchist, a key shift that would lead to exoneration in the parlance of sanctions—whether or not any such shift in loyalties actually occurred.

Laxness toward Fascists and the slow pace of sanctions against them continued to embarrass Badoglio's regime. With his poor record in Apulia, Sardinia, and other places, it appeared that the marshal's attempts at sanctions were, at best, tepid. Under international pressure, voiced in the Armistice terms and the Anglo-American press, to democratize his regime, Badoglio had to validate it on defascistization as well as to legitimate its own existence among both Italians and foreigners. The clever marshal walked a tightrope, agreeing to serve the anti-

German crusade one moment and plotting for more independence the next. On occasion he accomplished these goals quite ably. Badoglio's surprise arrangement for Soviet recognition of his regime was a true coup de main. It came as a complete shock to the Allies and was a major step in the international legalization of the Regno del Sud.

At other times the marshal succumbed to pressures, mainly from Roosevelt and the New Dealers who had his ear, that the Regno del Sud appear more democratic. The memory of the Darlan experiment was still fresh, and neither Roosevelt nor Churchill relished a repeat performance.[64] That debacle must have loomed large in their minds when the Anglo-Americans vetoed some of Badoglio's functionaries, such as Jung and Pieche. On November 12 General Mario Roatta was also pressured into resigning.[65]

Some cabinet members also began to appreciate the discrepancy between defascistizations in AMG Italy and king's Italy and were soon moved into more action. The minister of justice, Vincenzo Arangio-Ruiz, noticed a "gross disproportion" in late April 1944 and warned Badoglio that the Allies had little faith, *un atteggiamento alquanto dilatorio*, in the Royal government. On April 22 the minister of war also advised Badoglio that the Allied Commission perceived a lack of seriousness in his government's handling of the purge. And on April 3 the minister of national education reported that the Allies were pressuring him to start firing Fascist employees.[66]

THE REBIRTH OF POLITICS

If there existed among Italians any popular resentment against Badoglio's choice of men like Roatta for high government service, it was not vocalized in the early autumn of 1943. Except for anti-Savoyard melees, the streets witnessed few manifestations of appreciable magnitude for defascistization, at least anything on the scale of what would occur at the end of the war. Three reasons must explain this docility: (1) the confusion of the war—the Italian mainland was in the process of being invaded by the Anglo-Americans; (2) the absence of opposition parties capable of forging this sentiment into action; and (3) the early leadership in southern Italy of the Royal House and the military. Political parties were few and at best nascent and structurally weak. They had no say in the composition of Badoglio's government until April 1944.[67]

Badoglio could control these embryonic organizations, but he could ill afford to ignore official Allied pronouncements for a freer Italy. To address that pressure, he permitted a free political meeting for January 1944 at Bari.[68] This "Congress of Bari" embraced members of the newly emerging parties that had united in the Committee of National Liberation (CLN): Communists, Socialists, Action party members, Liberals, Christian Democrats, and Labor Democrats. Adherents to these factions had resumed public life during the Forty-five Days and by early September had engineered among themselves the CLN.[69]

The Bari Congress, however, backfired in Badoglio's face. His worst fears were realized there as his regime and the monarchy were branded corrupt and Fascistophile. Each orator placed the responsibility on various segments of society for Mussolini's regime. Generally, the objects of their anger might have been the ruling classes, big business, or Royal institutions; but in virtually all of the speeches Victor Emmanuel bore guilt and was clearly placed at odds with the entire anti-Fascist political spectrum.

The assembly was chaired by old Tito Zaniboni, the Socialist who had tried to shoot Mussolini in 1926. His quixotic assassination attempt captured imaginations and approached legendary status. However, although he spent most of the *ventennio* in confinement, and his sincerity was beyond reproach, his mental state, always a bit in doubt, seemed to have worsened with age. Zaniboni was no friend of the Royal family, and his preliminary remarks at the Bari Congress blamed the sovereign for much that had happened. But the harshest assaults on the crown came from others—Benedetto Croce, Adolfo Omodeo, and Carlo Sforza.

Croce's speech launched the Congress at the Teatro Piccinni. Bent over, in an overcoat to protect himself in the unheated building, the old Liberal philosopher framed a surprisingly vitriolic tirade against Victor Emmanuel, whose twenty-year flirtation with totalitarianism had condemned Italy to the current catastrophe. Speaker after speaker continued the attacks. Among the most stinging were those delivered by the republican Carlo Sforza, the former foreign minister who was fresh from exile in the United States, and by Adolfo Omodeo, the liberal historian and friend of Croce, who went so far as to shout death to the king.[70]

The monarchy aside, Badoglio's record of defascistization also appeared particularly dismal to the CLN politicians at Bari. Nevertheless, the marshal presented the Congress with a fait accompli, something that might have taken the wind out of his critics' sails. Just before the Congress, he announced a new measure to punish Fascists: Royal Legislative Decree (RDL) 29/B of December 29, 1943.[71] Much of it sounded similar to Badoglio's August measures. Its first stipulations removed from government certain categories of officials who had occupied major positions in Fascist organizations. Decisions for dismissal were to be based on investigations carried out in two ways. The ministers themselves were to deal with the most important functionaries: officers down to grade 6 (e.g. vice prefect). Lower officials were to be dealt with by the separate Ministerial Commission, which had vaguely existed for some time under the presidency of Professor Omodeo.

But the decree RDL 29/B was stillborn. The target categories for this plan of attack were vague, and no framework was provided for enforcement. Badoglio's only modification of the plan before his April 22 cabinet shake-up was RDL 110 of April 13. This measure created a High Commission for a National Purge of Fascism and entrusted it to the old Socialist Tito Zaniboni. The program was so ineffectual and unpopular, however, that when Zaniboni took charge, he was immediately chastised by his comrades on the Left, and his career was ruined.

Attempts to put teeth into RDL 29/B, undertaken within Badoglio's government, were doomed to failure. The minister of justice, Ettore Casati, one of the most determined voices for true reform, pushed for an enactment to get the ministers involved in the purge and advocated easier suspensions and loss of salaries. Badoglio and his other ministers unanimously condemned the measure. The marshal felt that Casati's suggestions were too harsh. His minister of finance lamented their "excessive rigor," and they were also compared to the Anglo-American measures that had been applied "with disastrous consequences." As late as April 7, the Allied Control Commission complained, "So far as is known, neither the Council of Ministers nor the Ministerial Commission ever sat. The Ministerial Commission has never been appointed."[72]

Since Badoglio possessed a near monopoly over what power the Anglo-Americans allowed the Italians, he remained a virtual dictator of the Regno del Sud through April 1944. All anti-Fascist measures, contrary to what happened in Allied territory, stemmed from his authority. The spring of 1944, however, heralded a new age of mass politics that more and more would affect the punishment of Fascists. After the first expression of political sentiment at the Bari Congress, *sub rosa* consultations and byzantine maneuvering led to the formation of the first government to include representatives of popular parties. Formed on April 26, 1944, Badoglio's new government included, for the first time, members of the CLN: Communists, Socialists, Christian Democrats, Liberals, and Labor Democrats. Now, real potential existed for sanctions.

The spring, however, signaled an accelerated Allied drive against the Germans, and the imminent fall of Rome delayed defascistization. Reforms like RDL 29/B predated the Nazis' evacuation of the Eternal City in June and had only anticipated that event. On May 26, however, Badoglio went ahead and issued a decree for the punishment of Fascist offenses that included the death sentence and life imprisonment.[73] The final text also listed more categories of offenses beyond membership in the *squadristi*, participation in the March on Rome, and participation in the Sciarpa Littorio. All *federali*, ministers and undersecretaries who held their positions after January 3, 1925, and those who appeared on the 1929 PNF electoral list, were designated for sanctions.

Ample evidence suggests that outlines for even more stringent measures were deliberated in the ministerial debate over the application of the May 26 decree. Badoglio himself took no part in those discussions, as the move was sponsored by the republican Count Carlo Sforza, the Communist leader Palmiro Togliatti, and a Sardinian member of the Action party, Mario Berlinguer. Two proposals had been drawn up for the meeting: a mild one devised by two legal experts, Professors Ugo Forti and Altavilla, and a harsher measure posited by Badoglio's now former justice minister, Casati. Casati had even planned for punishments, in one form or another, against all PNF members, regardless of rank. The harshest sanctions included the death sentence for certain crimes against the state connected with the Fascist seizure of power in 1922–25. Sforza later told a British officer that Casati's had been a "very radical, far reaching and sweeping plan for the punishment of all Fascist criminals." His energetic measure, however, was immediately and severely modified by the new minister of justice, the Liberal Vincenzo Arangio-Ruiz, who enjoyed the support of Badoglio and Croce.[74]

The May 26 decree was nevertheless the most important action undertaken to resurrect the dormant December measure, RDL 29/B. At the same time, Zaniboni was removed from his position in order to become the high commissioner for Sardinia. Debate turned toward his replacement as chief purge administrator with the new title high commissioner for the punishment of the crimes and illegal acts of fascism. The Liberals adamantly refused to have anything to do with it and put up no candidate. The Communists expressed interest but refused to have one of their own replace Zaniboni. Finally, after a long attack on the "milk and water" nature of the plan, Count Sforza was successfully promoted by a ministerial group headed by Togliatti. As coordinator of the sanctions program, Sforza was received differently than had been Zaniboni. Due to the more promising atmosphere presented by the May 26 decree, the impending liberation of Rome, and his own esteemed reputation, the count's prospective tenure was generally hailed as a positive step toward things to come.

Warning signs appeared, however, to qualify this early optimism. For example, conflict and doubt surfaced within the Badoglio circle. On May 28 a test case was presented at a meeting of the Council of Ministers. General Alessandro Pirzio Biroli had been a military commander in occupied Albania and Yugoslavia, where his reprisals against anti-Fascists and nationalist freedom fighters had become notorious. The Serbian Resistance leader Josip "Tito" Broz demanded that Pirzio Biroli be tried for the murder of 7,000 compatriots. Badoglio, however, vehemently interrupted the colloquium with assertions that no proof existed of Pirzio Biroli's guilt and squelched any more talk about prosecution. The military would not acquiesce to an investigation, and Sforza would have to choose someone else guilty of more obviously political crimes.[75]

Another jarring indication of doom was the state of the administrative machine at Sforza's disposal. What the high commissioner inherited was a desk with nothing on it; the sanctions program had accomplished practically nothing since December. Only the creation of a small staff for Omodeo's moribund commission on the purge of lower-level bureaucrats served to demonstrate that, indeed, nothing at all had been accomplished. A report on the conditions of this staff indicated the miserable progress that had been made on defascistization almost a full year after the fall of Mussolini. In July 1944 Benvenuto Piovani and Nino Contini, the two secretaries, wrote to Omodeo. The tone of the letter reveals that the chief could not have been very aware of what was happening. The two complained of an absence of every reasonable tool for their job. For example, they and their staff of three did not possess a single copy of defascistization laws or decrees. They requested agents, more staff, and even some form of transportation. Piovani and Contini reminded Rome that the defascistization commission had not really gotten off the ground until May 1944. Without tools, "without the use of even a single pencil, or a sheet of paper," nothing could be accomplished.

Despite these handicaps, the commission was able to perform some investigations. Piovani and Contini listed 182 preliminary "inquests" and 72 other cases that had been sent to higher authorities such as the AMG, Zaniboni, or later on, Sforza. These "inquests" were apparently little more than registrations of simple accusations.

Piovani and Contini wrote that, in AMG areas, a more positive attitude toward sanctions existed and the Allies seriously endeavored to establish purge commissions. In Royal Italy, and more specifically in the area where Omodeo's defascistization commission was theoretically "operating," that is, mainly Salerno and in the Apulian cities of Brindisi, Bari, Lecce, and Taranto, nothing was happening, despite the importance of haste. To be effective, the purge must begin and begin quickly. A delay could spell disaster in the defascistization process. The two warned that, after a lapse of a year or two, the government would never be able to purge someone for his Fascist past.[76]

Events in the late spring of 1944 had begun to force change onto the rigidly conservative Regno del Sud. The petty, narrow-minded king and his prime minister held out as long as they could contain the roar of CLN political expression first heard at Bari and again in April at Salerno. With the liberation of Rome, this tide would be manifested in a more democratic government and in a real attempt at sanctions against Fascism.

CHAPTER THREE

THE PROBLEM OF ROME

In the spring of 1944 the German line cracked. North of Naples, at Monte Cassino, and east along the Sangro River, the Allied offensive gathered steam for the push to Rome. Pope Pius XII and others had been negotiating with the Germans in the hope of saving from destruction the city's magnificent religious, artistic, and human treasures. Fortunately for Western civilization the Nazis and Fascists opted to evacuate without a fight.[1] They left the city as the king had nine months before, under cover of night; but this time the Allies moved in to replace them. And for a moment the capital waited in that strange silence that often haunts the vacuum between old and new regimes.

One Allied officer remembered the moonlit drive into Rome—the stillness, the quiet—as one of the most vivid impressions of his life. Through suburban Velletri, Genzano, Albano, "the warm air," he wrote, "brought with pungency a baffling succession of odours: the scent of thyme and jasmine and oleander alternating with the stench of corrupting flesh." He continued along into the city, past the aerodrome, past a burning factory, within earshot of sniper fire. He drove across the Tiber and up to St. Peter's Basilica. June 5, 1944. Rome was liberated.[2]

ROME

The capital of Italy, liberated Rome proved an enormous psychological victory for the Allies and for the Regno del Sud. More than Naples and Palermo, Rome had been the ultimate urban symbol of government and fascism. Its liberation, furthermore, triggered significant political consequences for the new Italy: the end of the Victor Emmanuel/Badoglio dyarchy and the foundation of a more sincerely democratic and popular CLN government. As a reflection of this importance, Anglo-Americans and Italians focused their attention on Rome to see how the new regime and the Roman people would deal with followers of Mussolini. The *romani* themselves would now be scrutinized for their own popular reactions to the end of fascism in their city.

Most measures against the Fascists since September 8, 1943, had been in the form of decrees, either Allied or Badoglio's. They had been undertaken within the closed chambers of government, and no significant popular pressure affected this early "elimination" of Fascists. Whether as public demonstrations or acts of violence, in fact, that element had hardly appeared. The famous scenes of happy crowds pulling fasces off the sides of buildings or burning portraits of the Duce all occurred immediately after July 25 or during those brief moments when towns were liberated by Anglo-American troops and newsreel cameramen. Beyond that first picturesque euphoria neither the Allies nor Badoglio's police took notice of many large-scale demonstrations against fascism.

The single important exception to the passive southern attitude was found in the unique and inspiring example of Naples, where the anti-Fascist uprising of September 1943, the *quattro giornate*, justly ranks among the great moments of modern Italian history.[3] Without significant Allied help, the people of Naples rose up against their Nazi overlords and, after four days of heroic fighting, helped to liberate their city. In its drama and magnitude, the *quattro giornate*, however, stands as a glaring exception to the rest of the south.

The few other cases of popular political violence before June 1944 tended not to be specific and directed but rather sporadic and not very purposeful. An October 1943 AMG report noted that a "mob" near Potenza had killed a town secretary and attacked a troop of Carabinieri. On another occasion a group of people attempted to burn tax and communal records.[4] But not many of these reports were recorded, and they appear to have been exceptional events. The attacks generally took the form of setting tax logs and government buildings on fire and were not specifically directed against Fascists. They were probably manifestations of traditional discontent, aggravated by the war.

The peculiarities and mistakes of geography account in part for this public treatment accorded Fascists. The south had always experienced a different type of regime than did the north, where resistance against fascism was more urban, organized, or pronounced. Even before Mussolini's overthrow in July 1943, most trouble, like the giant strikes that March, had occurred in northern industrial centers. September 8 further emphasized this important geographical dichotomy. Except for the area immediately south of the capital, no part of the Mezzogiorno had suffered under the Nazis and their neo-Fascist allies for more than a few days. The bitterness and hatred had not gestated there to the degree found in the north by the time of its liberation.

Another factor that tempered public antifascism stemmed from the conservative nature of the Regno del Sud. Whereas the regime paraded itself as anti-Fascist, the royalist and military monopoly of power worked against a serious and popularly motivated antifascism that had the potential of getting out of control. Mention has been made of the slowness in opening up Italian politics to opposition parties. Badoglio's record against dissidents also illustrated the continued presence of authoritarianism in the Italian government. The marshal's iron fist had already been felt during the Forty-five Days in August 1943 at Bari and Milan, when Royal troops were ordered to shoot protesters. That Badoglio would not tolerate anti-Fascist manifestations (while he was technically at war with fascism!) indicated how sensitive such questions remained as long as he held the reins of power and Victor Emmanuel sat on the throne.

Rome, however, was different and presented both problems and opportunities for defascistization. Not only was it the capital, it was the first important city to fall since the pivotal September days, and consequently, it had experienced a significant period of time (about nine months) under the RSI flag. As such, Rome witnessed a new brand of mass terror under a ruthless, Nazi-controlled administration, a type never experienced in the south. The brutality of this rule might have acted as a catalyst for popular and violent antifascism.

After the disaster of September 8, the Fascists had returned to Rome with a bloodthirsty form of their old street-brawling and murderous tactics, *squadrismo*, embodied in a police state never before seen in Rome. Uniformed bands of criminals and sadists held the city in a grip of terror; and to be dragged into the Via Tasso headquarters often meant death. The massacre of 335 innocents on March 24–25, 1944, at the Ardeatine caves was the most horrible, but far from the only, nightmare of this period.[5]

The terror affected every sector of society, including the world of political leaders. Many of the anti-Fascists who had emerged into public view during the Forty-five Days were forced back into hiding by the reappearance of Mussolini's police state. Such experiences must have profoundly affected many of the most important CLN leaders who were destined to pilot Italy after the fall of fascism. Some, like the Christian Democratic leader Alcide De Gasperi, were harbored in the security of the Vatican. Others, like the CLN president, Ivanoe Bonomi, and the Socialist Pietro Nenni, were hidden in cellars and back rooms. Many of their comrades, friends, or relatives were murdered or deported to the Third Reich. When the Nazis and Fascists, in June 1944, evacuated the Via Tasso, they picked fourteen prisoners from their cells and dragged them along for insurance. Included in that sad lot was Bruno Buozzi, the Socialist labor organizer and personal friend of many CLN leaders. These unfortunate people were butchered about five miles outside the city at La Storta.

Considering the enormity of the crimes the Nazis and Fascists had inflicted on them, the Romans remained in a fairly calm and nonvindictive mood when the Anglo-Americans entered the city. Partisan attacks took place on Fascist and German police headquarters on the eve of the liberation. But even these assaults were mild, and the captured blackshirts were handed over to Allied authorities without incident.[6] The rest of the liberation was completed with even less trouble. Along with the aforementioned explanations for tranquil populations in the south, other, peculiarly Roman, reasons may also account for this oddly quiet response and might also explain subsequent treatment of Fascists in other places.

For one thing, the Romans had more pressing problems than bringing Fascists to justice. There were severe food and power shortages. Recalling the occupation experience since the first landings in Sicily, the problem of feeding the population was an acute and constant concern for all.[7] The newly appointed American governor of the city, Charles Poletti, remarked that the people were restless and undernourished, but the food problem lingered on through the autumn and into the winter of 1944–45 with no end in sight. Upon his entrance into the Eternal City, the American promised "more spaghetti and less chatter" and promptly increased the food rations. In February, however, Poletti would ask in despair, "How do they live? How long can they stand it? The ration is not enough, prices are at a tremendous level, many things are unattainable, and, sooner or later, become necessities."[8]

The strategic visibility of Mussolini as the chief Fascist remained a powerful image for Romans and also helps to explain the mild anti-Fascist reaction upon the liberation of Rome. The Churchillian notion that one man, and one man alone, was responsible for the regime still made much sense to many Italians. The war was far from over, and that "one man," Mussolini, still headed a Fascist government in the north. Again, the symbolic and strategic nature of the political class confused the issue of defascistization.

Terminology and perceptions of situations revealed by key words illustrate other aspects of the problem. When Anglo-American units rolled into Rome, they "liberated" it. The universal use of "liberate" (*liberare* in Italian), in both the English-language and Italian press, presented an image of finality. Like Naples and Sicily, Rome had now been liberated from fascism, and, outside of a counterattack, a liberated place has nothing more to fear. Thanks to the Anglo-American forces of democracy, Mussolini had been expelled from the south and Rome had been liberated. The war seemed essentially over.

The profound symbol of Mussolini and the importance of September 8, 1943, on the psyche was not limited to any one political persuasion. This fashion of thought worked its magic on both Left and Right; the Socialists, for example, often fell prey to it. *Avanti!* stated on June 5 that those who had inflicted starvation on Rome were gone. They had "gassed up their cars" and vanished "like fog under a hot Sun."[9] From now on, for most Italians to fight fascism meant to enlist in the Royal army or the partisan ranks and to join the march on Salò. Thus Colonel Poletti could write in his January 1945 monthly report that the resolution of many problems, including retribution against Fascists, would have to wait until the "liberation" of the rest of Italy. "All eyes," he wrote, "in the political sense, are turned [toward the North]."[10]

Confusion in the press also reflected inability or reluctance to work out comfortable definitions of Fascists and Fascist crime. Arrests or purges of "Fascists," regardless of their rank, were usually announced in abbreviated stories on page 2. A general or a *federale* might easily receive the same, or occasionally, even less space than a policeman or even girlfriends of prominent Fascists.

The interest in love and prostitution particularly reveals the general inability to identify Fascists. The notoriety of lovers and mistresses created a peculiar and special place for them in the "strategic elite." They embodied a kind of corruption that many associated with fascism. This vision of morally rotten Fascists and Nazis stays with us even today. It is a difficult idea to lose. Indeed, Mussolini's love life and those of his *gerarchi* still elicit comment in the popular press and on the screen.

The first of these love interests in the Roman press concerned the Pensione Trinità dei Monti. The well-known hostess of the Pensione, Stefania Rossi and her daughter, Bibi, were arrested on July 26. The *Risorgimento Liberale* reported that Stefania was the "official lover" (*amante ufficiale*) of Prince Ruspoli and "friend" of her most prominent lodger, the Gestapo boss of Rome, Eugene Dollmann. The police roundup included the porter and others "involved in the unhappy activities of the two women."[11] Coverage of the stories was distinguished by very little political content, and the slant was decidedly prurient. Perhaps, after twenty years of living in a "Revolution," the Italians had grown tired of politics.

Another explanation for the mildness of the anti-Fascist reaction can be ascribed to official policies designed to curb partisan activity. As in the south, the Allied intention to keep local politics quiet and the conservative nature of the Badoglio regime had combined to maintain a peaceful, orderly city. The Anglo-Americans would not tolerate any infringement on their monopoly of power. On June 7, the official Allied *Corriere di Roma* ordered that all rifles be handed over to the AMG while lamenting that it must be a great pain for a partisan to surrender his "faithful weapon." However, this sacrifice was necessary "for obvious reasons of military security." Besides, more weapons were needed by their partisan brothers in the north where, ostensibly, these arms were to be sent.

The press, even the Left press, supported the Allies in the contention that the emergency had passed and the time had come for a return to normal life. In an interview with Education Minister Guido De Ruggiero, the *Italia Libera* stated that "the insurrection is just about over."[12] Even the Socialists' fiery *Avanti!* warned that "looting is a crime" and that, although the Fascists stole from the people, the Romans must not turn into vigilantes, embarking on acts of retribution. The press campaign, backed by Allied military might, paid off for the AMG. In his first monthly report as governor of Rome, Charles Poletti boasted that there had been no clashes between the demonstrators and the police for any reason; public order was very good. There would not be a popular anti-Fascist massacre in Rome.[13]

The conservative mood of the liberated city and its government was also exhibited on June 5, when two important ACC analysts were welcomed at City Hall on the Campidoglio by members of the new political order. Accompanied by General Allen of the Third Division, the Allied Commission's Harold Caccia and Samuel Reber met the CLN's military commander of the city, General Roberto Bencivenga, who "drove up in a large black limousine escorted by about two dozen motorcyclists, with goggles, crash helmets and breeches on, wearing the armband of the Committee of Liberation. Several people remarked that the guards had only changed their clothes and that they were last seen as Fascists."[14]

Despite the authoritarian style, the choice of Bencivenga had been a concession to the CLN. Marshal Badoglio had appointed him underground commander of Rome in March after a furor over his original choice, General Armellini, whom the new leaders considered to be thoroughly Fascist. Bencivenga could, indeed, boast of an anti-Fascist past as a protégé of Giovanni Amendola and as an inmate of Fascist prisons for five years. Still, many members of the CLN were also dissatisfied with Bencivenga. Alcide De Gasperi felt that Badoglio had succumbed to "a rich Italo-Americano who was in touch with an American secret organization." The Christian Democrat felt that Bencivenga wanted to twist the CLN into a Unione Democratica with himself as commander surrounded by a personal bodyguard of "green shirts."[15] The paper of the newly organized Action party, *Italia Libera*, worried about Bencivenga's Ordinance Number 3, which allowed everyone in public service to remain at his desk. It appeared that all Fascists could carry on undisturbed in their jobs. This, however, was inevitably a moot question. The arrogant Bencivenga badly overstepped his authority, and the AMG never tolerated his behavior. He was relieved of command and his directives were immediately nullified by the Allied government.

ROME AND THE NEW POLITICS

Along with its popular ramifications, the liberation of Rome acted as a catalyst for three political phenomena that affected the course of defascistization: Victor Emmanuel's surrender of power, the transition from Pietro Badoglio's government to one headed by Ivanoe Bonomi and the Committee of National Liberation, and the inauguration of a lively debate in the political press over sanctions.

The issue of the crown perpetually confused actions taken against Fascists. Despite his limited political consequence during the Duce's regime, the monarch had come to symbolize Royal and aristocratic betrayal of Italian liberty to the blackshirts. Victor Emmanuel served the purpose, as did Mussolini, of being a living emblem of Italy's government. Like the Duce, he possessed a strategic, political status, but, unlike the Fascist, he was also a pillar of the older ruling class. The king's involvement in the July plot against Mussolini undoubtedly gave the crown some breathing space by erasing some of the guilt of the *ventennio*. But it could not save Victor Emmanuel. He had to go.[16] As for a successor, the first alternative was his heir, Umberto. But the crown prince was in his forties, and his own past—for example, as a commander in the 1940 invasion of France—revealed his collusion with, if not enthusiasm for, the old regime. Another solution might have given the reins to Umberto's son, Victor Emmanuel IV, still in minority; Croce was usually mentioned as regent in this schema. The final compromise, nevertheless, would give Umberto the Royal duties as lieutenant general of the realm, but not the crown, which was to remain on his father's head. The issue of monarchical responsibility would thus be partially defused and partially muddied.[17]

After discussions earlier in the year with Liberal leaders Enrico De Nicola and Benedetto Croce, and under heavy Allied pressure, King Victor Emmanuel III finally had consented in April to resign in all but name and relinquish the day-to-day affairs of the Royal House to Umberto. It was also decided that no political party would question the existence of the monarchy until a suitable period after the war had ended, an arrangement that came to be known as the "institutional truce." Upon the liberation of Rome, the king adhered to his part of the bargain; he was not even allowed to enter the city and retired with Queen Elena to their villa near Naples. Crown Prince Umberto then took the reins as "Lieutenant General of the Realm." Victor Emmanuel would never serve in prison, but he had, de facto, relinquished the throne, and in 1946 he would go into exile in Egypt. He died in Alexandria in 1947. Regardless of how the succession arrangement was reached, this was a victory for the anti-Fascists.[18]

Replacement, or, as one historian has put it, defenestration, of the Badoglio government with one comprised of CLN leaders was the second consequence of the liberation. This was an alteration of the political climate that had not been arranged and that few, certainly not the Allies, had foreseen. The first important Allied official on the scene was the ACC chief, Scottish General Noel Mason-Macfarlane. Like most of the Anglo-Americans, he had not been overly concerned with the drift of Italian politics, and when pressure for a new political arrangement manifested itself, he was content to invite the CLN leaders to AMG headquarters, the Grand Hotel, so that they could "have a go at it." When they emerged, Italy had a new government composed of the CLN anti-Fascist coalition and without Badoglio, a government that opted to swear an oath not to the king but "to the supreme interests of the nation." On June 8 Crown Prince Umberto was informed that Ivanoe Bonomi, the head of the Rome CLN, had replaced the marshal as prime minister.[19]

Representation by the CLN parties—the Christian Democrats, Liberals, Socialists, Communists, Labor Democrats, and the newly added moderately left "Actionists"—in the Italian government was not new. A broader Italian cabinet had already been accomplished in the marshal's April 1944 cabinet. Now, however, Badoglio was gone and the CLN coalition claimed total authority.[20]

In London, Churchill was infuriated. The prime minister berated the ACC command in Caserta for allowing Mason-Macfarlane to take such liberties and roared to Eden that the Scot "seems to have been completely helpless." Within a few days he was replaced by Commodore Ellery Stone, an aged American naval officer brought out of retirement to staff the occupation.[21] Churchill railed at the CLN and its presumptuous move to power since it appeared to him that the new regime threatened British interests, the monarchy, and his personal commitment to Badoglio. He insisted that the CLN could claim no legitimate authority and attempted to discredit it. On March 13 the prime minister wrote to Roosevelt, "I do not believe the ambitious wind bags . . . have any footing. I fear that if we drive out the King and Badoglio at this stage we shall only have complicated the task of the armies." On June 10 Churchill again wrote to the president, "I think it is a great disaster that Badoglio should be replaced by this group of aged and hungry politicians." Roosevelt answered neither of these notes. An oss report, in fact, applauded the new government, which fulfilled the goals of the Moscow Declaration and "accomplished to a point even beyond the expectations of the most hopeful persons in and out of Italy."[22]

Despite Churchill's tirades, the Bonomi ascendancy within the Rome cln and that organization's victory at the Grand Hotel proved to be a great blessing for London's interests. Although British influence in Italy did indeed decline during Bonomi's tenure, it was mostly a consequence of the inevitable expansion of American power, a phenomenon occurring around the world. But the new Italian government did not signal disaster for Churchill's crusade to salvage the monarchy. With only a mildly Socialist past, Badoglio's successor was no revolutionary and stood to the right of center in the cln coalition.

Born in Mantua in 1873, Ivanoe Bonomi earned fame before World War I as a reformist Socialist. His moderate opinions, however, strained relations with the left wing of his party. An interventionist stance in the Libyan War was the final straw, and the Socialists, led in part by Mussolini's faction, ejected him in 1912. Bonomi learned from his mistakes and soon acquired fame as a moderate and a fence-mender, dodging controversial issues. This reputation gained him the prime minister's chair from June 1921 until February 1922. It had been rumored that Bonomi assisted the Fascists in their climb to power, and indeed he was later embarrassed by certain comments made in support of the regime. Nevertheless, during the *ventennio* he did not accept office. Neither, however, did Bonomi engage in anti-Fascist activity during the 1930s. He reemerged as a political figure only after the July coup but soon was forced into hiding when the Germans took the city in September. None of this deterred the Salò propaganda machine, which enjoyed broadcasting the cln prime minister's endorsements of Mussolini. The programs were interspersed with charges that Bonomi was a fraud and liar of the first order.[23]

Bonomi's presidency ensured that the cln would be guided by a leader who stood against social upheaval for the sake of defascistiza-tion. Bonomi assured a PWB intelligence officer that "the first task of an Italian Government was to secure a maximum Italian war effort." This he promised to do by relying on high-ranking officers and the crown, "the only guarantee of Italian unity." To Roosevelt, the new prime minister professed a "profound sense of solidarity and admira-tion with which Italian democracy . . . [would follow his] activity and work." Bonomi guaranteed, furthermore, that his government would be composed "exclusively of men absolutely free from any fascist contamination."[24]

Bonomi proved to be a loyal subject of the House of Savoy and a friend of the United Nations. America's recently installed ambassador, Alexander Kirk, reported that "the Advisory Council for Italy . . . con-sider that in all circumstances this Government should prove satisfac-tory in furthering the main purpose of the Allied powers which is the final defeat of Germany." Kirk did, however, add two caveats: that Bonomi fulfill all obligations to the Allies agreed upon by Badoglio and that the monarchy question remain submerged until the end of the war.[25]

Although it meant the end of the Badoglio regime, the CLN victory did not signal Churchill's apocalyptic vision of Left hegemony and an anti-Fascist massacre. In August, the British prime minister under-took an inspection trip of the Italian front and made the effort to visit Rome. Churchill may not have enjoyed the trip—he seemed only to take pleasure in the company of the pope and of Crown Prince Umberto—but it could only be interpreted as an endorsement of the CLN regime.[26]

Bonomi served the Allies as a conservative, stabilizing factor, but his new government was a coalition, and within that coali-tion there existed little agreement beyond the necessity of military vic-tory over Hitler and Mussolini. Sanctions against fascism, particularly and significantly, divided the parties. All CLN factions—mainly the Com-munists, Socialists, adherents to the "Action" Party, or *azionisti*, Chris-tian Democrats, and Liberals—advanced their own approaches to the problem. Their points of view were tempered by both ideology and experiences during the *ventennio*, and they took the form of a lively journalistic debate which began soon after Rome's liberation. Each party,

through its press organ, expressed opinions on the nature and parameters that sanctions should take.[27]

The Communist party position had shifted radically by June 1944.
Through 1943 its organization in Italy had in effect been relatively
independent from Moscow. After it was outlawed by Mussolini, the
party's leadership had left the country, gone into hiding, been put in
prison, or dropped out of politics altogether. As a result, what remained
was a weak clandestine organization, all but nonexistent in the south
and pretty much on its own elsewhere through the late 1920s and
1930s. Because the party and its leadership became scattered within
Italy and in foreign exile, it soon developed two natures, one identified
with Palmiro Togliatti and oriented toward Moscow, and the other associated more with those who stayed in Italy, often in prison. During
the fall of 1942, the PCI in Moscow had begun to formulate new directives and transmit them to party adherents back home. In order to
defeat Mussolini, the new "national front" policy sought to forge alliances, not only with Socialists and other leftist parties, but with Catholics, the military, monarchists, and even dissident Fascists.

The new policy circulated in Italy during the months before the
collapse of the Duce's regime in July 1943. In June, PCI leader Concetto
Marchese confided to Liberal friends that his party would collaborate
with the king to rid Italy of Mussolini. But many other Communists
resisted the new arrangement and preferred to deride the Royal House,
the military, big business, and the entire ruling class. Led by many
veteran stalwarts like Pietro Secchia, Mauro Scoccimarro, and Velio
Spano, these dissidents refused to abandon their traditional stance
against those who had betrayed Italy and plunged it into the catastrophe of war. After September 8, while the PCI's immediate task remained
the defeat of nazism, all of Italy, particularly the ruling classes, must
be purged in order to build democracy. In his resistance to a serious
restructuring of Italian society and his maintenance of the nation's
traditionalist ruling class, Badoglio received the scorn of these mal-
contented Communists. Toward the end of 1943, they launched an
appeal to the people, charging that the marshal represented Italy's
most reactionary forces and as such ignored defascistization in order
to favor his sneaky friends among the *gerarchi* and other criminals.[28]

PCI dissidents, however, abandoned their objections and radical views
during the volatile months that followed the establishment of the Regno

del Sud. The issue was settled in March 1944 when the party's leader, Togliatti, returned to Italy from his Moscow exile and enforced the new policy. This astonishing about-face, known as the "Salerno turnaround" (*svolta di Salerno*), guaranteed the adoption of the national front. The PCI endorsed the Badoglio regime and modified its intransigent stand on sanctions.[29]

In April 1944 Togliatti was taken into the government as minister without portfolio. The new and somewhat incongruous arrangement was reluctantly endorsed in May by the PCI ideologue Pietro Secchia. Recently released after years in Ventotene Prison, Secchia was pressured to concede that, to combat fascism effectively, Communists must take orders from others, "even when they are members of other parties with ideas different from our own." The pragmatic Badoglio welcomed the about-face and developed a "full and happy" working relationship with Togliatti, something abhorred by Socialists and Actionists who were unburdened by orders from Moscow. Thus, the Communists were to follow commands from those who, a few months before, had been labeled "exponents" of the reactionary forces that had led Italy to the catastrophe of war.[30] Applied to sanctions, the *svolta* meant that the PCI would support Badoglio's actions, a far cry from its earlier dicta. Togliatti would go so far that in April 1944 he announced in the party journal that sanctions against fascism meant ferreting out saboteurs and spies, nothing more.[31]

Communists could never, of course, abandon completely their demand of sanctions against Fascists. With the liberation of Rome, *L'Unità* continued to endorse an effective purge. To end its support of one would have been a serious mistake, and the paper applauded Colonel Poletti's first steps in that direction. But anxious not to embarrass or worry any right-wing factions within the government, which had been guaranteed its support, *L'Unità* added that the purge was to be neither a personal nor an anti-Fascist vendetta against the old "*aguzzini*." The party's vision of the all-embracing purge that would cleanse Italy for the new people's democracy had been replaced by one of moderation in the national interest.[32]

Gathered under the temporary banner of the Italian Socialist Party of Proletarian Unity (PSIUP, later PSI), the Socialists surpassed the PCI's original line. Gathered around party leader Pietro Nenni, most among the radical wing would not consider abandoning their harsh

57

sanctionist stance in return for cordial relations with Badoglio. Although even Nenni had flirted with fascism in its early days and had counted himself among Mussolini's oldest, though ersatz, friends, under his leadership the PSIUP became the most powerful force for effective defascistization and for the punishment of the maximum number of Fascists. The August 26, 1943, issue of *Avanti!* was immediately clear on this point; the July coup was portrayed as a palace plot and a sham intended to whitewash the ruling classes. The Badoglio regime was a fraud engineered by reactionaries and big capital and had no intention of restoring liberties, much less democracy, to the Italian people. Accordingly, *Avanti!* called on a worker's movement to destroy "the bourgeois state."[33]

Unlike the Communists, furthermore, the Socialists were not confused with a *svolta di Salerno*. Party views were never hinged on the dictates of Moscow, so PSIUP participation in Badoglio's April and Bonomi's June cabinets did not affect its early intransigent stance on defascistization. Nor did the liberation of Rome alter Socialist policy. If anything, the party stood out on the left and appeared even more radical since it had been abandoned by its Communist allies. In the June 5 *Avanti!*, the PSIUP proclaimed its faith in a purge that spared no important Fascist and declared that no collaborationist should ever receive a position in the free Italian government. The paper predicted that some would try to disguise their pasts and slink back into office. For them the Socialists promised "rigorous punishment."[34]

The PSIUP demanded not only stringent measures but also their application over a broader spectrum of Italian society, beyond the narrow political class. Their first target and the object of their most heated attacks was the crown. For example, Socialists attacked the institutional truce, something that the Communists would not do. On June 7, a Nenni editorial blared, "Victor Emmanuele Get Out!" (*Vittorio Emmanuele, se ne va!*), blaming the Royal House for much of the Fascist regime and the disasters of the war. The lieutenant-generalcy was labeled a stunt, a sham, a last-ditch attempt to preserve an immoral monarchy that, in its icy silence, had been secretly sheltering Fascists.[35]

Attitudes of the numerically weak Action party were as vehement as the Socialists'. Primarily a grouping of intellectuals and white-collar professionals, the Action party was an outgrowth of the fiercely republican left wing of the old anti-Fascist Giustizia e Libertà movement; and its intellectual and moral weight within the Resistance movement and the CLN was much greater than numbers could indicate. The party's views on sanctions were first printed in a clandestine edition of *Italia Libera* in January 1943 and were conceived in much the same terms as those of the Socialists, holding that fascism had not been merely a corruption of society or a dictatorship by a few thugs and criminals. Rather, they concluded, the ruling classes had bankrolled Mussolini's regime and were collectively responsible for the *ventennio*. In order to eradicate fascism and bring democracy to Italy, those culprits must be dealt with severely. The monarchy must be abolished, large capital and industry must be nationalized, and radical agrarian reform, including the breakup of the great *latifondi*, must be implemented.

The Action party was the only CLN faction to seriously treat the church in its platform. This was a particularly sensitive subject in that relations between the church and the Fascists had run hot and cold over the years, although for the most part it was a symbiotic affair. The *azionisti* considered essential an analysis of the church's role in their new Italy, but even they could not lay much blame on the institution and in the end called rather blandly for separation of the two spheres. This important exception aside, however, the Action party was as inclusive as any other in its condemnation of the ruling classes for the crime of fascism.[36]

The liberation of Rome did not signal any change in the Action party's stance, and its newspaper attempted to categorize the problem by identifying four Fascist "types." The first and largest of these was the least culpable: men and women on the street, whose crime was one of conscience. Appropriate penance here might include reeducation. The three other, more blameworthy groups were the career Fascists, the thieves, and those responsible for the 1925 coup d'état. This last category implied a dynamic role for the ruling classes as instigators of a plot to launch the Fascist dictatorship.[37] In an interview with a PWB agent, the Action party ideologue Ugo La Malfa reiterated that the blame for fascism must be placed on the ruling classes. He saw much of the problem in the extreme gulf between rich and poor. The governing groups in Italy were simply too powerful, and some means of curtailing their domination had to be discovered.[38]

The *azionisti* carried the left banner of the Giustizia e Libertà movement. Its right banner was held by those in the Liberal party who congregated around the overwhelming figure of Benedetto Croce and the organization's mouthpiece, *Risorgimento Liberale*. As self-styled representatives of traditionalist Italy, however, the Liberals could easily be subjected to criticism from the *azionisti* and the Socialists, who, if they wished to, could logically include many PLI leaders in their sanctionist nets. Croce, of course, was not a Fascist. He and his followers, nevertheless, were obliged to walk a very narrow path within the CLN and worked hard to disassociate themselves from fascism. Their arguments echoed those of Badoglio, labeling Mussolini's followers as traitors and refusing to categorize fascism as a class phenomenon, as the Socialists and *azionisti* had done, but by emphasizing personal choice in the matter of political alignment. This was reinforced by a quite sincere elaboration of Liberal philosophy. Grounded in the Hegelian tradition, Croce considered the problem as a corruption of the individual spirit. As there were murderers, criminals, and social deviants, so there were Fascists. The upper classes were responsible only insofar as they did not use their moral weight in an all-out battle against Mussolini. But they were not collectively guilty. Certainly there were Fascists in the ruling classes, but Fascists existed in all classes. The prison guard was as guilty as the minister of the interior.

Croce published one of the most famous polemics on this subject in the October 29, 1944, *Giornale di Napoli*. Soon acknowledged as the standard Liberal line, his article "Who Is Fascist?" ("Chi è fascista?") conceptualized Mussolini's regime as an intellectual and moral illness (*morbo intellettuale e morale*) that affected all ranks. Quick to challenge Marxist accusations that, as part of the ruling political structure of the country, middle-class parties like the Liberals were particularly guilty of fascism, Croce wrote that the *ventennio* was "a crisis born in disillusion not only with rational liberalism but also with Marxism." Croce insisted that to look for the roots of fascism meant more than an analysis of Italian class structure. It meant exploring the dark corners of the psyche, something very difficult to do, as Croce admitted. But to put Italy on the mend, one had to purge individual minds and spirits.[39]

Upon the liberation of Rome, Croce's thoughts echoed in the *Risorgimento Liberale*. A June 14 article entitled "Harshest Punishments" ("Severissime Pene") branded the Fascists as "traitors," traitors to the real Italy of humanism and liberalism. It praised the May 26 decree that extended the Zaniboni Commission into all liberated Italy and treated Fascists as traitors and, thus, aberrants. This sentiment was emphasized on June 23 in another treatise, this time by the Liberal ideologue Manlio Lupinacci. In "Guarantees of Justice" ("Garanzie di Giustizia"), he countered, once again, leftist insinuations that, as a bourgeois party, the Liberals were partly responsible for fascism. In turn, Lupinacci attacked the Left as wholly sectarian in its zeal to punish. On June 30 the *Risorgimento Liberale* reiterated in its editorial "Giustizia" that any purge or punishment must be directed at individuals and not at social categories.[40]

The Catholic position was the most distinctive and did not correspond to those of the other parties.[41] The intellectual bases of the Christian Democratic movement were found more in traditional religious philosophy than in Enlightenment and nineteenth-century materialist and class-centered beliefs. Many DC leaders condemned the entire post–French Revolutionary political system that had introduced both Hitler and Stalin to Europe; they also urged a reevaluation of a world gripped in ideology and thus artificially divided. Christian Democracy (DC) postured as the champion of all people, rejecting special interests, be they interests of privilege or social revolution. As an avowed "mass party," it labored to maintain and extend its constituent base among the Italian bourgeoisie, made serious claims on the loyalty of the working class, and was undoubtedly the most popular force among peasants, especially in the south, and later, Lombardy and the northeast. It refused to defend or attack social groups in the way that the Socialists attacked the ruling classes and the Liberals in effect defended them. The party never urged or even intimated notions of revenge or overt harshness in punishment. And while the DC could always be suspected of defending its own bourgeois constituency and shielding the church, its religious tradition necessitated that mercy and a resistance to radical measures be incorporated into its stance on sanctions. Christian Democracy could, therefore, urge conciliation and forgiveness in the debate, as virtues unto themselves, and not sound entirely self-serving.[42]

The Christian Democrats' most nagging problem, however, was that the church was heavily compromised by the Fascist regime. As a foreign state, the Vatican was, of course, beyond the reach of sanctions; but a clerical network numbering in the tens of thousands embraced

Italy. Certain well-placed officials, such as Milan's Cardinal Ildefonso Schuster, Father Enrico Rosa of the *Civiltà Cattolica*, and Father Agostino Gemelli, rector of the Catholic University, were among the many influential churchmen who publicly supported the regime. Lest that clergy be implicated in punishments, the Catholic party sidestepped this issue. And it was highly successful: a purge of the church was never seriously considered, and, except for a few Salò fanatics, no cleric ever served a prison sentence for his role in the Fascist regime.

Despite its evasions, the DC presented some embryonic opinions on punishment in a series of clandestinely published articles, mostly written by Alcide De Gasperi, in December 1943 and January 1944 editions of its organ, *Il Popolo*. These editorials illustrated that Christian Democracy's approach to sanctions did not conform to the strict dogmas of the more materialist parties. While, in "The Word of the Christian Democrats," *Il Popolo* called for fairer distribution from "excessive concentrations of riches," the newspaper was careful not to threaten the plutocracy with a purge. The most innovative thought here was an allusion to generational guilt for fascism. Christian Democracy claimed to be a union of the young and the old but made little reference to the middle aged. It professed to speak for a continuity between two extreme generations: the Catholics who fought the *squadristi* in the early 1920s and Resistance heroes of the mid-1940s. The notion was certainly an interesting one, but the Christian Democratic ideologues never followed up on it.[43]

The DC groped for a nonclass-based handle on sanctions but could not find a satisfactory one. As a result, most party statements seemed inconclusive. Emblematic of Catholic defascistization notions was the call to transform the Via Tasso torture chambers into a "haven of charity" (*un asilo di carità*), just as a church, St. Agnes in Agony, had been built over the spot where, in antiquity, the Roman soldier "attempted to rape the innocent Roman virgin."[44]

Christian Democrats had also already begun to question the wisdom of past anti-Fascist measures. In June 1944 G. Margotti wrote in *Il Popolo* that Badoglio's May decree had been "a juridical and moral error." Another, unsigned article suggested that Poletti's defascistization measures contained the risk of hurting the small, "the weak, next to the criminals," and that universal consensus and cooperation were required to determine responsibility for fascism. The DC maintained, nevertheless, that reform and proper punishment must come from above, not from the people. Margotti advised the Romans to put their faith in government justice.[45]

Another presence in the political fray, although unrepresented in the CLN coalition, was the crown. A monarchist movement formed, nevertheless, and its newspaper, *Italia Nuova*, was among the first to attack the broad sanctions. The newspaper claimed that a purge based on wide-ranging Socialist and *azionista* parameters would create deep fissures in the social rock upon which Italy was built. Any defascistiza-tion program should practice special caution since the nation was at war, and tampering with its fragile government could not be afforded. Harsh punishments would harm the government's ability to fight the Nazis and serve the Allied cause. Already, by June 14, before any seri-ous purge had even begun, *Italia Nuova* claimed that fear of one had gripped the state bureaucracy in a paralyzing terror.

However, the royalists could not appear too enthusiastic in their con-demnation of a purge, so instead of taking issue with CLN objectives, they focused on the alternative enemy—Salò. The identification of Mussolini and the RSI as the persistent and undefeated Fascist menace worked well for the monarchists. Umberto could appear as the man on the white horse, leading liberated Italy against frondeur rebels at Salò. In this regard, the monarchists emphasized an argument that distinguished the RSI from the *ventennio*. The more the public forgot October 1922 and remembered September 1943, the better it would be for the crown.

But the monarchists complicated the argument one step further. The Badoglio government had previously emphasized September 8 as the crucial date to define Salò treason. If one had decided, on that date, to follow the Fascists north, then he was a collaborator. The prob-lem here was that many, probably over half, of the Rome bureaucracy had remained in the capital between September 8 and the liberation. Under Badoglio's distinction, all were guilty of collaboration. Further complications arose from orders by the retreating *gerarchi* demanding that functionaries retire north with them or suffer the consequences. Anyone who remained in Rome thus found himself in serious trouble, theoretically, with both sides. *Italia Nuova* opted to defend the bureau-crats and insisted that, while those who went north in June 1944 should receive the most severe justice, those who stayed in Rome to face the

Allies and the new government represented a complex problem that required perhaps not exoneration but more compassion.[46]

Besides their collaborationist/loyalist dichotomy, the monarchists added another distinction that echoed Liberal and Badoglian arguments: criminalization of selected Fascist political acts. The monarchists adopted the position that a difference existed between well-meaning card holders and those Fascists who had abused their powers for illicit ends, that being a Fascist per se was no crime, but the abuse of Fascist power was. For example, on July 14, *Italia Nuova* advocated sanctions against those who used their past merits, like participation in the March on Rome, to obtain illegal advancement in the state machine. No one could disagree with that position, and it appeared as if *Italia Nuova* were adopting a slightly more progressive line. But this editorial was tempered with the caveat that summary justice and vendetta would solve nothing. The new government must treat the Fascists with "justice, tolerance, and magnanimity."[47]

Inauguration of the CLN government had pushed the lively debate on defascistization onto the front pages of the popular press. The five major parties could count on their positions being heard in the Council of Ministers and in their journals, while the monarchists could rely on their own press, as well as on the Royal House itself, for publicity. The only agreement between them was on the narrowest of foundations, that is, that someone or some persons should be punished somehow. How this was to develop into a policy was still anyone's guess.

FIRST SANCTIONS IN ROME

The liberation of Rome emboldened those who considered Badoglio's defascistization decrees as useless and stillborn. Many wished to redefine the task and refashion the weapons. Some might have forgiven the slipshod operation beforehand. But this was now Rome, the center of Italian bureaucracy. Until the CLN coalition could mobilize itself in that direction, however, the work remained primarily in Allied hands.

The importance of the city as fertile turf for defascistization was obvious enough. Even under Salò, Rome had remained the bureaucratic cornerstone of the RSI. Mussolini moved the highest administrators to offices in the north, but most of the staffs remained at their desks in the Eternal City. When the neo-Fascists evacuated, furthermore, all bureaucrats were ordered to follow. Severe penalties such as loss of pensions and even prison sentences were to be exacted on noncompliant functionaries. Many employees bowed to this pressure and retreated north with the Fascists. It is impossible to determine how many of them did so, but the numbers were significant. For example, in September 1944 the British ambassador, Sir Noel Charles, reported to London on the status of the bureaucrats in the old Fascist Ministry of Popular Culture. He reported that of the agency's 550 permanent civil servants and 524 temporary employees on the payroll, 251 permanent and 141 temporary staff members retreated into Salò territory.[48]

Chances for an effective purge in Rome were enhanced when the Allied regional commissioner of Rome was chosen. The most capable and indefatigable administrator in Italy, Charles Poletti, arrived shortly after the liberation. His fame stemmed from his administration of Naples and Palermo, as well as from his athletic corpulence and broad smile, which soon became daily sights for many Romans. Macmillan called him "a real American, a one hundred per center."[49]

On June 26 Poletti launched his purge with Administrative Order Number 1. This measure originated in his tenure as governor in Naples, where he authorized and engaged his staff in a plan to formulate punishment guidelines. The actual authors were Poletti's assistant Maurice Neufeld and the Neapolitan Socialist lawyer Rosalbino Santoro. Santoro had been married to an American woman before the war and headed an Italian association of World War I veterans. He was reluctant to work with the Allies in devising a defascistization strategy but was pressured into it. Years later, as Italy settled into a more normal routine, Santoro's private business suffered due to embittered Fascists who had been displaced by his actions.[50]

The new purge measure was released as Region III (Naples) Administrative Order Number 3 on June 2 and then as Administrative Order Number 1 in Rome on June 26. It appeared rather rudimentary, but perhaps its simplicity hid an admirable efficacy. A commission of Allied officers was established to review cases of accused Fascists. This commission was to work alongside an advisory board made up of twelve CLN members, two from each of the parties. Within two days of the announcement, *Italia Libera* could report that an incredible

65

3,750 cases had been deliberated and that 1,700 agents of the Fascist PAI police would be dismissed. The Action party newspaper announced optimistically, "The purge has begun."[51]

A PWB report noted that the Left in general welcomed the new Poletti decree, a measure that aimed at the goals advocated by the Socialists and *azionisti*. If anything, for them, Order Number 1 may have been even too complete, too sweeping to be applicable. Indeed, conservatives certainly considered the measure as unreasonable and extreme. Poletti had overstepped his bounds once before in March when he envisioned a purge of private industry and was quickly rebuked by Badoglio. The marshal complained to the Allies that Poletti was "sovietizing" Italian industry, and the project was squelched. Furthermore, a PWB observer reported that many socially privileged Romans greeted Order Number 1 with little enthusiasm. The analyst discerned "a noticeable tendency among the leisured classes to decry these decrees as altogether too radical and likely to endanger the structure of Italian society."[52]

If newspapers were any measure, then the PWB was correct in its estimation of Left and Right reaction to the Poletti purge. The Communist *Unità*, anxious to reconcile its national front stance with its ideological predispositions, preached a "purge without quarter [*salvataggi*]," and sided at once with Poletti without the reservations found in the conservative press. The Socialist *Avanti!* ran a cartoon that summarized its view of monarchist reaction to defascistization. Behind an oversized crown, two Fascists were quickly changing clothes. One says to his *camerata*, "Hurry, throw away your blackshirt and shout '*Vive il re!*'" On the other side of the spectrum, the monarchist *Italia Nuova* warned Romans, even before Poletti announced his decree, that a purge was a dangerous method of defascistization. However, to denounce a purge at that time would be highly impolitic. Of course, the monarchists argued, a purge was necessary, but it must be a careful one of moderation.[53]

Announced and trumpeted by the Allied newspaper, the *Corriere di Roma*, Poletti's purge of Rome had begun on an encouraging note. On July 5 it boasted that five hundred people, all Fascists, had been suspended from Rome's communal administration. The *Corriere* announced on the same day that "the first step [had] been taken" at the University of Rome. With the assistance of Giuseppe Caronia, professor of infectious diseases and future rector of the school, Poletti formally suspended a number of high-level Fascists who taught courses at the Sapienza. The list included luminaries like Giuseppe Bottai and Giacomo Acerbo. But action against them was a dead letter since these *gerarchi* had long before vanished. Many others conducted courses in politics or law with an obvious Fascist slant. Men like Francesco Coppola, who taught the history of international relations, and Emilio Bodrero, who lectured on "The History of Fascist Doctrine" and signed the Manifesto of Fascist Intellectuals in 1925, were fired.

The *Corriere* also announced a crackdown on the Fascist police. Mussolini's questore of Rome, Pietro Caruso, was the prime catch. Early on the morning of June 5, as the Anglo-American advance units neared the gates of the city, Caruso and some followers evacuated their offices and the legendary torture chambers of the Via Tasso. Within a few hours, however, the long arm of the United Nations had reached the ex-police boss. Caruso's auto had smashed into a German vehicle on the way out of the city, and his body was left on the side of the road by the retreating Fascists. Shortly afterward he was located in a nearby hospital. The Liberal newspaper, *Risorgimento Liberale*, breathed a sigh of relief in its June 7 edition. "Now we expect to see these sad figures, who have spread grief and tears over the city, put up against the wall."

Two and a half hours later, the new head of police, Enrico Morazzini, occupied his desk. The *Corriere di Roma* described his first day on the job, emphasizing the orderliness of the new occupation. The questore walked into his office and found all of the functionaries at their posts ready to start the new day. The work of the police would continue but "on bases and on principles quite different from those that characterized the long Fascist period." Morazzini announced that twenty-seven functionaries would be immediately fired. The period of informers, spies, and tapped phones was over. The political office was to be entirely revamped and dedicated to the restoration of the human liberties that the Fascists had so flagrantly and brutally violated.[54]

On July 9 came the announcement of the AMG's arrest of the local OVRA boss, Gesualdo Barletta. The Anglo-Americans promised to turn Barletta over to the local officials for trial; but their hunt did not end with him. On the same day Lieutenant Colonel Pollock of the Public Security Subcommission declared a purge of the Regina Coeli prison, and seventeen days later the governor of the institution, Donato Carretta, and five of his staff were fired.[55]

In an effort to leave no stone unturned, Poletti investigated Fascist corruption of the arts. In that nest of intrigue he discovered the world-famous opera star, Beniamino Gigli. Gigli had many fans of all political persuasions but had maintained close contacts with the Germans during the occupation. He had graciously given a command performance for the notorious "smiling" Nazi boss of Rome, Lieutenant General Kurt Maelzer. This could not be forgiven. Upon the liberation Gigli planned to give another performance at the Teatro Reale for the Allies, but Poletti chose to cancel it. Later the artist would write that, "having 'sung for the Germans,' I now discovered to my astonishment that I was a traitor." Like Mussolini, or like Stefania Rossi, the proprietress of the Pensione Trinità dei Monti, Gigli represented that emblematic or strategic aspect of the regime. The famous opera star's career coincided with fascism's in the 1920s and 1930s. The suspension of celebrities like Gigli often received the greatest press, not only in the *Corriere* but in other papers as well.[56]

Inspired in part by Poletti and often in conjunction with the Anglo-Americans, the Italians also made some progress on sanctions. The waning Badoglio government had already activated the old Zaniboni Commission throughout all of liberated Italy. But since that commission hardly existed even on paper, the order was hollow. Wheels had begun to turn, however, and by June 27 *Italia Libera* announced that for the first time criminal charges had been filed against Fascists. Four defendants were scheduled to appear before the court, three of whom were Neapolitans: Ciano's banker, Giuseppe Frignani; the prefect Domenico Soprano; the industrial magnate and political boss Achille Lauro; and Mussolini's foreign minister, Dino Grandi.[57]

The proposed trial in Naples complemented other achievements, foremost among them the incarceration of Vincenzo Azzolini, governor of the Bank of Italy. Rome's military commander, General Erskine Hume, personally arrested him at the banker's home. The Liberal *Risorgimento Liberale* hailed this as the conclusion of a long period of *malgoverno* for the nation's first financial institution.[58] On July 27 the *Corriere di Roma* announced yet another crackdown on Neapolitans. Four important directors of state concerns, including the southern communications czar, Ugo Pellegrini, were suspended.

The Allied Control Commission expressed real faith in the Poletti juggernaut. At an August 22 meeting, Commodore Stone bragged about Poletti and "this hard-hitting epuration commission" that had "thousands" of leading Fascists turned out of their jobs and "hundreds" arrested. Stone continued, "Without a thorough and rugged clearance of leading Fascists from positions of public trust and influence, a new Italy of liberty can never arise."[59]

But despite the glowing words, Poletti and his men were soon committing the same mistakes found in previous purge attempts. Added to logistical dilemmas, lack of clear direction, and the growing political pressure discussed earlier, Allied officers were also often lulled into social contacts with members of the Italian ruling classes. Whereas the political parties debated the nature of sanctions and wondered whether they could be extended beyond narrow political-class confines, many conservatives in the ruling class had been maneuvering quietly to strengthen their ties with the Anglo-Americans. The governor's assistant, Maurice Neufeld, complained of that lack of discernment, which had hampered the Neapolitan purge and now persisted in Rome. He cited the case of a number of American and British officers who were invited to the home of an Italian aristocrat for lunch. The Allied officers had no idea that their hostess had been just as friendly with the Germans and Fascists. The affair was spoiled by an abrupt intervention by Allied Counter Intelligence forces who arrested some of the Italian guests, including the chief propagandist of the defunct Fascist radio station. The famous historian and anti-Fascist Gaetano Salvemini complained of similar circumstances to an American readership. In an article published in the *Nation*, he recounted the collusion between Roman aristocrats and Allied officers. Many such examples concerned American wives of Italian noblemen.[60]

Neufeld and Salvemini were not alone in lamenting the easy fraternization between the new authorities and potential purge cases. In London, a Foreign Office official recorded the same discontent after a luncheon conversation he had with a CAO fresh from Italy. The CAO, a Mr. Young, chastised the higher-ups as "dug-out senior army officers who do not even pay lip service to anti-Fascist ideals," and among the Italians the new prefects were nothing more than disguised Fascists. The Foreign Office official suggested in his report that Mr. Young's bitterness be taken with a grain of salt. "He was consumed by the Fascist bogey and honestly believed that every Catholic and Conservative was a potential Mussolini or Hitler."[61]

Beyond the campaign against sanctions that was waged in the press by their political surrogates, traditionalists in the ruling classes relied on their powers of social, extrapolitical contacts, and many Anglo-American officers, homesick, lonely, or easily impressed, were more than willing to oblige. The AMG personnel may or may not have connected their gracious dinner companions with their Fascist enemies. The "dug-out senior army officers" in Young's complaint were, figuratively, the same men who drank the wine and tasted the sweet life of Italian refinement. They liked what they saw and must have doubted the necessity of punishing their hosts for what seemed to be, at worst, past indiscretions.

On the other end of the spectrum, the obvious military danger posed by active neo-Fascists and fifth columnists occupied the primary attention of the Anglo-Americans. Military decisions being paramount, saboteurs and spies were treated first and most severely. Allied worry was well justified, for the RSI had indeed been involved in violent subversive acts in southern Italy. Covert activity occasionally took the form of clandestine links between Salò and the south, such as in the Martini affair in Sardinia. On other occasions, the Allies were faced with small groups of neo-Fascists, often teenagers, who occupied themselves by obstructing the war effort, minor acts of violence, or scribbling Fascist slogans on walls. As early as October 1943 a group of neo-Fascist boys was arrested in Trapani, Sicily, for cutting communication lines between Vittoria and Gela. As was usually the case, the Allies took charge of the proceedings and prosecuted the gang. The Brindisi government rarely had any say in these affairs, which the Anglo-Americans considered purely military matters. The ringleader of the Trapani gang, also guilty of possessing a pistol, was sentenced to death and was shot. One member was given nineteen years and the others received lesser penalties.

Many other groups formed, both in the islands and on the continent, which tried to establish links with Salò. But these organizations, such as the Movimento Unitario Italiano in Catania or the Guardie ai Labari in Calabria and Campania, had emerged out of the rubble of defeat and displayed little or no continuity with the fascism of the *ventennio*. It was a nostalgic as opposed to a concrete fascism, with few direct contacts to any important *gerarchi* who remained hidden in the south. Nevertheless, the RSI maintained contacts with these groups and relied on them for information and sabotage.

The most important saboteur/spy was the leader of the Guardie ai Labari, Prince Valerio Pignatelli, once described as "a type of meridional d'Artagnan." Pignatelli was a maverick who never possessed real power in the PNF and who, more than once, was even tossed out of it. He was rich, dashing, had important friends in London and Washington, and, it was claimed, was related to Henry Ford. Upon the urging of the Fascist *gerarca* Carlo Scorza, Pignatelli assembled an RSI spy network from his Neapolitan palace. Allied secrets soon found their way to Salò as a result of lavish parties thrown by the prince in honor of the Anglo-American liberators. But the first crack in Pignatelli's ring occurred in a February 1944 roundup. Finally, attempts in April by the princess to hoodwink Allied intelligence units backfired and resulted in her and her husband's imprisonment.[62]

Neo-Fascist infiltration of the Italian military and security forces posed another dilemma for the Allies. Among all segments of the Italian government, London and Washington bestowed perhaps the highest role to the Carabinieri and other security forces in that it was they who were relied upon to keep the peace and allow the Allies to focus on the war at the front. Any links between Badoglio's police and Mussolini's RSI, therefore, could have catastrophic consequences for the war effort. Nevertheless, the security forces were among the official agencies least touched by sanctions.

That problem stemmed mainly from one of Badoglio's early, disastrous mistakes, his integration of the Fascist party Militia into the armed forces. It was a mistake that could not easily be undone. A thorough purge of the military would be a colossal, probably embarrassing task that neither the Allies nor the Royal government relished. During the *ventennio*, most of the military had rallied around the king in, at best, a slight opposition to the regime. Conservatives hoped that the royalist officer corps would keep control of the military and security forces to ensure their places in the Center-Right political bastion. Meanwhile, the loyalty of the security forces to the crown was another trump card held by the monarchy, a trump card the Allies did not challenge.

Some members of the supposedly reliable security forces were, nevertheless, still linked to Fascist elements, and Anglo-American observers felt obliged to report these connections to their home governments.

On March 10, 1945, Ambassador Alexander Kirk indicated to the State Department that thirty-five Carabinieri members were involved in a PRF "cell." They even circulated their own paper, *Onore*. Kirk's letter was only one of many observations made on this matter in diplomatic channels, in Italian government circles, and in the press.[63]

The liberation of Rome had opened a new phase in both the punishment and the conception of punishment of Fascists. For the Anglo-Americans and for the Italians, the issues became more pressing and more political. But the problems were also more confused and clouded than they had been in July 1943. The Allies appeared far more willing than the Italian government to purge through this period, and their actions reinforced this view. However, such actions were locally conceived and applied. The AMG was not a monolith, and a man like Poletti could exist in the same administration with those Anglo-American officers who dined with Fascists. The only complete agreement among the Allies concerned crackdowns on saboteurs and spies, like those in Trapani, which had very little to do with the broader Italian issues.

Through June 1944 little recorded sentiment appeared among the broadest spectrum of the population for serious prosecution and purges of Fascists. Both the people of Rome and their southern cousins remained relatively quiet, a complacency that must have encouraged the traditionalist forces. Part of this quiet stemmed from other causes related to wartime emergency, but much of it was the result of the way Fascists were perceived. The most famous leaders had vanished. And the dearth of any serious and popular signal toward social revolution seemed to indicate that the ruling classes had been successful in disassociating themselves from the defunct regime.

With the return of free expression, political parties and their journals launched a spirited debate on sanctions. Their arguments revealed serious fissures within the CLN coalition, divisions illustrating that politicians and ideologues themselves faced difficulties identifying Fascists. The crucial point of contention concerned the extent of defascistization. How deep must a purger's scalpel cut into the nation's body? Was punishment aimed against a class or against individuals? To conceive of fascism not as a narrowly based dictatorship but as a mass and national phenomenon was a task that still eluded many.

THE PROBLEM OF ROME

The most interesting ideological argument here was found in the ranks of the Liberal party, whose determination to blame individuals and not classes implied sanctions geared not at fascism but at Fascists who were criminals. Of all the parties, the PLI's stance best reflected the reality at work that viewed fascism as dead and associated the movement with its strategic elite and highly visible personalities. Who would be on trial—the ideologue, the bureaucrat, the lover, the profiteer, or the general? Someone like the notorious PNF secretary, Achille Starace, or Stefania Rossi? Despite the obvious differences in rank and importance, both Starace and Rossi served as Fascist icons. Vivid and strategic, they were the easiest symbols to grasp.

The Allies, officially at least, and the Left parties, however, pressured the Bonomi government to construct some sort of Fascist policy. Badoglio's actions had clearly failed and could never be applied to the gigantic Roman bureaucracy. Upon the liberation of the capital, Bonomi would be forced to oversee a program to deal effectively with Fascists in the government. The response would be the keystone of anti-Fascist measures: DLL 159, July 27, 1944, which set the standards and the machinery that framed the parameters of all subsequent actions. The most important part of this measure created the Alto Commissariato per le sanzioni contro il fascismo, a High Commission for Sanctions against Fascism.

CHAPTER FOUR

SANCTIONS AGAINST FASCISM

The weeks after the liberation of Rome and the formation of the Bonomi government inaugurated a new and more complex phase in the story of punishments of Fascists. Badoglio's sterile regime had ended, and the introduction of free politics could not but dramatically alter the situation. The result was the cornerstone decree for sanctions against fascism, Decreto legislativo luogotenenziale number 159, July 27, 1944. Shortly after the decree was made public, Prime Minister Bonomi proclaimed that the direction would now shift from Anglo-American into Italian hands and that the nation was on the verge of creating an entirely new ruling class. Both statements required very important qualifications.[1]

Complications guaranteed immediately that the new law would be applied only with great difficulty. First, wartime logistics created headaches. Obvious and pressing details of establishing new government machinery in the middle of a war curtailed hopes. Shortages of fuel, paper, and personnel automatically restricted what could be accomplished. The new legislation was voided in effect when these difficulties were reinforced by the actions of conservatives and traditionalists who opposed the program. Strong impetus for the program suffered as well from indecision among its champions. The Left, which theoretically advocated broad and severe application of sanctions, was in reality divided between rigorous Socialists and *azionisti* and more malleable Communists, who undercut the program.

The task was also complicated by the fact that, outside of the earlier weak-hearted attempts and half starts, the new government still groped in the dark. Marshal Badoglio had devised his early ineffectual anti-Fascist actions without precedents and had constructed them within a political context still heavily Fascist. There had never been a sanctions program from which to draw experience. Mussolini had been the first Axis dictator to fall, and southern Italy in September 1943 was the first territory in western Europe to submit to Allied occupation. The invasion of France did not occur until June 1944, and after Italy the first of Germany's allies to break was Romania, two months later. Thus, even in mid-1944, both the Allies' administrative machinery for Italy and sanctions against Fascists were still experimental.

In this regard, Badoglio's first attempts, regardless of their motivation and effectiveness, were important if only as precedents. His defascistization left a heritage of narrow visions: timid measures selectively directed, which ignored the extensive presence of fascism in Italian society. A dictatorship of twenty years had not been so successful because a handful of ideologues and bureaucrats in the government made it so.

The new measures of July 1944 may not have been perfect, but they systematized an assault on the bureaucracy and signaled the first real volleys from the camp that favored true sanctions, sincerely and effectively applied against Fascists. The Right had easily tolerated Badoglio's tactics of selective or slipshod punishments and of focusing blame on the Duce, Starace, and the rest of the "important" and newsworthy Fascists. Now, however, the attack would turn on the nameless, faceless government machine; the net would be cast wider. The purgers now aimed beyond the charismatic, notorious, or strategic elements of the Fascist dictatorship and began to look at the bureaucracy, the more "permanent" element of the Italian government. If these administrators could be subjected to sanctions, then roads might be opened beyond—roads leading to private business, certain professions, or the Quirinal Palace.

DECRETO LEGISLATIVO LUOGOTENENZIALE NUMBER 159

The Italian government's measure, DLL 159, issued on July 27, 1944, superseded all previous provisions against Fascists. It created the High Commission for Sanctions against Fascism, the government machinery to investigate and punish. The law was divided into five parts or titles. The most significant titles, the first and the fifth, spelled out the parameters of Fascist crime and set up the High Commission.

Article 2 of Title 1 proclaimed the intent of the new decree: "The members of the Fascist Government and the *gerarchi* of Fascism guilty of having annulled constitutional guarantees, destroyed popular liberties, created the Fascist Regime, [and] compromised and betrayed the nation's destiny in the current catastrophe are punished with life imprisonment and, in cases of graver responsibility, with death."

These sanctions, however, as harsh as they appeared on paper, were insufficient to lighten the prosecutors' handicaps. All of the bureaucratic machinery created in the measure did not alter fundamentally the scope of Badoglio's earlier decrees. Definitions remained vague, and Rome seemed to abdicate its responsibility, leaving interpretation up to the jurists and purgers themselves. Who, for example, were to be the objects of prosecution? Who had destroyed popular liberties or had created the Fascist regime? What specific acts had these people committed to establish their guilt? Did someone throw a bomb or beat up a Socialist? Did someone make a political deal? Investigators used the old *scheda personale* to evaluate cases, but that document merely described, rather than created, categories of guilt.

Other sections of Title 1 dealt with Fascist crime, but none sufficiently addressed it. Articles 3, 4, and 8 faulted some for using the regime to further their own careers. Article 8 in particular was the great catchall in that it contained a nebulous provision for "acts of special gravity which, while not in the bounds of crime, [were] considered contrary to the norms of sobriety and political decency." It called for punishments like "temporary interdiction from political office," loss of political rights, or internment in agricultural colonies for up to ten years.[2] Once again, clarification was left up to others.

Only Article 5 of Title 1 established a clear crime for which people could be prosecuted: collaboration with the enemy after September 8—that is, treason against the Royal government. Here was an offense, an obvious violation against the Regno del Sud, that allowed the government to take full measures against Fascists, albeit the neo-Fascists of Mussolini's Social Republic. Article 5 emphasized the ideas drawn from Badoglio's measures and the *scheda personale* that distinguished between the Fascists of the *ventennio* and those of Salò. According to Article 5, anyone who, after September 8, 1943, had committed treason, "delitti contro la fedeltà e la difesa militare dello stato," would be punished according to the Military War Code. Both civilians and soldiers would be prosecuted under this code, but they would be tried respectively in civil and military courts.

But even this prosecution had its limitations. As clear a crime as treason is, Title 1 provided an escape clause: Article 7 noted that the penalties, life imprisonment or death, could be reduced to five years in the event that the accused had "actively participated" in the struggle against the Germans. It would be a handy tool for many Fascists upon the liberation of the north. Emblematic of the nagging doubt over sanctions, Article 7 created an obvious escape clause that existed only to be utilized; and it was.

Title 5 of DLL 159 gave the program its teeth—the new High Commission for Sanctions against Fascism. Placed in charge was the high commissioner, of equal rank to top magistrates.[3] With a well-defined office and task, at the end of July the leadership question was finally settled. Count Carlo Sforza, who had agreed to replace Tito Zaniboni shortly after the May 26 decree, would carry on and expand Zaniboni's duties. Adolfo Omodeo also left both his vague defascistization post and his minister's chair to return, as rector, to the University of Naples. Sforza could now clearly and rightfully claim sole directorship of the government's program of anti-Fascist sanctions.[4]

Sforza's task was to direct four offices, each concerned with a different type of sanction. One office, or *commissariato aggiunto*, dealt with criminal proceedings, another with a government purge, a third with confiscation of ill-gotten profits, and the last with sequestering Fascist party property. Day-to-day operations were directed by the high commissioner's four assistants, the *commissari aggiunti*. These vice administrators were equal in rank to third-level judges.

Much of the Alto Commissariato was activated in three auxiliary decrees: DLL 198 of September 3, 1944, which launched a High Court to try the biggest Fascist criminals; DLL 238 of October 3, 1944, which clarified personnel details; and DLL 285 of October 23, 1944, which set procedural rules for the High Court and the purge and which first faced the task of extending the purge out of Rome and into the provinces.

DLL 159's purge was initially limited to the Rome-based central government and did not extend into the private sector, the military, or, initially, even the provinces. Certain observers saw at once that the purge envisioned in the measure would not be sufficiently thorough. G. M. Gancia, an American officer in the AMG, expressed little faith in the "Sforza law," which was not as rigorous as the superior anti-Fascist decrees issued by the Anglo-Americans. He wrote to Rome's governor, Charles Poletti, that "there are remarkable discrepancies between the Poletti orders and the Sforza law. The former automatically ousted all Fascists and all the weight of the bureaucracy was brought to bear against them in their appeal. In the Sforza law, all the weight and the inertia of the bureaucracy hampers the operations of justice in ousting the guilty."[5] Gancia's words would prove prophetic.

At the helm of the High Commission, the staunchly republican Sforza was more a politician than an administrator, more imperial than clerical. Tall and elegant, his haughty eyes peered down past a white goatee. His political roots extended back before World War I, notably at the 1906 Algericas Conference on the Moroccan Question, and then through Foreign Ministry service for the last pre-Fascist governments. A man of enormous ego who spoke of himself in the third person, Sforza left Italy, ironically enough, shortly before Mussolini purged the Palazzo Chigi of many old-line royalist diplomats. He subsequently spent many years in Belgium, France, and the United States and presented himself as a symbol of antifascism. At best moderately liberal, the count abandoned support for the crown when he returned to his native soil as an independent republican. He was generally, but not wholeheartedly, supported by the Roosevelt administration, particularly Adolf Berle. Churchill, however, loathed Sforza, whom he considered an opportunist traitor to the Italian crown.

The count possessed a titanic ambition and always kept his eye on higher goals, such as the prime minister's office or at least the Foreign Ministry. Sforza harbored no great wish to direct sanctions for any extended period of time; such a program would have probably been too controversial to serve his political plans. In fact, he insisted on interfering and caused so much trouble at the Foreign Ministry that an important undersecretary, Count Visconti-Venosta, threatened to resign if the meddling did not cease. For the time being, Sforza reluctantly settled for the high commissioner's chair. In a conversation with an American officer, Sforza displayed an embarrassing ignorance of the technicalities of DLL 159 and the Alto Commisariato. Although it cannot be denied that the count sincerely believed in the mission of sanctions, he saw himself more as coordinator than a crusading leader.[6]

Despite his new position in the Bonomi government, Count Sforza did not soften his antimonarchical positions. In the months after his angry discourse at the Bari Congress, Sforza had lost none of his hatred for the crown and its policy, or lack of one, toward Fascists. A few days before the announcement of the July decree, he granted an interview with the *Risorgimento Liberale* in which he declared that earlier sanctions taken by the king's "neo-Fascist" regime insulted democratic Italy. "I don't know if [Badoglio's decree 29/B] was more of a joke or a tragedy," he added." The high commissioner promised a new, tough program that would severely punish the higher-ups while indulging the lesser functionaries of Mussolini's dictatorship. Attack high and indulge low became the professed modus operandi for sanctions.

Sforza chose his assistant *commissari aggiunti* from the ranks of the CLN parties. DLL 159's Title 5 allowed him to nominate them and present the list to the prime minister for final approval. For his commissioner of sequestered Fascist property, the count chose a personal friend of Bonomi, F. S. Stangone. Stangone had been an anti-Fascist journalist and was a member of the Labor Democrats. The Christian Democrat Mario Cingolani was picked to oversee the office on illegal profits. The two most important commissioners were those for the prosecution of Fascist crimes, Mario Berlinguer, and for the government purge, Mauro Scoccimarro.

An *azionista*, Mario Berlinguer was a wealthy Sardinian landowner and lawyer who had remained in Italy during the *ventennio*. He never cooperated with the Fascists or took out membership in the party. He kept a low political profile but maintained contacts with the anti-Fascist *Giustizia e Libertà* groups abroad and spent a brief period in prison. Berlinguer sincerely held humanitarian values and was esteemed as a decent man by many who met him. On the other hand, Mauro Scoccimarro was unable to keep a low profile during the *ventennio*. Born in Udine in 1894, he was known as a tough, high-ranking member of the Communist party at the time of its dissolution by the Duce in 1926. A protégé of Antonio Gramsci, he represented the PCI in Moscow as well. Along with many comrades Scoccimarro was sentenced

79

in the anti-Communist trials of 1927–28 and spent a decade and a half in Fascist prisons. He was released after the overthrow of Mussolini in July 1943 and resumed his role in the party's directorate.[7]

The backgrounds of the two men, one legalistic and humanitarian, the other combative and a partisan in the class struggle, set the tones for their respective commissions. Both were true in their determination to eradicate fascism, but each went about it in his own way.

Berlinguer's classical, humanistic education was reflected in his aims. Although he was an *azionista* and later a Socialist, his trials never upset the social equilibrium he was anxious to maintain. Berlinguer would not attack the ruling class through the courts, and arguments concerning legal sanctions against Fascists remained within the bounds of liberal juridical propriety.

Where legal scholars might argue loopholes and intent, however, Scoccimarro concerned himself with firing Fascists. He confided to an oss informant that he was "essentially" happy with the new law and that its real value depended on a "rapid, just, and severe" application. The commissioner predicted an effective purge with "no fear of reactionaries and imperialists."[8] The letter of the law did not much concern Scoccimarro; rather, it was in the spirit of its application. He said as much in his September 8, 1944, circular to the purge staffs.[9] The *commissario aggiunto* would attempt to use DLL 159 as a spearhead in a broader attack, and he found himself in the maelstrom of the first and greatest controversy over sanctions.

THE PURGE

Many took great interest in Sforza's tasks and feared that the problems faced in DLL 159 would surface most apparently in Scoccimarro's subcommission. It was universally acknowledged that timing was crucial and that it was imperative to strike while the iron was hot. If action did not begin immediately, it never would. The often skeptical *Risorgimento Liberale* noted and applauded the high commissioner's dicta of aiming high, indulging low, and setting in on a speedy purge. The AMG also acknowledged the importance of celerity. Colonel Upjohn of the AC met Count Sforza on July 30 and stressed the "importance of these [purge] Commissions getting to work very quickly, with which view [Sforza] said he was in entire agreement."[10]

But time proved to be an impassable obstacle against Sforza's and Scoccimarro's efforts. Like most of the world in 1944, Rome was a city in chaos. Both the Italians and the Allies were fully aware that the question of delays was becoming acute. Reporting to Commodore Stone a conversation he had had with Scoccimarro, Major Upjohn complained of foot dragging already in the first week of September. Upjohn told a meeting of the Advisory Council on October 6 that Sforza also recognized the problem and was issuing directives to accelerate the purge.[11]

Nothing not directly related to the war effort could be swiftly accomplished. The taxing details of provisions, the day-to-day essentials of operating in government, were ever present and exasperating. Dislocation, destruction, and bureaucratic confusion hampered all sorts of operations. Scoccimarro complained to Major Upjohn that many essential records had simply been lost or destroyed and that this severely hindered his work. The High Commission had no autos until the spring of 1945, when it received two.[12] An elderly chief prosecutor, De Villa, often took the tram to court. Much of the chaos could be blamed on the war, but Sforza, Scoccimarro, and Berlinguer faced other, more insurmountable tasks.[13]

The problem of personnel was also particularly acute, a potentially dangerous dilemma that forced the High Commission to rely on ex-Fascists to punish other ex-Fascists. There were purgers, lawyers, stenographers, and judges to procure. Judges were particularly needed to staff both the trials and the purge commissions. But they were in very short supply, and their whereabouts were often unknown. After one purge commission waited months for its magistrate to arrive, Sforza received a letter from the judge's wife thanking everyone for the honor but noting that her husband had, unfortunately, been dead for about a year. Consequently, premiums were placed on all jurists, with little or no mention made of their conduct during the Fascist dictatorship. The Alto Commissariato was even forced to search through prisoner-of-war camps and pension records for retired ones.[14]

The High Commission needed policemen but ran into trouble here as well. As with the magistrates, Sforza was forced to rely on established government functionaries in order to enforce sanctions. But the royalist Carabinieri ranked among the least enthusiastic and receptive

to the high commissioner's overtures. On September 16 the commanding general of the Carabinieri, Taddeo Orlando, turned down Sforza's
request for men. The commissioners would have to make do with what
they had.[15]

More serious problems arose from elements in society: the bureaucracy itself and powerful conservatives, who determined to limit or
destroy the sanctions program. To fight Sforza and Scoccimarro, government functionaries undertook a typically bureaucratic mode of
operation: quiet, institutional maneuvers. This opposition was conducted on a lower level, but it was more immediate and more desperate than was the "traditionalist" opposition that came later, which was
more ideological and was played out in the press and between government ministers. When Mauro Scoccimarro launched the purges in the
summer of 1944, his efforts were initially hampered by the first group,
a stubborn, large, and powerful bureaucracy. Sensing the impending
attack from the High Commission, large segments of the state apparatus closed ranks.

Scoccimarro spent much of August and September sending out *schede
personali* to all government employees and forming his purge commissions. Each ministry and government agency was to host a three-person
panel of which one member was appointed by the minister or head of
the office; another was to be a magistrate "of untarnished reputation";
and the third member was to be chosen by Scoccimarro.

The panels reviewed the *schede* to separate the wheat from the chaff.
All questionnaires filled out by the top ranks of the civil service, and
"questionable" ones filled out by some lower-level bureaucrats, were
then sent for final decision to a central commission that sat in Rome's
Piazza dei Santi Apostoli and to Scoccimarro, who maintained his desk
at the Viminale Palace. In practice, a harsh verdict could mean suspension, often on reduced pay and ration cards, or dismissal, usually
with pension (one-twelfth normal pay). Loss of political rights often
accompanied these judgments. Most punishments meted out by the
Alto Commissariato, however, would be *sanzioni minori*, nothing more
than letters placed in the person's file.

Generally, many bureaucrats in government offices under scrutiny
quietly worked within their own confines against the purge. Occasionally, however, some functionaries went outside their realms, creating a
flurry of correspondence with officials on whom they felt they could

count. The officials in those cases largely seem to have been found among the Allies or within the forces of "traditional" Italy, in the Vatican or, quite often, in the prime minister's office.[16]

One example of the quiet approach was made by the Avvocatura Generale dello Stato, the Advocate General's office. Very little documentation exists on the events of the purge in that agency, but what does exist reveals a resistance, and the final figures clearly indicate the failure there of the sanctions program. On September 27 the advocate general sent the *schede*, completed by employees of grade 6 and above, to Bonomi's chef de cabinet, Marcello Flores.[17] But the action ground to a halt by the end of November when most of the staff had been whitewashed. A December 5 progress report to Flores indicated that, of 382 employees in Rome and in RSI territory, 182 had been examined, none had been suspended, and the case of one grade-4 employee had been sent for judgment.[18]

Shortly after the report, however, Scoccimarro reviewed two other cases, both "substitute advocates" (*sostituti avvocati*), sent from the Advocate General's office. One concerned a member of the defunct, conservative Nationalist party who had joined the Fascists before the March on Rome.[19] The other concerned a functionary who had been an official in the Militia from 1928 to 1930. Both were absolved of all guilt since neither had "exhibited overwhelming sectarian behavior" (*prova di faziosità, settarietà od intemperanze*). In the case of the second man, the High Commission felt that, as a Jew, he had suffered enough at the hands of the Fascists.[20] These two cases illustrate that, as Gancia had warned, DLL 159 was flexible enough to allow bureaucrats to slip past serious scrutiny. Almost a year later, on August 21, 1945, another purge status report from the Advocate General's office listed 255 reviews, nineteen of which had been sent to higher authorities. But none of the employees had been removed. The agency had weathered the storm.[21]

The purge at the Istituto Centrale di Statistica, the Central Statistical Institute, reveals another story. Here, Scoccimarro's men appear to have been far less compliant than those at the Avvocatura dello Stato and more determined to attack the Fascists. But in this case, the bureaucrats, led by the director of the institute, forced a direct confrontation with the Sforza Commission.

The purge commission for the Central Statistical Institute was inaugurated on August 22 and was chaired by a councillor from the Court of Appeals, Giovanni Senerchia. The High Commission's appointment, Francesco Papa, and the institute's personnel director, Ulderico Trillò, rounded out the panel. The trio took seriously its task, and the numbers of reviews were proportionately among the highest of any commission. In mid-December Senerchia reported that of eighty-five employees, thirty-eight had been suspended and, after the final judgment, eight had been removed. Ten employees were also in the process of presenting appeals.[22]

The commission's most controversial member was Ulderico Trillò, the institute's representative. He did not cause rancor in the purge panel but rather among the employees and head of the agency. Trillò became very unpopular at the institute, so much so that on December 15 he submitted his resignation for reasons which he did not elaborate. The following day, the institute's director general, Alessandro Molinari, wrote to Flores that he would forthwith name a replacement. At this point it appears that Trillò displayed some reluctance to leave; letters from Molinari and other employees of the institute imply that the purger was still on the job.[23] The scandal, however, had only begun to surface.

On December 20 Molinari wrote to Bonomi's undersecretary, the Christian Democrat Giuseppe Spataro, to complain that Trillò had overstepped his authority by himself making denunciations, including one against Molinari. According to the director general, Trillò had adopted the roles of both accuser and judge. Molinari suggested to Spataro that, as president of the Council of Ministers, Bonomi should intervene and clean up the mess.[24]

The tables may have been turned when employees of the institute stepped in to defend their boss, an act that clouded the picture of who had been the real Fascist, Molinari or Trillò. The director general was supported by a group of his underlings who, in a junta of the CLN parties, formed a counter-purge committee and sent three indignant manifesti to the prime minister's office. These proclamations were signed, however, only by members of four of the main parties, the Communist party being the exception. Sent on December 18, 20, and 28, the letters defended Molinari, who, they claimed, had been the only functionary in the office never to have joined the PNF and, indeed, had always been a "notorious anti-Fascist." On December 28 the committee declared that the purge was a farce if a former PNF member, Trillò, used it against a completely innocent person while at the same time admitting twelve former *squadristi* back into office. The employees lamented that Trillò had created an atmosphere of fear and had caused a paralysis in the institute's work.[25]

On December 18, after receiving Molinari's nomination for Trillò's replacement, Bonomi stepped into the fracas. The prime minister agreed with the director general that the purge had gone too far and, on December 22, accepted Trillò's resignation and appointed a Professor Pietro Battara in his place.[26]

In replacing Trillò, a task that should have been left to Sforza or Scoccimarro, the head of the government risked either overstepping his authority or entering into an arena where the purgers did not want him. The High Commission soon made this apparent by firing some volleys of its own at the Palazzo Viminale. On the same day as Battara's appointment, Scoccimarro sent Bonomi the upsetting news that "this High Commission has rejected the resignation presented by Dr. Trillò," thus, in turn, invalidating Battara's nomination. Scoccimarro was supported by Senerchia, the president of the institute's purge commission. On January 8, 1945, he wrote to Bonomi that, since Trillò's resignation had never been accepted, he could not accept Battara as a replacement. The two sides were at loggerheads, and the effective purge of the Central Statistical Institute ground to a halt.[27]

The Trillò case revealed an important problem of defascistization, that we have no real proof of anything beyond charges and countercharges. Trillò could have been a Fascist just as easily as he could have been a sincere anti-Fascist. Like the central figure in Alberto Moravia's *The Conformist*, pointing the accusing finger at his former associates, Trillò might have been playing the same game for his own survival. During Joseph Stalin's Great Purges, Lavrenti Beria is reported to have done the same thing against his former comrades in the Caucasus in order to save his own life. Similar personal animosities and rivalries are rarely documented but must have been important factors in the history of sanctions.

Events at the National Research Council, or Consiglio Nazionale delle Ricerche (CNR), reveal other collisions between the purgers and the bureaucracy. The original contention concerned two of the purge commissioners. One was Scoccimarro's representative, and the other came from the CNR itself. Both had been assistants of the notorious biological racist and ex-Consigliere Nazionale, Sabato Visco.[28] The CNR and the Sforza Commission immediately found themselves at odds, and, as a result, no purge could be accomplished at the CNR.

On October 2 the CNR's Internal Commission met at the biological institute to discuss the membership of Visco's two assistants on the purge panel. It was reported there that the CNR's Commissario Straordinario, a Professor Castelnuovo, had sent a letter to Sforza protesting the nomination of the two members. The Internal Commission, in turn, alleged that Castelnuovo had been misguided by faulty information from those who wanted the purge "sabotaged," expressing, furthermore, complete faith that the two were guided by truly anti-Fascist instincts. By October 7 the Ministry of Public Instruction had discovered the controversy, and, as evidenced in a pro memoria for the minister, Guido De Ruggiero, its attitude was to get rid of Visco's ex-assistants.[29]

Academics have never been known to keep secrets, so the squabble broke quickly before the public. The rigidly Communist *Ricostruzione* printed the story on October 4, reminding the Romans that, as Visco's helpers, the two purgers had worked at that "racist and ultrafascist address," the University Institute of Biology. The presence of the two "indubitably constitute[d] a grave offense." On November 1 *Ricostruzione* uncovered more trouble. Another alleged Fascist who had never been removed was Ferruccio Banissoni, the head of the Experimental Center for Applied Psychology (Centro Sperimentale della psicologia applicata). He had served as an important officer in the Fascist Gioventù Italiana dell'Littorio, an offense specified in all purge guidelines. He was a vociferous PNF member and a Germanophile Axis booster who organized a celebrated meeting in 1941 of Fascist and Nazi psychologists. *Ricostruzione* cynically suggested that Banissoni organize a meeting between the Italians and the Americans.[30]

Since formal instruction under Mussolini was heavily tainted with political indoctrination, an abnormally high number of Fascists lingered in the ranks of the Ministry of National Education and in the school and university systems. Because of this concentration, Scoccimarro found a purge of academe difficult. On September 11 he requested the "immediate ostracism" of the University of Rome's administrative director, Dr. Nicola Spano. On 22 September, a skeptical

Minister De Ruggiero asked Bonomi whether the case could be opened up for further scrutiny. After more letters of denunciation and defense, the matter was submitted to one of Italy's finest legal scholars and historians, Arturo Carlo Jemolo, who, on November 13, recommended that Spano be declared innocent. His argument lent credence to the notion of two fascisms—one before the July coup and a different one after September 8—and after September 8 Spano had maintained a clean record. Actions taken in the *ventennio* meant less and less. On December 23 Bonomi concurred and stopped the case, noting that the administrator was of more use in the university than out of it.[31]

To keep track of his attempts at an extensive purge of the entire government, Scoccimarro compiled statistics. The figures present a valuable picture of how far the purge had proceeded under its vigorous commissioner. He reported that 112 of the proposed 157 commissions were functioning. These commissions claimed to have examined 28,399 cases "up until two o'clock on 30 November, 1944." Of these, 6,859 had been judged serious enough for higher review; 1,199 of the 6,859 were recommended for suspension, and, the bottom line, 495 state employees had been "disposte," which seems to have been the accepted euphemism for "sacked." At the higher level, the purge of the top grades of the bureaucracy, Count Sforza also reported that of 3,210 decisions, 1,355 were acquitted, 1,316 received minor sanctions, and 539 were purged.[32]

Numbers in these High Commission reports, however, often conflicted. Tallies of purge cases varied from report to report and prohibit any clear conclusion on how many were really affected. For example, Scoccimarro's figure of 6,859 cases does not reappear elsewhere. And though much of that figure is explained by reasonably detailed statistics, large gaps remained in the overall picture. Employees of quasi-governmental organizations such as the *enti pubblici*, agencies in the national interest, comprised much of the 6,859. Scoccimarro listed that 1,705 employees of these organizations, the largest single figure, had been brought up for review. But if he requested that any of these 1,705 be suspended, record was not made of it.

Purge figures also reflect an imbalance between the various ministries. The Interior Ministry, one of the largest government employers, claimed the dubious honor of having the most workers, 1,430, deferred to judgment. Of these, Scoccimarro requested 422 suspensions; 176 of those were listed as *personale civile*, and 246 were personnel of the *pubblica sicurezza*, a national police force.[33] On the bottom line, 86 bureaucrats and 158 PS seem to have been purged at that point. While the Interior figures were among the most drastic found in the Council of Ministers, others were far less severe. The Ministry of Public Works, for example, a traditional job mill, surrendered 304 workers for review. Suspension requests were made for 18 of these but none were purged.

The Treasury and the military services were among the ministries most representative of traditional, conservative Italy. Of 654 reviews in the Liberal Marcello Soleri's Treasury, 10 requests for suspension were made and 5 were complied with. In General Piero Piacentini's Air Force, the figures, which included only civilian bureaucrats and not military personnel, were 351, 200, and 2. In Admiral Raffaele De Courten's Naval Ministry, the numbers were 152, 17, and 2. The odd agency in this group was the War Ministry, which purged more—54 out of 99 requests—than the others combined. Perhaps the explanation lies in that the minister of war was a civilian, the Milanese Liberal Alessandro Casati, who saw potential in a purge and seems to have favored it more than did his Liberal colleagues. As minister of war he went so far as to suggest a serious sweep of the marshals and generals and recommended to Bonomi that the first two on the purge list be Badoglio and Messe. He also insisted that, since such a sweep required an enormous show of strength and nerve, Bonomi himself chair the commission. This never materialized.[34]

Despite the efforts of the High Commission, the purge was largely confined to Rome and a few other large cities south of the front, like Naples. Out in the provinces, purge commissions were to be composed of a member appointed by Scoccimarro, one by the local prefect, and one by the CLN parties. This was not a hard and fast rule, and some purging seems to have been carried on by prefects or CLN committees on their own. In his study of the purge in Forlì, Dino Mengozzi tells us that the hand of Rome was felt there but once: when Scoccimarro appointed the High Commission's purger. Everything else was left up to the Forlivesi.[35] The situation there, Mussolini's birthplace, was probably typical of similarly sized cities and smaller ones.

The effectiveness of the purges in the provinces depended on local conditions: the position of the prefect, CLN strength, local business and church leaders, Allied presence, and so on. That no comprehensive log of the provincial purge has been found serves as an indication of the problem and Rome's lack of interest in it. Some available figures, however, illustrate a haphazard affair. According to a report from Scoccimarro's office, on December 3 only one person had been *disposte* from "the provinces," a claim that makes little sense.[36] But final figures for some regions compiled in January 1946 reveal more discrepancies. Nothing indicates, for example, the composition of the pool of purge targets. Were they all local or were some refugees? What were their ranks? The puzzling figures certainly could not have represented only government employees. For example, in regions liberated by the end of 1944, the most exhaustive examinations were in Tuscany, where 10,090 *dipendenti* out of an accounted-for 21,990 had been examined; in Umbria, with 5,950 of 6,824; in Lazio, with 3,019 of 5,298; in Sicily, with 29,713 of 37,023; and in Puglia, with 10,780 of 20,130. The worst record seems to have been in Sardinia, with 423 of 2,385. However, these regional figures were not complete. In certain places, like Palermo, Brindisi, and Aquila, virtually everyone had been examined. In others the work had hardly begun. Ragusa purgers had looked at 120 out of a potential 1,807. In Chieti 305 of 3,868 were vetted, and in Grosseto the figures were 985 of 4,073. Other provinces such as Enna, Foggia, Benevento, and Pisa had not reported anything.

These select final figures also reveal that very few people were being removed from office. The Sardinia numbers were all compiled in Sassari province, where, out of 2,385, 6 were removed. Of 128,837 employees in Naples, 23 were forced out. Five left the ranks of 26,636 Palermitani. A high ratio of punishments to employees was the exception. But exceptions did exist. In Lecce, 57 out of 263 employees were examined. But of those 57, 25 were removed. Those figures were approximated in Terni and rivaled in a few other places.[37] Counting all of the figures cited in this incomplete report, about half—143,781 of 277,701—of all provincial employees were examined. Of those, 13,737 were felt important enough to judge formally. And from that figure about one-tenth, 1,476, were removed.

THE TRIALS

If the purge touched few people, fewer still were affected by the trials against Fascist criminals. DLL 159 and its corollary decrees created the High Court (Alta Corte), within Mario Berlinguer's subcommission to judge those most responsible for the regime and the disaster of the war. Regular lower courts would handle Fascists of lesser rank.

But as with Scoccimarro's purge, Berlinguer's prosecutions were beset with troubles that reflected the general doubt over sanctions. The capstone to the whole program, the High Court, illustrated this problem. As only one court, its scope was necessarily limited and could not possibly have been devised with the idea of punishing all *gerarchi*. A single bench was established for show trials, not for effective, broadly based sanctions. The proceedings, one trial at a time, went slowly and were complicated by the enormous amount of attention focused on them. The early cases, particularly the first one against Pietro Caruso, were presented at the very least as much for public and Allied consumption as they were an effort to rid the Roman bureaucracy of Fascists.

Berlinguer was also plagued by the incessant and never-resolved battle of legal scholars, journalists, and the public on the parameters and limits of guilt. The stated purpose for the High Court, as defined in DLL 159 and auxiliary decrees, was to try key criminals of the *ventennio*, aiming at the pervasive fascism before 1943 and not at the imposed, Vichy-like puppet RSI. As it turned out, however, although military courts were designed to process traitors, the trials often concerned RSI personnel and the treasonous crimes committed, not between 1922 and 1943, but after September 8. Beyond the time frame, furthermore, the parameters were still quite narrow: government officials. In both cases the dockets were filled with targets—"strategic" figures closely tied in the public's mind to the regime. Thus, while conservatives may have grumbled about the trials, they did not enlist the same kind of frontal assault against Berlinguer as had been thrown at Scoccimarro. There was no need for such drastic measures. No doubt many may have shuddered at the idea of trials—uncertainty regarding one's own relationship with the Fascists or one's position within the defunct regime could easily determine a stand against too-effective legal sanctions. But not only was most of the traditional "establishment" safely beyond the limited goals of the trial program, it could also rely on a sincere and important faction within Italian society who believed that sanctions were morally questionable.

Many well-intentioned Italians, the *benpensanti*, were simply reluctant to prosecute Fascists. Ex post facto application of ill-defined offenses, complicated by the threatened use of the death penalty, were foreign to legal tradition. Before 1943 the most important sanctions in modern Italian history had been conducted by the Fascists during the 1920s. This was not an admirable standard to emulate. In August 1944 a group of eighteen prestigious legal scholars, all of them anti-Fascists, published a manifesto condemning a legal campaign that prosecuted people for violation of laws that had never existed.[38]

The composition of the High Court was announced on August 2. Its president, or chief magistrate, was Ettore Casati, former *primo presidente* of a cassation court and justice minister under Badoglio. He was assisted by eight jurists, mainly lawyers, judges, and officials, such as the minister of industry, commerce, and labor in Badoglio's second government, Attilio Di Napoli; the vice mayor of Rome, Guido Lay; and a future undersecretary in the Foreign Ministry, Eugenio Reale. Judge Casati, however, was gravely ill and was replaced before the first trial by one of the eight, a *consigliere* from the cassation courts, Lorenzo Maroni. Maroni was among the few high officials in the sanctions network whose tenure would last for practically the entire life of the institution, in his case the High Court.

Maroni's role also illustrated an important flaw in the program that concerned the magistracy. The chief judge was typical of many who had pursued a career through the *ventennio*, and he found himself in that great gray area between the Fascists and the apolitical population at large. Worse, however, was that Maroni was criticized for hidden ties to the old regime. The right-wing historian Luigi Villari related the story told to him by one of the judge's close relatives that, during the dictatorship, Maroni would "go off the deep end" when someone criticized Mussolini's government in his presence. Later, during one of the High Court trials, the Duce's henchman Cesare Rossi defiantly reminded the assembly that Maroni had often judged cases during the *ventennio* with a black shirt on underneath his robes.[39]

The first High Court trial was the most important one. The accused were Salò's questore of Rome, Pietro Caruso, and his assistant, Roberto Occhetto. Caruso had served the Nazis by rounding up partisans and innocent victims for slaughter. The trial was significant for four reasons. First, a riot broke out during the proceedings and seriously damaged the credibility of the Sforza Commission for Bonomi, the Allies, and much of the press. Second, a dangerous precedent was established by the defense attorneys in their argument that if an accused secretly aided anti-Fascists, playing what was called the "double game," his guilt was partly or even wholly exonerated. Third, the crimes of Caruso and his cohort had no strong connection with the *ventennio*. Nor were they overtly political but were traditional crimes of violence and treason against liberated Italy. Fourth, despite the vile nature of Caruso's crimes, many considered that he was a scapegoat, a victim of Sforza's show trials.

Caruso had been a fringe character in the Fascist hierarchy. He was an early party member from Naples but held no important position before the establishment of the RSI. He appeared in Verona as head of police at Mussolini's trials against the "July Traitors." In February 1944 he was installed as the police boss of Rome, commanding a bloodthirsty gang of sadists and thugs who tortured and murdered for the Duce and the Germans. Caruso's name will forever be tainted by the deaths of hundreds of Romans. The Ardeatine Caves was the site of his most monstrous crime in March 1944. After a partisan attack on a German unit marching up Via Rasella, Caruso and the Nazis retaliated by rounding up 335 innocent men, women, and children—many of them Jews. The people were transported to the Ardeatine Caves in the hills south of the city near suburban EUR. There they were butchered and the entrances to the caves sealed.

The site of the Caruso trial was the mammoth and garish Palazzo di Giustizia on the Tiber near the Castel Sant'Angelo. On a hot September 18, well over 300 people jammed themselves into a courtroom that was built to accommodate sixty. Some were issued guest passes, but they were joined by Allied observers and journalists, a camera crew, Mario Berlinguer, and a crowd of people, mainly women. Most were the mothers, wives, and sisters of victims of the Ardeatine Caves massacre. These people knew Caruso for the cutthroat that he was.[40]

His horrible crime was no secret, particularly to the loved ones present in the Palazzo di Giustizia. They demanded justice. For security the PS and the Carabinieri allotted 450 guards to the building. But only 320 were present, and most of those were in the "lower reaches of the building." Few, often only two or three, guarded key doors.[41]

The first prosecution witness was the former director of the city's Regina Coeli prison, Donato Carretta, who himself represented another ambiguous challenge for defascistization. He had been removed by the Poletti administration, but, because he had displayed some anti-Nazi activity, charges had not been brought against him. Colonel Poletti and the Bonomi regime felt that Carretta "did everything in his power, exposing himself personally to serious risks, to help the political prisoners." The warden had defied the retreating Germans who insisted on taking captives with them by successfully arguing that many prisoners were ill and could not bear the rough journey.[42]

Before Governor Carretta entered, Colonel John Pollock, the AMG's public safety officer, recommended that the courtroom crowd was too large and unruly and that the place be cleared. But his suggestions came too late. Carretta was ushered into the chamber, where his appearance ignited the spectators, particularly those connected with the massacre victims, into a fire of rage.

There was some question whether the people mistook Carretta for Caruso, but, whatever the case, they immediately attacked him. The assault was led by a woman, Maria Ricottini, whose son had been shot by the Germans on May 8.[43] Berlinguer jumped onto a table and implored that the crowd get a hold of themselves, but his pleas were drowned in demands to lynch Carretta. Shouts of "Paris, let's imitate Paris" heard in the courtroom indicate that the crowd was inspired by new radical measures then being taken by the French government against Vichyite collaborators.

With a couple of guards trying to protect him, the ex-jailer was jostled and beaten by the mob. His body was dragged out of the building and down the front stairs. All attempts by the police to get him away failed. The guards implored some Americans to put Carretta in their jeep, but they refused to get involved. Carretta was dragged onto the Ponte Umberto spanning the Tiber, and his body was stretched over tram tracks. An approaching trolley slammed on its brakes and screeched to a halt inches before crushing the ex-warden. The infuriated crowd tore the hapless motorman from his berth and beat him

93

until he broke away and ran for his own life. Still the people had not had enough so they carried the bloodied and motionless Carretta to the side of the bridge and tossed him into the river. They were astonished to see the pathetic figure attempt to stay afloat and make for shore. Some young men, bathers on the bank, then finished the job by pummelling Carretta to death with oars. His body was dragged to Regina Coeli and hung there, feet first, for the Romans to contemplate.

Carretta's death was a tragedy on a high level revealing that a submerged and undirected resentment persisted among the population. The events of September 18 revealed also a government incapable of understanding and powerless in controlling its citizens. The riot represented a broad failure in the sanctions program.

Newspapers across the political spectrum deplored Carretta's death. The prison director was seen at once as a symbol and a victim of Fascist oppression. As would be suspected, his death was interpreted differently depending on the editorial staff. The monarchist *Italia Nuova* took the line that a tragic murder of an innocent had occurred. Who was to blame? Nobody really; the tragedy was one of crowd control. The monarchists felt that more police protection was needed and that a scandal was brewing. The Liberal *Risorgimento Liberale* used terms like "the law of the jungle" to describe the disgraceful scene. *Italia Libera* painted the same picture in an editorial, "Blood in the Tiber." The Action party termed the incident "a bestial, horrendous explosion of base mob instincts." *Avanti!* bemoaned the death of a man at the hands of the mob. But here Carretta was colored more as an object of disdain than pity. The Socialist daily claimed that the people knew full well that he was "hated for his cruelty and inhumanity." But even Pietro Nenni displayed sympathy in an editorial, painting Carretta as a sad scapegoat of the times. Nenni felt the fault for the riot rested in the state and not the people, chastising the police as a nest of unpurged Fascists who represented no moral authority for the Italian people. He also wondered why the trial was taking place three months after the liberation of the city instead of three days.[44]

The Allies were horrified by the Carretta lynching and immediately contacted the Palazzo Viminale to discuss the matter with Bonomi. Within hours of the incident, the American ambassador, Alexander Kirk, accompanied Colonel Poletti to the prime minister's office and warned that Allied troops might be called out to preserve order. Bonomi concurred, adding that he would issue a statement deploring the shameful event and suspend all Carabinieri and PS officers involved. The next day Britain's ambassador, Sir Charles, reported that Allied Commissioner Stone and Poletti had also been at the Viminale to confer with the prime minister and Sforza. The Italians were forced to sit through a tongue lashing that again threatened Allied intervention, "and [Bonomi] would realize the serious consequences that this would entail." In his memo Charles added, "I agree with Captain Stone."[45]

The British ambassador's memo was circulated among high Foreign Office personnel, and their marginal notes reveal a distrust of Sforza and his campaign of sanctions against Fascists. A. D. M. Ross commented,

> This disgraceful incident suggests 1) That the Italian Government are not able to keep order in the area handed over to them. 2) That we should be chary of making any statement complimentary to the Italian Government for the time being. 3) That the Allied Control Commission were not in sufficiently close touch with the situation, which could easily have been foreseen. 4) That the censorship system which permitted such discreditable reports as those which appeared in the British press . . . needs overhauling. 5) That Count Sforza is not a suitable person to be in charge of the investigation of Fascist crimes.

Sir Orme Sargent agreed with Ross and went further to denounce the high commissioner. "As regards Count Sforza," he wrote, "it would be very satisfactory if we could incriminate him sufficiently to get him removed from the Government, but I doubt whether this would be possible." Finally, Anthony Eden added his own, terse opinion of Sforza: "I should like to see him in trouble."[46]

Back in Rome, the Caruso trial continued in a new venue: from the eclectic Palazzo di Giustizia, it was moved to the baroque splendor of the Palazzo Corsini. Security was tight and the crowd was more sedate. *Avanti!* noted a sharp contrast between the Italians: Carabinieri resplendent in full dress, Judge Maroni seated on a red and gold throne beneath a mammoth eighteenth-century painting; and the shirt-sleeved Allies, stretched over leather chairs. The Socialist daily sensed that the beautiful hall fitfully provided a dramatic stage for a ritualistic show trial of both tragedy and circus.[47]

Because of his abominable crimes and because this first trial was clearly a showcase, Caruso's fate seemed to have been a foregone conclusion. He was not attacked as a creature of fascism but as a thug, a mad dog. One prosecutor charged that Caruso was not a career bureaucrat but rather a kind of mobster, "an authentic hired assassin."[48] But the assumption of guilt did not alter a paradoxical split image of him as monster and victim. Incredibly, Caruso managed to elicit some pity. Released from his stay in the hospital, the broken police boss entered the hall on crutches, and if anyone looked like a scapegoat, he did. Even *Avanti!* felt a little sympathy for one who "might be taken for any poor devil." Caruso presented a calm, perhaps resigned figure, and, it was noted, his defense lacked any conviction.

The examination of Caruso's assistant, the *segreteria particolare della questura* Roberto Occhetto, added new dimensions to the trial. Unlike Caruso, the press always portrayed Occhetto as overly sure of himself, someone who, even if on trial, seemed to hold the right cards. He had been involved in the same atrocities as Caruso, but the lieutenant had insured his safety by a clever manipulation of the Resistance forces. He played what *Avanti!* and *Italia Libera* both termed "the double game." By forging Caruso's signature, Occhetto had released partisans from jail and even procured for them false papers. Those tactics saved his life. *Italia Libera* insisted that they did and seriously questioned the entire legal process against Fascists if this double game could guarantee lightened sentences.[49] When the verdicts were read, Caruso appeared exhausted, destroyed. He was condemned to death. The ex-questore leaned over to his assistant and whispered in his Neapolitan cadence, "I am dead, but I hope that you can save yourself." Upon hearing the verdict, those nearby reported that a tear came to Caruso's eye, and even *Avanti!* discerned, perhaps, some air of redemption in this touch of humanity. On the other hand, the crafty Occhetto, while scribbling on a paper and chewing gum, calmly received a sentence of thirty years.

Maroni's decision to have Caruso shot triggered doubts and questions held by many, including those on the Left, over the wisdom of such extreme measures. Accounts of the September 22 execution betrayed broad ambivalence toward the use of the firing squad even for murderers like Caruso. Reports of the event were often tinged with sentimentality. The *Risorgimento Liberale* devoted a great deal of space

and detail to it, such as the prison chaplain's account of Caruso's preparation for an honorable death, comforted with a copy of Saint Augus-
tine's *A Christian Life*. The execution was to take place at dawn, but
Berlinguer arranged a postponement for the condemned to write some
final letters. There was a limit, however, to the sympathy Caruso would
get in the press: *Italia Libera* reported that he spent his last few hours
not in prayer or in thoughts of loved ones but rather "dozed off."[50]
Upon the fateful hour, 2:00, Caruso refused the blindfold but held
Rosary beads. The old police boss bade the troops aim well and shouted,
"Vive Italia!," his last words.[51]

From Salò the Fascists warned that should any harm come to Caruso,
there would be reprisals. Upon word of his death before the firing
squad, twenty-one people were reportedly shot in Reggio nell'Emilia,
Turin, and Bologna. Thirty more unfortunates were sentenced to thirty
years in prison by an RSI court in Bologna. Falsely reported among the
reprisals were Togliatti's brother and Badoglio's son.[52]

Caruso's execution left many unanswered questions concerning the
propriety of the trials, particularly the extreme punishments. It exhibited, once again, that progress of sanctions left many Italians
unsatisfied or unsettled. Something was wrong; something was missing. That this doubt spread across the political spectrum is best illustrated in the pages of the Socialists' *Avanti!*, which feared further dis-
appointments in the upcoming trial of the governor of the Bank of
Italy, Vincenzo Azzolini. While Caruso had been portrayed as a poor
devil, nursed by his instincts and drunk with power, he was nevertheless a tragic victim of a witch hunt that did not justify severe retribution, least of all the death penalty. While it still expressed doubts, however, *Avanti!* believed that the banker's story was different. Here was "a
crafty and intelligent man who knew exactly what he was doing."[53]

On the charge that he had transferred 120 tons of gold behind German lines, Azzolini was hauled before President Maroni. A PWB report
described the governor of the Bank of Italy as a calm, substantial-
looking Neapolitan, whereas the defense witnesses presented "a rather
sorry spectacle." For a moment one of them even forgot where he was
when he looked to Maroni and mistakenly gave the Fascist salute.[54]
Such memory lapses were not the exclusive terrain of the defense
witnesses. At one point, both Azzolini's lawyer and the prosecutor referred incorrectly to the High Court as the notorious Fascist Special

Tribunal. Besides friendly witnesses in court, Azzolini could boast of international support: a number of letters on his behalf from bankers in Switzerland and Sweden. Count Sforza protested to the Allied Psychological Warfare Branch that this was unfair foreign meddling in an Italian trial and requested that journalists not print the letters' contents.[55]

Azzolini's defense was based on lack of any motive for collaboration and was bolstered with another cry to prosecute the genuinely guilty and leave the little fish alone. The main defense lawyer emphasized the *ventennio*/RSI dichotomy by insisting that the real criminals were not bureaucrats, like Azzolini, but were the others, mainly generals, who had delivered Italy over to the Germans in September 1943. On the last day of the trial the crowd in the courtroom answered the attorney's pleas to bring the real criminals to justice with a concerted, "They're coming." Maroni added, perhaps with some chagrin, that eventually all would answer for their crimes. On October 14 Azzolini was given thirty years.

The initially optimistic *Avanti!* quickly turned sour and found two faults with the trial. First, the thirty-year figure seemed arbitrary. Second, as in the Caruso trial, only the lesser figures seemed to be prosecuted. Here, the Socialists clearly contradicted their earlier belief that the accused was a true and important Fascist culprit. Azzolini turned out to be yet another victim of a policy that hunted scapegoats and permitted the real criminals, the wire pullers, to go free. Where were the truly authentic Fascist criminals?

On 24 October *Italia Libera* insisted that further time not be wasted in bothering with the likes of Azzolini. The real culprits were to be found in the Palazzo Quirinale—the king, the crown prince, and the camarilla. Fascism's stain would never be eradicated until Italy was rid of them. But within the Left could still be heard more determined voices endorsing severe sanctions. In Naples a debate took place between Eugenio Reale's "social communist" *La Voce* and the Liberal *Il Giornale*. Reale argued that legal niceties had their place but that Azzolini was "overwhelmingly guilty." The people knew it, they felt the truth deep inside, and Maroni should have forgotten the rules to listen to them. The Liberal journalist Manlio Lupinacci retorted that demagoguery had no place in Italian courts. Should Maroni adopt the social communist recommendation, then trials would resemble the Colosseum, with Emperor Maroni watching for a thumbs-up or thumbs-down signal from the mob. Sanctions had to maintain a sensible and orderly course.

Even the monarchists were disappointed in the Azzolini verdict. Strangely suggestive of Eugenio Reale, *Italia Nuova* posited that Maroni had in fact succumbed to the mob, and it charged the court with cowardice in its arbitrary punishment. The newspaper felt that the sentence should have been either very light or death, for collaboration. Once again, the crown was attempting here to legitimize itself as the alternative to the RSI. Azzolini's crimes fit nicely into the monarchy's attempts to pose as a champion of justice. But most agreed that Maroni took the easy way out with the middle road, and few were satisfied.[56]

Those hoping for a showdown with the military received their wish in the third trial of the High Court. On December 14 Generals Riccardo Pentimalli and Ettore Del Tetto appeared before the High Court on charges of conspiring to surrender Naples to the Germans.[57] For the armed forces the crime of collaboration with the enemy was delineated in Article 51 of the Military War Code. Article 51 was very important for the Maroni court and all courts prosecuting Fascists. However, if the accused were an officer in the services, he would be judged by a military tribunal, where presumably he would receive a more sympathetic hearing from peers who might have been themselves guilty of similar crimes. A loophole contained in DLL 159, however, stated that "in cases of exceptional gravity," officers could be tried by the High Court.

Socialist and Communist journalists keenly awaited the trial. The unpurged military, thoroughly monarchist and tarnished by a record of collusion with fascism that few could match, would be up for serious scrutiny. Ambassador Kirk cabled Washington to say that the two officers had already been tried and condemned in the Left press. They were being referred to as "the traitor generals" by ideologues in *Avanti!* and *L'Unità*.

The trial of Pentimalli and Del Tetto held even more importance for the Center-Right, which feared that the normally moderate Berlinguer, who requested the arrest, might be overstepping certain bounds. Certain "notoriously" Fascist officers like Rodolfo Graziani or Gastone Gambara might have been considered liable, or perhaps acceptable, for sacrifice to the purgers. But Pentimalli and Del Tetto were different; they were simply "good" soldiers. In fact, the latter had been demoted over his opposition to Mussolini's aggressive Balkan policy. The generals had not been considered as *gerarchi* during the *ventennio*. They were not thugs like Caruso nor even occupants of Fascist sinecures like Azzolini. Like Chief of Staff General Giovanni Messe and Marshal Badoglio, they were soldiers of the king; the prosecutors had crossed over into the non-Fascist Right. It seemed as though Sforza and Berlinguer were on the verge of extending prosecutions beyond the narrowly Fascist political class. Discussing the matter with a PWB officer, a magistrate on Berlinguer's staff confessed that a great deal of opposition to the trial existed among high-ranking officers. General Messe, for example, had tried to sabotage the indictments, "but the commission had decided to carry on . . . in spite of him."[58]

Fears over Pentimalli and Del Tetto also extended beyond the military. The PWB reported that everyone on the Right was "very aware" of the trial's implications. The *Voce Repubblicana* had already contributed to the worries through a call for prosecution of other military leaders, including the prince of Piedmont. The specific fates of the two generals were rarely discussed seriously. The PWB concluded that Pentimalli and Del Tetto had certainly handed Naples over to the Germans and that they should be "unquestionably shot." But that was not the point. Who would be next?

The trial lasted about a week. The southern Pentimalli's slight, dark stature contrasted with the Piedmontese Del Tetto's tall corpulent frame. The latter presented the more memorable figure, often breaking into sobs, insisting that he was a "poor ragman" (*straccio*). The prosecution focused on an order, the so-called Memoria 44, from the Italian Supreme Command for the defense of Naples, which the generals insisted never came. Maroni asked to see a copy of it but was told by the prosecution witness, General Mario Arisio (Pentimalli and Del Tetto's commanding officer!), that it had been burned. The public minister, Pietro Traina, asked for death, but, on December 23, the two generals received twenty years for abandoning their posts. The other charges were dropped.[59]

The two sentences fueled still more flames of dissatisfaction. Even after the third trial, broad disagreement persisted over the type of people who should be prosecuted and over the confusing and narrow aims of DLL 159. Much of the press complained once again that the prosecutors were missing the mark. The guiltiest, those at the highest levels, enjoyed their freedom while Pentimalli, Del Tetto, Azzolini, or Occhetto languished in jail. A dissatisfied Pietro Nenni led the denunciations in *Avanti!*. In his December 23 editorial, "Lessons from a Trial," the Socialist leader blamed the surrender of Naples on men more important than the two generals. The responsibility rested with Badoglio, who "plays bocce in Rome," and with Victor Emmanuel, who "finishes his days in the quiet of the Villa Guariglia at Salerno." Nenni felt that if truly important *gerarchi* had experienced any discomfort thus far, it was due at most to a few days spent in Regina Coeli prison. "Others, very many, have not been disturbed for a day, not even for an hour." The Socialist's answer echoed those cries in the Caruso riot to imitate the French and establish more popular courts. Demands for justice represented "one of the strongest positive elements" in liberated France that condemned "without pity [the] miserable collaborators." In Italy, corruption and persistence of the old ruling classes, so heavily compromised with fascism, were effectively killing all hope of real sanctions.[60]

In December 1944 an officer with the Allied Commission was prompted to investigate the French example for himself and visited anticollaborationist courts in Dijon, Toulon, Marseilles, Lyon, and Paris. He concluded that far more local authority was placed in the French courts than in the Italian ones and that the system there was facilitated by two factors: that all the crimes had been committed in the last four years and that they were sins of collaboration. On the other hand, the Italian problem concerned a native regime of over twenty years with no allegiance to a foreign power. Although the observer felt that the Italian methods were sound, he conceded that the French ones were simpler, speedier, and better.[61]

Indeed, events in Italy contrasted with what was occurring in France, where courts reviewed cases with greater speed and displayed much greater propensity to use the death penalty than their Italian counterparts. Through the end of 1944 and into the next year, executions of Vichy personnel were regularly reported in the Roman press while Caruso, a collaborator, remained the one Fascist who had been sent to the wall. On the other hand, few RSI functionaries, who appeared more like Vichy collaborators than officials from the *ventennio*, had been caught. Most of them were still in the north with Mussolini. When the

Salò Republic collapsed at the end of April 1945, a style more evocative of the French would be applied to RSI collaborators. Until then the Italians would continue in their inability to come to terms with the crimes of Mussolini's *ventennio*.

Parallel with Maroni's High Court, legal sanctions against fascism also occupied the lesser courts: the Corti di Assise and the military courts. Italian records are closed or scanty, and little quotidian attention was paid in the press to these trials. Our knowledge is limited to the more notorious cases. A December 28, 1944, article in *Italia Nuova* stated that 257 "political" investigations (*posti istruttoria*) occupied places on dockets in Rome's ordinary courts. Most of these cases regarded offenses specified in DLL 159. Colonel Upjohn's April 1945 report listed 4,398 cases pending in the lower courts.[62]

For the most part, judges for these lesser courts were regular Italian magistrates: either brought out of retirement, taken from prisoner-of-war camps, or continuing at their benches. Virtually all had served fascism, and their links to Sforza and Berlinguer or with the Allies were tenuous at best. There was no apparent coordination of policy among these lower courts, and the verdicts were wildly uneven from judge to judge.

Among the most important and controversial proceedings emblematic of this imbalance was the long-awaited trial of important Neapolitan Fascists, which took place in October 1944. A military tribunal reviewed the cases of five men including the communications czar Count Ugo Pellegrini and the former prefect of Naples, the notorious Domenico Soprano. On October 18, the five were acquitted on grounds that their actions did "not constitute a crime." The term *non costituisce reato* quickly became a standard phrase signaling that charges would be dropped.[63]

During the last part of 1944 some lesser court trials were held against real *gerarchi*. The built-in limitations of Maroni's High Court necessitated that most blackshirts would answer their accusers in the ordinary system. These affairs were nevertheless moot since the defendants were virtually always in absentia. In December the first of these trials—of Attilio Teruzzi—was held. The Ninth section of the Rome Tribunale declared the former Militia boss and minister of the colonies guilty of misuse of public office and continued outrageous acts. He received six years and three months. This sentence must have been welcome news to him since, if he had chosen to return south from the RSI, his prison term would have been relatively short.

But these verdicts were uneven, and not all merely exonerated Fascists or called for light sentences. Some defendants received harsh terms despite minimal roles in the maintenance of the regime. The victims of these punishments hardly or never possessed political or social power. Later on, with the fall of the north, many of them would be low-level policemen or soldiers who had been involved in roundups. In 1944, however, a disproportionately high number of these cases involved women. Their strategic or symbolic role is obvious. The public images of them as either guardians of morality or temptresses made charges of collaboration against them strike responsive chords. Punishing "Fascist" women seems to have been strangely connected in the popular and political media with a purification ritual for Italian womanhood. With the exceptions of the Duce's daughter, Edda Ciano, and wife, Rachele Mussolini, no women connected with fascism would receive more attention than mistresses. Upon Salò's collapse, papers would be filled with stories of the Duce's mistress, Claretta Petacci, and of the RSI party boss, Alessandro Pavolini's lover, the actress Doris Duranti.[64]

The fascination in trials with women defendants reflected the deep uncertainty that permeated the applications of sanctions against fascism. Unable or unwilling to define guilt, the Italians chose to concentrate both their attacks and their interest on easy symbols such as the bloodthirsty Caruso, the shady Azzolini, or the frivolous immoral lover.

The most important trial against a woman before the liberation concerned one of Mussolini's lesser mistresses, Cornelia Tanzi. She wielded no power during the *ventennio* nor held any office. Her guilt was purely by association; the crime of unwise loves. She was privy to some information about a hidden cache of partisan arms and betrayed it in her boudoir conversation.

The attractive thirty-six-year-old Tanzi was the perfect choice for a show trial. She had been the Duce's lover in 1936 and subsequently slept with such *gerarchi* as Alessandro Pavolini and Alfredo Cucco. Newspapers could not resist her flamboyant personality and artistic background. They bestowed upon the trial headlines like "The Lover Danced While Mussolini Played the Violin" and portrayed the defendant as a flippant Salome mired in the lust of fascism. Her trial received front-page attention, and, although not held in the High Court, it competed with all others in Roman press coverage.

The assembly convened on December 20 in a packed Roman courtroom. Tanzi launched her defense by playing a role, that of the frivolous artist, perhaps hoping to charm the judges. Wearing brightly colored dresses and heavy makeup, she virtually flirted with the authorities. Her behavior did not produce results so she changed her style, wearing more somber, black outfits and bursting into tears to implore the grace of God. At one point Tanzi interrupted the court with an emphatic plea, "Lord, Lord, help me. What have I done wrong? Why do they hate me?" On December 23, based on the violation of Article 51 of the Military War Code, the artist was sentenced to thirty years in prison. The Carabinieri had to pull her, screaming and crying, out of the courtroom.

The great irony of the Tanzi case was that it coincided perfectly with the Pentimalli and Del Tetto trial, and the verdicts were easily contrasted. From whatever political bent, sentences of twenty years for the generals and thirty for Tanzi were shamefully unjust. The embarrassing comparisons were compounded by the conclusion of yet another trial on the same day as Tanzi's. The *ex-segretario federale* of Naples, Domenico Tilena, received a sentence of six years, eight months. Even the American ambassador felt the Tanzi verdict sufficiently odd to relay back to Washington.

The lopsided sentences were so glaring that the trials were universally condemned. *Italia Nuova* felt that the problem lay in the fact that a military tribunal was not allowed in the generals' case. It was about the only thing that the monarchists could have said without coming out completely against the Sforza Commission. Had there been a military tribunal, the generals might have gotten off with slaps on the wrists. *Italia Libera* was "surprised" to learn of the generals' verdict, especially in the light of Tanzi's. The *azionisti* appeared sincerely baffled as to how this could have been possible. The paper asked: "What were the two generals doing in Naples when it was handed over to the Germans? Were they taking a walk? Were they on vacation? How could their sentences conceivably be lighter than Tanzi's?"[65]

Mario Berlinguer's High Court trials and those before the ordinary magistrates revealed the same sorts of problems that plagued Mauro Scoccimarro's purges and the Sforza Commission in general. Logistics hurt their progress but was not enough to derail them. The inability or reluctance to come to terms with the nature of fascism in society, in its broader, more profound terms, and reliance on the limited notions of the July decree hindered meaningful action. The problems were rendered insurmountable by the amount of opposition, particularly to the purges. At this early stage of application the resistance came from the front line of those affected. But behind that was the stronger force of the traditionalists among the ruling class, a strength that would reveal itself in November and December 1944.

From their inception in July until the end of 1944 the form that sanctions would take was still largely unclear. By late December, however, only one thing had become apparent: the program as it stood was, by all standards, ineffective. The narrowness of DLL 159 had become manifest. Leftists feared that an indictment of the entire ruling class was not coming, and important segments of the state bureaucracy had launched a determined resistance against Sforza. On the other hand, Crocean-Liberal intentions of intelligent and selective punishment seemed also to fail.

The whole program appeared at least tactically if not morally mistaken. Most of the highest *gerarchi* had vanished with Mussolini, so the obvious targets were gone. Many feared that if a purge was being accomplished at all, only lesser bureaucratic figures and fringe elements were its victims. The High Court defendants—Caruso, Azzolini, and the rest—were considered either as thugs per se or as scapegoats. Not one of them had been a key figure under Mussolini, particularly before the July coup. And the lower court trials were erratic, exonerating Domenico Soprano and condemning Cornelia Tanzi.

The Scoccimarro and Berlinguer subcommissions began to run into trouble from the most threatened Center-Right forces. Initial opposition had come in quiet bureaucratic avenues like the Advocate General's office or the National Research Council. Bureaucrats by themselves, however, could not destroy sanctions. That required more powerful artillery. The assault would begin in the November crisis of the first Bonomi cabinet, when the CLN coalition would rupture over challenges to sanctions and the High Commission. The crisis would reveal how broad and serious was opposition to sanctions. The traditionalists had found their footing, recognized their strength, and issued open pronouncements against sanctions, something that would have been political suicide in the summer of 1944.

CHAPTER FIVE

SCOCCIMARRO AND THE OPEN RIFT

By November and December 1944 Italy's new sanctions against fascism languished in rancor and difficulty. The recalcitrant bureaucracy's opposition to the measures was soon reinforced by objections from traditionally minded members of the higher orders—the crown, the military, capital, and the church—who, in turn, were backed by their political allies—Liberals, monarchists, and factions within the Christian Democracy. This combination of forces would close ranks while protecting their first line of defense: the state employees. Mauro Scoccimarro's controversial purge, which aimed at broad segments of society, although this was still only a threat, continued as the focus of most suspicion and bore the brunt of contravention. Mario Berlinguer's tenure, on the other hand, suffered less than Scoccimarro's. His trials had come to be criticized for their uneven sentences, but by and large they were not considered as assaults on whole parts of society and had escaped the conservatives' wrath.

As 1944 drew to a close, defascistization had emerged as the hottest issue in domestic Italian politics. Arguments concerning the Sforza Commission, by November, were creating deep divisions in the ruling CLN coalition and forced the ultimate crisis of the first Bonomi Ministry. Within the cabinet, the conservative vanguard of the Liberal party called upon its allies, mainly elements within the Christian Democrats and the service ministries, and demonstrated for the first time in free and post-Fascist Italy how powerful the political Right was. The November-December crisis also illustrated two other phenomena: how weak the Left was in the face of such opposition, and how important the swing votes in the Center were, essentially those of the Christian Democrats.

The Center-Right played its hand in the cabinet emergency, and Bonomi marshaled it to victory: by holding the prime minister's chair, by ridding the High Commission of Sforza and Scoccimarro, and then by muzzling it under his own auspices. Consequently, in early spring 1945 Italy witnessed a renewed and emboldened political Right, which enjoyed an inverse relationship with the slow and disappointing course of the purge and the trials.

Some observers had been monitoring the new and rising confidence on the far Right, those beyond the CLN spectrum, since the black mark and embarrassment of fascism had begun to fade. As early as December 2, 1943, Croce had written, "This morning I thought how practically no one now talks of Mussolini; not even to rant against him," and he feared that soon historians would "set about discovering bright and generous traits in that man."[1] By the following November 29, Corrado Barbaglio in *Avanti!* bemoaned that many Italians were recalling the *ventennio* with some fondness and noted the growth of a "certain nostalgia" for it. Perhaps the old regime was not so bad after all, and a hasty, or even unnecessary, purge would upset the nation's society in the face of a rising Marxist menace that seemed particularly strong in the anti-Fascist resistance.[2]

Ironically, the liberation of Rome and open politics also nurtured fresh doubts over the perilous existence of sanctions. By October 1944 Colonel Poletti had detected a growing popular restlessness in Rome and a more heated political debate over the program. The fight between traditionalist forces, which opposed the High Commission, and the Left, which supported it, could not but alter the goals of defascistization, narrow as they may have been, and transform them into symbols in a highly polarized and partisan struggle. Any semblance of nonpartisan sanctions vanished as the High Commission became a political football in an increasingly embittered atmosphere.[3] By November that controversy had fallen squarely in the lap of the Bonomi government.

SANCTIONS AND THE FIRST
BONOMI CABINET CRISIS

The cabinet fight over the Sforza Commission was sparked by the publication, in the November 10, 1944, *Avanti!*, of an interview with Mauro Scoccimarro in which the *commissario aggiunto* launched salvos against the upper reaches of the Bonomi government. Scoccimarro had been complaining privately for some time, and Italians had not been the only targets of his rancor. He had also singled out men in the Allied Commission who maintained too many friends among "the likely and legitimate subjects of *epurazione*." Scoccimarro's tactic, as he had already told an Allied informant on October 16, was to lie low and work for the end of the Bonomi regime. Only then could an effective purge be engineered.[4]

When *Avanti!*'s Achille Corona approached Scoccimarro for the November 10 interview, the subject was ready to talk. Sitting at his desk in the Palazzo Viminale, the adjunct commissioner illustrated his position with two colored pencils placed in front of him. A black one represented reactionaries and Fascists, while a blue one stood for democracy. Scoccimarro used his hand as a symbol and placed it between the pencils. Here were the well-meaning conservatives or moderates, "democrat[s] of the old type," who acted as obstacles to a purge. Scoccimarro undoubtedly saw Christian Democrats as the bulk of that segment. The problem with the purge was that the hand leaned toward the black pencil. More specifically, within government ranks, the stumbling block was the high bureaucracy that had served the Fascists for twenty years but had never truly been Fascist. Although those officials were not purge matériel, they fought it with a "passive resistance" that facilitated "Fascist and reactionary . . . sabotage."

Scoccimarro continued. Purge decisions sent to the ministers fell on deaf ears. He cited many instances where no action was accomplished despite the best efforts of the High Commission. He mentioned the National Research Council, the Court of Accounts, and the Treasury, where only one bureaucrat had been fired out of eight requests. "Among the service ministries," he said, "the Navy is particularly notable: of seventeen cases, only one has been taken care of." Because of this opposition, the purge had dragged on for three or four months rather than the one or one and a half that it should have.

Scoccimarro had foreseen this trouble, some days before, when his chief met with many of Bonomi's ministers to discuss sanctions. Sforza complained at that conference that Byzantine ministerial channels, through which he was forced to work, hampered his task; he suggested that his commission be given the power to directly suspend functionaries. Perhaps to the high commissioner's surprise, everyone at the meeting agreed. Soon after the meeting, however, resistance to the idea developed. Many ministers turned to block Scoccimarro's purge efforts, and some labeled him a partisan Communist bent on the destruction of the state administration. How can one conduct a purge, he concluded to *Avanti!*, when the ministers are against you and when some of them, specifically Raffaele De Courten at the navy, were "not able to respect even the terms of the law?"[5]

The impact of the *Avanti!* article was compounded with the publication, on the same day, of another piece in *L'Unità*, which concerned wrongdoings in the Treasury. The report charged that the Liberal minister, Marcello Soleri, had been suspiciously quiet over the tenure of certain high officials in the Exchange Office (Istituto dei Cambi) who had held the same positions during the Nazi occupation.[6] The Scoccimarro interview and the *L'Unità* piece caused an immediate backlash in the Council of Ministers.[7]

The first reaction came from the Treasury. Soleri complained to Bonomi on November 11 about the *Avanti!* and *L'Unità* articles and reminded the prime minister of an agreement reached at the last council meeting that "before publishing attacks against the Government or against its measures, one must take the questions to the Committee of Ministers without Portfolio."[8] Soleri also penned an angry note to Scoccimarro to say that the interview had left him flabbergasted (he read it "con molto stupore"). In his defense, Soleri claimed to have suspended eight of the nine high (grades 3 and 4) officials requested by the High Commission and thirty of the fifty-three lower-level employees under scrutiny.[9]

Soleri's second letter to Bonomi, on November 12, was even more explicit, charging that the purge had created a terror and paralysis among his Treasury employees. The High Commission's objectives had been too sweeping, and his methods were unnecessarily harsh, repeatedly requesting the suspension of top men, including the minister's "best" inspector general, his "best" division head, and his own *chef de* cabinet. Soleri defended many of these men, including one accountant (*ragioniere*) on whose behalf, he claimed, the Allies currently pressed for a promotion. The minister cited other government agencies, including the Bank of Italy, the State Printing Office, and the Exchange Office, which were under attack. The functionaries in those institutions had become lethargic and demoralized, halting necessary services while "the sword of Damocles" hung over their heads. In conclusion, Soleri threatened to resign since such conditions, and his own poor health, rendered productive work impossible.[10]

Soleri's anxiety was at least equaled by that of Admiral Raffaele De Courten, minister of the navy. At the November 9 Council meeting he complained of a press campaign that had already begun against him and the ministry. *Italia Libera* and *Avanti!* had been printing inflammatory articles about the naval brass and their resistance to the purge; and the Scoccimarro interview had been the final straw.

In a November 14 letter to Bonomi, De Courten challenged Scoccimarro's assertion concerning the lack of response to the seventeen suspension requests made to the ministry. But De Courten's challenge was more defiant than Soleri's. No excuses were offered. In fact, the admiral insisted that the seventeen should not be ousted at all. He cited a September 4 circular from Bonomi stating that, regarding the suspension of Fascists, action should be taken only when continued tenure would endanger the administration or, significantly, cause a public outcry. De Courten wrote that Scoccimarro had never given him a reason for the suspension of the bureaucrats nor an explanation of why their presence constituted a danger. Thus, he saw no reason to apply sanctions.[11]

De Courten concluded his letter by opening all guns on Scoccimarro:

> But the fundamental problem, which affects the function and the tenor of the Government as a whole and among its individual members, is that constituted by the menace that Scoccimarro has permitted to be aimed against the ministers in general and against me in particular. . . . Before the gravity of these words, the significance and meaning on which I do not have to linger, since they have not escaped Your Excellency's political sensibilities, I cannot but repeat for the record that which I had the honor to verbally communicate to Your Excellency the other day; and that is that

my continued tenure in this high position is impossible if Scoccimarro remains in his position or if the Government gives its tacit agreement to his declarations in regretful interviews. To put Your Excellency in a condition of complete freedom of action to be able to bring the question before the Council of Ministers, I hereby submit my resignation as Minister of the Navy.[12]

Bonomi had no intention of sacrificing his naval chief to the purge and refused De Courten's resignation. Confident of the support both of the Allies and of Bonomi, the minister of the navy resumed his battle against Scoccimarro. The climax came at the November 24 meeting of the Council of Ministers, where an infuriated De Courten thundered that unless Scoccimarro were removed and the naval purge lightened, he would order all of his men to leave the ships and go home. General Messe at the Supreme Command soon joined the naval minister with two letters to Bonomi in which he urged caution in any move to purge the military.[13]

Bonomi sided with the admiral and pointed his finger at the High Commission as the government's source of all evil. The prime minister insisted that valuable, trained personnel were being unnecessarily suspended and discharged and that the bureaucracy had ground to a halt. He demanded the resignations of Sforza and his four assistants. The crucial juncture had been reached as Bonomi, De Courten, and Soleri assembled before the other ministers and forced the issue of who would possess power and how that power would be used to approach the issue of sanctions against fascism.

The issue was also forced for the Left. The moderate Socialist Giuseppe Saragat argued that the High Commission stand firm, free from meddlesome cabinet ministers, and urged Sforza not to cave in to Bonomi's demands. Appeasement of Bonomi, he claimed, would signal a return to dictatorship. Saragat's move on behalf of the Socialists forced his reluctant Communist ally into choosing sides. Togliatti was cornered. He had to support Bonomi or Saragat. He chose the latter and announced, with some partisanship, "I support Scoccimarro." Finally, the Christian Democrats avoided a strong stance. De Gasperi pleaded for "indulgence: justice tempered with mercy."[14]

The alternatives were clear: Scoccimarro or De Courten, and all that that implied. On November 26 Bonomi tendered his resignation to

Umberto, revealing the prime minister's intention to rely on the monarchy in addressing leftist pressure. Although his CLN government had refused in July to adjure to the Royal House, Bonomi now enlisted Savoyard help to ensure his tenure and guarantee a Center-Right solution to the crisis. Bonomi stayed on with a caretaker regime to weather the storm. The first CLN government had collapsed and, with it, hopes for Sforza and Scoccimarro at the High Commission.[15]

THE ALLIES AND THE CRISIS

Among the Anglo-Americans the war effort continued to pose more constant demands than did a change in the Italian government. Nevertheless, a pattern of military victories and Bonomi's triumph coincided with their own general and growing pessimism over defascistization. Not every indicator, however, pleased the Jeremiahs. For example, the Allies' newly adopted policy of less interference in Italian affairs, Roosevelt's so-called New Deal for Italy, continued to endorse defascistization. The Allies still kept ultimate control over everyone hired in the Royal government, although as a general principle they conceded broader freedoms to the Italians. In a February 24, 1945, note, Harold Macmillan wrote that in keeping with the New Deal, Allied veto over government employment was to be relaxed. Only in the most strategic agencies would the Anglo-Americans exercise serious scrutiny. These included the Ministries of War, Navy, and Air, the undersecretariat of telecommunications, the PS, the Carabinieri, and the railroads. Some Allied administrators, like Charles Poletti, continued to apply themselves toward defascistization. Others, however, had already begun to ignore the problem. Commodore Stone commented to an underling that, with DLL 159, "the purge is the responsibility of the Italian Government. The function of the Allied Commission is to see that it is conducted in harmony with the guidelines imposed on the Italian Government by the Armistice. The Allied Commission is not a tribunal where Italian laws are administered or decided."[16]

The Allies, particularly the Americans, would not abandon their endorsement of sanctions as a positive step in democratizing Italy, and they pledged their offices to help. But their policy, as sincere as it may have sounded, was not advocated exclusively in the spirit of altruistic democratization. The threat of Communism was a factor of increasing importance that affected the sanctions issue as the war neared its end. Less than one hundred miles away from the Apulian coast, a Greek civil war had erupted between moderates and Communists and created a great fear of something to be avoided in Italy.[17]

Concern that Communist trouble not spread across the Ionian Sea complemented London's ingrained uneasiness regarding leftist influence in Italy. Secret correspondence reveals that British calls for a purge had been partly motivated to counter Communist and Socialist propaganda. Already in June 1944 Orme Sargeant in the Foreign Office had linked the purges and Communists in a note to Ambassador Charles in Rome. In this early letter, London expressed disappointment that the application of sanctions was proceeding so slowly. Orme Sargeant may have been quite sincere when he wrote that "the extirpation of Fascism is . . . one of the leading aims of British war policy . . . [and] we do think that you should, through the Control Commission, make a point of encouraging the Italian Government, whenever possible, to take vigorous and effective measures." The letter, however, emphasized the need to "publicize" these encouragements "both to counteract propaganda by the Communists to the effect that they are the only true anti-Fascists, and by leftist sources generally to the effect that we are apt to support the conservative, and even reactionary, elements in Italy and elsewhere."[18]

By late autumn of 1944, however, private British doubts on a truly sweeping purge began to surface. For instance, reacting to a letter from Air Vice Marshal W. A. B. Bowen-Buscarlet on sanctions in the Air Force, A. D. M. Ross of the Foreign Office attached to it a confusing note on British, and perhaps American, attitudes. The airman lamented a failed purge but for two contradicting reasons: it was not effective, and it was too effective. He portrayed the judicial apparatus mired in debilitating legalisms and infighting; "[the judges] cannot see the wood for the trees [and could not] get on with the necessary job of purifying the Service." On the other hand, Bowen-Buscarlet complained about the successful purge of an unnamed "old *squadrista* general" who he felt did not deserve such bad treatment. Despite his blackshirt past, the general "had collaborated loyally with the Allies since the Armistice and had proved himself a capable officer."[19]

Meanwhile, at the Foreign Office, A. D. M. Ross approached the problem from another angle. Like Orme Sargeant, Bowen-Buscarlet, and the rest of the Allies, he felt some necessity in ridding the Italian government of Fascists and praised Allied actions toward that end, especially those of Charles Poletti. However, Ross continued, "what we really mean, I think, is that epuration must be thorough [which allows it to be fair] and *above all rapid*." He doubted whether the constant sword of Damocles, "the fear of being hauled out of a job to answer to the tribunals," had any value. Ross felt that the purge was getting out of hand when technocrats and valuable civil servants, "men whose tactical knowledge would be of great value to Italy and to the Allies," were staying out of public life due to fear of attack.

The Anglo-American hand was forced in December by rumors that Sforza intended to arrest Marshal Badoglio. Once again, crucial support for the Center-Right came from London, not Washington. On December 6, Ambassador Charles complained to the Foreign Office that the meddlesome Sforza intended to capitalize on the confusion of the government crisis by going after Badoglio. The British envoy feared "that the situation [was] becoming grave. The Purge Commission, by attacking Badoglio, [were] aiming eventually at the monarchy and they should be aware that the Marshal's arrest is an insult to His Majesty's Government."[20]

Later that day Badoglio appeared at the British embassy with news that Sforza planned his arrest for the following morning. Charles acted at once to protect the marshal from the High Commission. While he arranged for Badoglio to remain as a ward in the embassy compound, the ambassador telephoned an official in the Italian Ministry of Foreign Affairs, Renato Prunas. Together, Charles and Prunas went to see Bonomi. At the Viminale the prime minister adamantly insisted that the Government had absolutely no intention of arresting Badoglio and, in the ambassador's presence, telephoned the High Commission to make this clear. Nevertheless, the still-apprehensive Charles searched for a safe place for Badoglio to pass the night. With no luck at the Vatican, the marshal stayed on in the embassy. The press was told that he had become ill at dinner and would have to remain there in bed.[21]

In London, Churchill told Anthony Eden that "the execution of Badoglio by Sforza" would be a "most odious breach of faith" for the Americans as well as the British.[22] The Allies could not afford to have attention focused on Badoglio, since that might reveal embarrassing military and diplomatic secrets.[23] The British ordered their ambassador in Washington, Lord Halifax, to explain that a trial of Badoglio would bring to light sensitive information regarding the Armistice, particularly "the cancellation of the [Allied] air-borne landings on which the Marshal would probably say he confidently relied." It was not yet common knowledge that the Anglo-Americans had contributed to the fiasco of September 8, when the forces they promised to the Royal government were not airlifted into Rome.

But Washington did not esteem Badoglio as highly as the British did. Roosevelt's answer to Churchill's exhortations is not recorded. Furthermore, evidence points to an American reluctance to defend the marshal. When London again interceded with the Parri government in 1945 on his behalf, the State Department would not join them.[24]

While Badoglio remained in the British embassy, soundings were made to secure his safety. Despite further assurances from Mario Berlinguer, Badoglio would not trust his own government and pleaded for British protection. Charles concurred and wrote to the Foreign Office that "I have therefore arranged for him to stay two days with a British Military Unit where his presence will be kept entirely secret." The ambassador doubted that these precautions would suffice and felt that the best course would be to get Badoglio out of the country altogether. Philip Broad at Allied Headquarters in Caserta recommended that Badoglio be removed to Malta pending negotiations with the Americans and the Italians.[25]

Churchill intervened again. In a December 8 letter to Charles, he illustrated his deep concern for Badoglio's safety as well as for the close ties uniting the Allied and Italian armed forces, ties he deemed quite noble. The prime minister emphasized the principle of military honor involved between Badoglio and those high Allied officers "with whom he dealt so favourably." This, no doubt, was a reference to the Armistice and treaties signed with Eisenhower and Admiral John Cunningham. Churchill entrusted his representative with the responsibility "for the Marshal's safety and sanctuary in the British Embassy or in some equally safe place."[26]

Although it revealed London's attitudes toward the High Commission and sanctions against fascism, much of the British anxiety over the Badoglio affair appears to have been unfounded. Sforza and

Berlinguer were not seriously interested in his arrest, at least at that time. The High Commission was embroiled in enough controversy, and there was no need to add fuel to the fire. Most important were Berlinguer's constant assurances that no such prosecutions were planned. However, due to the marshal's paranoia, the guarantees were never heeded. Neither Charles nor Churchill would believe the High Commission. They instead trusted Badoglio.[27]

Badoglio was not the only high-level Italian officer involved in British machinations. General Mario Roatta had been included in the marshal's first two governments, and only after Allied pressure had he been removed but not incarcerated. Roatta's record had already warranted great suspicion among the anti-Fascists and the Anglo-Americans. It is one of the many mysteries and incongruities of the sanctions program that he still enjoyed freedom while Generals Pentimalli and Del Tetto and Cornelia Tanzi languished in prison. The American columnist Drew Pearson may have provided part of the answer when he uncovered a keen interest in Roatta on the part of Churchill. The British secret service, wrote Pearson, had developed connections with, and had relied on, Roatta for information. Churchill was anxious that this relationship not be exposed, particularly by Sforza. But the high commissioner had plans of his own, and according to Pearson, it was Roatta's arrest on November 17 that enraged Churchill and had sealed Sforza's fate during the cabinet crisis.[28]

Admiral Raffaele De Courten was another in whom the British took an interest, and he took advantage of the situation. In a December 6, 1945, letter to Charles, scholar Elizabeth Wiskemann related an incident that resulted from the relationship. During the first Bonomi administration, she reported, De Courten complained to British admiral Cunningham of persistent leftist press reports that publicized his past links with Mussolini. An indignant Cunningham promptly went to the Viminale to admonish the prime minister, "whereupon Bonomi ordered the press to hold off." Pressure from the British admiral had effectively curbed the Italian newspapers.

To explain the Cunningham incident as a case of British influence being used to protect Fascists requires some caveats, the most important of which considers motivation. Charles wrote later that he did not judge De Courten a Fascist. In a note to London the ambassador said he believed the admiral was a "nationalist and a monarchist" but not really purge material. De Courten represented as much as anyone the problem of the purge and of sanctions against fascism. He was not an ideologue, and his Fascist party affiliation was probably tenuous at best. He may have sympathized with Mussolini's regime, but his worldview was anchored in the monarchy and the navy, and when it came to a test of loyalty, as it did on September 8, the admiral sided with the king over the Duce. Of course, his king was heavily compromised by the regime, but where did that leave De Courten? As a reactionary, did the admiral's royalist sentiment and determined stance against the Left and sanctions constitute the criteria that should interest the purgers? London thought decidedly not.[29]

DOMESTIC POLITICAL REACTIONS TO THE CRISIS

Anglo-American anxiety over sanctions against fascism coincided with a growing disquiet among the Italians themselves. Even the leftist newspapers grew less confident in the efficacy of the purges and trials, while many on the Right considered the experiment misguided and sunk in sectarianism. The division in the press both reflected and contributed to the growing polarization of Italian politics at the end of 1944. Governor Poletti's November report noted that party activity was on the sharp rise, and, he believed, animosity between the Left and the monarchy was "out in the open."[30]

During the late autumn of 1944 all party newspapers affirmed their positions in preparation for what they knew to be the coming battle. The Socialist *Avanti!* toughened the most of all. Pietro Nenni and his followers had excluded themselves from Bonomi's new government, and free of CLN compromises, the PSIUP opened fire with abandon. In the November 28 issue of *Avanti!*, in the thick of the crisis, Nenni forecast a critical period for sanctions; Italy had reached the threshold between the "moderate" state and "tomorrow's democracy." He applauded Roatta's arrest on November 17 as a sign of a new, more severe, course. But now it was time to give Sforza the tools so that he could finish the job. The High Commission should be strengthened and not muzzled.

On December 9, Nenni viewed the sanctions problem in rigid Marxist terms. The battle in 1944 was essentially the same one he had fought
in the 1930s. For him, the struggle was simply one that pitted the new
nation of the democratic CLNs, reinforced by the Anglo-Americans,
against traditional Italy of the crown and Fascist generals. Viewing the
issue in black-and-white terms, Nenni had fallen essentially into the
trap of an over-politicized society. For him, one was either a Fascist or
an anti-Fascist. To oppose sanctions meant to support Mussolini.
Whether or not his thesis was valid, Nenni was contributing as much
as anyone else to the polarization of Italian society into two camps of
Left and Right.[31]

Still hesitant and opportunistic, the Communist stance was quite different from that of the Socialists. Velio Spano, the ideologue editor of
the PCI organ, contributed a number of articles for L'Unità during the
crisis that lacked the immediacy of Nenni's call to arms. His "Purge: a
Problem to Resolve," on January 3, 1945, displayed doubts over the
High Commission and sanctions. Spano wrote that the Communists
were not out to destroy the careers or lives of everyone who had ever
been carried away with fascism. Fears over a bloodthirsty PCI bent on
the destruction of Italy through a decapitation of its entire political
class were unreasonable anxieties spread by obfuscating conservatives.
Spano knew that a Reign of Terror would disrupt the lives of millions
of Italians, force hundreds of thousands from their jobs, and result in
government paralysis. That broad axe approach would create a disaster. Yet Spano's solution oddly reflected what essentially had been
Croce's: selective purges and trials of top-level Fascists. That this program had not been successfully promoted, Spano felt, was the problem with sanctions.[32]

During the cabinet crisis the Liberal newspapers had taken the most
blatantly antisanctions stance. In fact, more than any other political
newspaper, Risorgimento Liberale advocated the crisis in order to bring
the matter of defascistization to a head. During the fall it charged that
the purge progressed too slowly to be of any good and invited both
Scoccimarro and Sforza to use its columns to defend their positions.
Their two replies reached the same conclusion: that the High Commission was moving as fast as it could, and, to accelerate operations,
the law needed revisions. Despite the offer of its space, the Risorgimento Liberale launched, on November 11, a full attack against the

High Commission. Scoccimarro bore the brunt of the assault, contained in the article "The Purge and the Masses." He was accused of the worst sectarianism and of using the purge to increase the power of the Communist party.[33]

The monarchists naturally echoed the Liberals but walked on thinner ice. Monarchists had to be careful how far they attacked sanctions against fascism in that a relentless assault would appear self-serving. So, on January 4, 1945, *Italia Nuova* insisted that "The Purge Must Be Accomplished." The unsigned editorial deftly urged a hard-hitting attack against the *gerarchi* and the profiteers. Needless to say, the House of Savoy was never mentioned in that group. The object of sanctions should be the political "crook," and the ideal crook for *Italia Nuova* had no political scruples nor allegiances. He opportunistically flirted with all ideologies and, before 1922, had funded leftist *camere di lavoro* and Fascist *squadristi* at the same time, and then handed Italian workers over to the German slave-labor Todt organization during the war.

In discussing the cause of the cabinet crisis, the chief monarchist ideologue, Enzo Selvaggi, felt that Sforza's moderating influence at the Alto Commissariato had faded in the face of growing "social communism" and charged that Scoccimarro's Communist vehemence had corrupted any positive aspects that had been found in sanctions against fascism. Scoccimarro had stolen the purge machinery and was using it for his own ends, namely to broaden the parameters and attack the Treasury, the armed forces, and the police, institutions dear to traditional Italy.[34]

The Catholics' more ambivalent position posed problems that grew complex as discrepancies arose within their camp between the official Vatican organ, *L'Osservatore Romano*, and the Christian Democratic *Il Popolo*. Safely behind Bernini's columns, the Vatican had doubted the purge for quite some time. Not that the church stood squarely against punishment of Fascists; it did not. However, *L'Osservatore Romano* worried that a purge might get out of hand. Much of this criticism was based on moral grounds. In April the Vatican paper urged moderation: "let him who is without sin cast the first stone." On July 4, 1944, the organ of Catholic Action, the very powerful conservative lay organization, called for justice and not vendetta against the Fascists. And by October, the Vatican specifically criticized what it deemed were the purge's excesses. In "The Purge at the Zoo," the church paper reported that the chimpanzees had been expelled for giving the Fascist salute to passersby. By the time of the November cabinet crisis the Vatican's clear opposition to Sforza's commission was well known.[35]

In June and July, Christian Democrats were also skeptical about a blanket purge that could destroy the fabric of the nation and harm innocent people. *Il Popolo* had stood very much against Badoglio's earlier May 24 decree as antijuridical and politically in error. The DC also criticized the Poletti decrees on moral grounds, believing that the orders, in their breadth, could cause unnecessary pain to innocent people. Those doubts, however, were modified after DLL 159, for which the DC was in part responsible.

But Scoccimarro's presence provided the DC with an easy way out. In November *Il Popolo* also worried that the Communist had carried the purge too far and sacrificed justice to further his own ideological ends.[36] In "Causes and Aspects of the Government Crisis," the DC felt that the purge, which it still supported and which "should proceed rapidly and justly, [had] become often slow and partisan," threatening to "paralyze some of the principal administrative organs of the state."

The party, however, had not turned against the sanctions as clearly as the Liberals and the Vatican had done; and the Left recognized this. A secret report to London during the crisis revealed that the CLN's Left had not given up on the Christian Democrats and preferred De Gasperi over Bonomi as the next prime minister. The skeptical British observer added, however, "for the reason probably that they would be able to continue their ruthless purge."[37]

RESOLUTION OF THE CRISIS

Despite his November 26 resignation, Bonomi remained a caretaker in office, determined to kill the Sforza Commission and to form a new ministry. At the same time, the high commissioner and his assistants persisted and tried to push sanctions even further. Berlinguer's work continued, and the Pentimalli and Del Tetto trial took place unimpeded. Scoccimarro also developed plans for a speedier purge. On December 6, he ordered a radical suspension of everyone in the four senior grades of government service, including the armed forces. The purge commissioner could not have been serious, and the feisty Communist's drastic threat was probably a test for Bonomi. Such a plan had, after all, already been discussed in September and was opposed by both the Allied Commission and the prime minister.[38] When Scoccimarro resuscitated the issue in December, Bonomi reached the limit of his patience and told Ambassador Charles that he had "put his foot down."

Confident of broad support from Center-Right parties, agreement from the Allies, and PCI ambivalence, the prime minister acted.[39] Charles reported on December 10, "It is probable that Signor Bonomi may be able to take the machinery of the purge out of the control of the Communists (and Sforza) and hand it over to the judiciary."[40] The premier was particularly confident of British support against Sforza, who he knew was loathed in London. The high commissioner also knew it and tried to defuse British mistrust with a peace letter to Anthony Eden. The count insisted that he had been a positive force in Rome and had never "actively opposed" the CLN government. "I give you my word that the contrary is true [and] Bonomi knows it." London, however, remained indifferent to Sforza's plight. Charles wrote to Orme Sargeant in the Foreign Office, "You notice that even in his apologia Sforza cannot resist the temptation to exaggerate."[41]

Bonomi's new cabinet, revealed on December 12, reflected a clear victory for the traditionalist ruling class and its Center-Right political forces and did not bode well for serious sanctions against fascism. De Courten and Soleri remained at the navy and the Treasury. Scoccimarro was forced out of the Alto Commissariato and into the newly created Ministry of Occupied Italy. All CLN parties continued to be represented except for the Socialists. Among the loudest voices for effective sanctions, Nenni and his party withdrew into the political wilderness. The *azionisti*, determined but numerically weak, and the Communists, powerful but cautious, became flagbearers for sanctions. Togliatti became vice president of the Council of Ministers while De Gasperi took the Foreign Ministry. On December 27 Carlo Sforza resigned as Alto Commissario.

Bonomi himself restructured the High Commission in January 1945, a reorganization that the dejected and outcast Nenni felt "had all the characteristics of a first-class funeral."[42] The office charged with confiscated profits was conveniently submerged into Soleri's Treasury. Scoccimarro was replaced by the Neapolitan Communist Ruggiero

Grieco. The choice of Grieco, one of the most stalwart of party leaders and Togliatti's chief collaborator for many years, was certainly a concession to the PCI, but, perhaps in return, the new man proved more pliant than his predecessor. The office in charge of trials remained under Mario Berlinguer. Bonomi evidently felt that he could be dealt with, while conceding that such an important part of the sanctions could not be eliminated.

Most important, the high commissioner's chair went to Bonomi himself, and the Alto Commissariato became a tightly regulated function of the Council of Ministers. Bonomi could not devote his full energies to the management of sanctions, so he placed an assistant between himself and the *commissari aggiunti.* Handling its day-to-day functions, this assistant became in effect the most important man in the High Commission. Bonomi chose Renato Boeri for the post. A Milanese lawyer who never joined the PNF, Boeri had remained loyal to the Liberals until recently, when he moved over to the Action party. In an interview with the PWB, Boeri felt that his tenure as Bonomi's assistant might help to evade an anti-Fascist bloodbath at the end of the war. He urged that the government "show the people how efficient, speedy, and thorough are the means in liberated Italy for disposing of Fascists." Boeri considered that "Sforza's tenure had been dismal" and that a new path must be taken to rectify the "complete failure" of the present system. Among the first manifestations of this new direction was a January 10 circular from Bonomi's desk, no longer Sforza's, stating that henceforth, no consultants or part-timers (*ufficiali di complimento e della riserva*) would be subject to the purge. The prime minister also lifted the temporary ban from public office for suspected Fascists that had been prescribed in the July decree.[43]

THE NEW RIGHT EMERGES

The new complexion of the High Commission revealed the growing pessimism over sanctions and interwove with the reemergence of a non-Fascist political Right. While a call to arms for unrepentant Fascists would still have been suicidal, support for sanctions was no longer a political necessity, and public criticism of the program became increasingly acceptable. Members of the Royal House, the military, major newspapers, and politicians began to act and sound as though the High Commission had been a mistake, and some went so far as to imply that fascism left Italy a heritage not completely negative. As traditional Italy perceived a frightening rise in left-wing political membership perhaps some of that heritage might be reconsidered. Three phenomena illustrated this new boldness on the Right after the formation of Bonomi's second ministry: the duke of Aosta incident, the emergence of the Uomo Qualunque movement, and the Salvarezza affair.

Since the formation of the Regno del Sud, the Allies had concerned themselves with links between Salò and the king's military forces in places like Sardinia. But after the launching of Bonomi's second ministry it became clear that these ties reached into higher levels, into the House of Savoy itself.

Monarchist and military sentiments were sometimes revealed in gaffes, the most glaring having been made by the king's cousin, the duke of Aosta. The duke, an admiral, held a March 1945 dinner party aboard a cruiser in Taranto harbor. During the festivities he raised a glass and called for the execution of the High Court judges. Among the guests was *Manchester Guardian* correspondent Sylvia Sprigge, who a few days after the party circulated the story of his indescretion. Upon learning of the incident, Judge Maroni sent a note of protest to Bonomi. It was decided at a meeting of the prime minister, De Gasperi, Ruini, Brosio, and De Courten, that the duke should be disciplined, and an embarrassed Quirinale accepted his resignation.[44]

Another and more popular indication of the right-wing rebirth was the appearance, on December 27, 1944, of a new journal, *L'Uomo Qualunque*. The newspaper bore the same name as the movement that spawned it, Qualunquismo, and was chaired by the Neapolitan humorist Guglielmo Giannini. With a reputation as an amiable wit —monocled, robust, and dapper—Giannini had led a public life through the *ventennio* while maintaining an apolitical profile. A writer who hung around the stage-door crowd, he was a popular contributor to comedy and theater magazines and had founded a cinema review, *Kines*. Secretly, however, he had been "subsidized" by Mussolini's Ministry of Popular Culture. For Giannini the war was a clash of ideologies that he probably did not care to understand. He professed to hate the hot air of political debate, hot air that would only scald the "common man," the *uomo qualunque*. His arguments probably stemmed most of all from personal feelings: he blamed ideology for the combat death of his son. Giannini was greatly affected by that loss, and he joined the political fray with a vengeance. The *uomo qualunque* was a reaction to the brutality and corruption of fascism, the devastation of the war, and the quagmire of Bonomi's regime. The movement took root in the middle class, and, despite its competition with the DC for votes and its exclusion from the CLN coalition, the organization grew into a major political phenomenon. According to Sandro Setta, the leading student of the movement, Giannini and Qualunquismo were symbols "of those vast sectors of moderate public opinion where filo-Fascism was a state of mind of more or less accentuated benevolence toward Mussolini and the regime, without serious compromises."[45]

What Setta termed "accentuated benevolence" toward Mussolini Giannini called "passive resistance." Responding to a January 7 article in *L'Unità* that claimed that *qualunquisti* were merely ex-blackshirts, Giannini wrote that his followers were neither Fascists nor anti-Fascists, at least since the latter had abandoned a purpose and had become a profession. On October 17 he responded again with his own claim that 90 percent of Communist party membership was ex-Fascist.[46]

Giannini's bitterest commentary concerned the CLN, the recent cabinet crisis, the sanctions program, and abstract notions of Rome and big government. *L'Uomo Qualunque*'s inaugural issue agreed that Fascists had oppressed Italy for twenty-two years. But now, wrote Giannini in his terse, often vulgar style, forty-five million Italians were suffering under the yoke of 10,000 windbags, boondogglers, and crooks, otherwise known as professional politicians. Many of these "carpetbaggers" had been *fuorusciti* who had spent the *ventennio* abroad, perhaps on the Riviera or in Paris, while the hapless *uomo qualunque* coped with the regime in Italy. In another article Giannini personified the *uomo qualunque* as the victim of politics. "I am the guy who, meeting an *ex-gerarca*, asks, 'how did you get to be a purger?' . . . I am the guy who looks around and says, 'These are Fascist methods and systems' . . . [and] I am the guy who no longer believes in anything nor anyone."[47]

Qualunquismo, however, was too challenging for the end of 1944. Its style was overly abrasive, and the Bonomi government was still fragile enough that the new and increasingly popular movement appeared as an immediate threat. Not a member of the CLN coalition, the movement was, furthermore, vulnerable to attack from the Left. The assault came from Ruggiero Grieco, the new purge commissioner. On February 5, 1945, he recommended Giannini's name to the independent purge panel for the journalistic profession. The panel chair, Mario Vinciguerra, agreed and suspended him on February 27. From March 1 until April 25 *L'Uomo Qualunque* was not published, but the movement remained strong and, indeed, continued to grow.[48]

More important than a loose-lipped admiral and more sinister than Qualunquismo was the Salvarezza affair, which occupied the Roman press throughout the first half of 1945. Here was proof that important military commanders and the Royal House maintained contacts with fascistic elements linked to Salò. The public became aware of the case with the news of a police attack on a partisan hero, the sixteen-year-old hunchback Giuseppe Albani, nicknamed "Gobbo." In some working-class Roman neighborhoods, Gobbo had gained notoriety by enduring terrific Nazi punishments and escaping from the Via Tasso. The anti-Fascist celebrity enjoyed particularly warm accolades from the monarchist press. In return, he granted an interview to *Italia Nuova* where he regaled the reporters with stories of Nazi brutality and joked, "they beat me so much they almost straightened out my hump."[49]

But Gobbo's record tarnished on closer examination. No freedom-loving opponent of Nazi brutality, he had been playing the double game and, in fact, had not escaped from the Via Tasso but rather had walked out through the front door. After June 4 he ran a black-market operation, as well as extortion and blackmail rings that victimized, among others, opera star Beniamino Gigli. On January 15, Carabinieri forces ambushed and shot Gobbo. Three days later, 800 policemen stormed the Giordani, Quarticciolo, and Garbatella districts and smashed what remained of his organization. An entire wing of Regina Coeli was reserved to house the 350 arrested. Further investigation revealed that Gobbo's interests went beyond the black market.

It was learned that Gobbo's ambush occurred as he approached the headquarters of a shady fringe political party, the Unione Proletaria (UP). On January 23 *Avanti!* discovered that, two days before his death, Gobbo confided to a friend that he had been employed by Umberto Salvarezza, leader of the UP. Salvarezza had a long record of skirting politics; included among his titles had been secretary to Liberia's delegation to the League of Nations. During the Nazi occupation he maintained questionable contacts and, in 1944, formed the Unione Proletaria, a monarchist splinter group with an incongruous name. The connection proved immediately embarrassing to *Italia Nuova*, and the paper ceased its long panegyric to the fallen angel, labeling Gobbo and Salvarezza as "political gangsters." On January 21 it intimated that the two had formed weak links in a Communist plot and that Gobbo, for some strange and dark reason, had been gunned down by UP assassins in the pay of the PCI.

More concretely, others in the Roman press discovered an intricate political web linking Salvarezza to important officials on both sides of the Gothic Line. That he had influential friends was evidenced in an earlier investigation of him that was squelched, as well as subsequent police reluctance to reopen the case. On one occasion, a search of his offices promptly ceased after the mysterious Salvarezza telephoned one of his well-placed friends. His main contact in the Royal army, a General Vanetti, had served Salò in Rome before the liberation, and he had been tied to Mussolini's minister of the interior, Guido Buffarini-Guidi, and the German commander of the city, Lieutenant General Maelzer.

Through Vanetti and other officers, Salvarezza secured entrance into the Quirinal Palace where, disguised in bandages as a wounded soldier, he was clandestinely introduced to Umberto. What was discussed at this meeting remains unknown, but *Avanti!* claimed that the two were dividing up the ministries: the Interior for Salvarezza, and Justice and War for two generals, Tomassi and Dall'Ora. Whatever the subject of the conference, the affair became hotly followed and debated in the press until Salvarezza's arrest on February 4. Even then, the order of capture emanated from the High Commission and was met with resistance from the questore. Only at that point was Salvarezza turned over to the Roman police.

On April 16 Salvarezza's trial began in the lower courts. He was charged with rather pedestrian financial crimes such as illegal use of the offices and furniture of the Fascist Gioventù Italiana del Littorio for his own ends. Despite the low-key handling of the case, however, the hearing's political nature could not be ignored. Damning Unione Proletaria archives had been seized by the police, including one strange file, "Relations with the Duce" (Rapporti al Dux), that tied the UP to Masonic lodges, a coalition of twenty splinter parties, the Vatican, the Carabinieri, the Rome Questura, the Soviet Union, and Charles De Gaulle. At least one of these allegations was borne out when secret OSS reports connected Salvarezza to Rome's questore, Enrico Morazzini.[50] On May 11, Salvarezza was sentenced to seven years.

In and of itself, the affair did not affect the course of sanctions. However, together with the duke of Aosta's dinner party and Qualunquismo, it revealed in public the lengths and complexities of connections between the crown and military on one side and filo-Fascist political groups on the other. The dynamic of these connections was part of an ongoing process during the first half of 1945. Through political struggle and examples set by Royal and military leaders, together with the poor and controversial record of purges and trials, sanctions against fascism had been subjected to ever more open criticism.

FURTHER COMPLICATIONS
OF SANCTIONS

Muted and altered, doubted and criticized, sanctions against fascism nevertheless continued as public policy after the inauguration of Bonomi's second government. In January Bonomi reiterated his commitment to a purge as integral to his policy. Among the foremost aims of his administration, he said, was "the advancement of the work of the purge in a quick and impartial way."[51] The fall of Berlin was still a long way off, and the Fascists still constituted the enemy. Furthermore, the Left was a strong force to be reckoned with and, in general, prodded the application of sanctions. While still constituting the major support faction for sanctions, however, the Socialists had abandoned the CLN governing coalition.

After his resignation, Carlo Sforza published an essay and some documents on the Alto Commissariato, a work that coincided with a letter he sent to Bonomi on January 5. In the essay's preliminary observations, Sforza saw a real need for collective introspection on the nature of sanctions and on the direction they should take. He encouraged this discourse in a public arena since Italy did not yet have a popular or national assembly where sanctions against fascism would normally be debated. He added that the lack of argument was in part due to the

Allied tendency to get directly to work while frowning on discussion. Charles Poletti's dictum, "More spaghetti, less chatter," seems to have left an impression on the count.

The former high commissioner nevertheless urged Italians to stay the course with sanctions; but his suggestions were littered with reservations. DLL 159, he felt, was basically sound. It was a thorough measure that was not oppressive and "assured the most ample guarantees to the accused according to the best Italian traditions." The task was not to discard it but to streamline the law. On a more abstract level, however, Sforza presented the same doubts about sanctions that increasingly plagued many others. Despite his glowing commentary on "the best Italian traditions," he admitted that the notion of purging and of putting people on trial for acts committed when there were no laws against them was doubtful legal procedure. Nevertheless, perhaps cynically, Sforza urged Bonomi to continue and perfect the program of sanctions.

Inaugurating Bonomi's second government, however, ensured that Sforza's recommendations would fall on deaf ears. The first half of 1945 marked the low point of both the purge and legal activity until their demise. By March the Ufficio Studi, a general legal and research advisory agency within the prime minister's office, began to recommend that DLL 159 be reconsidered. Its verdict was that the early sanctions measures had been formed "in the heat of the situation" and perhaps needed revision. Bonomi, in fact, had already begun to modify the measure.[52]

By January 1945 the purge had ceased altogether in many government sectors. The most glaring example of this probably rested in the military. Since the High Commission's power only ambiguously touched military personnel, much of the armed forces was left to purge itself. At the War Ministry, Alessandro Casati relied on his territorial commanders for a cleanup of fascism in the army. Among those entrusted with the purge, for example, was the commander of Territory VII (Florence), General De Simone, a regular general who had accepted command of Fascist blackshirt divisions in the invasion of Ethiopia. It was no surprise when Casati was informed by Allied authorities that parts of the armed forces were "compromised" with the former regime and even with the RSI. Casati noted in a January 22 circular to his officers that this dilemma illustrated how ineffectual a self-purge had become: once again, he noted that the push came from the Anglo-Americans, who were themselves critical of a military purge.[53]

Beyond the military, as the war worked its way up the Italian peninsula, the sanctions dilemma presented itself anew in the liberated regions. In his report on the purge for the first half of 1945 the new adjunct commissioner, Ruggiero Grieco, conceded difficulties on the "periphery." He blamed the problems on three things: lack of proper legislation to extend sanctions beyond Rome, the Allied military occupation of much of central Italy, and the "complex, varied, and difficult political situation in the provinces." The last cryptic cause was probably the most important one.

Tuscany was freed in stages between the summer of 1944 and the final push against the Germans in the spring of 1945. The record there of sanctions against fascism echoed the inactivity and frustration that had plagued earlier provincial attempts. The frustration was no doubt heightened because the Tuscan anti-Fascist resistance embodied the first instance of a more violent trend that would culminate in the chaos of May 1945. Historian Claudio Pavone has lauded Tuscany's CLN as "the first . . . that knew how to live with dignity . . . both in its rapport with Rome and with the Allies."[54] Immediately upon the liberation of Florence a purge panel was established to investigate the public administration. The chairman was a Socialist, Emilio Gabrielli, who was assisted by a Communist and an *azionista*. In the first days of the AMG administration Gabrielli submitted to the Allies a list of those he considered to be dangerous Fascists for roundup.

But action was not immediate. Response from Rome was lax, and, as late as September 30, no formal purge commission had been formed. The Florentines soon grew impatient. Occasionally Fascists were attacked in the streets, and many feared the rise of more widespread vigilante action caused by the perceived mistaken or sabotaged purge.[55] The local purgers abandoned their original reliance on denunciations from directors of public offices, quickly concluding that these were not the best sources of information. As a result, they started over and released all who had been jailed. Gabrielli then established autonomous boards of inquiry to weed through the bureaucracy. These boards suggested sanctions, and their recommendations were sent to a deciding panel headed by a Sicilian judge, Giustino Notarbartolo. By March

9, 1945, seven months after the liberation of Florence, three thousand cases were still under consideration, of which only one hundred decisions had been delivered.

The Florentines complained that part of the reason for the delay stemmed from the Byzantine administration that characterized sanctions in the provinces. For the more important cases the final word had to come from the High Commission in Rome, which disturbed Gabrielli, who told a PWB officer that the Florentines did not trust the Romans. This suspicion had been aggravated in September 1944 when Bonomi appointed a notorious career official, Giulio Paternò, as prefect of Florence. The new man adopted a confrontational policy toward all post-Fascist reforms advocated by the partisans, and relations had grown so bitter that, although his superiors bore some responsibility in the choice, the Allied provincial commissioner surmised that Rome had sent Paternò to Florence to suppress the Tuscan CLN.[56]

But Rome was not the only problem. A February 23 PWB report noted that the Florentines entertained an "erroneous opinion" that the Allies were also lenient with Fascists. Despite his cordial relations with the Allies, Gabrielli confided to their representative that the Anglo-Americans quietly resisted his attempts to remove the vice prefect, "against whom we have collected an enormous amount of evidence. We have made direct representations to the High Commission for his immediate removal. Somehow he still holds his job."[57]

As the purge in Florence mirrored the logistical problems and opposition that had occurred in the south, so it was reflected in other areas. The Livorno purge commission experienced the same kinds of difficulties that plagued sanctions everywhere else. The head of the Livorno panel complained that the process had barely begun in late January, five months after the liberation. As a result, he said, "many Fascists are . . . still going about freely and the people complain of this. They complain above all that in Livorno, as elsewhere, not a few Fascists have been taken on in various capacities by Allied bodies and organizations."[58]

The trouble was not limited to newly freed areas. It also persisted in the south. A Christian Democratic journalist confessed to a PWB agent of his anxiety over growing fifth-column operations in Naples and elsewhere due to the persistence of Fascists in teaching and in labor. A group of *azionisti* complained to Rome of a renascent movement in

Basilicata. Another controversy in Salerno's local purge commission confused many there. One of the commission members, a Liberal, had been the right-hand man of the regional Fascist railroad boss and had been "the most eloquent of Fascist speakers for war propaganda." The man's defense, that he had not been a member of the PNF, held no water since it was discovered that he tried a number of times to join but was always rejected. In *Avanti!* Pietro Nenni focused attention on Sicily, where, he claimed, fascism had practically been reinstalled. The island's administration had become a disgrace to the new Italy and to the Allied cause. An OSS observer noted that the situation was so bad that the Palermo PCI had taken matters into its own hands and formed a "Red Guard" to punish Fascists and clean up the black market. Even Benedetto Croce admitted that the Sicilian administration was back "in Fascist hands."[59]

Popular responses to the purge and trials appeared to change from place to place and from time to time as the Allied armies inched their way toward the Austrian border. Intelligence reports and newspaper articles give us basic information on the mood of the people during this period, and two general conclusions can be drawn: that broad discontent persisted over defascistization, and that more anti-Fascist violence would be encountered in the north. The relatively complacent southern population described above stood in contrast to the northerners, who would adopt more violent solutions. There were simply more cases of bloody reprisals against Fascists during the last days of the war when a final reckoning witnessed thousands of Mussolini's followers shot down in the streets. On the other hand, it is almost impossible to discern whether this northern fury represented a truly popular undertaking or whether it was the action of smaller groups.

Much of the reason for more violence in the north stemmed from the simple fact that the war was drawing to a conclusion. With the liberation of Rome, the landings in Normandy, and the spectacular Soviet advance from Stalingrad and Kursk, by autumn 1944 Germany's defeat had become a foregone conclusion. Some concern over V-2 rockets and rumors of other secret weapons caused second thoughts, but a look at the map illustrated to everyone that Axis collapse would be only a matter of time. In 1943 Italy's fate had still seemed to hang in the balance; the battle line could still have gone either way. But after a year the Germans had become the victims of a pattern of nearly constant defeat and withdrawal. This no doubt emboldened many on both sides of the front into an antifascism that many would not have displayed had the National Socialists fared better.

Although it was on the perpetual defensive, the persistence of Salò's rule in the north was another cause of heightened anti-Fascist feeling. Deportations to Germany, hostage roundups, censorship, Fascist socialization blunders, and murder constituted the horrible and macabre nightmare of the end of Mussolini's dictatorship. Not only the size of the partisan forces but the fact that very few Italians volunteered to come to the aid of the RSI illustrate the final bankruptcy of the regime.[60]

THE PURGE AND THE TRIALS

Events in Florence, Livorno, Forlì, and in the south seem to belie a claim made by the *commissario aggiunto*, Ruggiero Grieco, that the purge in the provinces had been a "particularly intense" operation. In July 1945 he submitted a report on the course of his tenure that was intended to complement the one issued by Scoccimarro in January. The new commissioner wrote that his administration marked a distinct break with that of his predecessor. There were two phases to the course of sanctions: Scoccimarro's 1944 period, which Grieco portrayed as a rather unsuccessful hunt for high-level bureaucrats, and his own 1945 phase, which turned to investigate the middle and lower ranks of the government. Considering the sorry state of sanctions against important bureaucrats by January, the shift was a clear indication of Bonomi's attempts to defuse the purge. Sforza's goal of aiming the purge and trials against high-level officials and indulging the lower ranks had been abandoned with the inauguration of Bonomi's second government. To keep the program alive it had to be directed precisely against those middle and lower bureaucrats whom Sforza, and even Badoglio, had been so anxious to spare. Despite the general failure of sanctions against important government figures, this attack on middle and lesser functionaries was sadly misplaced.[61]

Grieco offered statistics to substantiate his claim that Rome's lower bureaucratic ranks were being thoroughly investigated and purged. From January 1 through July 15 the High Commission processed

12,507 names for judgment, as opposed to Scoccimarro's 5,184.[62] However, while over half of all denunciations against Fascists, 11,384 out of 17,151, had been lodged during Scoccimarro's tenure, the predecessor had removed only 539 of a total of 2,553 bureaucrats. But Grieco's use of the statistics might have been questioned if one looked at the figures for appeals. During the first half of 1945, 1,718 recourses were presented to the appeals board. Added to the 227 submitted during the Scoccimarro period, fully 2,045 of the 2,553 cases were in review. Only 508 decisions were still secure by the time of Grieco's report, even less than the 539 purged before January 1.

Berlinguer's prosecutions of Fascists continued through the spring of 1945, but his efforts were again discredited by unfortunate incidents, lethargy, and inefficacy. The season was dominated by the trial in the Maroni court of General Mario Roatta, along with other high-ranking Fascists and their assistants, most notably Foreign Ministry officials Fulvio Suvich and Filippo Anfuso and Alberto Jacomoni, chief administrator of Albania and an associate of Count Ciano. Roatta was charged with graft and international terrorism. The crimes included the murder of the anti-Fascist Rosselli brothers, the assassination of the Yugoslav king Alexander and the French foreign minister Louis Barthou, and acts of sabotage during the Spanish civil war.

Here was the first trial directed against important Fascists whose crimes were committed during the *ventennio* and not the German occupation. Much was to be gained in clear presentations of the case and in a real debate on political crime during Mussolini's regime. But the trial was complicated by the presence of Mario Roatta, who had served not only the Fascists before July 25 but the Badoglio regime and the Allies as well, as an important official and as a double agent. Churchill's anxiety over the Roatta arrest has been noted. A PWB agent, furthermore, discerned anxiety in Italy. A lawyer from the Action party, "well-connected in Rome and Florence," told him that the Italian General Staff in particular would staunchly protect Roatta from prosecution.[63] The trial itself provoked another crisis, something that, like the Caretta incident, exploded into a riot and further discredited the sanctions program.

As with earlier trials, the press was anxiously optimistic over Roatta's.

On November 16 and December 8, *Avanti!* repeated the now fading and stale hope that Italians could look forward to a public display of "some of the most famous and nefarious crimes committed by Mussolini's henchmen." The depravity of the *ventennio* would be illustrated for all to see, and finally, in this regard, the trial would be no disappointment. Sensational evidence of murder and corruption surfaced throughout the hearings, from sabotage and assassination during the Spanish civil war to graft in Albania that implicated large concerns, Breda and Ansaldo. The level of these crimes shocked even Pietro Nenni; but in the January 21 *Avanti!* he urged that verdicts not carry the tinge of vendetta. Rather, the trial's purpose should be to contrast the sheer horror of Fascist guilt with the justice of the new Italy, meted out on behalf of heroes: the Rosselli brothers and all of Mussolini's victims.

All optimism ended on the night of March 4. Roatta had been complaining of ill health and had received quarters in the military hospital in Rome's Via Giulia. On that evening the general left his bed, walked out of the building, and disappeared. That this was more than the case of an old sick man who somehow wandered out of a hospital became immediately apparent. Questions of complicity arose at once when it was revealed that Roatta's handful of Carabinieri guards had been absent from their posts. The political Left was determined not to let this one pass and mobilized within hours. The Communists led the way, launching their attack not against the Bonomi ministry, which it was anxious not to confront publicly, but against the security forces. The PCI demanded immediate suspension of those "on which falls the legitimate suspicion of everyone for having organized the flight."[64]

Bonomi responded with the removal of two officials. On March 7 he replaced General Taddeo Orlando at the Carabinieri with the "colorless" General Sogno. Within a few hours, however, it was clear that Sogno's past was also suspect, so, very quietly the next day, General Brunetto Brunetti was in turn chosen to replace him. Brunetti's past, particularly a tenure in Yugoslavia, would later prove embarrassing to the Allies and the Italian government but, for the time being, his appointment was generally accepted. Bonomi also endeavored to douse the fire by formally disbanding, but in fact camouflaging, Roatta's old intelligence operation, the SIM. The prime minister pulled the nameless but still-intact organization out of the General Staff and transferred it to Casati's Ministry of War, renaming it the Office of Information. The Allies keenly appreciated the work of this intelligence operation and were fully aware of Bonomi's administrative trick. They expressed no objections, provided that an SIM unit that worked in Allied headquarters remain there intact.[65]

But many Romans were too restive to accept some bureaucratic reshufflings and call it "case closed." Popular attitudes shifted, and prefectural reports detected a significant anxiety. Shortly before Roatta's escape, on February 4 the prefect Persico had observed that the trial held no interest on the street, that for the most part people were not concerned with it. But after the escape Persico reported a great resonance and fears of a government crisis. "Important arguments," he wrote, "are forming in all sectors of society."[66]

The Left CLN parties announced a popular rally at the Colosseum to protest the Roatta escape. A secret report from the Allied public safety subcommissioner claimed that the rally had been organized by the Soviet embassy. Informants had alerted him that PCI leaders Palmiro Togliatti and Velio Spano had been instructed to discredit the Carabinieri by staging a demonstration. According to the secret missive, the two Italians were instructed that, at the demonstration, "bombs have to be thrown and there must be a victim." This strange report helps to reveal at least the heightened partisan atmosphere affecting the sanctions debate. Assuming it was false, the Allies proved quite willing to believe their informants and succumb to anti-Communist fears and alarms. On the other hand, despite Togliatti's formal commitment to the CLN government, there was enough ambiguity in the PCI's stance as well as plenty of motivation on the part of the Soviet Union to suggest, as at least plausible, some intrigue toward destabilization.[67]

On March 7 a crowd of 15,000 assembled at the Colosseum, where they listened to a range of speakers berate the government for its poor sanctions record. The air was charged and aggressive. Hoots and whistles, red flags and placards were everywhere. Signs read "Death to the King!," "We want a real purge!," "Shoot the war criminals!," and "Clean up the police!" About a thousand of the protesters decided to take their message directly to Prince Umberto and marched en masse up the Via dei Fori Imperiali toward the Quirinale. They were met at the palace by 200 mounted Carabinieri. Conflicting stories described the initial ugly confrontation and the outbreak of violence. The troops fired warning shots above the crowd's heads. Both sides charged, and in the middle of the scuffle a bomb went off, killing a young demonstrator, Giuseppe Lasagna Mancini. Although some accused the Carabinieri of throwing explosives into the melee, this was probably not true. The bomb exploded in Mancini's hand. Nevertheless a martyr —specifically a leftist martyr—had been created: the incensed people put his body on a truck and marched, ever more threateningly, toward the Viminale and Bonomi. Some entered the palace, but they were quieted by Velio Spano and General Armando Azzi, a troubleshooter from the military who had gained some notoriety as a voice for purge within the army. While the hostile crowd waited below, the two met with Enrico Molè, an undersecretary in the Interior Ministry. No one reached Bonomi. Spano then announced to the protesters that the prime minister was prepared to resign. Although this news was based on a questionable rumor and was proved by events to be untrue, the crowd accepted it and soon dispersed.[68]

Although Allied spies insisted that the Communists were behind the original demonstration at the Colosseum, it is significant that when it shifted to the Viminale, a PCI leader helped to act as a brake. When things got out of hand and the ministerial offices were invaded, Spano, with Azzi, took charge and diverted the crowd's energies away from further violence. The next day, Molè of the Interior Ministry telephoned Spano and thanked him for his calming hand. Spano himself insisted to a PWB reporter that both the Quirinale and the Viminale demonstrations had been entirely spontaneous. The protests were over ineffectual sanctions and were quite sincere.

On the other side, Bonomi's safety must have been in more peril that day than it had ever been during the Fascist era. He soon petitioned Stone for more protection, once again leaning on the Allies to prop up his tottering government. He was emphatic: "I have already pointed out to you—after the invasion of the Viminale—the very great need to reinforce the armed forces in the capital. The Government cannot run the risk of seeing its offices invaded again." Macmillan nevertheless considered it at least a temporary victory for Bonomi, "The Government has survived," he wrote. "I think the Communists shall feel it better to wait."[69]

Like the Caruso verdict, the results of the Roatta trial were anticlimactic. Anfuso was sentenced to death in absentia. Roatta and two assistants were given life, which was moot since only one of the three was present. Suvich and Jacomoni were among the few on hand to hear of their twenty-four-year sentences. The others received punishments ranging from ten to twenty years.

There were other trials after Roatta's, but the importance of the High Court would rapidly decline. The number of Fascists brought before Judge Maroni's court was never significant compared to those on trial before regular courts; and with the collapse of Salò many more thousands, including high-ranking *gerarchi*, would be processed outside of the High Court. A less-newsworthy phase of trials against RSI thugs Federico Scarpato and Pietro Koch and "at-large" Fascist officials such as Giacomo Acerbo and Giuseppe Bottai completed the task of the Maroni bench. Only a judicial review of the status of Fascist senators was entrusted to the High Court after its "active" phase ended in October 1945. This was another meaningless endeavor since the Senate had been disbanded and it would not be reconstituted with a clean slate until after the war. It was becoming evident that the Maroni and the lower, regular courts, which continued to hand out wildly uneven sentences, did not constitute the correct combination to administer sanctions against fascism. Some new system waited to be devised.

By the time of the Roatta trial, grand events were occurring across Europe: World War II was coming to an end. Fascist governments in Berlin, Salò, Sigmaringen, and Oslo were all collapsing into a flaming Götterdämmerung. Throughout much of the continent, partisan troops and popular insurrections were hastening the collapse. Many, including Italians, looked upon these mass uprisings not only as hopeful for the defeat of fascism but also as a chance at redemption. On April 1, Nenni wrote that the last struggle would be won with the decisive element of partisan and popular forces. In that way, he felt, Italy would regain the world's respect.[70]

It was impossible to ignore the popular input in the collapse of Fascist power, and the Italian case was among the most vivid examples. In many areas, such as Domodossola near the Swiss frontier, partisans of the north Italian CLNs, the CLNAIs, had already evicted the Fascists and established independent, if short-lived, republics. All of this would have a determining effect on sanctions against fascism; Salò's collapse would change all the rules. The forces of the Center-Right, gaining momentum through the spring, faced a potentially major threat. And beyond the fear of social and political revolution, the slow process of democratization that sanctions had been experiencing would be completed: the people themselves would take charge in punishing Fascists. In April a huge looming force of very determined men and women, mainly connected with the CLNAIS, demanded strident and often extreme measures against the blackshirts. Giuliano Vassalli called in *Avanti!* for new forms of castigation for all *repubblichini*. Those who had accompanied the Duce north would be considered collectively guilty. On the verge of the insurrection, an oss analyst commented that the prospect of sanctions was "perhaps the principal internal issue that will face Italy on the Liberation of the North."[71] The choices of September 8, to serve the king or the Duce, now came back to haunt Mussolini's followers. They had become traitors who had lost a ferocious, bloody civil war.

CHAPTER SIX

INSURRECTION AND POPULAR JUSTICE

Europe has never experienced anything quite like the cataclysmic horror of the collapse of Hitler's Empire: first the blood orgy of dying National Socialism, then government, commerce, families, and men and women caught between retreating Germans and advancing Allied armies. In the last weeks of April 1945, northern Italy fell into this chaotic, ultimate struggle. A dual conflict of national liberation and civil war ranged over the whole of the north: from Bologna to the Brenner, from the Val d'Aosta to Trieste. On April 24 and 25, the German line broke along the left bank of the Po River, and within five days the Anglo-Americans reached the Swiss frontier. Milan, the last capital of Fascist Italy, fell on the twenty-sixth to the semiautonomous northern Italian CLN, the CLNAI (Comitato di Liberazione Nazionale dell'Alta Italia). Fighting had been conducted by various military groups that can be loosely organized into two headings: the *autonomi*, generally composed of RSI deserters and army regulars who had been in the bush since September 1943, and the Corpo Volontari della Libertà (CVL), which was predominantly, though far from exclusively, Communist inspired. It was not until April 29 that Allied troops reached Milan, and only on May 2 did Anglo-American administrators arrive. The war was over, but old scores remained to be settled.[1]

Like September 8 and the liberation of Rome, Axis military collapse altered the course of sanctions against fascism. New complexities arose, some alliances were strengthened, others were weakened. The stage was broadened further by the real multiplication of voices, the voices of northerners from all walks of life who had themselves contributed to the Resistance against Salò and the Germans.

The first complication posed by the events of April came in the simple but important fact that World War II was over. The battles ended, as did National Socialism's attempt at world domination. This held two immediate consequences for Italians. First, the Anglo-American forces on their soil no longer concerned themselves primarily with defeating the enemy in Berlin and could afford the time to consider Italy's future. Inevitably, Washington and London would focus more attention on the nation's government and politics.

The second effect of peace in Europe was the quick transformation of the nature of the anti-Fascist struggle, from a civil war into a combination of popular violence and sanctions against a defeated enemy. The violence was predominantly one sided. Mussolini's Social Republic ceased to exist, and blackshirts were rendered largely physically defenseless against vendetta. During the weeks after the liberation, several thousand Fascists died violently at the hands of their political enemies. How random or organized was this popular justice remains problematic.

No doubt anti-Fascist retribution was openly endorsed by many. The chorus, however, was far from universal, and the "justice of the piazza" itself was limited largely to left-wing zealots and radical elements within the working class. Unless Fascists could hide, find protection, or leave the country, they would also be harassed by another foe: the government. But only later would this second factor, the more conservative hand of Rome, moderate the popular attacks and oversee more formal sanctions against fascism.

Another complication to affect defascistization was the different socio-economic structure found in the newly liberated area. Actions undertaken in the south could not easily be reapplied to the north. The two were now politically rejoined, but it was not the fusion of two identical halves. Unlike the agricultural south, there existed in the north heavy industrial concentration. Italy's uneven economic development meant that most large manufacturing concerns were located in cities such as Turin, Genoa, and Milan, far from the southern purges that had already taken place. Consequently, no special measures had yet existed to address issues raised by the north's intense, but largely private, capital concentration. Until the liberation, an attack on the magnates of commerce and industry had remained on the back burner.

In April 1945, sanctionists could not rely on many precedents since few directors had been prosecuted in the south. Poletti, for example, had jailed certain Neapolitan cotton bosses mainly for black-market activity. But they were exceptions, and they paled in importance next to their Lombard, Ligurian, and Piedmontese counterparts at Pirelli, Ansaldo, or FIAT.

This northern structure guaranteed that the narrow statist framework of sanctions against Fascists, which had persisted since Badoglio's first decrees, would not remain unchallenged. Collusion between money and fascism emerged as an issue difficult to ignore, and the obvious complicity of many industrial and commercial leaders served to force the case for a broadened definition of "Fascist." But an assault on collaborationist capital threatened to cross the crucial line between the political and ruling classes. Thus far, sanctions had been applied to government employees and to very few others, with only spotty effectiveness. Most conservatives within the ruling class had been able to avoid inclusion into the list of sanctions targets. But popular sentiment to purge big capital fit into a vague and larger theme, particularly strong in the Left Resistance, to redistribute wealth in postwar Italy. And these ideals were simply too strong, for that moment, to ignore. Historian Romolo Gobbi has noted that the projected assault on capital was the most extreme phase of the purge, which was, in turn, the most radical expression of the liberation.[2]

Upon the liberation, a significant impulse for broadened and intensified sanctions came from partisan formations, usually on the political Left. Important leaders, ready to lead free Italy into the promised land of popular democracy, emerged from these ranks. Sandro Pertini, Roberto Battaglia, Luigi Longo, Rodolfo Morandi, Leo Valiani, Edgardo Sogno, and Ferruccio Parri, among others, all had engaged in clandestine struggle against Salò. Together with their more moderate allies among the Christian Democrats and Liberals, these powerful underground, anti-Nazi organizations transformed themselves into legitimate political factions within the existing parties. In June, the leader of the Resistance, Ferruccio Parri, would carry the CLNAI ideals to Rome and replace Ivanoe Bonomi as prime minister. From Parri on down to the rank and file came a fresh impulse to purge and prosecute Fascists.

But these diffuse partisan fighters and anti-Fascist groups were often more divided than they were agreed. Theirs was a coalition, essentially the same CLN coalition that ruled in Rome, and they approached the sanctions problem in three ways. First, despite Allied orders to surrender their arms, many undertook a clandestine and violent campaign against the blackshirts that would continue for three years after the formal end of hostilities. This persistence of killing especially affected the Po Valley and Emilia-Romagna, which earned itself the sobriquet "the triangle of death" from historian Paolo Alatri. The intensity of this wave of violence has also prompted some to term the period a civil war.

A second option was to abandon violence and punish Fascists through formal or semiofficial organizations. This required faith in not only the High Commission but also new vehicles, primarily the newly created "extraordinary assize courts" and CLN purge commissions within factories. The third, more general alternative was to endorse the prospect of a CLNAI government in Rome, a more democratic Italy, and the end of the Fascist monarchy forever.

THE SALÒ REPUBLIC AND
THE CULTURE OF DEATH

With all of the struggles over defascistization after the liberation, it should be remembered that Mussolini's Salò regime practically had killed itself. The internal history of the RSI was one of defeatism and political suicide: a puppet government that devoured itself. After the fall of the Duce and the creation of the Salò Republic in 1943, the Nazis and Fascists conducted a thorough and brutal housecleaning of their own. Most of the Grand Council members who voted against Mussolini in 1943 had the good sense to get out of the country, like Dino Grandi, or to go underground until the Allies arrived, like Giacomo Acerbo. But other *gerarchi* were caught and tried by the blackshirts. After the Verona trial of January 1944, many of them were executed. These included Marshal Emilio De Bono, one of the *quadrumviri* who marched on Rome with Mussolini in 1922, and Count Galeazzo Ciano, the Duce's son-in-law.[3]

The civil war against the partisans had also devastated Fascist ranks. Important *gerarchi* such as the Milan police boss, Aldo Rasega, and the philosopher Giovanni Gentile were assassinated during the last two

143

years of the war by underground enemies, while others, like party boss Alessandro Pavolini, had been wounded. In his essential work on the subject, Ricciotti Lazzero has described and cataloged the enormous casualties suffered during this period among the Fascist Black Brigades. Examining organizational rosters to discern which men died at the hands of the partisans, he listed, for example, 220 men and forty-seven officers of the Turin Black Brigade "Ather Capelli." Of the officers, six were killed before April 26, 1945, and seven in the month after the Armistice. About one-third, including the commanding colonel and his chief of staff, died. Lieutenants were the hardest hit; six of ten were killed. This must be explained in part by the fact that many of the other ranks who survived were desk personnel, procurement staffs, and so forth, and that lieutenants were the essential field commanders most visible to the public. Overall, ninety-three of the 220 men in the "Ather Capelli" were killed: fifty-five of these died shortly before the liberation, and twenty-eight in the month after.[4]

By 1945 RSI leadership consisted mainly of new men. The most important relics of the *ventennio* were Guido Buffarini-Guidi of the Interior Ministry, Renato Ricci, the old Militia boss, and Marshal Rodolfo Graziani in the armed forces. Some others, notably Roberto Farinacci and Achille Starace, haunted the chancelleries and jockeyed for position with the Germans. Most of the other leaders were men of minor or peripheral rank before the war. The party secretary, Alessandro Pavolini, was a writer who secured the Ministry of Popular Culture only in 1940. Paolo Zerbino, the last minister of the interior; Colonel Valerio Borghese, head of the elite Decima MAS commando force; and Vittorio Mussolini, *éminence grise* at his father's court, all commanded minor roles before 1943.

The RSI bureaucracy realized that the last act had been played out and was ravaged in these last months by a psychological malaise, *attesismo*, waiting out the end. Government officials seemed merely to go through the motions and kept their heads low until the Allies arrived, causing some party sticklers to complain. The prefect of Cremona moaned to the Interior Ministry that his provincial administration was scarred by an "utter disregard for rules during office hours." Management had completely broken down, and the prefect lamented that his staff wasted time in "illicit relations." He admitted that the questore personally intervened at two hotels "to break up a deplorable situation."[5]

More than anything else, the Duce himself represented the pallor that tinged the whole regime. He had given up on public rallies; the last was his December 16, 1944, appearance in Milan to address an assembly in the Teatro Lirico and visit, ironically, the birthplace of the movement, the Piazza San Sepolcro. All accounts of this event attest to a strange euphoria, a last hurrah of fascism. At any rate, the excitement vanished immediately, and the Duce began to refer to himself as "the late Mussolini." In March he granted two interviews which were not for publication where he constantly spoke of his own mortality. To journalist Maddelena Mollier he lamented, "Death has become a friend; it does not frighten me any more. . . . I've made my mistakes and I'll pay." On the twentieth he said to Ivanoe Fossani, "I have no illusions about my destiny. They will not give me a trial . . . they'll probably kill me and say that I committed suicide, a victim of remorse." Despite a dubious record as a prophet, this time Mussolini was not far from the mark.[6]

THE LIBERATION OF THE NORTH
AND ANTI-FASCIST VIOLENCE

Popular violence against Fascists reached its fever pitch during the liberation and would determine the extralegal nature of sanctions after the Axis surrender. The April-May retributions cannot be understood without seeing them as the final phase of the civil war of 1943−45, and they were unique to Italy among the Axis nations. Germany and Japan never experienced anything remotely similar to the enormous wave of popular justice against RSI officials. Other countries, however, particularly France, Norway, Belgium, and many of the eastern countries, did. Evidence also points to popular justice against collaborationists in the Philippines. Much of the difference between these public reactions stems from the types of wartime administration encountered in each nation: native regime or collaborationist. Germany's government was native; France's was collaborationist. Italy from 1922 until 1945 experienced both.

Four considerations aid in our understanding of the violent measures undertaken against collaborationists. First, regimes such as Salò or Vichy were established to serve, or at least to placate, a foreign power:

Nazi Germany. Their existence is inconceivable without the historical fact of Hitlerian conquest and hegemony. The element of treason here is obvious, and Mussolini's followers in the RSI had been branded as traitors by the Regno del Sud and by all of the CLN parties. Second, the collaborationists were extremely brutal as they complied, often quite willingly, with National Socialist demands for forced labor, anti-Semitic policies, and stringent police measures.[7] Third, Resistance forces had arisen that enabled anti-Fascists to take up arms against the "German invader." These important partisan elements acted from ideological premises that gave political directions to their vague antifascism. In the CLNAI, Italy possessed one of the greatest European resistance movements—armed and sworn to vindication against Salò. Finally, in Italy, extra significance was bestowed on the partisans in that the Allies refused the Royal army participation on any noteworthy level against the Germans. Elsewhere, Anglo-Americans had supported the Free French forces and viewed them as an integral factor along with Resistance units in national liberation. In Italy, on the other hand, the Resistance, primarily alone, had to exonerate the nation from the disgrace of fascism. Baptized in blood, a national uprising would show the world that Italy had destroyed its past and was ready to rejoin the community of free nations.[8]

By the end of the war physical danger had become a fact of life for the Fascists. The ferocity of the civil war was proof enough of that. On February 8, 1945, the CLNAI had issued "death warrants" for various RSI personnel including ministers, undersecretaries, *federali*, *questori*, judges on the Special Tribunal for the Defense of the State, directors of political journals after September 8, and officers in blackshirt formations.[9] The partisans had also undertaken more systematic and quasilegal steps to deal with blackshirts. Even before the apocalypse many transported their vengeance from the battlefield into special clandestine courts. On February 27, 1945, the Turin CLN headquarters, the *comando piazza*, announced the creation of "insurrectional tribunals," clearly a reaction against the sad course of sanctions in liberated Italy. The partisans considered their popular courts necessary, due to the "lack of exemplary provisions" undertaken by both the Bonomi government and the Allies in Rome, where the only laudable accomplishment had been the execution of the police boss, Pietro

Caruso. The *comando piazza* then listed capital offenses. Those slated for possible execution included all authority figures in the RSI who had been listed in the earlier February 8 decree.[10]

The more conservative Milan headquarters tempered Resistance politics, and the stringent measures of Turin were never fully implemented elsewhere. Instead, from the Lombard metropolis less-severe directives against Fascists were issued before the liberation. Many of them specified parameters for a purge. On June 2, August 30, October 26, and November 28, 1944, the CLNAI directed the establishment of purge committees in government and private business; work had even begun toward hearings. On March 27, 1945, each provincial capital was authorized a panel staffed by members of all CLN parties. The Milanese also approximately endorsed Rome's sanctions, acknowledging that the guidelines for these commissions had been delineated in DLL 159 as well as CLNAI decrees. Also reminiscent of Rome was a bit of advice from Guglielmo Savio, the Communist representative on the Piedmontese purge commission. "The . . . decisions," he said, "must be effective, rapid, and ready to be implemented at the moment of the Liberation."[11]

Despite milder Lombard attitudes many rank-and-file partisans held radical goals for sanctions, ignoring Milan and implementing their own. In some places before the end of the war clandestine courts were established and Fascists were executed.[12] Beyond the summary tribunals, general prospects for popular justice loomed large upon the liberation. From his listening post in Bern, Switzerland, the American counselor of the legation gleefully reported that the neo-Fascist militiamen were particularly "despised by the population and will doubtless be exterminated by the good people . . . on 'D' Day."

No one doubted the inevitable wave of recriminations. The question was how many would die before normalcy could return. On the eve of the final insurrection the CLNAI issued its last declaration to the blackshirts. Mussolini and the *gerarchi* were to be shot. Plastered on buildings and poles all over northern Italy were the simple, chilling words, "Surrender or Perish!"[13]

In the last week of April, the first days of the liberation, loose popular courts were established to judge whatever blackshirts could be dragged before them. CLNAI representatives also attempted to channel anti-Fascist anger into their more structured popular tribunals, *commissari di giustizia*, where the accused might have some semblance of a trial before they were executed. In effect, there seems to have been little difference in the two. They might be held by citizens' committees or partisans acting on vague orders from higher-ups. No one is sure how many of Mussolini's followers were tried in makeshift popular courts and executed or simply shot on the spot. Justice was often accomplished hurriedly before more rigorous public order could be imposed by regular partisan units or by the Anglo-Americans. Harold Macmillan encountered some evidence of this as he entered newly liberated Bologna. When his jeep pulled into the Piazza Maggiore, he noted that the splattered brains of the Fascist *questore* still clung to the wall of the Municipio.[14] This is the way Mussolini and his entourage, including Zerbino, Pavolini, Farinacci, and Claretta Petacci were shot.[15] The events of the Duce's death are well known. Shot' at Giulino di Mezzegra on the shore of Lake Garda, his body was brought back to Milan. The corpse and those of fourteen companions were hideously beaten, trampled, and spat upon until they were barely recognizable as human beings. Photos of the dead Duce reveal something inhuman: caved-in eyes, twisted, misplaced features. He had no face left. Beaten and blood stained, the bodies were then hanged upside down at a gas station facing the enormous dusty Piazzale Loreto, where the Fascists had publicly executed fifteen partisans some months before.

Undoubtedly most blackshirts who died were never given the benefit of due process and were immediately killed at the hands of the people and partisans. One Allied administrator wrote in June that recriminations were so extensive that "any person tainted with Fascism has been extremely fortunate if he has remained alive . . . with the result that not a great deal has been left to do in respect of epuration. The methods have been cruel and summary—perhaps sometimes unjust—but thorough." The chaos, furthermore, rendered complete tallies of the dead impossible. The CLN claimed that in Milan city, four hundred had been done in before the arrival of Allied forces. Separate Allied sources estimated two thousand, of which, the Americans felt, four hundred had been processed through summary courts. From Swiss sources *Italia Libera* reported that three thousand had been shot in Milan province. The May 6 *Avanti!* claimed that about seven hundred Milanesi had been killed, of whom 170 lay in the city morgue and many of the rest dumped at the gates of Musocco cemetery. On July 4, the Allied *Corriere d'informazione* reprinted an article from a Turin paper claiming twenty thousand dead in the north. Piedmont, according to this piece, accounted for eight thousand, Lombardy for four thousand, and Emilia for three thousand.[16]

Although complete figures were never compiled, the Allies and Royal government spent most of May recording as many of these deaths as possible. Daily and weekly communiqués kept general counts for random localities. In a May 17 report, the Carabinieri commander, Brunetto Brunetti, logged thirty-one deaths in a three-day period around Forlì alone. His report included a few sentences on suspects and their backgrounds, labeling some culprits as partisans, others as "probably partisans," and a few as "unknown." All shootings were of RSI personnel, and mostly of militiamen or police officers. One was a woman, Iolanda Gridelli, an RSI operative who had reportedly secured the executions of many partisans.[17] Another report listed the deaths from a small town near Padua, Piove di Sacco. From April 28 until May 16, seventy-eight cadavers were found there, of which only eight were recognized as former locals.[18] Another Carabiniere officer wrote that from May 5 until May 15, seventy-nine people had been killed in Genoa "by persons unknown."[19]

Not all cases concerned violent death. Many of the luckier blackshirts were put into prisons and created problems of overloaded jails. When the Anglo-Americans arrived in the northern cities, they often found them filled with people who, only hours before, had been rounded up by partisans. Quite often the new jailers had no idea of the captives' names or the charges against them.[20] Allied makeshift jails also sprang up around the country, with the most important concentrations just south of the old Livorno-Rimini Gothic Line.

Existing prisons filled immediately. By mid-May *Avanti!* reported that Milan's San Vittore contained 3,682 political prisoners, far more than the usual number. They filled the entire place and could be seen sticking their heads out of the windows, shouting to their families and friends on the street below. Because of the overcrowded conditions, the spillover often went into Carabinieri barracks, then converted factories and warehouses, such as one in Terni. The largest of all the prisons was the mammoth Coltano outside of Pisa. The men's compound there held over thirty-two thousand. The prison problem would stay with the Italians for months after the liberation and would later prove embarrassing for the High Commission.[21]

One group that escaped execution only to endure incarceration were some Piedmontese psychiatrists who later, in 1947, complained to Rome of their treatment. Their statement about the liberation recalled the pervasive confusion of that period. So many events merely seemed to happen, leaders seemed to appear, and records to explain it all seemed to disappear. At 10:30 on the morning of May 1 the psychiatrists were arrested on orders from the hospital's new director, who also headed the institution's CLN and was a member of its "provisional administrative junta." (No mention was made of the former director.) There was no legal basis for this takeover, but events like it occurred frequently. The doctors were placed into separate cells for the criminally insane and kept there in isolation for sixteen days. Their families petitioned for a release and cited the May 5 Allied ordinance that prohibited illegal imprisonments, but it was not until the sixteenth that the new questore ordered them transferred to a jail in Turin. The doctors were then interviewed by a regular magistrate in the city who ordered them immediately released. Unfortunately for them, the new staff was still headed by the CLN leader, who denied the psychiatrists their old positions.[22]

Some other Fascists and business leaders who had the money and pull were able to get to some shelter or haven in Switzerland.[23] The Milan Communist *Volontà del Popolo* reported that on the morning of April 26 hardly an important boss could be found at his desk; they had all simply vanished.[24] Nevertheless, some stayed in Italy and courted the opposition. Rumors abounded of industrial magnates inviting workers into their houses for coffee and sweet cakes, doling out handfuls of cigarettes. They might have been able to buy their way out of trouble, but lower-level Fascist employees who could not get away or who had no black-market goods to sprinkle around were often gunned down in the streets. The industrialists and capitalists will be dealt with below. It should be noted here, however, that their situations differed greatly from less-fortunate militiamen and police officers.

Into this violent scene stepped the Allied armies. Anxious to contain the political hothouse in the north, the Anglo-Americans strung around it a cordon sanitaire, prohibiting civilian travel between north and south. Only on May 11 did the Allies permit eight ministers and four political leaders from Rome to make the trip, and on May 14 most top-ranking officials were allowed to go. General travel remained severely restricted.[25]

The partisan challenge was formidable and was taken seriously by the Allies. However bedraggled and ill trained the patriots were, they represented a large and armed (it has been estimated that the partisans hid at least 40 percent of their weapons from the new authorities) alternative to Rome and to the Allied Military Government, and many considered that to be reason enough to disband them.[26] In canceling armed partisan defiance, blackshirts might also avoid being dragged out into the streets and shot; their safety could be ensured.

To help meet the perceived partisan threat, Rome and the Allies could examine a parallel situation existing in France. There, General Charles de Gaulle had been dealing with similar trouble posed by Resistance forces and solved his problem by disbanding them two days after his entry into Paris in August 1944. The Italians were about to do the same thing by dissolving the CVLS.[27]

On April 27 Commodor Stone emphasized that the new relationship between the Anglo-Americans and the partisan formations would remain cordial if certain provisions were acknowledged. While, he declared, CLN representatives "must be treated with the courtesy due to their political position and past labors," they did not possess legitimate authority in northern Italy and must surrender their weapons. The Allied forces were free to accept or reject any advice the partisans might offer, but "it must be made plain to the prefects and to other officials that they are to be servants of [the] AMG and can take no orders from [the] CLN." To the dismay of more determined revolutionaries, Resistance leaders agreed to these measures, urging the partisans to lay down their arms and put their trust in government.

In Milan, newly installed Colonel Charles Poletti's first acts were to order a cease-fire and to replace CLNAI authority with Military Government. However, while Poletti insisted that his was the "only authority which could emanate decrees or ordinances or confer public office of any type," the new administrators, in effect, relied on CLNAI personnel for much of their work. The Allies chose not to interfere at first, and de facto management of Milan was entrusted to the partisans for much of May.[28]

Urban and provincial administrations were manned with CLNAI operatives who held power in the name of the Allies, but they soon surrendered much of their authority to them or acted in their name.[29] On April 30 Milan's Socialist prefect, Riccardo Lombardi, decreed, "By virtue of the powers conferred in me today by the Allied Military Government, I order the immediate suspension of arbitrary executions and summary trials by volunteer formations or by self-proclaimed like organizations." The popular tribunals had to cease, and all cases were to be brought to the CLNAI *commissioni di giustizia* or to Milan's San Vittore prison. Finally, on June 1, the Anglo-Americans assumed direct control of the north.[30]

On May 6 the Allies permitted one last display of CLNAI military strength, a grand parade through the streets of Milan. At the Castello Sforzesco, the coordinator of partisan military units, General Raffaele Cadorna, and Ferruccio Parri stood alongside British, American, and Royal officers as formations passed them in review, each Resistance group marked off by different colored scarves. Red dominated, interspersed with *azionista* and GL orange, *autonomi* green, and Christian blue. But these soldiers had no weapons. Although it was a victory manifestation, the parade represented a weakened Resistance whose ideas and sentiments may have lived on but whose military and political power had waned.[31]

Although the partisans had surrendered their authority and much of their fire power, the attack on Fascists did not end. As spring turned to summer, and then to autumn, intermittent violence persisted in northern Italy. Inflamed passions and heated political debate remained particularly rampant in the notorious "triangle of death," Emilia-Romagna.[32] Certain left-wing journals fostered, or at least sympathized with, the vigilante spirit. By early July the Modenese edition of the Communist *Volontà del Popolo* proclaimed that "the people ask bread and justice, not promises," and complained that those who believed in a purge had been abandoned by the system. The more impatient joined mobs or procured weapons and went after people whom they judged guilty. Many of the police reports during the second half of 1945 indicate that action was taken by Italians who had lost faith in Rome's anti-Fascist measures. On June 5 an "exasperated" crowd of four thousand attacked a jail near Siena to lynch an RSI soldier locked inside. They were held off by calming words from the vice-mayor, the Carabiniere commander, and CLN members. In the Chianti region on August 6, a town council sat to consider the readmission into service of two purged bureaucrats. A crowd of five hundred formed to protest the action. Near Pisa five hundred stormed the Carabiniere barracks where two women consorts of Fascists were kept. The crowd, mostly women, broke into the place and cut the hair off of the unlucky pair.[33]

More sobering and lethal were the well-planned and well-executed attacks by fewer but better-organized people. In the second half of 1945 easily hundreds and perhaps thousands of Fascists were killed by determined persons in small groups or working alone. Some deadly strikes targeted entire families, and though not normal, it was far from uncommon to read of women, children, and the aged being shot along with some Fascist police boss. In mid-June, the ex-cashier at the Ravenna *fascio* was murdered along with his wife and son. On another occasion a schoolteacher who had headed the local *fascio femminile* and her seventy-four-year-old father were shot by partisans. On September 30 a group of "unknowns" broke into the home of a former Fascist police official near Imola and machine-gunned him, his wife, and his twenty-five-year-old daughter and seventeen-year-old son. In late June, the Ministry of Foreign Affairs also expressed concern over the number of murdered priests. According to an investigator, the clergy in the lower Romagna were particularly paralyzed with fear.[34]

The attacks went beyond private households and churches. Small groups began assaulting government authorities to reach Fascists who they believed were being shielded from the public. In mid-June, ten men armed with machine guns entered the Modena jail and killed thirteen internees. At another location, a police motorcade transferring Fascist prisoners from Verona to Imola was attacked and twelve were killed.[35]

The worst incident occurred on July 17, when a group of masked partisans entered Schio prison near Vicenza and massacred fifty-five Fascists. The tragedy at Schio made a great impression on the AC's regional security officer. It illustrated for him the polarized sectarian hysteria that had gripped the north. In a note to the governor of the Veneto, Brigadier General Dunlop, he wrote, "one gets the impression that half [of the residents of the town] are pleased with what happened and the other half are afraid to speak."[36]

Ambassador Kirk wrote to Washington that murders were taking place all over and that "all of these outrages were committed by people calling themselves partisans, although in no case was their exact identity determined." A leading Christian Democrat lawyer in Bologna was not so unsure. He told a PWB agent that the murders were the work of partisans in the pay of the CLN's Left parties.[37]

DEFUSING ANTI-FASCIST VIOLENCE

The Anglo-Americans determined, among their immediate tasks upon the liberation, to save as many Fascists as possible from popular justice. Obviously during the war both the Allies and partisans agreed perfectly on the necessity of killing Fascists. Upon the cessation of hostilities, however, the Allies often, in effect, protected RSI personnel by declaring them prisoners of war and by either moving them into the "safety" of prisons and concentration camps or out of the north altogether.

Marshal Rodolfo Graziani was one such case. Mussolini's most loyal officer managed to dodge his more radical partisan pursuers until he surrendered at CLNAI headquarters, the Hotel Milano. After Graziani spent a few days at the city's San Vittore prison, a monsignor friend of his worked out his transfer into Allied hands. The Anglo-Americans brought "the Butcher of Ethiopia" back to Africa, to Algeria, where he and his American captor enjoyed "a bottle of very fine old cognac." Graziani stayed in Africa until February 1946, when the Allies felt it was safe to relocate him in Italy. He was then placed under the Italian authorities at Procida Prison.[38]

The Anglo-Americans' announcement on June 3, 1945, that RSI soldiers captured after the liberation would be considered prisoners of war gave them an internationally recognized legal status and saved many from denunciations as traitors or rebels. The declaration flew in the face of every Italian definition of their status since Badoglio's proclamations in 1943. RDL 29/B, for example, had specifically labeled all who professed allegiance to Mussolini after September 8 as traitors. Events had eroded that distinction, particularly toward those bureaucrats who labored in Rome under the Fascists through June 1944. But no one had yet exonerated RSI troops, and the Allied declaration was a major step in that direction.

What appeared a clear-cut decision, however, actually was not. Disagreement persisted within Allied ranks over the status of Mussolini's troops. Brigadier General Lush wrote to the chief administrative officer at AFHQ to explain that the AC's attitude was to let the Italians handle everything their own way, whereas the Fifth Army put Fascists in the camps and refused to surrender them to the local authorities. Meanwhile, both Rome and the Allies pointed out to the judiciary that the soldiers' status as prisoners of war should not affect the court decisions against them.[39] Milan seemed to have been in another world from Rome because in the Lombard capital the order exonerating Fascist troops was apparently ignored. On July 10 Prefect Lombardi complained to Poletti that his decree to arrest all RSI enlisted men and members of the Black Brigades would continue to overload the jails.[40]

Upon the collapse of Salò, the Allies also began to transport *repubblichini* south, often to the Taranto area or to North Africa. On May 24 *Italia Libera* reported that 150 Black Brigade members were spotted on a special train headed for Taranto, and in July 1946 the prefect of Bolzano would write that 645 neo-Fascists had just returned from "campo 'S'" at the southern port. One Questura report called for added security at train stations because of violent incidents where crowds awaited arrivals to see if any Fascists were on board.[41]

Through May and June 1945, Roman and Allied measures combined with a natural tendency toward calm, and northerners started to resume more normal lives. The insurrection against the Nazis was over. Attacks against Fascists would continue for some time and fueled hot debate, but the extreme violence and dislocation of the liberation were beginning to subside.

The established parties in Rome did not promote and generally lamented most of the violence. But many understood the necessity to blow off steam, such as in the death of Mussolini, and on some points the entire spectrum was in near perfect agreement. In the first days of liberation even the pacific Christian Democrats stood back and let events run their course. Stuck in Rome, the leadership was only able to piece together shreds of news from the north. That a massacre was occurring was common knowledge, and *Il Popolo* understood that the Milan morgue was filled with Fascist corpses. How many and who had been shot was unknown, but the journal was "sure that justice would reach everybody."[42] Alcide De Gasperi nevertheless counseled moderation and on May 1 urged "no rash convulsions or Jacobin improvisations but free popular decisions according to the laws of democracy."

For many, May 1945 represented a clean finality, a good point to end, or at least to envision an end to, the campaign against fascism. Mussolini's corpse was a tangible symbol of the final terrible end of his revolution. It was a powerful image, and many were impressed by it. A great deal of the tone in the political journals conveyed that feeling of resolution. For example, despite its dubious legality, Mussolini's execution was applauded as a necessary conclusion to fascism's final act. The demise of the Duce and the rebirth of a new Italy were often described in tones of hope, and sometimes of Christian resurrection. *L'Unità* insisted that the partisans had opened the way for a democratic Italy. For the *azionisti*, the execution signaled "the necessary conclusion of a historic phase (and) the end of the insurrectional struggle which is a sign for the Patria of rebirth and reconstruction." Pietro Nenni said about the same thing in *Avanti!*. It was necessary for the "resurrection of the nation; not a vendetta but the implacable fulfillment of an unpleasant mission." Rodolfo Morandi, the Socialist CLNAI leader, proclaimed to his comrades that the Italian state, gnawed at for twenty years by a cancer, had collapsed. "The public administration is smashed," he said, and "Rome attempts in vain to govern with the debris of this great ruin." The Communist partisan leader, Luigi Longo, felt that the death of Mussolini defused much public anger and "truncated" violence and vendettas. And on April 29 the CLNAI issued a proclamation claiming that the Duce's execution was necessary for Italy to make a clean break, "un taglio netto," with fascism.[43]

The *Risorgimento Liberale* noted that fascism was finished but, looking at the far Left, warned of other dictatorships that might replace it. *Italia Libera* stressed the same idea but left it a bit open ended when it announced that "the elimination of Mussolini and his *gerarchi* represents the tragic and deserved end of Fascism, in its symbolic exponents and structure. . . . now we must look to reconstruct. . . . The past must never resurface in any form." The Christian Democrats successfully maintained their centrist position throughout the liberation. *Il Popolo* expressed in ironclad terms the desire to end the nightmare without offending either the far Right or Left. Mussolini's dangling corpse in the Piazzale Loreto was for them "a symbol of a past forever dead. . . . justice has been done . . . and now the cadavres are better in graves than piazzas." The DC called for an end to all the unnecessary violence since now had come the time to forget. "We have the strength to forget! Forget as soon as possible."[44] On the seventh the PWB, perhaps optimistically, downplayed the violence and reported that all interest in the execution of Fascists had subsided. Except for the scandal sheets "which appeal to the morbid curiosity of the uneducated," the people no longer concerned themselves with an issue that belonged "forever to the past."[45]

THE PARRI GOVERNMENT AND THE THREAT OF INCREASED SANCTIONS

The liberation also altered the political situation in Rome. Until the spring of 1945 the ruling CLN coalition had been maintained among natural enemies in the hope of defeating Hitler. When that threat passed, polite veneers quickly vanished and hard animosities came into the open. Sanctions against fascism again assumed a crucial position in debates concerning Italy's future.

During May, CLNAI leaders met with Roman officials to form a new, postwar government. Pietro Nenni, still outside the government coalition, had lobbied for two months to secure the prime minister's position and was endorsed on May 24 by the Communist Giorgio Amendola and by Leo Valiani of the *azionisti*. Nenni's candidacy was opposed by Christian Democrats Alcide De Gasperi and Mario Scelba. Their resistance, furthermore, revealed severe fissures within the Left bloc's support for the Socialist. On one side it appeared that PCI faith in him was at best tepid. Togliatti's continuing endorsement of coalition arrangements between the Left and conservative forces, in fact, has been criticized as sabotaging the Nenni candidacy. On the other, the Action party began to crack as its moderate wing, led by Ugo La Malfa, pulled away from the Nenni candidacy. What emerged on June 20 was a new government under a compromise candidate: the *azionista* Ferruccio Parri, highly respected among the CLNAI but unknown in the south and a political virgin. Nenni would have to be consoled with two positions—vice president in the Council of Ministers and high commissioner for sanctions against fascism.[46]

Parri brought with him a high-mindedness rarely seen in the Viminale. Tall, bespectacled, and mild mannered, his gentleness and scholarly mien contrasted with Badoglio's old soldier bearing and Bonomi's craftiness. Parri had been a stalwart of the anti-Fascist Giustizia e Libertà movement since the 1920s. In and out of jail, he had taken a position with Italian Edison but had gone underground during the Salò era and had organized *azionista* partisan formations. Extremely popular among his Resistance followers, Parri was soon dubbed "Zio Maurizio." Passionately devoted to the end of fascism not only as a political reality but as a condition of minds and hearts, he stood for sweeping social reforms and democratic renovation.[47]

After the liberation Parri used his celebrity status to popularize his visions of a new Italy and more effective, fairer sanctions. On May 13, before an entirely sympathetic audience in Rome's Teatro Eliseo, he tearfully recalled partisan sacrifices. In the midst of this extraordinarily emotional moment, Parri launched into a tirade against the monarchy. Such an attack from the man who one month later was to become the prime minister was a clear declaration that the institutional truce was dead and the issue was very much alive. Parri reminded his audience that many comrades died not only in Fascist prisons but in Royal ones as well. Let no one forget that much of the responsibility for the Fascist disaster stemmed from the Quirinale and its allies. The Carabinieri with their royalist sympathies were singled out as a force to be purified. Particularly in the north they were discredited, and their ranks were to be filled with the democratizing partisan elements.[48]

Although he demanded punishment for the worst Fascists, Ferruccio Parri was no revolutionary. Before the CLN Congress on September 1 the prime minister claimed to represent "a middle road, I would say, a line of mediation . . . to which I remain rigorously faithful." Parri also urged that Italians should place their faith in the Allies because it meant "bread, coal, and credit." The new prime minister was far from the bloodthirsty monster many feared him to be, and had he been one, the Anglo-Americans would never have acquiesced to his government. The prime minister recognized this and later commented that his regime had at first been very popular among the Americans and members of the Allied Commission.[49]

But Parri's ascent to power, on June 20, along with the Socialists' reentry into the government, gave the CLN coalition a more pronounced leftist slant and frightened many on the Right. The aged pre-Fascist prime minister, Vittorio Emanuele Orlando, for example, lobbied against Parri. He told Ambassador Kirk that this was no mere change of government but rather a change of regime. Historian Antonio Gambino has written that fear of Parri also extended beyond the rarified atmosphere of high politics and into the bureaucratic rank and file. The police, the armed forces, the state functionaries, and the parastate employees did not regard the new prime minister as their leader. They all bemoaned a loss of status they accounted to the CLN victory, not to their conduct under the Fascists. Anxieties heightened over the appointment of Nenni as high commissioner. Through his articles in *Avanti!* he had become notorious as among the most determined advocates of a severe purge.[50]

The heightened fear of radicalism also infiltrated Anglo-American ranks. Ambassador Charles warned Churchill that Nenni in the cabinet "should give us cause for preoccupation," although the British felt that Togliatti and the PCI would exert a moderating influence on him.[51] To Washington, Ambassador Kirk wrote on June 18 that the new government marked a "distinct turn to the left." A political amateur, Parri himself was not considered a threat, but with "extremist" advisors, namely Nenni and Togliatti, "the future trend [was] obvious." Kirk advised that the new administration could not fulfill its obligations to the Anglo-Americans as Bonomi's had done. To complete the picture, the ambassador passed on an inference from the Quirinal Palace that the Allies "would be justified in interfering."[52]

Anglo-American perceptions of Parri and his CLN government were also colored by increased international tensions that aggravated Italy's Left-Right struggle. Rome had been thrust peculiarly into European politics by the Yugoslavian Josip "Tito" Broz's invasion of Istria and Venezia Giulia on the Yugoslav border and by the Greek civil war. To make matters worse, as early as the winter of 1944–45 Italian Communist partisans in the Friuli region had sided with Tito's army. But other, more conservative groups refused to follow their lead. Of course any PCI or Socialist sympathy for Tito was interpreted as treason by self-styled patriots.[53] Deep animosities in that area split the liberation movement, rifts that became horribly apparent when, on the northeast frontier, twenty DC and *azionista* underground leaders were massacred by their erstwhile Communist allies.[54] From April on, the conservative press was obsessed with the fate of the Italian population in the northeast, where a national struggle between Italians and Slavs overwhelmed the concerns about sanctions.

Similarly, Italian interests were affected on its southeast flank by the possibility of a Communist government in Greece. In a temporary lull by summer 1945, the ferocious war there preoccupied both the Italians and the Allies, who supplied the anti-Communists with massive amounts of aid. Consequently, the Anglo-Americans had more reason to suspect the motives of the numerically powerful Italian Communists and Socialists.

The euphoria of victory over nazism, however, could not last, and populist triumph in the north and in the Council of Ministers would prove illusory. Ever perceptive, Palmiro Togliatti sensed this before the liberation. On April 7, 1945, in a speech to the PCI Congress, where he continued to advocate a national front with the Christian Democrats, Togliatti announced that the Center-Right was stronger than the Left. "There is something," he claimed, "stronger than we are, and stronger than all of the democratic bloc."[55]

Togliatti undoubtedly sensed that Parri would not occupy the prime minister's chair very long. And he was right. The new prime minister had been spared an immediate Allied veto only because the Anglo-Americans considered his government as, essentially, a transitional one that would be modified by the more traditionally oriented of the CLN parties. With the war over, divisions among the anti-Fascist forces, particularly concerning the form Italy's government would take, were becoming more apparent.[56] With full confidence that Parri's administration would be short lived, his foreign minister, Alcide De Gasperi, bided time until he assumed the reins of state. As leader of the Christian Democrats, De Gasperi took charge of a secret government, an anti-Parri one, with which the Allies preferred to deal. Already, on June 26, 1945, Ambassador Charles described the DC as representative of the peasants, the lower middle class, and some workers, as well as being his own party of preference.[57]

THE PURGE

The heady days of the liberation guaranteed, at least, that the purge would live on and, indeed, take another turn: a serious attempt to apply it to the private sector. Since their earliest manifestations, sanctions had been limited to government employees. A fiction had been maintained that fascism had existed only in Rome. The private sphere and society in general had been largely ignored or avoided. There existed some voluntary purge organizations, notably in the journalistic profession, probably due to its political nature. But, until the liberation of the north, the application of the purge into the private sector had been consistently blocked, publicly and secretly, by the traditionalist ruling class.

The collapse of Mussolini's RSI signaled a two-pronged purge aimed at both government and business. The first was merely Parri's continuation of Badoglio's and Bonomi's failed program. The second was a muddled blend of both official and partisan activity that, despite a strong impetus from below, never knew real direction from above. But sentiment for severe measures in private commerce was important enough to elicit response and opposition from business, government factions, and among the Allies.

The Bonomi government knew that this issue would be raised with the fall of the RSI and planned for it with, among other things, DLL 149. Its origin was in the Ministry of Industry, Commerce, and Labor, headed by the left-wing Christian Democrat Giovanni Gronchi. With some Allied prodding, in March and April 1945, Gronchi petitioned for such a measure, but even he advised going ahead "with extreme caution." The purge chief, Renato Boeri, wrote to Bonomi that the government might issue some kind of declaration calling for "the elimination from positions of command" of northern social and financial leaders. He added that it would be dangerous "not to give the impression that we are taking immediate steps to eliminate them." The result, however, DLL 149, April 26, 1945, was stillborn. Ellery Stone intervened at the last moment and told Bonomi that the Allies had not been sufficiently informed of deliberations over the decree and that he would not implement it in the north. In his letter of June 8, Stone stated that DLL 149 was too vaguely written, established superfluous commissions, and duplicated measures already contained in DLL 159.[58]

Upon his assumption of power, Parri broadcast on June 22 a radio address to the nation concerning the new situation and the place of sanctions. Some of his stance seemed to soften, his tone more pacific and reminiscent of Croce's suggestion that "civil re-education" was the key to defascistization. He urged the partisans to end their "arbitrary acts of justice [that] compromise us with the Allies and, above all, offend our spirit of justice." "Thugs" was the term he used for those engaged in popular justice against the Fascists, and he urged all partisans to place their trust in Rome and to "cooperate for the defense of law and order which our own revolution secured for us."[59] But regarding sanctions against fascism, Parri still had an agenda. The prime minister appointed new personnel for the Alto Commissariato. He scrapped Bonomi's tight control and relinquished authority to the dreaded Pietro Nenni. Mario Berlinguer remained in charge of the trials, while in July the purge was placed under an *azionista* Piedmontese judge, one of the best legal minds in Italy, Domenico Peretti Griva.

As was the case in Naples and Rome the year before, the first purge law applied in the north was an Allied measure, Ordinance Number 35. But Anglo-American efforts were enhanced by a new, more radical Ordinance Number 46—aimed at private commerce and industry. Under Parri and Nenni two other laws, DLL 472 of August 4 and DLL 702 of November 9, contributed to DLL 159's provisions, extending the purge into the business world and aiming at the higher bureaucrats. Despite new legislation, however, Rome's official purge in the north never amounted to much. By the summer of 1945 it appeared that the application of sanctions in the newly liberated areas would be as dismal as it had been in the south. From July 3 to 16 the Alto Commissariato in Rome sent an investigator, Roberto Franceschelli, north to measure the situation firsthand. His report was submitted to Nenni on the twentieth and described the overall situation in the blackest terms; the purge was "chaotic, generally retarded, and in some cases grave."

Rome's lackluster purge in the north did nothing to inspire anything among the partisans and was, in fact, briefly eclipsed by the activity undertaken in industries by the many CLN factory councils (CLNA). After the AMG had annulled DLL 149, the CLNAs owed much more to Allied decrees, Ordinances 35 and 46, than they did to Roman measures in taking action against the owners of big capital.

Franceschelli found, moreover, that in many areas High Commission panels had yet to be formed, and in other places they were riddled with corruption, such as in Venice, where a Liberal member was caught blackmailing the wife of a detained Fascist. In Milan no one who had weathered the liberation had been suspended. Also, like Rome, the local governments were succumbing to paralysis, with sanctions hanging over their heads.[60]

Those who harbored doubts about a purge of the private sector need not have concerned themselves solely with ideological reasoning. Much of the key resistance to a business purge came from the many technocrats and economists who doubted that Italy's fragile postwar economy could sustain this attack. Among the skeptics was one of Rome's administrators in the north, the *commissario straordinario* for industrial production, Roberto Tremelloni. On June 28 he wrote to the CLNAI's Central Economic Commission in Milan regarding companies that had been heavily associated with collaborationism. He declared that while the government should accord preferential treatment to less-tainted concerns, sometimes it was impossible to do so. Each case required separate examination, and there were likely to be contracts awarded to companies with strong Fascist connections. By September the moderate purge commissioner, Peretti Griva, added his voice in defense of the captains of commerce. DLL 472, the August law, was on the books, and Nenni's office pushed for a new purge law to include the top executives. Tremelloni advised Parri to think twice about such a move. "I don't think that I'm out of place in observing," he wrote, "that in these difficult times it would be harmful to the private and the public economies."[61]

Frustrated with Rome, the CLN factory councils, or CLNAS, often acted on their own, and it was within these grass-roots efforts that the most serious purge activity in the north was found. At the first congress of regional CLNAIS, held in Milan on June 6 and 7, 1945, delegates from all over the north, although mainly from the Left parties, exalted the vision of serious purges carried on by the CLNAS in the private sector. Rodolfo Morandi claimed the northerners must achieve results to redress the blunders of Rome, a city "who's eye [was] always focused on the south." The Communist Emilio Sereni stressed the necessity of a real factory purge waged by real factory workers. He castigated another Allied proposal to include managers on the panels, although he claimed that the CLNAS' more radical measures had been endorsed by Colonel Poletti.

Looking for authority from Parri and the Allies, the CLNAS were determined to push through effective sanctions and were given a good head start; the Anglo-Americans postponed their effective administration of Milan until the end of May and, to a degree, held aloof for a while even after they took control of the city and other provinces. The commissions were thus able to maintain some autonomy. This gave the CLNAI the opportunity and authority to establish purge commissions in factories and offices. The coordinators of this activity were a lawyer, Giovanni Naldi, and his assistant, Dr. Marco Simoni. Eventually, however, in an effort to control them, the Anglo-Americans appointed the chairs of the purge boards, a not too drastic move since most candidates were recommended by the CLNAI.[62]

The autonomy worked both ways for the commissions. Without the Allies or Rome breathing down their necks, they were able to innovate and occasionally accomplish quite a bit. But like everything else with the purge, these commissions were composed of uneven talent, zealots, and saboteurs. Each large concern and many small ones experienced a purge, but the particulars and results varied in extraordinary degree. An observer from the British consulate in Bern was generally correct when he wrote that some of the big magnates would go into temporary retirement and divest some of their war profits. "But," he continued, "it is not thought that in the long run they will be completely eliminated, as big industry in Northern Italy is so largely tied up with these personalities and their collaborators."[63]

At the time of the liberation, arrest warrants for many of the north's most important industrial and commercial leaders were issued by the CLNAI and the Allies. Many of them, like Arnaldo Mondadori, a publisher, Guido Donegani, the general manager of Montecatini, and Franco Marinotti of the scandal-ridden Snia Viscosa, had maintained connections with the Fascists that were simply too glaring to ignore. Some of these leaders made it to the Swiss border or to Spain, while others were arrested. Only occasionally were their names brought before a CLNA commission, and even then often in absentia.

Most industrial and commercial leaders were able to hold onto their desks through two methods: by bringing outside pressure to bear on the CLNAs or by opting for a "double game" defense, as Occhetto had done a year before in the Caruso trial. The double game, or *gatto-pardismo* (essentially, changing one's spots), was so widespread at the end of the war that it is difficult to determine whether commercial leaders had aided partisans out of sincere or cynical motives. The double game had been endorsed, in a manner of speaking, by past measures from Rome, such as DLL 159 and the *scheda personale*, which distinguished between "good" Fascists of the *ventennio* and "bad" Fascists of Salò. It was also sanctioned by the CLNAI, which on April 28 declared that those seeking justice against Fascists must discriminate in favor of those who aided the cause.[64] As early as 1944, the Allies were receiving reports of wealthy northerners "paying off" partisans. Benedetto Croce told an OSS agent of an 80 million lire payment by Genoese industrialists. The Liberal was particularly incensed by the industrialist Parodi Delfino, who had made "huge profits" from Fascist war contracts yet "brazenly said to some of his intimate friends . . . that he hopes to receive preferential treatment and a certain amount of forgiveness when the Communists will be the dominant power in the Italian government."[65]

However, as with all other aspects of sanctions, it would be an error to claim that all corporate leaders had been Fascists or that they should have all been purged or jailed based simply on their above-board relations with the old regime. Many industrialists, like the Venetian Vittorio Cini, had been actively anti-Fascist. Enrico Falck, a major figure in Italian heavy industry, was a Christian Democratic representative and treasurer of the Milan CLN. One PWB report described the armed resistance of a Milanese Liberal industrialist, Bruno Perelli. He had led a band of four thousand, mostly Communists and Socialists, that persisted in executing Fascists up until May 5. Perelli complained, in fact, to the investigator that the Allies had arrived ten days too soon; given more time, he and his men would have solved the sanctions problem. Even Franco Marinotti, an otherwise notorious pro-Fascist, had participated in abortive German/Allied negotiations in Switzerland as early as October 1944.

In addition to individuals, corporations adopted secret policies to aid partisans against the Fascists. Charles F. Delzell tells us that major financial institutions such as the Credito Italiano and the Banca Commerciale Italiana had helped to fund the underground by depositing money for its use in dummy accounts that were often listed under the names of major corporations such as Falck and Edison. Naturally, some of this secret financial support must be viewed with some skepticism. But the aid did exist and was substantial. It also must be remembered that Mussolini's socialization measures, the brutality of Salò, and German bully tactics strained relations between the private sector and the Fascists.[66]

CLN factory committees nevertheless leveled charges that described complicity between managers, owners, and the Nazis. In Milan's industrial suburb, Sesto San Giovanni, the principal accusation brought against the managers of the Breda plant was that they compiled lists of troublesome workers for deportation by the Germans. Five highly placed administrators who worked on the lists were fired without indemnity.[67] But such drastic action was the exception rather than the rule.

Both reliance on the Allies and a defense based on the double game were employed when the FIAT (Fabbrica Italiana Automobile Torino) purge commission was able to bring before it Giovanni Agnelli's second in command, Vittorio Valletta. Valletta was the most powerful manager in the country and, since Agnelli was on his death bed, he ran the FIAT empire.[68]

Already in February 1945 clandestine and energetic CLNAI purgers inaugurated a hearing against Valletta and other Turin industrialists. Their decision, delivered on April 7, prescribed that Valletta leave his position at FIAT. Upon the liberation, partisan units attempted to obstruct him from entering his office, and Valletta filed an appeal with the Piedmontese CLN on May 3. In August a five-man commission chaired by Alessandro Galante Garrone met to review the case. Valletta had worked on his defense for months and arranged for a barrage of supporting witnesses, mainly workers, and for letters of support from influential people like Ellery Stone. Valletta also maintained contact with other industrialists, Piero Pirelli, Enrico Falck, and Angelo Costa; with politicians, Giovanni Gronchi, Marcello Soleri, the ambassador to London, Count Nicolò Carandini, and Alcide De Gasperi, who read Valletta's defense with interest and pressured the CLN on his behalf; and with military men like Stone and Colonel Robert Marshall, the regional commissioner for Piedmont. Oss evidence indicates that Valletta also used economic threats against the British to elicit support for his cause. According to a secret report, he menaced that FIAT would not accept credit for the purchase of British finished goods unless His Majesty's Government came to his aid against the purgers. Colonel Marshall, whether prompted by threats or not, went so far as to write a letter to the head of the Piedmont CLN, Franco Antonicelli, stating that the Anglo-Americans believed in and supported Valletta.

Valletta's own defense was that he did not actively promote the Nazi cause, that before the liberation he only granted bonuses to workers as incentives for increased production; on the other hand, he had in fact aided the partisan cause by maintaining secret contacts with the Allies via a clandestine radio—all of which was essentially true. CLN witnesses for the defense also validated Valletta's claim that he had donated 500 million lire to the partisans. Valetta's defense, however, did not impress the purgers, who voted, over the objections of the Liberal and Christian Democratic members, to uphold the earlier sanctions. Valletta was forced to turn to the Allies, who supported him against the CLN. By 1946 he was back on the job and continued to lead FIAT through the fifties.[69]

Another who jockeyed between the Nazis and the partisans was the administrative director of Genoa's giant Ansaldo and Dalmine works, Agostino Rocca. Rocca appealed to the Allies for help against the "viciously inspired" purge commission of Dalmine. To the Anglo-Americans he emphasized his CLN ties and claimed a pivotal role in saving the port from Nazi destruction. The Allies aided in his defense and surrendered to the CLNAI a file that the Germans had kept on Rocca.[70] On November 23, the chief Allied economics officer, Morley Fletcher, wrote to the Dalmine commission that the Alto Commissariato was examining Rocca's case and that their internal investigation was unwarranted. Rocca battled against his own *epurazione* but eventually gave up the fight and moved to Buenos Aires.[71]

Every one of these cases has its own peculiar twist. Some administrators kept very close ties to the Fascists yet stayed on in their positions. Others had less-embarrassing pasts but experienced more trouble.

Ares Azzarino, founder and director of a Milanese insurance company and director of two other concerns, wrote often to Lombard and CLNAI officials protesting a one-year suspension against him. He insisted that "it [was] untrue, absolutely untrue" that the majority of his workers had voted against him. Azzarino boasted a long and distinguished anti-Fascist past that included harboring the Liberal ex-Premier Luigi Facta during the *ventennio*. Finally, two weeks after the suspension decision, Azzarino abruptly showed up at a stockholders meeting and took a seat. The CLNA protested that this move was "absolutely incompatible with the decision reached fourteen days ago." But no letters exist to indicate that anything further happened. Apparently Azzarino had won.[72]

Along with directors, many lower-level bureaucrats and blue-collar workers were brought before CLNA purge commissions. Two important sets of records, from Milan's Breda and Brown Boveri (TIBB) plants, exist that enable some insight into the proceedings. Regular hearings in both places did not begin until September 1945 and lasted for one or two months. These meetings were generally open to the workers, and as many as two hundred could be present. Sanctions roughly paralleled those called for in DLL 159. The accused from any sector of operations might be exonerated; a letter might be placed in the file; he or she might be suspended with or without pay, or fired. Occasionally some were turned over to the authorities for criminal prosecution.

Some cases seemed trivial or personal. The director of the Breda cafeteria was brought to task for her liaisons with known Nazis. One worker, who carried a PNF membership card, found trouble by hitting another for singing the Communist "Bandiera Rossa." An office head at Brown Boveri was unanimously "admonished" by the staff because they "detested" him. Among the most important and frequent of the charges leveled was enrollment in the RSI's armed forces or the Black Brigades. Sanctions varied. One such worker who gave "sporadic" service to the Republican National Guard was suspended for a year. But another, who tried the strange tactic of presenting a good-conduct paper from the old Fascist *federale*, was absolved. Family considerations and extreme youth were other bonuses that lightened or eradicated sentences.

The purge at Brown Boveri was far less extensive than Breda's.[73] Whereas the former firm might review three or four cases in a single day, the latter would dispatch twenty. All told, thirty-six purge cases were deliberated at Brown Boveri: nine workers (*operai*) and twenty-seven white-collar employees (*impiegati*). The second category, *impiegati*, was a very vague term that could include an office clerk or a well-placed manager. Sentences were in general fairly harsh. Of the nine Brown Boveri *operai*, three were absolved; two were suspended, one for a year and the other for a month; the remaining four were purged. Of the twenty-seven *impiegati*, seven were absolved; sixteen were suspended, none for over a year; and four were purged.

During the same period, the Breda CLNA called 187 people before the purge commission. Not counting ambiguously worded decisions and deleted references to occupation, 158 decisions were delivered, and almost two-thirds, 104, were purged. This number can be broken down among five occupation groups: *impiegati*, *operai*, foremen (*capo reparto* and *capo officina*), engineers, and administrators (*capo tecnico*, *ragioniere*, and *dirigente*). Forty-eight *impiegati* were judged, and thirty-three were purged. Another four received suspensions of a year or less. Among the *operai* forty-five of seventy-five were fired, eleven were suspended, and one was transferred. Nine of thirteen *ingenieri* were let go, one was "censured," and one was suspended. Twelve of fifteen foremen were purged, and one was suspended for six months. All seven of the *dirigenti* received punishment: five were purged, one was transferred, and one was suspended for a year.[74]

REACTION AGAINST THE PURGE IN THE NORTH

The factory purges were marked by determination or exhaustiveness not found in the government's. CLNAI and CLNA input was crucial to the accomplishment. But the long-term effects of these sanctions against fascism must be tempered by sub-rosa events that undoubtedly occurred on levels lower than Valletta's or Ares Azzarino's. Reports had already begun to circulate of suspended or fired Fascists being hired back by the government or the Allies. As early as October 21, 1944, the prefect of Naples had issued guidelines toward rehiring state functionaries who had been suspended by the AMG. In Chieti the post office and telephone service (PT) took back everyone whom the Allies had fired. This was accomplished with the acquiescence of the Anglo-Americans and the prefect.[75] In December and again in April 1945 the railroad workers union complained to Bonomi that, despite hundreds of their brothers without jobs, the British were accepting fired Fascists on construction projects.[76] In January 1945, an Interior Ministry report to Bonomi complained that the need for personnel at the communal level was so acute that there was no way out but to hire back the Fascists. The prime minister's secretary, Christian Democrat Giuseppe Spataro, responded affirmatively.[77]

We do not know how many people in the private sector simply returned to their posts after the noise of *epurazione* died down. It must have happened often because if the upper and managerial ranks of northern industry were being effectively purged, there would certainly have been more vocal reaction from the magnates and the politicians of the Center-Right. In his study of the period, Massimo Legnani was undoubtedly correct when he noted that the purge of the economic leaders was largely a matter of "veiled protests."[78]

Nevertheless, attempts to fight back in the factories could not be ignored, and according to as well connected a source as the Allied military commander of Italy, Field Marshal Sir Harold Alexander, a meeting took place on June 16 and 17 between six men, representatives of big capital from Milan, Genoa, and Turin, to organize "themselves to fight Communism." They decided on an annual expenditure of 120 million lire for a propaganda campaign, which was subscribed immediately and deposited in a Vatican bank. The six also discussed arming anti-Communist groups.

Many of these industrialists counted on Allied support against zealous CLNA purgers and trigger-happy partisans. They felt that they could, and with good reason. In his analysis of the above-mentioned secret conference, Alexander accepted the businessmen's motives as "a logical reaction to present Leftist activities."[79] The American consul in Genoa discovered the same sentiments in a July 29 conversation between the PWB and Rocco Piaggio, "one of the most important industrialists in Liguria." Piaggio, active in sugar, soap, and shipbuilding, was very anxious over a statement of Alexander's about the AMG leaving Italy earlier than scheduled. The project alarmed the Ligurian, who stated that Italy had been made "fifty per cent" slave under the Fascists and now the Communists were working on the other half. To prevent totalitarian subjugation of the nation, he pleaded to keep United Nations troops in Italy. If that were impossible, Piaggio promoted the creation of an Anglo-American stake in Italian big business through partial Allied ownership.[80] In order to preserve private initiative, the industrialists were willing to surrender some of their share.

Pleas like Piaggio's were not always well received. Despite so much Anglo-American intervention to end what they considered CLNA excesses or to defend industrialists like Valletta, the Allies still had not formulated a coherent and working policy on defascistization, and considerable optimism persisted within the Allied ranks for sanctions. Romano Canosa has correctly pointed out that while the Allies often intervened to save individuals from retributions, they never stood opposed in principle to a defascistization program. In fact, much of what had been accomplished could not have been done without Allied encouragement, aid, and tools like the *scheda personale* or Ordinances 35 and 46. The Allies had never officially changed their endorsement of defascistization and were concerned that antipartisan sentiment not be carried to any extremes. When Field Marshal Alexander's note on northern industrialists reached London, the Foreign Office contacted Ambassador Carandini to inform him that such actions smacked of the days before the March on Rome, and to "permit such methods to start again" would be "suicidal."[81]

The most famous and sincere of the Anglo-American purgers, Charles Poletti, furthermore, continued to endorse sanctions. From his new office in Milan, he continued to urge effective measures. He distributed instructions to Lombard regional purge commissions to persevere undaunted in their efforts, that they had behind them Charles Poletti and Allied authority. But even the colonel was beginning to have second thoughts.[82]

The number of prosanctions statements like Poletti's diminished after the war as the enemy switched from Fascist to leftist and as Anglo-American alarmism surfaced over partisan excesses. In his May report to the AC Poletti wrote that the CLNAS "have been too drastic in their actions. This situation, however, was also being met and [would] be under control before long through the cooperation of [organized labor]." Ambassador Kirk cabled Washington on June 14 to say that Communists were gaining control of CLN activity in the factories. Their armed guards stood at every office door and plant gate and forced reluctant workers into their ranks. "Still more important," he wrote, the factory purgers based all decisions solely on CLN denunciations without allowing the accused to defend themselves. The purgers were taking for themselves the right to "eliminate Fascist officials and sometimes even the owners themselves." Allied military as well as diplomatic circles were concerned with the problem. Field Marshal Alexander himself cabled the War Office in London that, although he did not believe the CLNAS could sustain their actions, the mere threat of "epuration is paralyzing responsible industrial staffs and, according to re-

sponsible Milan circles, leading to increased indiscipline in factories."
The Franceschelli report had also noted that the AMG's increased interest in the fate of private business formed part of broader plans for the
future of Italy. Originally, the Allies were to surrender administrative
control of the north on September 1, but by July they decided that the
situation warranted their continued presence.[83]

Undaunted, CLNAI pressure persisted for a purge of the private sector and often advocated actions more radical than those desired by the
Anglo-Americans. Conflict arose between two groups, especially in
highly charged Piedmont, where some of the bitterest fighting of the
civil war had occurred. Intent on an exhaustive and severe purge, the
Turin CLN requested over fifty commissions to judge industry. But the
Allies wished to establish only four or five. The Anglo-American officers
in Turin, headed by a Colonel Mencer, stressed to Franceschelli their
"grave" disagreements with the CLN.[84]

During the summer and autumn of 1945, more often than ever
before, the Anglo-Americans used their power to curb what they felt
were CLNA purge excesses. On May 25 the CLN commissioner for the
epurazione in Milan province, Dino Roberto, complained to Poletti of
Allied interference in the cases of a senator and an engineer at
Montecatini. Roberto felt the meddling jeopardized progress and had
to stop. He threatened the Allies with the only weapon left to the CLN:
popular opinion. If the Milanesi saw that the purges were going badly,
Roberto claimed, "it could have a negative influence on public order."
But by this time the Allies were not as obsessed with a tranquil nation
as they had been when Carretta was lynched or when Roatta escaped
from the prison hospital. The war was over.[85]

Norman Kogan and others have shown that the Economic Section
of the Allied Commission was specifically involved in these interven-
tions and was instrumental in securing reinstatement for many who
had been originally purged. Lieutenant Colonel A. G. Tubb, the AC's
regional finance officer, conducted one such foray into Milanese commerce. On May 31 he directed a letter to CLNAI headquarters on the
limits of a bank purge. The question of sanctions against financial
officers was "under consideration" by his office, and "in view of this,
[the CLNAI was] now requested to be good enough to withdraw the
committees at present installed at the various banks."[86]

Perhaps the most glaring crackdown on the CLNAI's attempt to carry on their own purge was made by the AC's regional commissioner for Piedmont, Lieutenant Colonel Robert Marshall. A bad situation came to a head when Marshall read an article in the July 20 Milan *Avanti!* on sanctions in the northwest. The head of the CLN-Piedmont, Franco Antonicelli, was quoted in the article as saying "no substitutions of administrative authorities, and prefects in particular, can take place without prior consultation with [his] committee." On the twenty-fifth, the lieutenant colonel wrote to Antonicelli:

> This statement, as well as the whole tone of this article, and certain acts by the CLN attempting to replace *sindaci* [mayors] both in Turin and in Aosta provinces causes me grave concern, and requires that I direct your attention to the fact that no CLN has the slightest degree of executive or administrative authority. Specifically I direct your attention to the fact that all functions of Government vest solely in the AMG. You are, of course, familiar with the fact that this is clearly recognized by the existing Italian Government and has been confirmed in writing. . . . It would be most unfortunate, and certainly very far from helpful to Italy, if at this late date and under current conditions it should become necessary to take actions against any persons for offenses of the type described above.[87]

THE TRIALS

Like the purges, post-liberation trials against the Fascists were convoluted affairs. Mario Berlinguer still directed what was left of Lorenzo Maroni's High Court in Rome. One of Bonomi's last acts, DLL 142, April 22, 1945, furthermore, braced the court system for the impending avalanche of collaboration trials by the establishment of the Extraordinary Assize Courts (Corti straordinarie di Assise) for each northern province along with an appellate Court of Cassation (Sezione speciale provvisoria della Corte di Cassazione) in Milan. The Assize Courts also assumed most of the responsibility for judging collaborationists who otherwise would have been prosecuted in the military tribunals. In October, the Extraordinary Assize Courts would cease, and their duties would be entrusted to "special sections" of the ordinary Assize Courts. All of these courts served as the most important vehicles in the punishment of Salò personnel. They consisted of a president assisted by four popular judges. Historian Antonio Repaci has termed them "the only revolutionary aspect of Italian political justice."[88] They were the closest parallels to France's anti-Vichy tribunals. The president was chosen from among a pool of judges by the chief magistrate (Primo presidente) of the Appellate Court (Corte d'Appello) and could not himself come from a rank lower than councillor of that institution. The popular judges were chosen from lists compiled by the provincial CLNs. The first of these Extraordinary Assize Courts was installed on May 4. More Fascists were processed and sentenced in the new Assize Courts than in any others. The records of the guilty verdicts, however, illustrate both uneven punishment and a predominance of severe sentences against minor but visible figures such as policemen.

In keeping with the trend of downplaying the *ventennio* and of emphasizing the crimes of Salò, collaborationists were the explicit targets of DLL 142. The Assize Courts were directed to judge officials of the RSI and not of the 1922–43 *ventennio*. The accused were to be examined according to both the earlier guidelines of DLL 159's Article 5 (collaborationism) and Articles 51, 54, and 58 of the Military War Code. The main crimes delineated were the holding of the following positions in the RSI:

ministers or undersecretaries of state
president or members of the Special Tribunal for the Defense of the State
provincial heads, secretaries, or *commissari federali*
directors of political journals
high officials in blackshirt formations

Provisions were also made for lower-ranking members of the RSI armed forces who were guilty of exceedingly grave or vicious acts of cruelty.[89]

Important *gerarchi* still remained to be tried, and their appearances in the new courts triggered raucous scenes filled with screaming audiences calling for execution. C. F. R. Harris held that the spectators at these events were often paid 200 lire each to scream for the death sentence ("a morte!"). Three of the earliest cases concerned high officials—Attilio Teruzzi, Guido Buffarini-Guidi, and Carlo Emanuele Basile—and illustrated the types of sanctions leveled against *gerarchi*.

Although Teruzzi's was coincidental, all three had connections with Salò.[90]

Among the first major officials tried was Attilio Teruzzi on May 24. As colonial governor, party leader, and Militia chief of staff, Teruzzi had been among Mussolini's most important and loyal lieutenants. His luxuriant beard had been a familiar sight to many, since he often appeared on podiums or balconies with the Duce. He had been arrested in the August 1943 roundup, but the Germans later freed him; and he had already been tried in Rome in absentia. Teruzzi held no offices in the RSI but was tried as a collaborator and received a thirty-year sentence. Unlike Caruso, he was not brought before the firing squad. This was no doubt due to two aspects of Teruzzi's career: first, although a more important Fascist than Caruso, he was not a police official responsible for the deaths of Italians; and second, all of his important positions were held before September 8 and Salò. Teruzzi's case was exceptional for another reason; he was among the few Fascists to die in prison, in 1950 of natural causes at Procida.[91]

The second trial of *gerarchi* concerned the most important man of the three. Guido Buffarini-Guidi pursued important careers both before and after September 8, 1943. Mussolini's assistant at the Interior Ministry, he built a bureaucratic empire so powerful that he was among the handful arrested in 1943 after the palace coup. Later, as a full minister in the RSI, Buffarini-Guidi was as responsible as anyone for the war against the partisans. His role thus approximated Caruso's, and he received the same punishment. Photographs of the trial illustrate a vivid scene where the Fascist appears to have been dragged out of San Vittore prison, beaten up by the spectators, then shot before the large crowd. *L'Uomo Qualunque* objected to a photo in a Communist journal of the terrified man listening to the sentence, his mouth open and his tongue hanging out. The Qualunquisti likened the display to something out of a "polynesian cannibal's newspaper." The execution itself marked another important event for the Corti straordinarie di Assise as the most extreme punishment taken against a high-ranking Fascist.[92]

During the 1920s, the third defendant, Carlo Emanuele Basile, had been an official in the Veterans Organization and a high-ranking bureaucrat in the PNF directorate in the 1930s. His real power came under the RSI, however, as prefect of Genoa and then as undersecretary for the army. Like Buffarini-Guidi, he was among those most responsible for civil war atrocities, and popular hatred of him was so heated that his trial was moved out of Genoa. But on June 15 the president pronounced that Basile had done "nothing precise" to warrant the guilty verdict. The hall exploded into a riot: one thousand workers charged the court, and spectators threw bricks at the officials. Back in Genoa two thousand workers protested the Basile trial, and the prefect, Martino, assured them that the Fascist would be brought to justice through a retrial in that city. Prefects from all over the north cabled Rome to protest the decision, and Pavia's Corte straordinaria held its own trial for Basile, finding him guilty and imposing the death sentence. He would be in and out of courts for over two years, but despite continued protests, as many as ten thousand in one Genoa rally, Basile eventually escaped severe penalties.[93]

What do these three trials against high-ranking Fascists tell us? Teruzzi was an example of a *gerarca* caught in the wrong place at the wrong time. He happened to be trapped in the maelstrom of the liberation and, although his connections with the RSI were minimal, he was tried before the first, greatest wave of anti-Salò sentiment had subsided. His familiar face probably elicited the verdict as much as anything else. On the other hand, Buffarini-Guidi was as archetypical a Fascist defendant as there was. His brutality against the partisans and anti-Fascists earned him the firing squad. Basile was more problematic. His crimes were as vile as Buffarini-Guidi's, but he did not receive the same punishment. None of the defendants were members of the traditionalist ruling class, but perhaps Basile maintained influential connections that cannot be traced. On the other hand, like Teruzzi, Buffarini-Guidi was a more infamous and notorious personality than Basile and represented, along with Mussolini, Starace, and Pavolini, a good example of a "strategic" member of fascism's political class. Whatever motivations might have prompted the courts, their uneven verdicts persisted, as did the inability of Italians to deal with their past.

The Corti straordinarie dockets displayed names less exalted than Teruzzi, Buffarini-Guidi, and Basile. Like lower-court trials before the liberation, those who appeared before the new tribunals represented all types of men and women from varied social classes and points of view. And also like the earlier trials, punishments were uneven. In the Lombard capital Maria Ferlat was tried for her role as translator for the German command. She was given twelve years, while the head of the German radio station, Agostino Papone, was absolved. As the intensity of the war experience varied from city to city, so did the severity of the verdicts. The Milan court was notoriously soft on *gerarchi*, while those in Piedmont were harsher.[94]

In Piedmont a journalist, Marco Ramperti, was tried for writing a number of pro-German and anti-Semitic articles and was given a sixteen-year sentence. A woman of Ivrea was charged with translating for the Germans and urging them to execute a partisan "to teach the people a lesson." She was given the death sentence, which was soon changed to life in prison. An exceptional case involved a collaborationist with other crimes that dated back over twenty years. Between 1922 and 1924 he had committed acts of assault, manslaughter, and murder. The president of the court ordered him jailed for thirty years. But this was an extraordinary case. By summer 1945, such trials involving "Fascists of the first hour" had become quite rare, as practically all prosecution was directed against RSI personnel.

At the Alessandria court, between July 5 and September 13 all seventy verdicts pertained to accusations of collaboration and none to the *ventennio*. The same held true elsewhere. Of fifty-six trials in Turin between June 6 and October 28, all concerned crimes committed under Salò. Romano Canosa calculated the same for Milan's Corte straordinaria. About 38 percent of these sentences dealt with roundups, arrests, torture, or executions. Twenty-nine percent related to denunciations or spying on partisans or Jews for the Germans. Most of the rest involved economic or political collaboration, propaganda for the National Socialist cause, or simple enrollment in the GNR (Guardia nazionale repubblicano).[95]

The defendants came mainly from the Black Brigades or the GNR. That Mussolini's troops were being tried indicates that the Allied decree on their status as prisoners of war was not taken seriously in the north and that the authority of these measures was still in doubt. In the hectic post-liberation atmosphere, early trials of soldiers generally ended with a high rate of guilty verdicts and death penalties. On June 6, the first sentences in Ivrea were imposed on two GNR troops who machine-gunned a fifteen-year-old boy. Charged with high treason and homicide, both were executed. In Alessandria the first six verdicts, pronounced between June 21 and 23, involved four death sentences.

Through the month of June, the Ivrea court judged nineteen cases, of which seventeen defendants were guilty. Four of these were given death, one received life, and five were dealt sentences of twenty-five years or more.

As the excitement of liberation subsided, so did the harsh sentences. The course of the Corti straordinarie di Assise can be traced as an initial explosion of activity and then a decline in mid- and late summer, and finally their demise in DLL 625, October 5, 1945. Their replacement by the "special sections" signaled, however, that the trials were not yet over. In Alessandria Dr. Mario Buscaglino and four popular judges examined twenty-nine cases in June and July, twenty-one of which contained guilty verdicts. Of forty-six defendants who passed before the same court during August and September, fourteen were held culpable. Eleven of these received their sentences in the earlier month. Industrial Ivrea gained a reputation for particular severity. In the month of June, judges there found seventeen guilty in nineteen cases. The figures remained high through September: fifteen out of twenty. But they began to fall in October: fourteen out of twenty-three. Although fewer in number, these later verdicts tended to be on the harsh side, representing the trend in the later trials to exonerate lesser criminals who might have been punished had they been examined in June, and to concentrate on the most brutal Fascist murderers whose guilt was too monumental to ignore and difficult to forgive.

The ambiguity and dearth of consistency in verdicts revealed a problem that had plagued the trials program since its inception—the lack of a purged judiciary. This obvious dilemma had never been seriously dealt with and reveals one of the most jolting arguments against sanctions: that they could never have been truly effective. Many hearings, even into 1947, were chaired by men who were terrified by sanctions or at least doubted their validity, magistrates who had never been purged and who inevitably had a hand in the end of the program. The problem also surfaced in Germany, where, one observer concluded, 60 percent of Bavarian judges and 76 percent of public prosecutors had been National Socialists. A historian of the French sanctions against Vichy noted a similar problem. In Italy, this problem had plagued the High Commission since its inception. As early as May 1944 General Mason-Macfarlane had recommended that, in order to procure magistrates, the Italian army's judge advocate general, Francesco Traina, be allowed to comb the prisoner-of-war camps to "see what's available." In a report one month before the liberation, Mario Berlinguer gravely doubted the ability of the judges to appreciate their tasks and lamented the unavoidable reliance on them. "One must always remember," he wrote, "that the *Alta Corte* . . . cannot judge more than the fewest number of cases (one can say one in a thousand); all of the others are the exclusive competence of the peripheral magistracy, where . . . hearings [*istruttorie*] are stagnating. Sometimes, due to an inability of the magistrates to interpret political norms, they conclude with an acquittal which causes popular unrest." Bonomi's minister of grace and justice, Umberto Tupini, had also condemned the recalcitrance of the regular magistracy and urged them to use their "exquisite political-juridical sensibility."[96]

Right-wing sympathies among northern magistrates triggered a number of complaints. The Ligurian CLN's Commission for Justice and the Purge discussed it in a report on judicial problems of defascistization that was sent to Parri and Nenni. It stressed that the regular magistracy was not able to judge political crimes. "In the North," it said, "there is no need to forget, the regular judiciary . . . served [Mussolini's] Republic . . . [and its work] should be viewed with suspicion by the people. On the other hand, one might fear that the regular judiciary believing itself suspect will wish to display excessive zeal and would not judge freely." In Emilia the Procuratore del Regno for Reggio's Corte straordinaria was very unpopular with the Left. A Carabiniere report noted that he was "not perfectly objective: many protests charge him with slowness, disorganization, and partiality."[97]

CRITICISM OF SANCTIONS MOUNTS

Opposition to sanctions from business, the Anglo-Americans, traditionalists, and others intensified through 1945. The two most specific attacks against the program regarded its essence and its application, particularly focusing on first, what many considered a perversion of the nation's legal patrimony in order to punish Mussolini's followers, and second, the conditions of prisons. Both attacks, but particularly the first, were profound in that they represented the thoughts and sensibilities of the educated bourgeoisie. The second argument was unexpected because, had sanctions been properly handled, prison conditions should never have been an issue. Both criticisms of sanctions were couched in certain tones of middle-class gentility and Christian morality that cried out to the rest of Italy, "This defascistization business does not suit us."

The primary arena for these debates was the legal community. The committee of eighteen scholars who attacked ex post facto application of laws in August 1944 submitted to *Domenica* the first of many articles that appeared when journals resumed publication at the end of that year and into 1945. The forms taken in these debates depended on the writers, but sanctions were criticized from all sides.

Among the first articles in 1945 were those from Mario Vinciguerra, a Neapolitan follower of Croce and a long-time anti-Fascist. He had edited Giovanni Amendola's *Il Mondo* in the 1920s and was fundamental in the organization of the National Alliance, a forerunner, albeit a conservative forerunner, of the Giustizia e Libertà movement. With its inauguration, Vinciguerra served the Alto Commissariato in various capacities and chaired the purge of journalists. But in the January 7, 1945, issue of Luigi Salvatorelli's *La Nuova Europa*, Vinciguerra doubted the wisdom of an administrative purge. Moreover, prosecution of Fascists went out of bounds, he argued; it went beyond the fine traditions of Italian jurisprudence to embrace the blood-stained legacy of the French Terror. Vinciguerra called for simple justice, not the vendetta he feared was taking place. He also commented negatively on the program of confiscation of profits, an indefinable concept that could never be enforced.

Vinciguerra was a moderate Liberal, and, like De Gasperi and Parri, his antifascism was unquestioned. His negative attitude was not a defense of the *ventennio*. He felt, rather, that his own beliefs need not be sacrificed in order to punish Fascists. Vinciguerra represented the many *benpensanti*, who did not advocate harsh measures because they seemed uncivilized. There was no need to sink to Fascist methods in order to punish Fascists. Vinciguerra was echoed by a British administrator in Germany who wrote in 1947, "the measures [of punishment] stand to be judged by allied objectives and standards . . . not by Nazi standards."[98]

Achille Battaglia also spoke for a wide range of well-meaning yet conservative anti-Fascists. A lawyer, he served the cause of antifascism during the 1930s in Rome, in an underground network with links to Mario Berlinguer and Guido De Ruggiero.[99] Battaglia was never a friend of fascism, but in a June 1, 1945, article, he doubted the validity of the government's legal campaign. His theme concerned the definition of crime found in DLL 159, that is, the concept of "significant acts" (*atti rilevanti*) that had maintained the Fascist regime in power. Not only was it a vague notion, it ran against legal tradition, a violation of *nullem crimen sine legge*. By sacrificing that principle against retroactivity, DLL 159 trampled on good sense. Here again the notion of civilized behavior and the superiority of Italian Christian culture played a role for influential jurists. Civil rights were treasured goals of the *fuorusciti* and of those who had struggled in the underground. Victory over fascism would be a sham if those rights were ignored in the punishment of old oppressors.[100]

In the summer of 1945, Arturo Carlo Jemolo, arguably Italy's most prestigious jurist and a distinguished historian of the Catholic church, took up again the position that he and the seventeen others had outlined in the *Domenica* piece. A scholar at the Universities of Rome and the Sacred Heart in Milan, Jemolo had served as a consultant to the High Commission.[101] For a man of his stature the vehicle for his message against sanctions was crucial; he chose Piero Calamandrei's respected Florentine periodical, *Il Ponte*.

The choice of *Il Ponte* was important also because it was a significant *azionista* sounding board, and its readership certainly favored sanctions. But Jemolo's article went beyond a discussion of the courts; it indicted all government measures against Fascists. Taken alone, his words would not destroy the program, but they revealed a widely held sentiment, an outlook that appealed beyond Center-Right ideologues who closely followed the course of sanctions. Jemolo's were notions attractive to the "well intentioned" (*benpensanti*) and the "solid citizens" (*buoni borghesi*), who were never Fascists, although many had probably been enrolled in the PNF. Their reactions to sanctions were not based so much on fear for themselves as on what they considered to be good sense and Christian mercy.

Jemolo apologized to *Il Ponte*'s readership for "unpopular thoughts" and professed loyalty to the CLN with a "readiness to serve the Government in devotion and faith." He felt obliged, however, to raise his voice over "the things which frankly displease me . . . the laws on sanctions against Fascism . . . poorly contrived and terribly applied." Jemolo attacked the Alto Commissariato's inability to purge while creating chaos in government. The question was not Fascist guilt; that was obvious. Rather, the nation's moral strength and its competence to face Mussolini's legacy were at stake. He traced a history of sanctions in other places and concluded that it was not the thing that truly civilized people did. The desire to punish political losers was mean spirited and unbecoming to decent people. As far as creating a new ruling class, Jemolo felt it was impossible. To renovate the government through an attack on the top four grades of the administration would destroy Italy, "and no politician would assume the tremendous responsibility of destroying a nation so far gone in the first place for the sake of justice."[102]

Piero Calamandrei added his own postscript to Jemolo's article. This editor of *Il Ponte* had his own complicated past with which to deal. Like Jemolo, Vinciguerra, and Battaglia, Calamandrei was never a Fascist and he hated Mussolini's regime. The *azionista* leader had, nevertheless, maintained a successful legal career under Mussolini. A very respected Florentine lawyer and professor, he helped to compose the 1942 civil law code for the Fascists and, in turn, would contribute to Italy's republican constitution. Calamandrei disagreed with some of Jemolo's notions, but his retort displayed much affection and respect for him. The Catholic historian-jurist was praised as "an eminent scholar" and a "coherent and utterly moral conscience." Calamandrei did not discount the article as a Fascist apologia, nor was he arguing with enemy journalists from *Italia Nuova* or *L'Uomo Qualunque*.

Jemolo and Calamandrei's polite debate reflected the growing doubt over the program within the highest ranks of Italy's political culture. But *Il Ponte* was an elite journal that did not appeal to a large audience. Symptoms of the declining sanctions program—controversies over the prisons and the continued violence against Fascists—reached a broader spectrum through the popular press. Here were issues unclouded by legalisms such as *nullem crimen sine legge*, issues that aroused emotions and furthered the decline of anti-Fascist sentiment and sanctions.

The prison program was a disaster from the start, and it became a cause unto itself that contributed to the growing distaste for sanctions. Critics of the prison camps charged that they were filthy and badly run. Simple humane passion made many feel sorry for the hapless inmates, and the miserable conditions altered the image of the Fascists from swaggering blackshirts into poor victims of an uncaring Roman administration. Thousands of people—men, women, and children—were held in an unhealthy limbo in the camps before most were released without charges.[103]

By the end of the war a complex network of jails had been created or converted to deal with Fascists. Some camps, including ones in Africa, India, and elsewhere, held prisoners of war, while others contained political internees. All were officially under Allied jurisdiction, but Italians often administered those in their own land. The first major one, holding about a thousand, was Padula, a former Fascist penal colony. Made up of long bunk houses, its inmates were separated along class lines, and its deluxe wing held some Roman princes, General Ezio Garibaldi, and the Neapolitan shipping magnate, Achille Lauro. Other institutions were either long-established jails like Rome's Regina Coeli and Milan's San Vittore or makeshift camps like Coltano near Pisa. There were also certain places for specific types of criminals; Terni and Casellina, near Coltano, were women's prisons, while many of the military officials were housed in Forte Boccea.

Conditions in these camps were often deplorable. Most were overcrowded and real health hazards. Coltano was the greatest disgrace of all these camps. It contained over thirty-two thousand inmates, overwhelmingly young men who had served in the RSI. Most of it was unpaved, and the internees survived in a sea of mud. Drinking water was scarce and food even harder to come by.

Protests reached authorities in Rome. The prefect of Pisa, Vincenzo Perluzzo, wrote to Parri on September 8 and described the situation there in alarmist tones. The prefect was sincerely shocked at what he saw, and the letter was remarkable for Perluzzo's sympathy toward the inmates. He emphasized that a great number of them were not guilty of serious crimes at all but were nevertheless endangered "from one moment to the next, I repeat, from one moment to the next" by Fascist thugs and murderers. The whole camp had sunk into immorality and disease. "As a Prefect and as an Italian," he concluded, "I feel that I must bring to your attention this grave situation and to urgently invoke immediate Government intervention."[104]

Response was quick. On September 25 Parri was advised by his minister of war that "the grave health, discipline, and morale within the

Coltano internment camp . . . have already caused notable public and political repercussions [and], notwithstanding the approaching rainy and winter seasons, have . . . given the Government the opportunity to close it immediately." Minister Stefano Jacini's solution was to transfer the most dangerous and guilty to other places. The majority of inmates were low-ranking soldiers—only 359 were listed as civilians—and they were safe enough to be released under police surveillance.[105]

The plan was adopted, and Coltano was phased out over the next few weeks. To screen the incarcerated soldiers, thirty-six three-man commissions were established made up entirely of Royal military officials. Five other commissions were formed to judge the civilian inmates, most of whom were transferred to other prisons. Two days after his letter to Parri, Jacini announced the release of between seven hundred and eight hundred men per day. On October 2 he reported that all the generals and colonels had left; some, like General Gastone Gambara, who had served Badoglio in Brindisi, were sent to Forte Boccea, while others were released on surveillance. On the fifth, Jacini counted 18,943 screened thus far, of whom 17,714 had been set free.[106]

By October 31, Coltano ceased to function. Prefect Perluzzo issued a final report on the destinations of the internees. Thirty thousand had been released and 2,700 remained in custody. Of the latter, 1,637 were transferred to a military camp at Laterina near Arezzo, 167 were sent to a naval compound at Narni, and 45 generals and colonels ended up at Forte Boccea. Three hundred and thirteen civilians were sent to various Questure throughout the kingdom. Mussolini's nephew Vito, the last editor of the Duce's own newspaper, *Il Popolo d'Italia*, and Vincenzo Costa, the RSI *federale*, were sent to Milan's San Vittore, while former PNF chieftains Francesco Giunta and Aldo Vidussoni went to Rome's Regina Coeli. Many others would later be interned on the penal island, Lipari.[107]

Coltano was the largest and most notoriously mismanaged prison in Italy; but other cases of poor administration discredited the incarceration system as well. The women's prison, Casellina, near Coltano, was one such case. The Florentine newspapers were filled with stories of pregnant inmates who shuddered over baptizing their newborns in those surroundings. One reporter listed "278 horrible stories arising from the chaos of war." The prefect of Florence noted that he could not close the camp because of legal technicalities between the Italians and the Allies. Nevertheless, he felt that Casellina must be terminated "out of the principles of humanity and civilization instilled in our people." *La Patria* of Florence criticized the camp where the "guilty, the innocent, mothers, babies," were kept in a long filthy wait to hear if they had committed a crime. In November the Red Cross stepped in, informing the prefect that they found the prison to be nothing more than a "cesspool" and adding that "the great majority of these women are surely innocent. Many are minors from good families." The report feared that the approaching winter would be hard on the many inmates, few of whom possessed heavy clothes or even shoes, and said that Rome should secure Allied permission to shut the camp before it was too late.[108] The women's camp was finally closed a few weeks after Coltano.

Sometimes the internees themselves generated trouble and further placed the prisons in bad lights. The oppressive summer heat, coupled with the stench of urine from poor sanitary conditions, sickened and infuriated inmates. Miserable overcrowding was aggravated by flared tempers among the polyglot group of prisoners, Fascist and now anti-Fascist. With the excesses after the liberation many partisans were sent to jail, often the same places that held the Fascists, and fights frequently erupted. Not only did the Milan prison hold four thousand Fascists; there were eight hundred common criminals and over one thousand partisans. San Vittore and Regina Coeli were sites of constant battles. On September 1, San Vittore's partisan inmates overpowered the jail's warden and the questore of Milan and held them captive until certain demands were met.[109]

Just as embarrassing were the never-ending stories of escapes. General Roatta's adventure in Rome was only one of innumerable successful slips. The camps and prisons maintained notoriously lax security to the point where Fascists simply walked out through the front gates. Prisoners had the free run of San Vittore, and an angry Liberal correspondent complained that they stood in the huge windows at the end of the corridors dressed in nothing but their underwear for all the world to see. Once they broke out, fugitive Fascists disappeared into the anonymity of urban life, assured that they would never see the inside of a courtroom. The lists of accused brought before the Corti straordinarie di Assise were often annotated with the telling word *latitante* (at large).[110]

The sorry state of the prisons was revealed most glaringly in the

Donegani scandal. During the heady days of the liberation the CLNAI prefect of Milan, Riccardo Lombardi, ordered the arrest of many important Lombard magnates including Guido Donegani, the general manager of the giant Montecatini chemical firm. Already on March 15, 1945, *L'Unità* had labeled him "among the principal architects of the catastrophe, the principal enemies of the Italian people, and the principal obstacles to her resurrection."[111] He was captured by the Allies and handed over to the Italians on June 22. At that point the mysteries of ruling-class influence went to work. In the Byzantine world of Fascist and post-Fascist governments, Guido Donegani maintained very important connections. On the twenty-ninth, the public minister from the Corte straordinaria intervened, contending before the Milan police that Donegani had been locked up without specific charges against him. On July 14, the General Attorney commanded Questore Elia immediately to release the industrialist. The legality of the order was extremely doubtful. But it was honored, and Donegani joined so many others who vanished into the Milan crowd, making his way to Switzerland. Investigations were made, officials were fired, and warrants were issued for the fugitive. All to no avail. He was later exonerated and died in 1947. Today central Milan boasts a street named, perhaps ironically, the Largo Donegani.

Reaction to the escape was immediate. The Communist journal *La Volontà del Popolo* proclaimed that, on the heels of the Basile affair, Donegani's shady release was an abomination. The paper spoke for all the Montecatini workers who slaved under his collaborationist regime and who felt cheated now that their boss sat back "to enjoy his ill gotten gains in one of his villas or castles." The workers spoke up for themselves in indignant letters to the CLNAI. Protests flowed not only from Montecatini employees but from CLNAs all over the province: railroad workers, Siemens employees, and private citizens.

L'Unità criticized the questore for not telephoning Lombardi and validating Donegani's release orders. But the Communists felt that, more than an oversight, there was corruption here, collusion between the police and the man who engineered the release, a Professor Narbone, who had maintained the friendly "tu" form with the questore in their discussions. Strangely silent was Christian Democracy's *Il Popolo*. Through the hottest days of the scandal, July 20, 21, and 22, nothing significant appeared in the journal.[112]

COMPARISONS TO SANCTIONS
AGAINST FASCISTS ELSEWHERE

Axis collapse added other dimensions to the history of sanctions. No longer did the Italian and Vichy French examples stand as the only programs to be studied. The obvious change in the broader European history of defascistization was its application to Germany. The connections and parallels between the two Axis partners were at once strong and tenuous. Both countries lived under Fascist (or National Socialist) regimes firmly entrenched in 1939. On the other hand, a German purge need not have to deal with the dual nature that characterized Italian fascism—Mussolini's 1922–43 *ventennio* and his collaborationist regime of 1943–45. In that sense, Italy could be considered as a bridge between Hitler's and Pétain's states, with aspects of both. The historian Peter Novick has claimed that the Italian case was so different from the rest of Europe that the two cannot possibly be compared.[113] However, it cannot be a coincidence that the Italians' mild reactions to fascism's 1943 defeat tended to resemble the Germans', while upon the April liberation they seemed to follow the more violent French model.

The Anglo-Americans concerned themselves much more with German denazification than they had with Italian defascistization. Through the end of 1945 the matter was the exclusive domain of the occupation forces, and not until 1946 was the work handed over to German administrators. One reason for this was that Britain and America considered Germany's position to be more critical than Italy's in the postwar world, and events there were subsequently watched and controlled more carefully. Only in the sensitive areas of Trieste and Venezia Giulia did the Anglo-Americans continue to exercise an important watch. Furthermore, the Nazis' reputation was more insidious. When the legacy of their brutal conquests and occupations combined with the revealed horror of the Holocaust, the Reich had clearly become guilty of some of the most unspeakable crimes in history. In popular perceptions Hitler and his ss murderers embodied evil the way Mussolini and his "clownish" blackshirts never did. As one American journalist put it, "Denazification is delousing."[114]

Nevertheless, the German denazification program met obstacles and suffered defeats similar to those encountered in the Italian experience. As in Italy, purgers in Germany faced logistical problems. Their own equivalents to the *schede personali* were the Fragebogen, or Meldebogen: 131-question litmus tests. Unfortunately, as one British occupation official wrote, categorizing seventy million Germans into innocent and guilty slots was "a sheer impossibility." America's overlord in occupied Germany, General Lucius Clay, also lamented the failure of these questionnaires.[115] The four occupation zones complicated the issue not only logistically but ideologically. The growing Soviet-Western conflict aggravated the problem through an inability to coordinate denazification programs. The Russians attempted, and to some extent succeeded, in addressing the pervasiveness of nazism not only in Germany's government and politics but also in society. On the other hand, the cautious Western occupiers were criticized for having in Germany, as they did in Italy, "preserved in its essentials, the social and economic system they found. They ... eliminated much of its most objectionable features, but hardly touched the foundations."[116]

The Nuremberg trials will forever be a symbol, specious or not, of denazification. Many of Hitler's murderers have been brought to justice through other means and channels over the past forty years. But whether Germany's bureaucracy and society were effectively purged of Nazis continues to be an object of heated debate.[117]

The Soviet factor did not loom over Italian defascistization as it did the German. But a general discrepancy between the British and American attitudes on denazification can be discerned. As was the case in Italy, the British in Germany tended to be softer on the old regime than did the Americans. The Americans, on the other hand, pushed for denazification "with undiminished vigor." Washington's first official pronouncement on sanctions against Nazis, JCS 1067, was met with horror in London, where officials considered far too drastic the provisions to fire all Nazis and "fellow travellers" in schools, universities, courts, and newspapers. Along the same line, the British never had the faith in the Fragebogen that Washington did.[118]

As in Italy, injustice and failure marked denazification in all four zones of Germany. Membership in the new Socialist Unity party of Germany aided many bureaucrats in the Soviet zone, while as early as summer 1945 it was reported that the French were hiring Nazis who had been fired in the American zone.[119]

Collusion between German and Western industrialists also blackened the denazification experiment. The directors of AMGOT's Financial Committee were the American William Draper and Britain's Sir Percy Mills. Both had ties to German big business. Before the war, Draper had served as treasurer for Vereinigte Stahlwerke's greatest American creditors, while Mills had been an important member of the Federation of British Industries, the group bound to Hitler's Reichsgruppe Industrie through a 1939 gentlemen's agreement. In his recent study on denazification, Tom Bowers insists that Mills was the central figure in dismantling the purge of German heavy industry. The attack on private business was also criticized by Germans themselves, as it was by Italians, for being counterproductive and promoting economic paralysis. Able executives in the private sector shunned public service for fear of scrutiny and attack. By 1946 the German people and government had abandoned serious hopes, if they ever existed, for sanctions against National Socialists much beyond the top political layer. The Anglo-Americans also gave up the fight. By 1950 the Allied chief of staff wrote, "Leave it to the Germans to decide what they wish."[120]

By the summer of 1945, Italy's sanctions against fascism had become interminably interwoven with the increasingly polarized political scene. The Left more and more viewed sanctions as a lost cause. Nowhere among Communists, Socialists, or *azionisti* were the trials or the purge hailed as successes. The Left reacted to this situation in one of three ways: by abandoning hope, which is probably what most of them did; by pressing for further measures; or by engaging in clandestine punishment such as the Schio execution. Only a small minority took the last option, but the Center-Right was very concerned with these. The Center-Right's opinion of sanctions remained the same: that they were a mistake. Some, like the Christian Democrats, were ambivalent. Others, like the military, the crown, the Qualunquisti, or the Liberals, were outright hostile to sanctions. By summer of 1945, despite Parri's victory and alarmism over vigilantism, the Center-Right had already won.

CHAPTER SEVEN

THE END OF SANCTIONS

The year 1946 marked the effective conclusion of sanctions against fascism. Three years after the July 1943 coup, an equilibrium returned to Italian politics in the form of a republic guided by an increasingly powerful Christian Democratic party, in the end of the sanctions program itself, and in an amnesty for most Fascists. A Constituent Assembly, furthermore, inaugurated in 1946 and piloted by Carlo Sforza, prepared for a renewal and improvement of the parliamentary system upon which the Fascists had trampled for twenty years. The revolutionary impulses of Resistance and liberation proved short-lived, and the "Wind from the North" was no match for the entrenched traditionalist segments within the ruling class, the state bureaucracy, and politics. Consolidated in 1948, DC hegemony guaranteed that the few remaining sanctions tools would be prudently applied until all activity could be terminated.

Alcide De Gasperi's government also renormalized sanctions after the fresh but brief infusion of populism during the liberation of the north. Initiated by a narrow camarilla gathered around a marshal and a king, by mid-1944 they reflected input from a spectrum of the CLN parties that constituted most of Italy's new postwar political spectrum. The April 1945 liberation added the final important popular dimension. The push from below to punish Fascists had become at least as important as direction from above.

Parri's defeat and De Gasperi's victory in December 1945, however, guaranteed that Rome would recapture the controls and that the traditionalist impulse that had tempered sanctions in the south would return to control them in the north. This was accomplished in two ways: first, the traditionalists and their Center-Right political allies in

Rome defused northern defascistization, particularly the factory purges and trials; and second, conservative forces crushed what remained of the anti-Fascist partisan movement and, albeit only partially, its legacy of opposition to the old regime.

Italy's institutional referendum of June 2, 1946, furthermore, which abolished the monarchy, combined with the amnesty for Fascists to affect the last phase of debates. Both convinced many that Italy was finally rid of its Fascist king and, by extension, its Fascist past. They also reinforced the argument that a healthy democracy proved its strength through magnanimity—even exoneration—of Fascists.

The referendum and the amnesty also cast new light on old problems that had plagued sanctions since 1943—the tendency to concentrate punishment on highly visible, or strategic, elements of fascism, and a general reluctance to punish people for ex post facto political crimes. These quandaries were still evidenced in the House of Savoy. Despite Victor Emmanuel III's certain complicity, the crown had not created Mussolini's regime. But the old king and his son, the Lieutenant-General Umberto, were thorns in the side of anti-Fascists. Victor Emmanuel's presence was more infuriating than threatening since, in any case, he was already stripped of power and his exit would be largely ceremonial. The monarchy had simply become so discredited that its political support dwindled until it was abandoned even by the Christian Democrats. Important traditionalists and the nation's largest political party took a lesson from the Italo-Swiss philosopher Vilfredo Pareto, who wrote that "elites could, while yielding where yielding was called for, maintain their power."[1]

Gradual but determined dismantling of sanctions angered many anti-Fascists who had pinned high hopes on the program as a step toward a new, more progressive and democratic Italy. Many took their resentment to the streets, and among the new prime minister's first tasks was that of grappling with the continued nuisance of leftist popular violence. Disorder also came in different forms in the late 1940s: attacks on southern latifundia, separatism in Sicily, labor trouble, and for our concerns here, popular justice against Fascists.

In its broader sense, opposition to anti-Fascist violence masked a struggle between the new order and the partisan legacy. Armed antifascism was a heritage that proved powerful enough to accentuate political lines well after the end of the war. The Resistance had been (and still is considered) in many regards a romantic episode in Italian history, a "second Risorgimento," which lent itself to mythmaking by the Left. Authors such as Carlo Levi, Elio Vittorini, Renata Viganò, Italo Calvino, and Cesare Pavese, in their own ways, contributed with their stories and novels to a Left culture that found its heroes among the partisans. They guaranteed that a CLN heritage would always remind Italy of its Fascist experience. On the other hand, the Center-Right's consideration of the Resistance did not figure as prominently or, in some cases, at all. Since 1943 the Christian Democratic, Liberal, monarchist, and, later, Qualunquista press had treated the dictatorship as a nightmare, an embarrassment, or as Croce's "parenthesis" in Italian history. The whole thing, from 1922 to 1945, was something to be forgotten, and not to be remembered as a glorious age of struggle and liberation. The Resistance heritage served as a vivid link to the *ventennio* and, in denigrating it, centrists and conservatives could bury and forget Mussolini's regime.[2]

The movement against antifascism was fought on two fronts. Conservatives demanded the cessation of ex-partisan outrages, and such great importance was attached to the problem that the government undertook an armed assault—a virtual military campaign—to crush it. They also waged war on the partisan legacy in Rome, where, in late 1945, a CLN government still sat. There, the attack aimed at two figures: the *azionista* hero Ferruccio Parri and his high commissioner, the Socialist Pietro Nenni.

THE END OF THE PARRI EXPERIMENT

As the tide of the liberation began to turn against them, many, although far from everyone, in the Left wing of the CLN continued to press for serious sanctions. In the face of inevitable conservative victory, the Parri/Nenni dyarchy appeared almost quixotic in its attacks on Fascists. For their part, the Socialists in *Avanti!* continued to launch broadsides on Fascists and their presumed allies among the traditionalist ruling class. They also publicized sanctions successes in other countries and attacked both the crown and Qualunquismo. In August 1945 the Socialists claimed that Marshal Philippe Pétain's trial was "the last act of the French tragedy" and through the end of that month, in glaring contrast to the dearth of Italian defascistization news, Norway's Vidkun Quisling case dominated their headlines.

Avanti! also emphasized the links between the Fascists and conservatives and stepped up attacks on the "Fascist Monarchy." Resurrecting stories of neo-Fascist spy rings around Umberto, Socialists claimed that the whole range "of Fascist organizations, the army, the high bureaucracy," rested upon both "the fasces and the Savoy coat of arms."[3] Giannini and his *qualunquista* following were also maligned. It was common to find references to them and to Mussolini's criminals in the same articles. For example, during the trial of the *gerarca* propagandist Ezio Maria Gray, *Avanti!* noted that the defendant passed the time in the courtroom arrogantly perusing copies of *L'Uomo Qualunque.*[4]

Active and thorough sanctions clearly interested Prime Minister Parri, who expressed complete faith in his Socialist high commissioner and, despite the sorry state of the purge, urged him to intensify it. On July 4 he wrote that Nenni should accentuate the Alto Commissariato's political character instead of its juridical side. Parri decided to broaden the attack to include big capital. To implement this he enacted DLL 479 and DLL 702. The former, released on August 9, extended the purge to large private corporations with assets over 5 million lire and aimed at the punishment of important business figures.

The more far reaching of the two measures was the "Nenni Law," DLL 702, November 9, 1945, which scrutinized top administrators in government, in publicly controlled businesses, and in private concerns with government contracts. The law, however, did not categorize the business levels included in the purge. Nenni nevertheless took it upon himself to specify that, regarding the government, all those over the eighth rank were to be examined. Offenses warranting dismissal concerned the RSI exclusively; included were simple enrollment in the Republican Fascist party or service in the Salò Regime. Lower-level employees were also susceptible to the purge, but their crimes needed to be far more serious—"extremely grave Fascist partisanship"—than those of their bosses.[5]

A panel of judges quickly chose 393 figures for investigation; the situation appeared foreboding. But the reality of DLL 702 did not live up to the anxiety it created: all had been specified before. Beyond Grieco's ineffective aberration, the notion of punishing the high and indulging the lesser had been a standard since the beginning. That the most important *gerarchi* should be included in the purge had always been a goal, perhaps the key goal, of the Alto Commissariato. By early 1946, however, some of the few CLNAs that still maintained purges voiced their preference for the old Allied General Ordinance 46 rather than the Italian measures. Despite Nenni's tough language, they still preferred the Anglo-American directives.[6]

DLL 702 was frightening enough, nevertheless, to bring a simmering ministerial crisis to a boil wherein the Center-Right moved to defeat Parri and Nenni. As early as October 3, the Liberal Manlio Brosio and the Christian Democrat Mario Scelba launched attacks in the cabinet against the Assize Court program. In his memoirs, however, the Socialist leader recalled that the fight really began on November 1 with his attempt to "reduce the purge to reasonable criteria," an accelerated campaign against the top government bureaucrats, a practical cease-fire on those from grade 7 down, and "a very restricted field of action toward the private employee." The ministers soon locked horns in a "huge battle." Considering Scoccimarro's earlier proposal to fire everyone in top government ranks, Nenni's aims were not at all unreasonable. Nevertheless the Center-Right, forever frightened by Nenni's specter, considered that revised measures, no matter how mild, represented a resuscitation of sanctions at the moment they appeared to be wheezing their last.[7]

Criticism of Nenni had by now become second nature for the conservative press, and fierce assaults on the high commissioner began immediately. As early as January 17, 1945, Nenni had been ridiculed by Giannini. In *qualunquista* style, a front-page cartoon depicted an angry mob chasing a caricature of the Socialist leader up a tree while they paraphrased the Fascist chant, "Camerata Nenni, A noi!" When the ministerial squabble broke out, the monarchist *Italia Nuova* blared that the new laws "put Italy at Nenni's mercy."

The deciding blow to the Parri-Nenni combination, however, came not from monarchists and *qualunquisti* but from Christian Democrats. Taking the lead from the Liberals, the DC had finally decided to move against the prime minister and to secure the government for their own De Gasperi. To achieve that end Nenni had to be neutralized, and that meant a denunciation of the High Commission.

The DC's public campaign to derail Parri and his Socialist ally began on November 4, at the beginning of the cabinet emergency when *Il*

Popolo published a three-column front-page editorial on "The Myth of the Purge." The choice of author, Guido Gonella, was a brilliant stroke. A mainstream DC leader very close to De Gasperi, his remarks could not be dismissed as rabid rightist drivel. "The Myth of the Purge" was, rather, a painful statement of disillusion from Italy's complex and powerful Catholic party.

Gonella wrote that, from the beginning, a national "rebirth" could never have come about through a purge. Italians needed to face questions "of earnestness [*serietà*], of stability, and of guaranteed rights [*certezza del diritto*]." But Gonella saw the sanctions program riddled with "uncertainty, doubts, reticence," where "the innocent [were] too often victims" while "double-gamers" and political "acrobats" were exonerated. To a friend's complaint of an unpurged Fascist co-worker who became more arrogant with every passing day, Gonella urged virtue rather than vendetta; virtue "that [was] a goal [*premio*] in and of itself." Italy's political rebirth could never succeed through the failed option of punishment. Purges and trials were foreign to Italy's humanistic tradition; sanctions were things applied by Fascist thugs not by Italian Christians. The problem required Croce's Liberal approach —although he was not cited in the article—of reeducation. Gonella warned that the purge was a mistake that worsened daily. The surgeon, he said, was not curing with his incisions, he was causing hemorrhages. "He began wrong and he is making it worse."[8]

Gonella's piece reinforced the position that the Vatican had taken long before. The DC attack came in the midst of a series of articles in *Civiltà Cattolica* that criticized sanctions. A noted Jesuit spokesman on politics and society, Mario Lener condemned the program as only marginally legal, "a constitutional *monstrum*." Particularly troublesome were the notorious *atti rilevanti* that served as a catchall for anyone who had ever associated with the blackshirts or attended a rally. Father Lener feared that anyone, outside of the most active anti-Fascists, could be prosecuted under that rubric. He insisted that Italians abandon their fraudulent campaign to prosecute at any cost and return to simple notions of fairness. "The special tribunals only create political victims. . . . Only justice does not change. What is justice today is always justice. . . . only [it] can bring about peace."[9]

Sanctions had to end. And with a De Gasperi government in the wings, the time was ripe to finish the job. The Christian Democrats and Liberals launched the attack, which was politically supported out-side the Council of Ministers by the *qualunquisti* and the crown. The monarchist *Italia Nuova* headline of November 24 blared, "Out with the CLN! Down with Extortionists!"

Since the middle of August both Parri and Nenni had known that enemies were coalescing against them. Parri himself identified the spearhead of the attack as a union of Christian Democrats and big capital represented in the industrialists' alliance, Confindustria. "One day I came to know," he later said, "of a colloquium between a Chris-tian Democratic member of the Government and Confindustria, be-tween Milan and Rome." Nenni also appreciated the situation and later wrote that the debate over his sanctions measures was only a cover, a decoy (*un falso scopo*) to bring about Parri's demise.[10]

In the face of the Center-Right onslaught, the Socialists continued to support their leader and his purge. Through the dark days of No-vember, *Avanti!* endorsed the Nenni Law and proclaimed that at last the government could begin a truly meaningful and fair houseclean-ing under Sforza's resurrected motto, "Attack high and indulge low." Important functionaries should worry, whereas lower-level bureaucrats, those under grade 7, would have nothing to fear.

But despite the party's support for its leader, the government was doomed: the Liberals and Bonomi's Labor Democrats triggered the actual cabinet crisis by resigning and attacking Parri and Nenni.[11] Parri realized that the end had come and, disheveled and confused, he called a press conference on November 24.[12] In what has been described by his foes as a rambling, incoherent tirade, he lashed out against the PLI and the DC, which he blamed for the destruction of his administration and hopes for popular democracy in Italy. He also maligned the Anglo-Americans, whose neglect of and disinterest in his experiment em-boldened the campaign against him.

Parri's collapse inspired a sigh of relief from the Center-Right. On December 10, Alcide De Gasperi formed his government. As a vote of confidence, the Allies announced that the AMG would cease in north-ern Italy, except along the Yugoslav border, on December 31. *Italia Nuova* trumpeted, "The CLN Government Ceases to Exist." One day earlier, a bitter Pietro Nenni lamented in *Avanti!* that the "Wind from the North" had died.[13]

Although it has been characterized by a Catholic writer as "the Restoration," De Gasperi's first government was no mere DC/PLI coalition of "White Terror." Communists, Socialists, and *azionisti* were also included in the cabinet. Togliatti, who indeed advocated the De Gasperi ascendancy, and Scoccimarro held the Justice and Finance portfolios respectively. Nenni was made vice president of the Council and minister for the Constituent Assembly, and he kept the High Commission chair. Actionist Emilio Lussu became minister without portfolio, and his confederate, Ugo La Malfa, gained the reconstruction slot. But the Liberals held on to the Treasury, represented by Epicarmo Corbino; War, with Manlio Brosio; and the job-rich Public Works under Leone Cattani. Back at the navy was the indestructible Admiral Raffaele De Courten. Among the major Christian Democrat prizes, De Gasperi kept Foreign Affairs for himself, while Gronchi retained Commerce and Industry.[14]

Italy's new prime minister, Alcide De Gasperi, was never a Fascist nor was he sympathetic to fascism. A Tridentino, his early life was spent as a citizen of Austria-Hungary, where he was active in Catholic politics and served in the Vienna Parliament. After World War I, his native Trent and the Alto Adige were incorporated into Italy, and De Gasperi refocused his attention on Rome. Among his first causes in the new locus was a campaign against a purge of those Tridentini who had served the Austrians. Although he was Luigi Sturzo's heir apparent in the Catholic Popular party, with the advent of Fascist dictatorship De Gasperi was drummed out of public life. After a year and a half in Mussolini's prisons, he found shelter behind the walls of the Vatican library, where he worked until the July 1943 coup.[15]

As a Christian Democrat, De Gasperi did not consider defascistization in the same light as did Nenni or Parri. His stand against Mussolini's regime was unquestionable, but his views on solving the problem differed from the Marxists. While the new prime minister certainly appreciated their analyses of class and struggle, his thinking was tempered by Catholic organic ideas, which, when applied to fascism, meant that everyone was guilty and everyone was innocent. Italian society endured the *ventennio*, but that nightmare was over, and De Gasperi, not Mussolini, was prime minister. De Gasperi's vision and the DC's official policy to implement Christian mercy and forgiveness favored the wish to end sanctions. With positions that did not fit neatly into the Left or Right, De Gasperi and his party could keep channels open in all directions. Many on the Left understood this and tolerated the DC's alliance with the Liberals. Strong PCI-PSIUP-Actionist factions still considered De Gasperi to be a member of the CLN coalition and were often quite willing to collaborate with him.[16]

THE END OF SANCTIONS

Antonio Bevere has written that November 1945 was a significant date for Italy in that De Gasperi acquiesced to PLI wishes to end all "element of renovation" in the state apparatus.[17] But, regarding sanctions, it cannot be said that his new administration signaled a significant change in their downward course. Sanctions, particularly the purge, had never enjoyed clear sailing and had been threatened with extinction from at least November 1944, when Bonomi's first cabinet collapsed. Parri's incumbency had represented the strongest impulse to turn them around, but the Left was not strong, coordinated, nor dedicated enough to carry through the promises of a real purge. De Gasperi merely adjusted sanctions back to their downhill track.

Continuity between the Parri and De Gasperi ministries, furthermore, was revealed in the endless squabbles within the High Commission itself. Throughout the late summer and fall of 1945, a battle had raged between two men in the structure, Renato Boeri's replacement, Spartaco Cannarsa, and Ruggiero Grieco's replacement, Domenico Peretti Griva. Upon the nomination of Nenni as high commissioner, Boeri's position reverted to one of general secretary. A Socialist, Cannarsa, was chosen for the deflated position and served his leader loyally, even collaborating on the formulation of sanctions measures. To head the purge itself, the *azionista* Peretti Griva replaced Grieco. The new Commissario Aggiunto was a magistrate of moderate political views who had worked with the clandestine CLN Piedmont. Upon the liberation he was regarded as a highly respected jurist with impeccable anti-Fascist credentials. He had grave doubts, however, regarding the prudence and justice of a purge and held strong reservations about the plans of Nenni and Cannarsa.

While Parri remained in office, the *commissario aggiunto*'s suspicions appeared as officious critiques of the Nenni decrees and goals. To counter the Socialists' aims, Peretti Griva audaciously issued orders of his own. For instance, an October 1, 1945, circular to the provincial purge commissions categorized the offenses that necessitated sanctions. Peretti Griva decreed that simple allegiance (*giuramento*) to the RSI, "deplorable" an act as it was, did not constitute grounds for punishment. Neither did holding a "Fascist rank" (*qualifica*), inscription in the Fascist Republican party, or following the Salò government north.[18]

Since Nenni's tougher guidelines were not applied anyway, Peretti Griva's criticisms were academic. But when De Gasperi assumed the prime ministership, attacks from the *commissario aggiunto* became bolder and more personal. Animosity toward Cannarsa, and thus toward Nenni, surfaced in a determined effort to secure his dismissal. On December 12, immediately after the change of government, Peretti Griva wrote to the prime minister of the secretary general's growing "rudeness" and "meddlesomeness," unwelcomed attitudes at a time when his staff had to be resolute in the completion of its work. A couple of days later, Peretti Griva followed this up with another letter to De Gasperi, complaining of a "demoralized staff" confused by the "uncertainty" of Nenni's decrees. But uncertainty was not the only problem. Nenni and Cannarsa were blamed for opportunistic manipulation of their positions for political ends, an underhanded tactic that could only bring sanctions "to a disastrous conclusion."

De Gasperi was slow to respond, and Peretti Griva pressed his case on December 19 by tendering his resignation, not to Nenni, but to the prime minister. He wrote that he had accepted his position in July despite great personal sacrifice and for the sake of civic duty. However, "I do not now feel that I can maintain these functions which would contrast with my moral sensibilities." In the same way that former Prime Minister Bonomi had been faced with the problem of De Courten and Scoccimarro, De Gasperi was now faced with an either/or situation: Peretti Griva or Cannarsa, normalization or more radical measures. A resolution was quick in coming. Within three days Cannarsa submitted his resignation, and the prime minister accepted it. On December 22 Nenni wrote to his friend that he was fully aware of the argument with the purge commissioner and "my opinion coincides perfectly with yours." The high commissioner urged Cannarsa to stay on until the transfer of power to a replacement. On his way out, Cannarsa told a journalist, "We can't purge; we can't arrest; we can't confiscate; we're useless."[19]

199

Cannarsa's resignation was not unique for the besieged Alto Commissariato. The entire purge program was on its last legs, and within months all of its personnel would be searching for work. In December 1945 government officials began seriously to discuss dismantling the Alto Commissariato, and a time limit was placed on Nenni's organization.[20] March 31, 1946, was designated the final day of operations. With his hands full as vice president of the Council of Ministers, Nenni quickly became a transitional lame duck at the High Commission.

In later reflections on his tenure at the High Commission, Nenni admitted that the purge was a failure. Even this most prominent voice for sanctions had already given up. His gloomy directive to provincial purge delegations, dated December 29, 1945, emphasized that his office would close on March 31 and that remaining work would be taken care of by the individual ministries.[21] On April 11, 1946, before his party Congress, Nenni confessed that he had realized the failure as early as summer 1945, when he accepted the Alto Commissariato position. He only agreed to the appointment, he said, to dispel accusations that Socialists shirked difficult tasks in Italy's reconstruction. This accounts both for Nenni's reluctance to defend his own purge and for his preoccupation with his other duties on the Council of Ministers. As PSIUP leader, his personal and then public abandonment of the cause meant that much of the drive behind the High Commission was gone. The Actionists, deeply divided themselves, could never command the numbers necessary for sanctions, and the Communists had never been fully committed to them. Without Socialist determination, defascistization had nothing behind it to withstand the onslaught of the Center-Right.[22]

To oversee the end of sanctions, on March 31, 1946, a coordinating Office for Sanctions against Fascism was established in the prime minister's State Council. Domenico Carugno headed this agency for the next few years in what essentially became an administrative "mopping up" operation. Real power had shifted to the cabinet. To that body all purge delegations surrendered their files and any more information that was required by the ministries.

The ministers themselves had already begun to assume more control of the purge. This was indicated in a December 13, 1945, summary of the military situation by De Gasperi's chief assistant in the prime minister's office, the pro-Catholic Liberal Giustino Arpesani. After a flurry of letters between Admiral De Courten and the premier's office, Arpesani wrote that the High Commission should review matters only after failure to reach a decision within the ministry itself.[23]

During these death throes of sanctions it is ironic that, in accordance with what remained of the Nenni law, one last attempt was made to create a purge commission for private industry. No comprehensive history exists of this committee. Its entire existence, spanning about two years, was marked not by an active implementation of sanctions but by interested groups trying to place their men on the committee. Its chairman, Gaetano Russo, and his assistant, Nicola Brunetti, were bombarded from all sides with requests to secure representatives on the panel in the unlikely event that it should ever become effective. Big capital, led by Confindustria and Concommercio, obtained seats for Battista Bardanzellu as a permanent member and for Mario Conti as a rotating member. Organized labor, the CGL, secured posts for Enrico Vinci and Vittorio Angiolini, while the Italian Banking Association submitted the president of Finsider, Oscar Sinigaglia. In the end, however, there is no record of anything at all being accomplished by this committee. On February 25, 1948, Brunetti announced to De Gasperi that the office was ending its operations and asked the prime minister to allocate his payment for the last two months' work.[24]

Furthermore, statistics indicate that almost no government purge had been applied since the end of the war. In January and February 1946 Rome reported its sanctions record to the Allies. Of 394,041 employees concerned, 1,580 had been formally dismissed. Of that figure, 728 were in the top seven grades of the bureaucracy; 531 others took early retirements; and 8,803 received *sanzioni minori*, a reprimand note placed in the person's file. In Germany, 1947 statistics indicated that 700 high public officials had been dismissed. A further 200 from private business lost their jobs.

Although Italian purge figures are higher than those found in Scoccimarro's and Grieco's earlier reports, they do not necessarily illustrate any accelerated government actions against Fascists. The 1946 statistics represent the reinstatement into the Italian government of the Salò veterans, roughly one-third of the Rome bureaucracy, all of whom, by the letter of the law, should have been fired. One might assume that the bulk of the increased numbers represented those RSI officials who probably never attempted to resume their old duties or, judging from the courtroom records, were still hiding out from the law. The bottom line figure in the 1946 report, 1,580, represents as many government bureaucrats as were purged. Few, if any, were dealt with after February 1946, while many more were readmitted to their positions and exonerated.[25]

For sanctions in general, 1946 also completed a process that had begun with a vague idea of punishment and had become a policy to forgive, or at least try to forget—a transition from sanctions to exoneration or a national loss of memory. Not only had the purge been halted and the High Commission begun to dismantle, dismissed Fascists were being rehired.

As early as June 29, 1945, reports from the Allied Commission no longer spoke of firing but rather of merely denying raises to RSI personnel. One circular ordered that "all such officials still in office are entitled to receive only the salary due to them according to the rank they held on 8 September 1943, without any recognition of the promotions in grade given by the Fascist Republican Government."[26]

In Rome, among the first to readmit purged personnel on a significant level was the Treasury's State Accounting Office (*ragioneria dello stato*). The minister, Marcello Soleri's heir, was Giovanni Persico. As early as August 16, 1945, he wrote to Parri that the *ragioneria dello stato*, "like the rest . . . of the other state administrations," was beset with "a grave personnel crisis" and advocated that the accounting office make use of those who followed the Duce north, about 130 "young men of sure value who could be immediately put into service."[27] By mid-September the rehiring had begun.[28] In five letters during the second half of the month, Persico announced that twenty-five RSI personnel had been taken back. These employees were probably the more important of those who had followed the Duce to Salò since their titles included section head, division head, personnel inspector, and various archivists.

Persico's efforts to find places for Mussolini's functionaries continued with his successor. Arpesani reported to De Gasperi that the Treasury minister considered the time ripe to reinstate RSI functionaries in the central government. Not all neo-Fascists were immediately reaccepted, but here it seems that exceptions bore out the rule: in April 1947 twenty-five of them petitioned De Gasperi for their jobs. They complained of unfair discrimination since other bureaucracies, particularly the military, bestowed "absolution" on RSI personnel. Documents like Persico's letters and the fact that those twenty-five disgruntled Fascists complained at all indicate that Rome must have been rehiring large numbers of bureaucrats.[29]

The northern factory purges had also run out of steam, and ex-Fascists were finding it easier to reenter business. CLN groups and workers' councils flooded Rome with protests against government leniency and the rehiring of blackshirts. The minister of labor reported to De Gasperi on May 9, 1946, that some die-hards among the Milan CLNAS had endorsed a return to Allied Ordinance 46 and an abandonment of the Italian decrees in order to pursue culprits in private industry more rigorously. For them, DLL 702 had already become a dead letter. In January 1946 the prefect of Milan wrote to the minister of industry that "with the end of AMG control, the [CLNA purge] commissions have suspended their work." The career prefect Triolo, who had replaced the CLN man (a common occurrence throughout northern Italy at the end of 1945 and government policy after January 1, 1946), added that "at some Aziende the situation has resolved itself by transferring . . . personnel, temporarily suspended in the purge, to other branches or plants."[30]

REPUBLIC AND AMNESTY: THE END
OF THE ANTI-FASCIST LEGACY

The High Commission formally ended its work on March 31, 1946. The press, regardless of politics, was strangely silent, and the demise passed virtually unnoticed. Later that spring Rome took two decisive steps to erase or cover up Italy's Fascist past in a referendum on the nature of the new government—republic or monarchy—and in an amnesty. These events had more of an effect on the trials than on the purge. The purge was a dead letter by June 1946, but prosecutions against Fascists continued after the amnesty and the victory of the republic. Resolution of the monarchy question and the amnesty, however, both illustrated that the Center-Right's attempts to erase civil war memories were largely successful and, furthermore, contributed to a lenience toward blackshirts.

Victor Emmanuel III's reputation as a Fascist sympathizer was equaled only by his ludicrously obstinate refusal to abdicate. Events in the spring of 1946 nevertheless revealed, even to him, that traditionalist segments within the ruling class and in the government had abandoned him. For indications of the national mood, long-awaited municipal elections held over five Sundays from March 10 until April 7 were closely studied. The contested positions were town and city council seats in Italy's 5,658 municipalities, and the Left's strong showing did not bode well for royalists. The conservative parties, excluding the Christian Democrats, won in 459 towns; Communists, Socialists, *azionisti*, and the new small Republican party captured 2,356 towns; and the Christian Democrats took 2,270 towns. Gaetano Salvemini claimed that the results were skewed to lessen the importance of the Left victory. Many of the "towns and cities" captured by Socialists and Communists, for example, were vital industrial centers, while the Liberals took villages. For instance, one PLI councillor was elected on forty-two votes, while a Socialist in Milan garnered 225,000. This was proof enough that the monarchy was in trouble.[31]

The greatest blow to the crown, however, came not from the elections but from its most important supporter, Christian Democracy, at its Rome Congress on April 24, 1946. Although De Gasperi revealed in private his desire to see the monarchy end, he urged upon his party the necessity to defend it. Not even he, however, could stem the disaffection and disgust felt by so many against the "traitor-king." The "taciturn" secretary, Attilio Piccioni, rose to announce the figures of a poll among the party's rank and file. His words were devastating: 146,000 favored the crown, 187,000 abstained, and 503,000 called for a republic. The royalist Christian Democrat Antonio Segni attempted to torpedo a move to endorse the republic in the coming referendum, but he was voted down. The DC had cast its lot against the king.

There was no hope for Victor Emmanuel. On April 25 the king summoned his aide-de-camp, General Paolo Puntoni, to the Quirinal Palace and informed him that the Anglo-Americans, "in agreement with the Lieutenant General [Umberto] and with the heads of the Center-Right parties have manifested the opinion that I must abdicate by June 2." The king's forty-six-year reign ended on May 9, when, with his queen, he sailed to exile in Egypt.

It was Victor Emmanuel, however, who had been sacrificed, not the monarchy. The king told General Puntoni that pressure had been applied so that his son, Crown Prince, now King, Umberto would be able to consolidate his position and "render more probable a victory for the Monarchy in the referendum."[32] But the Savoyard reputation was utterly bankrupt, and Victor Emmanuel's foolish refusal to abdicate had only worsened the situation. Nor did the new king's ascension deter attacks on the monarchy. Like his father, Umberto II had also been tainted with fascism. His "victory" tour of the north after the liberation had been a disaster. In Milan, he had been snubbed by Cardinal Schuster, and late one evening partisans riddled his villa with bullets. Umberto, furthermore, was personally ridiculed for his unfortunate marriage with the Belgian Maria José. The only way out for the dynasty would have been to surrender the crown to Umberto's son under a regent. A boy, he was free from accusations of having been pro-Fascist, and his innocence might have elicited popular sympathy. But the Royal House chose against that option.[33]

In its final days, the crown found its most vociferous supporters in the PLI, the *qualunquisti*, the church, and, naturally, the monarchists. In flagrant violation of electoral law, clerics ordered their flocks to vote against the republic, an action that, ironically, would also be a vote against Christian Democracy.[34] The monarchist campaign verged on hysteria in the last weeks. On April 30, *Italia Nuova* described a rally in Naples, the greatest pro-Savoy bastion in Italy. At the city's San Carlo opera house, Enzo Selvaggi urged voters not to swallow whole the claims of the Left. It was Victor Emmanuel who defeated fascism, not the CLN or the partisans. *Italia Nuova* thundered against both the Communists and the Christian Democrats throughout its May issues. The anti-Communist pronouncements were typical: Italy must prepare for a Red dictatorship, the PCI was plotting a civil war, and so forth. Some of the most bitter charges, however, were leveled at the traitor De Gasperi. On May 16, the DC leader was maligned as Togliatti's "Quisling." On the twenty-first, *Italia Nuova* claimed that the DC had betrayed Christian civilization through its choice to ignore the anti-Communist pronouncements from the Vatican, notably Pope Pius XI's 1937 encyclical *divini redemptoris*.

Although the outcome of the election never seemed to be in doubt, the number of ballots cast for the monarchy was surprisingly large. The republic won only by a vote of 12,718,019 to 10,709,423. The results were also important from a geographical vantage point. Prorepublic and Promonarchist regional majorities were cleanly split between north and south. Every region from Rome and south voted for the House of Savoy. North of the capital the tallies were exactly reversed.

On the same day the elections for seats in the Constituent Assembly were held. By capturing 204 seats, almost half of the total, the Christian Democrats could claim an enormous triumph. Their nearest competitor, the Socialists, earned 115. However, since the Communists and Socialists could command an even larger combined percentage, the DC would have to wait until the 1948 elections for their conclusive and overwhelming victory.

The passing of the highly visible monarchy mollified segments on the Left by adding to the notion that sanctions had been resolved. As reliable a journal as Piero Calamandrei's *Il Ponte* felt that the end of the Savoys contributed to the formation of a new ruling class. "The posts are empty," reported one editorial, "from the fresh forces of broad strata of people, the new ruling class is ready to step forward!" Another polemic claimed that June 2 represented "the reconciliation of a people" and that "peace with justice equals republic." Even Nenni commented that the battle against fascism and bourgeois capitalism had been twisted into one against the monarchy, and that battle had been "victoriously concluded with the plebiscite." In America, a skeptical Donald Downs wrote for the *Nation* that cynicism had won in Italy: "'Shall we have a king or a republic?' is about as far as the Italians have gone in the public debate. They seem to think that a decision on the one issue . . . would settle everything when of course it would settle nothing. . . . In this climate of opinion a purge of Fascists has become impossible."[35]

Along with the demise of the monarchy, the other factor in the sanctions struggle during 1946 was the amnesty. Based on the lessons of history, an amnesty toward the Fascists was inevitable. In eras before political parties established hegemony over public life, the vanquished in civil war, perhaps after periods of vengeance, often received exoneration through magnanimous acts from victors anxious to heal the wounds. Aristotle tells us of an amnesty after the First Peloponnesian War. When the Athenian leader Archinos saw how many of those who had fought against him chose to emigrate, he decided in a "fine and statesmanlike act" to compel "large numbers of them to remain . . . until they had recovered their confidence." The Athenians so wanted to settle their past feuds that when one malcontent sought to contravene the amnesty, Archinos "hauled him before the *boule* and persuaded it to have him executed without trial."[36] During the Renaissance, Machiavelli, cast out of Florence into years of exile, was eventually accorded a minor official position after an amnesty. The magnanimous impulse has perhaps eroded in our age of political animosities, but it persists; and modern civil wars fought between ideological adversaries have still often been resolved with forgiveness. The Restoration after Waterloo, the Third Republic, and the American Reconstruction were all launched in part with amnesties. In Germany, similar measures would also be undertaken toward the Nazis. The first one there occurred at about the same time as Italy's: in August 1946 an amnesty was declared for those born after January 1, 1919. The most important German scheme was announced in October 1947. After the Risorgimento, Italy's newly formed national army readily accepted officers from the defunct Neapolitan army, while the more radical Garibaldian elements that had infiltrated the royalist corps were purged. The establishment of the Italian Republic in June 1946 was no denial of this tradition.[37]

The irony of the 1946 amnesty that resulted in the release of so many, undoubtedly the majority, of Fascists still in prison was that it did not originate in the political Right, from which endorsement might have been expected, but rather from the leader of the extreme Left, the new justice minister, Palmiro Togliatti. Umberto II suggested an amnesty to the government after his father's abdication as a matter of course since Savoyard, and generally European, tradition dictated that one be declared when a new monarch takes the throne.[38] From that point, Togliatti decided on its parameters. The Communist leader opted for an amnesty based closely on the one commemorating Victor Emmanuel III's accession in 1900. Umberto II ultimately disagreed over Togliatti's application and refused to sign it. But the minister of grace and justice could afford to wait out the end of the kingdom, and the decree was among the first in the new republic.

Historian Antonio Gambino has termed the results of Togliatti's amnesty "catastrophic." It allowed the judges to "open every form of abuse" and invalidate most of the anti-Fascist sentences that had been handed down since the inauguration of judicial sanctions in July 1944.[39] All verdicts of under five years were canceled. Those with longer sentences, furthermore, also received indulgences, since all terms were reduced. Only those with very important Fascist positions and those guilty of particularly brutal crimes were to remain in prison. Death sentences were commuted to life, life was changed to thirty years, all other tenures were reduced one-third, and all financial indemnities were canceled. On June 22, 1946, De Gasperi approved the Togliatti amnesty, and its provisions were put into effect. So prepared for the decree were authorities that some prisoners seemed even to have been released in anticipation of it.[40]

The Communists' role remains problematic. Although the justice minister and his dominant faction in the PCI always advocated the sincere application of sanctions, they were never so adamant in this as the Socialists or even the *azionisti* had been.[41] Emboldened by their crucial role in the Resistance, the Communists were gaining strength against a declining Socialist party. The PCI, however, was still reluctant to use that power to support the sanctions program.

The obvious answer was that, as part of the CLN coalition, the PCI continued to adhere to the national front role it had adopted when Togliatti returned from Moscow. But since the liberation another explanation for the party's lukewarm attitude toward sanctions must be added. As a truly popular party (*partito di massa*), the Communists appealed to many Italians who had been denied political options during the *ventennio* other than the PNF. Of course the PCI shared this dilemma with the other parties. Like the Christian Democrats, the PCI realized better than did the Socialists and the Actionists that fascism, for twenty years, had been the only choice for the overwhelming majority of Italians.

Even before the war's end, Fascists had not only been disassociating themselves from the PNF and PRF but also had been playing their own double games by latching onto false partisan connections. Harold Macmillan noted how certificates issued by the Allied Commission that attested support for the armed Resistance were being sold for optimum prices on the black market, something he felt was probably a good thing.[42] After the war, some blackshirts naturally shifted into other parties that represented their own beliefs better than the Fascist monopoly had. Others moved to save their skins and positions. Complaints and suspicions of Fascist penetration into the Resistance parties had also surfaced at the first CLNAI Congress, held in Milan from August 31 to September 1, 1945. A report on the purge, entrusted to Giuseppe Brusasca, concluded that "too many Fascists have infiltrated into our ranks." He made special note of a case in the Milan Assize Court where the death penalty had been advocated against an ex-*squadrista* by a public prosecutor who had himself served with the accused.[43]

A popular deduction drew connections between Togliatti's amnesty and the feeling that an unknown but not insignificant number of Fascists had switched their allegiances to the PCI. The phenomenon of new allegiances was no secret, however, and Togliatti himself had often publicly invited former Fascists, particularly younger ones, to consider enrollment in the PCI. Events elsewhere also indicated that Communists welcomed "reformed" Fascists into their ranks. In Germany's Soviet sector, many ex-Nazis enrolled in the Proletarian Party of Socialist Unity, and in 1947 this was declared acceptable, and was indeed advocated, by the new government.[44] It would not be entirely unreasonable to assume that some Fascists might base their leap to the Left on ideological motives. Just as some Communists became Fascists, like Nicolo Bombacci had done in the RSI, others would lean the other way.

One important AC official recounted to the author that a Communist official had come to him urging leniency for certain Fascists already enrolled in Togliatti's organization. Another case was noted in the *qualunquista* press, always happy to embarrass the Communists. "Comrade Ulisse," the editor of the Turin *L'Unità*, was interrupted at a Genoa rally by a boisterous man in the back of the crowd. The heckler read aloud a speech Ulisse had made a few years before in defense of fascism.[45] An OSS investigation also discovered that many journalists, including Socialists and Communists, had been Fascists. Even the editor of the PCI *Ricostruzione* had been a member of the PNF and from it had drawn secret funds.[46]

The 1946 amnesty pointed most clearly to Togliatti's willingness to abandon the campaign of sanctions against Fascists. The Communist leader defended this to disgruntled members of his own party not as a move to exonerate a regime but rather as an act to forgive individuals. He claimed that the amnesty did not signal the end of the struggle, and, if needed, new legislation could be fashioned to prevent a Fascist revival.

The amnesty decree nevertheless proved embarrassing for many Communists. *L'Unità* devoted very little space to it, and what coverage was permitted took a hedging or even apologetic tone. Terming it "the pacification amnesty," the journal supported Togliatti and reminded readers that important *gerarchi* would not be released from jail and that this was only an act of clemency for the lower-level Fascists.[47] In the June 19 edition Togliatti himself wrote that because many Fascists, particularly young ones, had already been released from prison, an amnesty would not matter much anyway.

Others on the Left, championed by Nenni, stood against the amnesty. Socialists labeled Togliatti's act an abandonment of long-fought-for ideals and launched an attack on their Communist allies in the tenth sitting of the new Constituent Assembly. On July 22 the PCI minister of agriculture, Fausto Gullo, defended his leader before Sandro Pertini, the former CLNAI Socialist leader and future president of Italy. Gullo acknowledged mistakes in devising and applying the amnesty, but the essential thing to remember was that it was aimed at low-level personnel and that the *gerarchi* would remain in jail. Nor would prosecutions end. But Pertini was not satisfied, and Togliatti stepped in to defend himself. "This measure has been advocated," he said, "by all the parties: not excluding the extreme left and more or less by all strata of public opinion. . . . I believe that it is a manifestation of strength and not of weakness by the republican regime." Togliatti insisted that the Communists had not given up the fight and would always remain vigilant in their mission.[48]

The amnesty and the end of the monarchy hastened, but did not cancel, the exorcism of Italy's Fascist past. Although the former influenced the faltering trials by nullifying sentences, Togliatti and Gullo were correct that it did not end them altogether. Many, such as Marshal Graziani and Prince Borghese, still awaited trial. Other events that signaled the end were the demise of the Corti straordinarie di Assise and the end of the High Commission and subsequent incorporation of Mario Berlinguer's *commissariato aggiunto per la punizione dei delitti fascisti* into the Ministry of Justice. Both the court and the *commissariato aggiunto* had succumbed to attacks from the traditionalist camp.

Mounting problems in the courts had alarmed Togliatti, as minister of justice, since late September 1945. He warned Premier Parri that a crisis stage had been reached and that all work, particularly the inquests, had practically ceased. Togliatti demanded that something be done, but he had no suggestions of his own. He blamed the problems on forces of "Traditional Italy," in this case the magistracy and police. The minister of justice specifically complained of a tendency in the judiciary to consider mere warnings as final punishments. He also pointed his finger at the Questure for failing to furnish denunciations to the investigative boards and at the PS for a reluctance to supply information.[49]

Sub-rosa machinations by judges, the Questure, and the PS to sabotage the trials were strengthened by open attacks from the most important moral voice in the nation, the Roman Catholic church. Not only the Christian Democrats but the pope himself became acutely interested in the trials. In contrast to the past, the church chose not to rely on the DC to do its bidding but directly intervened with the Viminale. The Vatican was particularly critical of the adoption of the death penalty for grave Fascist crimes. On October 22 and November 14, 1945, Pius XII's nuncio to Italy, Archbishop Borgongini Duca, met with De Gasperi at the Foreign Ministry to express the pontiff's concern over the roughly 220 death sentences against Fascists. The envoy informed the Italian government "of His Holiness the Pope's desire that capital sentences pronounced at times when public feeling was especially exasperated should not be carried out."[50]

The British representative at the Vatican, Sir Francis D'Arcy Godolphin Osborne, intercepted another communication from Borgongini Duca to De Gasperi that emphasized Vatican satisfaction with the Council of Ministers' abolition of the Corti straordinarie, "a wise measure of precaution." But the church lamented that death sentences were still pronounced every day while others waited on death row. The cardinal reminded the foreign minister that the Holy Father received "long queues of mothers and wives, broken hearted by sudden verdicts . . . [who] make the pilgrimage to Rome to invoke pardon." Finally, on January 9, 1946, the Vatican secretary of state appealed to D'Arcy Osborne for help. His Majesty's envoy forwarded the note to the Foreign Office, adding, however, that he thought it was best left unanswered.[51]

Not every Vatican intrusion was a general plea to end the trials. Occasionally the Holy See intervened on behalf of particular defendants. On August 6, 1946, for example, the secretary at the Nunziatura, Monsignor Giuseppe Paupini, petitioned De Gasperi's office to reexamine the case of Vincenzo Azzolini, the convicted governor of the Bank of Italy. Paupini noted to the prime minister's vice chief of cabinet, A. Varino, that Togliatti's amnesty might apply to the banker in Procida prison. Varino agreed and reported back that Azzolini's case had been sent to the procurator general at the Rome Court of Appeals. De Gasperi's chief assistant, Francesco Miraglia, then informed the Ministry of Justice of the prime minister's interest in the matter. Azzolini was released, resumed his banking career, and settled back into Rome's fashionable Monte Parioli district.[52]

Other imprisoned Fascists had little need to rely on the Vatican since, in the collapsing juridical framework, decisions were being reversed and the amnesty was being applied. The Corti straordinarie di Assise, so functionally and symbolically important for the prosecution of Fascists, had been officially terminated in Parri's DLL 625 of October 5, 1945. Lorenzo Maroni's Alta Corte di Giustizia, created under DLL 159, was also canceled except for the ongoing judgments of senators. The Corti straordinarie were to be replaced by "special sections" of the regular Assize Courts, one for each provincial capital. They were manned by regular magistrates chosen by the president of the Appeals Court and included four "popular judges" picked by the president of the Tribunale from lists compiled by the local CLN. These special sections could rule on crimes specified in earlier legislation, mainly DLL 159 and DLL 142. DLL 625 also ended the Milan appellate Special Section of the Corte di Cassazione. Some Corti straordinarie continued to review after the inauguration of DLL 625. The last one functioned in Milan until December 1947.[53]

But whether special or extraordinary courts, there was a pronounced new conservative tenor to all verdicts by the end of 1945. The mood was reinforced by DLL 625's termination of the special section of the Milan Court of Cassation, created under DLL 142 as the exclusive body for appeals from the Extraordinary Assize Courts. With Parri's October reform, before De Gasperi had even taken office, appeals returned to the domain of the magistracy, free from CLN interference, in the regular cassation courts.

The continued existence of some of the older liberation courts and Corti straordinarie stand as exceptions to what occurred in the new special and cassation courts. In his study of the Milan court, Romano Canosa discovered a seriousness and activity that did not exist elsewhere. In 1945 the Corte straordinaria there accounted for 158 acquittals and 193 condemnations. In 1946 the numbers remained fairly high, 158 and 128 respectively, with 65 releases based on the amnesty. And although the number of cases decreased in 1947, the ratio of absolutions to guilty verdicts returned incredibly to that of 1945, 24 to 67, with 30 amnesties. Canosa also points out that, of 36 death sentences, only 2 were carried out.[54]

A sample of verdicts from the Turin Corte straordinaria illustrates less activity than Milan's. Although the Piedmontese Resistance had been perhaps the most intense in Italy, by 1946 much of the bitter edge had worn away, at least in the courts. From June 22 to July 12, 1946, eighty-two decisions were handed down, of which only thirteen had a guilty verdict. Of the thirteen, we know that one served out a sentence until 1962, another until 1954, and one had an appeal rejected with no further indication of status. The rest of the defendants were released soon after their guilty verdicts. Four were amnestied, and four more were freed after their sentences were "annulled" in the cassation courts. (The other two are unaccounted for in the Turin files.)[55]

DLL 625's creation of the Assize Courts' Special Sections altered the trial outcomes even more. The Turin pretrial inquiries in these new bodies determined much of the course by weeding out cases before they could be delivered for official prosecution. Between July 7 and 25, 1946, fifty-one cases were perused in them, and none were sent to court. The usual reason inscribed on the official record stated that the offense had been covered in the amnesty, invalidating any reason for a trial. It must be assumed that cases passed on from the inquests to the regular Assize Court were truly exceptional. Examples drawn from the trials in industrial Ivrea confirm this in their high percent of guilty verdicts. From April 10, 1947, until March 23, 1948, fourteen cases were reviewed in Ivrea. Only six were judged not guilty, and three of those were based on the amnesty. However, even here the sentences, generally for atrocities, were light: nine and a half years was the stiffest term, the rest being five years and under.[56]

The new Special Sections were not the only changes described in DLL 625. Equally important to the end of sanctions was the increased reliance on the regular cassation courts. After the amnesty, the appellate hearings staged in them resulted in the release of most Fascists who had been sentenced by all other courts.

The most famous, or notorious, of these cassation courts was its Second Section in Milan, under President Vincenzo De Ficchy. De Ficchy turned his proceedings into a virtual absolution mill by reliance on legal confusion and the amnesty. He accomplished this through the built-in ambiguity of sanctions legislation, in this case, the use of appellate courts. For example, according to DLL 198, September 15, 1944, verdicts rendered in the High Court were ironclad and beyond appeal. But the decree had been sufficiently unclear to enable De Ficchy and other jurists to interpret it their own way and use the cassation courts for indiscriminate review of all cases against Fascists. After De Ficchy established the legality of this procedure, he used the amnesty to exonerate Fascists, many of whom were very important figures.

Vito Mussolini, the dictator's nephew, was the first released by Milan's Second Section. The director of fascism's most important propaganda vehicle, *Il Popolo d'Italia*, he had been given a fourteen-year sentence in December 1945. But on July 18, 1946, De Ficchy used the coming amnesty and reversed the decision. Soon afterward the Second Section tested the validity of other rulings. Although condemned to death in absentia by Lorenzo Maroni, Filippo Anfuso had his case reopened. De Ficchy annulled the High Court verdict, stating that legislative ruling "[was] not *per se* sufficient to exclude recourse for [reasons of] incompetence and excess of power." Anfuso continued to be engaged in court battles for a few years, but finally, in 1949, he was completely exonerated and even elected to Parliament as a neo-Fascist deputy. The infamous Cristalli of fascism's dreaded Tribunal for the Defense of the State was another of the first released. Giuseppe Bottai, Dino Grandi, Giacomo Acerbo, Dino Alfieri, and Mario Roatta, among others in jail or in absentia, were all exonerated. "Thus," wrote Romano Canosa, "the road was open for the application of the amnesty to all *gerarchi*."[57]

The release of Fascist leaders was controversial enough, but De Ficchy went further and redefined Fascist torture in his court. Besides the *gerarchi*, the amnesty had specifically excluded RSI troops guilty of "particularly savage cruelty" (*sevizie particolarmente efferate*). But on March 12, 1947, he decided that "genital depilation and rape [*violenza carnale*] of a female partisan do not constitute particularly savage cruelty." Based on such rulings, De Ficchy released many RSI soldiers and Black Brigadesmen who had been condemned in earlier courts.[58]

THE END OF THE ANTI-FASCIST THREAT

Throughout the last weeks of 1945 and into the new year, the prime minister's office and the Interior Ministry were inundated with telegrams and letters demanding that sanctions not be abandoned and that justice be meted out to Fascists. These protests continued to flow in from individuals; but more often they came from groups: either workers' councils, usually associated with the CLNAI or CLNAS, or partisan organizations. Practically all letters from Milan called for "justice [that] is really justice" (*giustizia sia veramente giustizia*). Many of them specifically blamed the executive committee of the Liberal party for "aiming to sabotage CLNAI powers" and the purge.[59]

All over the north many gathered to voice their discontent over the course of sanctions, but their demonstrations in 1946 and 1947 tended not to have the intensity of the immediate postwar period. The speakers exclusively represented either the leftist partisan veterans association (ANPI, or Associazione nazionale dei partigiani italiani) or the "Chambers of Labor" (*camere di lavoro*). They varied in place and size: Venice witnessed fifty thousand demand justice against Fascists, two thousand protested in Castel San Giovanni near Bologna, five thousand in Ravenna, and two thousand in Piacenza, where the crowd, mostly workers, demanded a thorough purge of the telephone company, SEPRAL. Calls for severe justice, however, also came to be amalgamated into demands for other left-wing goals—such as cost-of-living reductions, increased food supply, unemployment relief, and land reform—or criticisms of American hegemony and aid.

After Togliatti's amnesty, the prefect of Alessandria described one suburban meeting of about one thousand people who protested the release of dangerous Fascist criminals. The mayor, a representative of ANPI, demanded four measures: that those who had been condemned to death be executed, that the releases from prison must cease, that purged Fascists not be rehired, and that more public works projects be inaugurated to cure unemployment. Other prefectural reports read more or less the same way.[60]

Reports to Rome, however, also revealed that the government was not frightened by these demands. Prefectural messages focused closely on popular opinion and concluded that the demonstrations did not represent a broad spectrum of Italians and dismissed the meetings as inconsequential.

Not all had resigned themselves to rallies and peaceful protests, however, and Rome was more genuinely concerned with persistent violence directed against Fascists. Although it had become a less attractive option for the far Left, the legacy of the "armed Resistance" continued to inspire. The prefect of Imperia noted that an ANPI speaker publicly threatened violence in retaliation for further lenient measures against Fascists. Threats occasionally turned to action. Two months after the amnesty a detachment of ex-partisans from Asti, mostly former policemen, abandoned hope and took to the hills in rebellion. Their demands included jobs, a ban on the Uomo Qualunque movement, and a revocation of the amnesty.[61]

Violence persisted into 1946 and 1947, particularly in Emilia-Romagna. In November 1945 the questore of Ferrara received an anonymous letter promising bloodshed if certain partisans were not released from jail, a threat officially condemned by the local CLN. At the same time, the city awaited the trial of its former RSI political boss, Carlo De Santis. The questore refused to act and was shot and gravely wounded in the chest.

The situation was serious enough to call for an Interior Ministry report on Emilia conducted by a PS official, Pesarini. Circulated in early 1946, its alarmist text counted acts of violence and murders against Fascists, focusing on Bologna, Ravenna, Ferrara, Modena, and Parma provinces and concluding with an appendix that summarized the police situation. Pesarini counted 489 Emiliani murdered after the liberation by former partisans who refused to lay down their arms. The fiercest fighting had taken place in Bologna, but, Pesarini noted, the worst had been curbed after the CLNAI questore had been replaced by a less "political" man chosen by the Interior Ministry, with AMG approval. The incumbent prefect, however, was still a partisan appointment who, Pesarini felt, had foolishly enrolled his comrades into the police force, men who displayed no sympathy for dead Fascists and who probably applauded the violence.[62] The number of deaths, he wrote, showed no sign of decreasing but rather was on the upswing in the countryside around the city. Some citizens were mobilizing their own National Guards to combat what was derisively labeled *partigianeria*.

Pesarini noted that much of the problem stemmed specifically from the high numbers of politicized partisans in the Public Security police force rather than in its royalist and conservative cousin, the Carabinieri. And it was to the Carabinieri that the Allies, as early as March 1944, had allotted a special place in their new order. The AMG's chief for public safety, Lieutenant Colonel Walter Doherty, remarked that those troops had become "invaluable" through "tactful usage, support, and combined use with the Military police of the Allied Forces . . . so much so that there is a general clamor for more and still more [of them]." Carabinieri numbers did indeed rise: from forty-three thousand in June 1944 to sixty-five thousand in July 1945.

Pesarini also focused on a Communist-Socialist coalition, "allied in order to conduct common action," which was particularly troublesome in the old Emilian battleground, where Red and Black had fought after World War I. There, politics were extremely polarized, and a bewildered population possessed little faith in Rome's ability to control the situation. Like many others, the investigator noted the large number of attacks on priests. He stated that violence directed against the clergy was labeled anti-Fascist by the Left but was in reality only masked Communist anticlericalism. Pesarini recommended a new purge aimed not at former blackshirts but, rather, at anti-Fascist partisans in the police force, strengthening it through reinforcements and appointing "career men" in Questura and prefectural offices.[63]

An alarmed Center-Right also attempted to impress on the Allies the seriousness of the situation. The Americans needed little prompting. After December 1945 meetings with the former CLNAI military leader, General Raffaele Cadorna, and Brunetto Brunetti of the Carabinieri, Brigadier General Francis Brady of the American embassy warned that the Emilian crime wave was "out of control." Police protection was "quite unsatisfactory," and the partisans' paramilitary forces possessed better equipment and higher morale than did the Carabinieri. Brady consequently advocated more effective measures to disarm the partisans. Their neutralization was essential for social peace.[64] Later, in July 1946, Premier De Gasperi and seven members of the DC promoted the emergency view to Henry Hopkinson, a political analyst for the British embassy. Hopkinson concluded that, while "perhaps not directly inspired by Communist Headquarters," partisan violence, such as the attack on Schio prison, represented "a general design to weaken the machinery of Government and intimidate moderate and conservative elements." The Christian Democrats and the British analyst agreed with the answers reached earlier by Pesarini: De Gasperi recommended a strengthened Carabinieri and an extended Allied presence.[65]

Rome soon exerted its authority. Bolstered with American backing, Alcide De Gasperi returned from a trip to the United States in January 1947 and prepared for the end of Marxist influence in the government. The stage was set through a crisis triggered among the Socialists by the moderate "autonomist" Giuseppe Saragat. Saragat had always opposed Nenni's flirtations with Togliatti and, prompted by Washington, pulled his faction out of the party. By May, De Gasperi felt that the time had come to expel the Communists and Socialists from the ruling coalition. The Action party had also disintegrated by this time in rancor and disillusion. Its members scattered into other camps—Socialists, Liberals, and the new Republican party under Ugo La Malfa.[66]

A year later, on April 18, 1948, the drama was completed when church exhortations and veiled threats of American military intervention ensured an overwhelming Christian Democratic electoral victory. The April election decided the composition of Italy's new Parliament. In the nation's most hotly contested and important vote after World War II, De Gasperi's Christian Democracy gained an absolute majority. In his study of the period, Massimo Legnani noted that the tense and belligerent statements from big industry before April 1948 were replaced by surer, more self-satisfied tones. Italy's membership in the Western bloc would never again be in doubt.

Suppression of the partisan legacy through police action had already begun by late 1946. Carabiniere reports from the end of that year and into 1947 summarized the political complexion of Emilia's prisons when Communist and other leftists made up the overwhelming majority of inmates. In Bologna, for example, 3 lonely Fascists languished alongside 321 Communists, 84 "communist sympathizers," 116 "aparatchiks," and 18 Socialists. In Reggio, 197 leftists were imprisoned with 6 Christian Democrats, an American deserter, and a single Fascist.[67]

But it was the overwhelming 1948 electoral victory that gave De Gasperi and the DC freedom of action to undertake the final push and to crush northern partisan violence. In the autumn of 1948 DC Interior Minister Mario Scelba directed paramilitary operations against the Emilian insurgents. From Bologna, a special 1,500-man assault mobile unit was armed with heavy equipment including grenade launchers and fifty flame throwers. By September 9 over three hundred partisans and workers were arrested in Bologna alone. Most of the jailed leaders were described in the press as ANPI veterans, and there were many charges of unreasonable police harassment. At Fanano the ANPI secretary was imprisoned for slapping an ex-Fascist in the face. The blackshirt had made derogatory remarks about a photo of dead partisans.[68]

Many commentators on the Left regarded these raids as part of a Christian Democratic ploy to distance the Italian people from the partisans and the Resistance heritage. In his study of denazification, Tom Bowers found the same phenomenon at work in Germany, where, by 1947, conservatives began to portray the Nuremberg prosecutors as dupes of Jewish-Communist treachery.[69] In Italy, participation in the war against fascism and support for sanctions became suspect, anti-Italian, and unpatriotic. *Milano Sera*'s Nicola Giudice claimed as much. "The Government," he wrote,"is attempting to turn around the historic relationship between the partisans and neo-Fascists, transforming the fascists into victims and the partisans into criminals." The Communist leader Luigi Longo agreed in *L'Unità*, insisting that Rome was determined "to cast aspersions on the partisan heritage and to favor a fascist rebirth."[70]

Naturally, Christian Democrat ideologues did not view the situation in such terms. The party vice secretary, Paolo Taviani, labeled Emilia "the test of democracy" and hailed the police action. He wrote in *Il Popolo* that, in Emilia, the Communists fought their last losing battle, "and their defeat spells victory, not only for Christian Democracy, but for all democratic parties, for free labor unions: it is victory for Italy, republican and democratic Italy."[71]

In one sense, at least, Taviani was correct: the partisans had lost the battle. Rome's military might had overwhelmed them so that, by December 1948, the commander of the Second Carabiniere Division announced to Rome that Emilia was pacified. After a tour of Bologna, Modena, Reggio, and other centers, General Filippo Caruso felt that despite "agitations organized by the left [*le sinistre*] the situation is under control, as it always has been under control, such that, I would advise, there is no cause for excessive worry." Caruso felt that it was now up to the magistracy to apply the law of the land "with proper rigor" so that Emilia "would rapidly come to a satisfying normalization." What was left of violent and popular antifascism had finally been crushed by Rome's troops. After forty years it has never resurfaced to levels even remotely matching the postwar era.[72]

EPILOGUE

Controversy and bitterness over sanctions against fascism still plague Italians. The issues of the mid-1940s have been submerged but never satisfactorily resolved: neither goals nor accomplishments have been clarified. What was the purpose of defascistization? Did sanctions aim at Fascists or fascism? Why, indeed, were sanctions applied at all? Was blanket forgiveness a more appropriate answer than a brutal purge or a bloodbath?

If eliminating "top Fascists" from office had been the goal, then prosanctionists must have received some satisfaction because the *gerarchi*, whether as political leaders of the *ventennio* or Salò, were out of power by 1946. The regime's highest visible elements were gone. Mussolini, Starace, Farinacci, and the rest of the top *gerarchi* were either dead, in jail, abroad, or in hiding. Of course the official sanctions program had less do with that than did the war and popular violence, but the results were the same.

On the other hand, Italian government sanctions, framed in Carlo Sforza's and Pietro Nenni's dictum of aim high and indulge low, cannot be considered successful. Traditionalist opposition against both the High Commission and the Resistance heritage; the pressures and complications of war; the tendency to blame visible, "strategic," members of the regime; and a general reluctance to chastise killed anti-

Fascist punishments. A few carried sanctions further than the government was willing to allow: CLNA factory purges and popular violence in the north were the most important of these attempts. Nevertheless, disturbed by actions taken against its authority and beyond its own criteria for sanctions, Rome successfully defused those alternate campaigns.

In order to evaluate the sanctions program, furthermore, one must consider two fascisms. First, as ideology, party, and regime, what remains of the blackshirt legacy? Between the two world wars, Mussolini used an old state bureaucracy and built on top of it one of his own. Constructing a self-consciously new system, Fascist philosophers and ideologues, men like Giovanni Gentile, Agostino Lanzillo, Ardegno Soffici, Mussolini, and others, sought to structure a new worldview for their faithful. What, then, became of those who believed and acted on those beliefs?

Second, as a condition of state and society, fascism's definition becomes broader and more difficult. A strong current in Italian society had "accepted" the dictatorship and benefited from it in a myriad of ways. After the war people who had been swimming in that current could state, often quite innocently, that their *tessera* had been taken out merely to preserve their careers or for other conveniences, while other important figures may never have possessed a party card. The High Commission and the rest of the sanctions program hardly addressed this broader picture of fascism in society. How seriously Italian democracy has been threatened by these persistent fascist tendencies in the mainstream of national life is a question that has occupied scholars for over forty years.

The lesser problem has been the resurrection of neo-Fascist groups. Organized neofascism came surprisingly soon after the defeat of Hitler. Some blackshirts, usually identified with the RSI rather than with the *ventennio*, staged a few rash acts in late 1945. In October they attempted an astonishingly ill-advised March on Rome to commemorate the twenty-third anniversary of the original one. There were other scattered incidents, such as a nighttime attack on San Gimignano's Casa del Popolo and CLN headquarters. The following April a small group took over a Rome radio station and repeatedly transmitted a recording of the Fascist hymn, "Giovinezza," until the police broke it up. The most bizarre act took place on the night of April 22, 1946, when a band of diehards "kidnapped" Mussolini's body from its unmarked grave. The corpse remained hidden for eleven years, buried beneath an altar in a Pavia church. The ghoulish ringleader, Domenico Leccisi, was later elected to Parliament on the neo-Fascist ticket.[73]

This Dark Age of neo-Fascist activity ended when it became apparent that more Italians would tolerate, if not condone, association with the old regime. The end of sanctions, along with Togliatti's amnesty, guaranteed the inevitability of more public expressions of profascism, something that might have been suicidal for a blackshirt in mid-1945.

An indication of the new toleration was the return of the exiles, in a strange sense, fascism's own *fuorusciti*. Giuseppe Bottai reentered Italy after service on the Franco-German border and in Indochina with the French Foreign Legion. He spent the 1950s as a journalist, working on memoirs and on various magazines such as the popular *ABC*, which he edited. Dino Grandi left Portugal for private business in Brazil and then returned in the 1950s to his farm near Ravenna. Giacomo Acerbo resumed professorial duties in agricultural studies at the University of Rome. Dino Alfieri became the head of a journalists' institute in Milan. General Mario Roatta emerged from hiding in Spain but returned in the 1960s to Italy, where he lived out his remaining years in retirement.

Publication of memoirs recalling life and politics in fascism's inner circles facilitated new acceptance. One of the first books to appear, in 1946, was written by the Duce's former police boss, Carmine Senise. An *apologia pro mia vita*, his *Quando ero capo della polizia* emphasized his machinations with the Royal House against Mussolini. Soon other Fascists followed Senise's lead and composed their own accounts of the *ventennio*. Giacomo Acerbo's *Fra due plotoni di esecuzione* presented the case, amid rambling and incredibly cluttered passages, that he was marked as a guilty man by both the Regno del Sud and Salò. Ermanno Amicucci was another neo-Fascist journalist who had been condemned to death in 1945 but lived to publish *I 600 giorni di Mussolini*, about life in the RSI. Among the most unusual was *Mussolini anedottico*, written by the former youth leader Asvero Gravelli. It was essentially a joke book—crammed with Mussolini's funny quips taken from the hilarious years of the dictatorship.[74]

Senise's and Acerbo's apologies differed from Amicucci's work, which was a thinly disguised pro-Fascist treatise. Amicucci was joined by others such as Gravelli, Rodolfo Graziani, Bruno Spampanato, Giulio Evola, Stanias Ruinas, Edmondo Cione, Valerio Borghese, Carlo Silvestri, and Giorgio Almirante, who, beginning in 1946, created a literature of neofascism, an oeuvre that grew in popularity when newsstands began to carry the journals of the renascent movement. Among the periodicals was Giuseppe (Pino) Rauti's 1946 *La rivolta ideale*. Other reviews founded later in the 1940s and into the 1950s included the influential Neapolitan *Nazionalismo sociale*, the official neo-Fascist party organ, *Lotta politica*, and the still reasonably popular *Il Borghese*.[75]

The new toleration bred a neo-Fascist arrogance. As early as 1948 one of the most aggressive of their lot, Carlo Silvestri, was sued by no less a figure than Ferruccio Parri. Condemned to death for his record as an RSI propagandist, the amnestied Silvestri launched a campaign in the review *Il Lunedí* to discredit the Resistance by focusing on its leader, Parri. He claimed that "Zio Maurizio," who had been captured and jailed by the Germans during the civil war, conducted deals with them to secure his release and safe transport over the Swiss border. Parri beat the case in court, but the fact that three years after World War II a Fascist could force the Resistance prime minister into a courtroom displayed not only what neo-Fascists were capable of but also of what the nation allowed them.

Finally, Mussolini's most die-hard followers opted to constitute themselves as a political party. But legal restrictions against neo-Fascist revival hampered their attempts to reenter the political fray. Among Badoglio's first acts after the July 1943 coup had been to outlaw the PNF. Furthermore, most subsequent anti-Fascist legislation, including the armistice terms, prohibited its resurrection. Despite these formal sanctions, Togliatti's amnesty and the establishment of the republic indicated that Italian society might tolerate public neo-Fascist activity.

The result was not long in coming. Six months after the amnesty, on December 26, 1946, a nucleus of RSI survivors gathered in Rome to found the Movimento Sociale Italiano (MSI), their new Fascist party. As its name implied, the MSI was more the ideological heir of Salò than of the *ventennio*. Its first years were dominated by the "Men of Verona," those who endorsed the socialistic measures employed by Mussolini in his final two years. Early rallies often ended in brawls with Communists, but by October 1947 the Movimento felt respectable enough to participate in the Rome municipal elections. The MSI garnered 25,000 votes, which put three representatives in the city council. These three immediately cast their lots with a local Center-Right coalition to maintain a Christian Democrat in the mayor's office. In the national elections of April 1948 the neo-Fascists won slightly under 2 percent of the ballots, enough to elect six deputies and a senator to Parliament.[76]

A few of Mussolini's *gerarchi*, notably Filippo Anfuso and Rodolfo Graziani, reentered parliamentary life as MSI candidates. The Fascist propagandist and veterans' leader Carlo Delcroix was elected in 1953 as a monarchist deputy. However, neo-Fascist political activity did not necessarily signal a return of the PNF of Mussolini's *ventennio*. Its appearance in the late 1940s angered many, particularly veterans of the Resistance, but the MSI was then, and still is, little more than a fringe organization that commands about 6 percent of the popular vote.

More profound than the MSI, and more elusive, has been the other consequence of the failure of sanctions: persistent fascist tendencies in Italian society and government. The most important case in examining the effect of sanctions, or their failure, is what had been the center of that storm, the state bureaucracy.

Robert Putnam's attitudinal study of British, German, and Italian government functionaries in the early 1970s clearly demonstrated that the last-named were the most antipluralist, antidemocratic, and alienated. Ninety-five percent of Italy's senior civil servants in 1971 had begun their careers before 1943. But Putnam also concluded that time was taking its toll, and, within eight years or so, the aged cohort would retire. Sabino Cassese also noted the weeding-out process in his 1974 work, prompting him to question whether Claudio Pavone's concept of "continuity" still held relevance. Although the makers of Italy's postwar state "passed over" the government workers, a profound change had begun that would affect everyone. By the 1950s, Cassese wrote, old prewar and new postwar bureaucracies stood side by side; and by the 1960s, a great mutation of Italy's governance had begun that would render irrelevant the legacies of Mussolini's regime. Furthermore, despite the antidemocratic sentiments noted in Putnam's study, Italy's bureaucracy, particularly its elders, has generally refrained from political action. Putnam attributed this in part to a bitterness, and also to Karl Mannheim's rule that "the fundamental tendency of all bureaucratic thought is to turn all problems of politics into problems of administration." Disdain and avoidance of political squabbles are strong impulses in the state apparatus, and Italy's was no exception in the twenty or thirty years after World War II. Italy's civil servants complied with the creation of the republic and with the nation's drift away from fascism. With the probable exception of segments within the military, Radical Right revivals and threats to overthrow the state have not originated or found strong support among state workers. In his work from the early 1970s, in fact, Mattei Dogan found Europe's most highly politicized and, perhaps, even most dangerous bureaucratic corps to be not in Italy but in Austria.[77]

The Fernando Tambroni political debacle of 1960 serves to illustrate that the wounds of Mussolini's dictatorship had yet to be fully healed, however, in other areas of Italian politics and society. The prosperous, dynamic Italy of 1960 appeared a far cry from the Duce's *ventennio*, but events at that time revealed that sympathetic elements had been waiting in the wings and would surface in political organizations other than the MSI.

Fernando Tambroni, a Christian Democrat known as a moderate leftist, had been entrusted the task of forming a routine stop-gap cabinet to see Italy through the summer of 1960 and the Rome Olympic Games. The DC had been hard-pressed to construct a government since it had kept Nenni's Socialist party out of ruling arrangements since 1947, and, after a decade of electoral shrinkage, coalitions had become more and more necessary to maintain Christian Democratic leadership.[78] In desperation, Tambroni assembled a single-party, or *monocolore*, cabinet based on DC strength and reliant only on an MSI guarantee not to vote against it. Thus, although no "missini" held cabinet positions, Tambroni's arrangement was in some form indebted to neo-Fascists. Even these narrow measures, however, enraged large segments of the population, and Italy suffered its worst riots since the war. Against the demonstrators, the prime minister employed the antiriot *celere* squads, which used traditionally Fascist tactics, including the blare of the trumpet before surrounding the disturbance with mobile units. Deaths in Reggio nell'Emilia, Palermo, and Genoa further infuriated the Left. The government collapsed and a broken Tambroni resigned, ending up as an obscure fringe character in the party until his premature death in 1962.

The crisis revealed that, even in 1960, strong and important currents remained in the population that might acquiesce to at least a Fascistic element in the government. Tambroni's arrogance and anti-Marxist belligerence may have been politically ill advised and certainly led to the collapse of his *monocolore* ministry. But the most remarkable phenomenon of his brief administration was the broad and vociferous support it received from the forces of traditionalist Italy. Big business, through its organization, Confindustria, and its journals, *Il Globo* and *24 Ore*, hailed Tambroni as "the investor's savior." Catholic support was also fundamental. Along with DC endorsement, Tambroni relied on important lay organizations such as the Christian Union of Business and Managers, Catholic University students, and the nationwide civic committees. Even key ecclesiastics, particularly Genoa's Cardinal Siri, applauded Tambroni. However, the Center-Right was not prepared to continue its support in the face of serious opposition. When the Left took to the streets, the traditionalists abandoned the prime minister as they had abandoned another one seventeen years before.[79]

The fall of Tambroni did not end right-wing intrigue. In 1964 a clique of officers led by General Giovanni De Lorenzo planned a coup d'état, but it never materialized. The left-wing press alleged the complicity of President Antonio Segni and Italian military intelligence in that aborted attempt. Another example occurred in 1970 when the "Black Prince," Valerio Borghese, who had been tried after the war for collaboration, led an unsuccessful coup that was closely tied to the MSI. His activities, like De Lorenzo's, were linked to highly placed government officials, military intelligence, and the American Central Intelligence Agency.[80]

But the most important plot was uncovered in the P-2 scandal of the 1980s. A Masonic lodge in Tuscany, the P-2 was the center of an entangled web that stretched from the Council of Ministers to the Vatican, big business, and military intelligence. The coordinator of the conspiracy was a neo-Fascist mattress maker from Arezzo, Licio Gelli. Gelli had served the Duce in Spain and later as a diehard in the RSI. After the war he moved to Argentina for a few years and gained some notoriety as a Peronista.[81]

On May 27, 1981, authorities raided the P-2 and discovered a list of 953 lodge members that included some of the most important men in Italy. Most of the nation's top intelligence officials were represented as well as thirty generals, eight admirals, forty-three members of Parliament, and three cabinet ministers. A diplomatic source indicated that the group's primary goal was to ensure that a Salvador Allende type of government would never surface in Italy. The blanket covering the P-2's aims and activities has yet to be completely uncovered; nevertheless, it has become apparent that the political tool of the plotters was not only the MSI but also important factions of other parties, particularly the Social Democrats and the DC itself.[82]

The problems inherent in the revival of the MSI, the Tambroni disaster, and the other postwar crises are much the same ones encountered in the story of sanctions against fascism. The questions center on the places both of fascism and of Fascists in Italy after 1945. Had the Italy of the 1920s and 1930s experienced a dictatorship of the most reactionary elements of a dying capitalism, or rather, in a narrower sense, the takeover of a radical right-wing political party? In its broad Marxian conception, fascism, as a manifestation of capitalist-ruling class control, had not been defeated in World War II. The forces of advanced capitalism that had fostered Mussolini's regime in 1922 had persisted and surfaced again in the Tambroni debacle and in the P-2 lodge. On the other hand, there can be no question that World War II ended Fascist control of Italy in the strict political sense that PNF power had been broken.

A defense of sanctions points to the absence of dictatorship in Italy after the war. What eventually replaced the regime was a constitutional, republican form of government, characterized by aims largely different from the Duce's. It is inconceivable today that the Italian Republic would launch any type of ideological militarization of society or expansionist foreign policy. Although the bureaucracy had emerged relatively intact after sanctions had ended, the government it served had been significantly altered. There was no longer any Fascist Grand Council in 1947. There was no OVRA, no Tribunal for the Defense of the State, and no Chamber of Fasces and Corporations. To be sure, some institutions remained. For example, the parastatal Istituto per la Ricostruzione Industriale (IRI), an organization established by the Duce in the 1930s that inaugurated a long history of important government intervention in the economy, was maintained and strengthened after the war. Mussolini's Opera Nazionale Dopolavoro (OND), the workers' leisure organization, is another that persisted as Ente nazionale assistenza lavoratori (ENAL). However, the IRI is not a bastion of Fascist power and is considered more as a political white elephant. ENAL, furthermore, is no OND. Victoria De Grazia has termed it "no more than a government social service funded by revenues from a national lottery."[83] In this sense, then, rejection of the thesis that the postwar Italian state was truly different from the prewar one requires serious modification.[84]

Sanctions against fascism, as studied here, moreover, were not directed at the state's machinery but rather at its members, functionaries, or leaders. And the lack of success against state employees ensured that the program would never be the first assault in a truly revolutionary restructuring of Italian relationships between power, wealth, and class. Those beyond the narrowly defined "state," those who controlled Italy's society and economy in 1948, emerged essentially from the same group who had controlled it in 1939 and in 1921. In their mild, final form, the sanctions battle ended as a victory of traditionalists in the ruling class over more radical Left forces. A moderate policy of selective punishment won out over aspirations to fit sanctions into a broader plan aimed at a restructured Italian society. The inherently slow and complex methods of a tepid purge and limited trials, whether undertaken consciously or not, was the wrong means to process and try large numbers of people, and it was an indication that few Fascists would languish in prisons.

Sanctions were then further sabotaged by the political Center-Right, the bureaucracy, and tendencies in Italian culture to avoid political punishment, to focus on collaborationists, and to concentrate on the visible elements within the regime. The sorry results of the sanctions program lend credence to the thesis of Claudio Pavone and others that fascism remained particularly among those who had most mattered in perpetuating the social status quo under Mussolini—many who had been cast from the same mold as those who had supported Tambroni and had probably participated in the P-2 Lodge.[85]

As postwar Italy's largest and strongest political formation, with the most socially diverse following among the CLN coalition, the Christian Democrats must draw particular mention in the balance sheet on sanctions. Their policies, and ambiguities, were decisive in determining the treatment of fascism and Fascists in the new Italy. The highest rank of the DC leadership was truly anti-Fascist as was much of its electorate; but the party also represented large segments of the middle class, which had bided its time and had fared not too badly during the *ventennio*. Sanctions must have made them uneasy. As a whole, however, Christian Democrats undoubtedly recognized that the threatened Marxist revolution would never succeed and, thus, neither would truly radical sanctions. Christian Democracy was acting from a position of strength, and its consideration of purges and trials were not based on fear. It could afford to approach them with a healthy element of propriety, fairness, and mercy, which were inherent components of its principles.

Much of the balance sheet also rests on the concept of sabotage from the Right and does not consider the failure of the Left to promote a revolutionary change. Important factions within the Resistance dedicated themselves to serious sanctions, but the Communists, particularly in Rome, along with certain moderately leftist forces, worked against them. Socialists and *azionisti* were honest and determined in their goals to make Italy more democratic and less fascist, but the Communists were not. Willing to abandon long-term ideals for short-term rewards, the Communist party must bear part of the guilt. Certainly much of this position was based on a frank analysis of the post-war situation: an armed socialist uprising in 1945 would have been suicidal. But the Left lacked even a concerted, serious plan to implement sanctions. The famous "Wind from the North" proved just that —wind. No storm followed it. By the end of the war the great power on the Left was no longer the waning Socialists but the Communists, and Togliatti's decision to soft-pedal stringent anti-Fascist measures cut the momentum of the Left in half.

Finally, one must return to the fact that Italy no longer suffers under a Fascist dictatorship. Unrepentant bureaucrats and the Byzantine machinations of right-wing industrial and commercial leaders have posed some serious threats; but Italy is not alone in this dilemma, and other countries with no Fascist legacies have also experienced it. Italy has faced these crises and has overcome them; it has become a republic with open politics and a voting public that elects its representatives. It is a troubled republic, to be sure, but it is not a police state. Italy is, in the Western sense, a free country. Institutional leadership still consists of the victorious CLN coalition: Christian Democrats, Communists, Socialists, and the "Lay" parties.

NOTES

CHAPTER 1

1. Warner, *Pierre Laval and the Eclipse of France*, pp. 411–16.

2. Interestingly, after his litany of invectives, Streicher's last words, spoken under his black hood, were discerned by reporters as "Adele, my dear wife." Snyder, *National Socialist Germany*, pp. 201–2.

3. Regime change or transition is a vast subject that, perhaps due to its overarching importance in history, has rarely been studied as a phenomenon unto itself. Regarding Italy, the topic has been dealt with in an excellent bibliographical treatise. See Diamandourous et al., *Bibliographical Essay on Southern Europe*.

4. A. R. Radcliffe Brown defined sanctions in the 1937 *Encyclopedia of the Social Sciences* as "a reaction on the part of society or of a considerable number of its members to a mode of behavior which is thereby approved (positive sanctions) or disapproved (negative sanctions)." In the 1968 revision of the encyclopedia, however, A. L. Epstein contended that Radcliffe Brown's analysis was too jurisprudential and did no go far enough to explain social control. Similar debates surrounded Italian sanctions against Fascists. The experience of World War II undoubtedly affected this definition. It is also interesting to note that the 1968 edition contained an entry on punishment, whereas the 1937 did not. *Encyclopedia of the Social Sciences*, 1937, s.v. "sanctions." *International Encyclopedia of the Social Sciences*, 1968, s.v. "punishment," "sanctions."

5. Regarding the Terror, see Palmer, *Twelve Who Ruled*.

6. Kirchheimer, *Political Justice*, p. 305. J. H. Plumb implied the same thing when he discussed the political processes at work after the Glorious Revolution in his *Origins of Political Stability*, Introduction.

7. An enormous collection of theoretical analyses and historical works deals with the nature of fascism. Among the most important must be included the thoughts of Mussolini and the leading philosophers of the movement. A number of useful English translations of the Duce, Giovanni Gentile, and others can be found in Lyttleton, *Italian Fascisms*, and Halperin, *Mussolini and Italian Fascism*. Some of the most important interpretations of fascism as an ideology include Nolte, *Three Faces of Fascism*; Gregor, *Interpretations of Fascism*; Laqueur, *Fascism: A Reader's Guide*; Salvemini, *The Origin of Fascism in Italy*; Renzo De Felice, *Interpretations of Fascism*; and Forgacs, *Rethinking Italian Fascism*. Also germane to the discussion are important works on the history of the Fascist regime such as Renzo De Felice's monumental biography of Mussolini, partic-

ularly, *Mussolini il Duce*; Denis Mack Smith, *Mussolini*; Lyttleton, *Seizure of Power*; and Aquarone, *L'Organizzazione dello stato totalitario*.

8. The list of contributions to this debate must include Gramsci, *Quaderni del carcere*; Togliatti, *Lectures on Fascism*; Gregor, *Italian Fascism and Developmental Dictatorship*; Juan Linz, "Some Notes toward a Comparative Study of Fascism in Sociological Historical Perspective," in Laqueur, *Fascism: A Reader's Guide*, pp. 3–121. Important works on the nature of society and power considered here include Mayer, *Persistence of the Old Regime*; Maier, *Recasting Bourgeois Europe*; Maier, "The Two Postwar Eras"; Keller, *Beyond the Ruling Class*; Michels, *Political Parties*; Mills, *The Power Elite*; Mosca, *The Ruling Class*; Pareto, *The Mind and Society*; Pareto, *The Rise and Fall of Elites*; and Pareto, *Sociological Writings*.

9. Renzo De Felice, *Mussolini il Duce*, 1:758; see also De Grazia, *The Culture of Consent*, pp. 221–24.

10. Andreotti, *Concerto a sei voci*, pp. 47–48.

11. Paolo Sylos Labini has presented data on working-class voting behavior that illustrates a strong conservative impulse. No statistical evidence of working-class political sympathies during the *ventennio* can be had, but subsequent polls illustrate that in no way can the workers be relied upon as a solid Communist or Socialist bloc. In the 1968 elections, of 15.7 million working-class ballots, 6.4 million, almost half, went to Christian Democracy, the Liberal party, and the neo-Fascists. Sylos Labini, *Saggio sulle classi sociali*, p. 191. See also B. Salvati, "The Rebirth of Trade Unionism, 1943–1954" in Woolf, *The Rebirth of Italy*.

12. Tannenbaum, *The Fascist Experience*, p. 3; Sauer, "National Socialism"; Sylos Labini, *Saggio sulle classi sociali*, pp. 73–79; Mayer, "The Lower Middle Class as Historical Problem," pp. 409–36.

13. Adrian Lyttleton stated that the Duce's "revolution" never won over all Italian conservative forces. "Mussolini's own personal freedom of action was restricted both by the resistance of the old order and the State Machinery." Lyttleton, *Seizure of Power*, p. 9.

14. Ibid., pp. 94–95, 241, 307. The role taken by Cesare Maria De Vecchi di Val Cismon as liaison between Mussolini and the crown and church also serves to illustrate the relationship between fascism and the old order.

15. Its leading student, Giorgio Rochat, considers the military the least democratic force in Italy. Rochat, "L'esercito e il fascismo," in Quazza, *Fascismo e società italiana*, pp. 89–123. Concerning relations between the armed forces and the regime, see also Lyttleton, *Seizure of Power*, and Knox, *Mussolini Unleashed*. For apologias, by a royalist officer, see Pugliese, *Io difendo l'esercito*, and by a Fascist officer, see Graziani, *Ho difeso la patria*. The military contained some sincerely progressive elements. During the immediate postwar years, which concern this work, the most famous was General Armando Azzi. Regarding Azzi, see *Italia Libera*, December 24, 1944; *Avanti!*, December 28, 1944; *L'Unità*, December 28, 1944; and *Manchester Guardian*, January 9, 1945.

16. The church, with its enormous network of lay organizations and its own diocesan structure, was, in effect, the largest and most powerful alternative to fascism during the *ventennio*. The standard works on church/state relations are Binchy, *Church and State in Fascist Italy*; Jemolo, *Chiesa e stato in Italia negli ultimi cento anni*; Webster, *The Cross and the Fasces*; Kent, *The Pope and the Duce*; Pollard, *The Vatican and Italian Fascism*; and the contributions of Richard J. Wolff and Frank J. Coppa in Wolff and Hoensch, *Catholics, the State, and the European Radical Right*.

17. Arno Mayer states that while, in the final analysis, Rome's "black" aristocracy supported the Duce against the forces of Bolshevism, it did so grudgingly. Mayer, *Persistence of the Old Regime*, pp. 123–27 (regarding the attitude of the Black Aristocracy toward the Italian state, see pp. 124, 149). Mayer's excellent transnational study serves further to illustrate that there still exists a great need for substantial work on Italy's aristocracy during the nineteenth and twentieth centuries.

18. Canosa, *La Magistratura in Italia*; Giuseppe Neppi-Modona, "La Magistratura e il fascismo," in Quazza, *Fascismo e società italiana*, pp. 125–81; Galante Garrone, "La Magistratura italiana fra fascismo e resistenza." The structure of the Italian magistracy was such that it placed itself in an inferior, almost bureaucratic, capacity under the Ministry of Justice. The Statuto of 1848 and subsequent laws simultaneously emphasized this position and confused it. Loyalties came to be split between Royal executive power and political executive power. Article 68 of the Statuto proclaimed that "Justice emanates from the King and is administered in his name by the judges which he appoints." Paradoxically, article 26, the Ratazzi Law of 1853, and the Orlando Law of 1907 (Royal Decree 511) emphasize the power of surveillance retained by the Ministry of Justice over the legal profession. Canosa, *La Magistratura in Italia*, pp. 7–12, 22–23.

19. See Sarti, *Fascism and Industrial Leadership*. See also Delzell, *Mussolini's Enemies*; Rossi, *Padroni del vapore e fascismo*, pp. 11–15, 50–51; and Sylos Labini, *Saggio sulle classi sociali*, p. 24.

20. Michels has written, "There is no essential contradiction between the doctrine that history is the record of a continual series of class struggles and the doctrine that class struggles inevitably culminate in the creation of new oligarchies which undergo fusion with the old. The existence of a political class does not conflict with the essential content of Marxism, considered not as an economic dogma but as a philosophy of history; for in each particular instance the dominance of a political class arises as a result of the relationships between the different social forces competing for supremacy, these forces being of course considered dynamically and not quantitatively." Michels, *Political Parties*, pp. 390–91.

21. Bottomore, *Classes in Society*, p. 5; Mosca, *The Ruling Class*, pp. 50–53.

22. Claudio Pavone has acknowledged that distinctions between the state and the Fascist party, detailed in the works of historians such as Alberto

Aquarone and F. W. Deakin, confuse the thesis of the continuity of the state through the postwar years. Pavone, "La continuità dello stato," in Piscitelli et al., *Italia, 1945–1948*, pp. 148–49.

23. Pareto, *The Rise and Fall of Elites*, p. 27.

24. Kirchheimer, *Political Justice*, p. 308–19.

25. Barton L. Ingraham devoted the first two chapters in his work to a discussion of the validity of the notion of political crime. Ingraham, *Political Crime in Europe*, pp. 3–36, 223. Otto Kirchheimer noted that trials for the "disposal" of political enemies was a "practice beyond the constitutional pale." Kirchheimer, *Political Justice*, p. 95.

26. Arendt, *Eichmann in Jerusalem*, pp. 250–52.

27. Matt. 5:7, 38, 39; 7:1–5; 18:21–22. Claudio Pavone and Costanzo Casucci have also noticed a moral argument presented by the Liberal party of Benedetto Croce. Pavone, "La continuità dello stato," in Piscitelli et al., *Italia, 1945–1948*, pp. 230–32.

28. Keller, *Beyond the Ruling Class*, p. 20.

29. Ibid., pp. 153–71. See also Weber, *Max Weber on Charisma and Institution Building*; Clifford Geertz, "Centers, Kings, and Charisma," in Ben-David and Clark, *Culture and Its Creators*, pp. 150–71; and Shils, "Charisma, Order, and Status."

CHAPTER 2

1. Regarding the Armistice and the events of September 8 and 9, see Garland and Smyth, *Sicily and the Surrender of Italy*, pp. 469–539. See also Bertoldi, *Contro Salò*, pp. 11–24; Degli Espinosa, *Il Regno del Sud*, pp. 11–20; Zangrandi, *1943*, pp. 379–440; Delzell, "Allied Policy," pp. 31–32; and Woodward, *British Foreign Policy in the Second World War*, pp. 461–500. Italy was not accorded full Allied status in the war against Hitler. Rather, as a former enemy, Italy had to, in Winston Churchill's words, "work her passage" at a lesser rank. See Harris, *Allied Administration*, pp. 129–32.

2. Harris, *Allied Administration*, p. 102; Mercuri, *1943–1945*, p. 366; Mercuri, *L'Epurazione*, p. 17 n. 2; Conti, "Aspetti della riorganizzazione delle forze armate nel Regno del Sud," pp. 85–120. War Ministry guidelines, dated April 5, 1945, which regularized the transfer from MVSN to the military, can be found in Archivio Centrale dello Stato (hereafter cited ACS) Presidenza del Consiglio dei Ministri (hereafter cited PCM) 1944–47 1/7 10124 s16-15, b. 111.

3. Roberto Battaglia, *Storia della Resistenza italiana*, p. 64; Zangrandi, *1943*, pp. 186–92. For an account in English of the Forty-five Days, see Delzell, *Mussolini's Enemies*, pp. 223–58. Regarding Badoglio's repression of public demonstrations elsewhere, see Ganapini and Legnani, *L'Italia dei quarantacinque giorni*, pp. 24–37, 214–76 (see particularly the accounts of the riots in Bari at the end of July, pp. 257–59).

4. Deakin, *Storia della Repubblica di Salò*, pp. 511–13; Ganapini and Legnani, *L'Italia dei quarantacinque giorni*, p. 147; Senise, *Quando ero capo della polizia*, pp. 225–28; Zangrandi, *1943*, pp. 225–34. The journalist M. deWyss estimated that seven hundred Fascists were arrested by Badoglio in the late August roundup. DeWyss, *Rome under the Terror*, p. 93. See also Bonomi, *Diario di un anno*, pp. 80–82.

5. Caccia to Macmillan, December 5, 1943, Public Record Office, Surrey (hereafter cited PRO) FO898 File 168; Psychological Warfare Branch (hereafter cited PWB) report, November 17, 1943, ibid.; Klibansky (British Intelligence) to Percy Lorraine (Foreign Office), November 23, 1943, ibid. See also Harris, *Allied Administration*, p. 135. Harold Caccia, one of the top Allied political analysts in Italy, considered Jung to be the best man in the Italian government, noting that inexperienced ministers deferred to him on many questions.

6. PWB report, November 18, 1943, PRO FO898 File 168.

7. Regarding Mario Roatta, see Scarlett to Dixon, October 1, 1943, PRO FO371 37360/9544; and Political Warfare Executive (hereafter cited PWE) report, October 6, 1943, ibid. In November the Allies pressured Badoglio to replace Roatta with General Giovanni Messe. Messe had commanded Mussolini's troops in the Soviet Union and in North Africa.

8. The case of Renato Prunas is particularly illustrative. In cabinet deliberations, Prunas's appointment as secretary general in the Foreign Office was opposed by the *azionista* Alberto Cianca and by the Socialist Giuseppe Saragat, on the grounds that he had served the Fascists in too high a position. Research and Analysis report 2688, March 17, 1945, National Archives and Records Service (hereafter cited NARS) RG59 Lot files.

9. Pieri and Rochat, *Pietro Badoglio*, pp. 773–74.

10. Missori, *Governi, alti cariche dello stato e prefetti*; Zangrandi, *1943*, pp. 129–89. Regarding employment of Fascists, including one as head of the Caltanisetta purge commission, see Research and Analysis report 2688, March 17, 1945, NARS RG59 Lot files.

11. Nicola Gallerano, "L'Influenza alleata in Italia," in Legnani, *L'Italia dal 1943 al 1948*, p. 94. In 1944 Pieche was placed on the reserve list and was made prefect of Ancona. Mercuri, *L'Epurazione*, pp. 121–22.

12. ACS PCM Gab 1943–44 Salerno 3/4 f. 2.

13. Ibid.

14. Ibid.

15. Harris, *Allied Administration*, p. 48; Mercuri, *1943–1945*, p. 149.

16. Harris, *Allied Administration*, pp. 106–8. See also James Edward Miller, *The United States and Italy*, pp. 131–33, 195–96; and Woodward, *British Foreign Policy in the Second World War*, pp. 501–8. For texts of the Short and Long armistices, see Garland and Smyth, *Sicily and the Surrender of Italy*, Appendixes C and D. Regarding the Moscow Declaration, see Harris, *Allied Administration*, p. 126.

17. Mercuri, *L'Epurazione*, p. 23.

18. Major C. A. H. Harrison to Division of War Plans, December 3, 1943, PRO FO898 File 168; Lucas to Percy Lorraine, January 5, 1944, ibid. For Churchill's opinions of the monarchy, see Churchill, *Closing the Ring*, pp. 201–2. In particular, see p. 188: "From the moment when the Armistice was signed and when the Italian fleet loyally and courageously joined the Allies, I felt myself bound to work with the King of Italy and Marshal Badoglio, at least until Rome should be occupied by the Allies and we could construct a really broad-based Italian Government for the prosecution of the war jointly with us. I was sure that King Victor Emmanuel and Badoglio would be able to do more for what had now become the common cause than any Italian Government formed from the exiles or opponents of the Fascist regime. The surrender of the Italian fleet was solid proof of their authority."

19. Delzell, "Allied Policy," p. 36.

20. Delzell, *Mussolini's Enemies*, pp. 198–202, 204–5. See also Diggins, *Mussolini and Italian Fascism*, pp. 414–21. Adolf Berle at the State Department was in regular contact with Carlo Sforza, although he held some reservations about him. On January 1, 1942, Berle wrote, "He is not ideal, and his anti-clerical views will make trouble, but I see nothing else." Berle and Jacobs, *Navigating the Rapids*, p. 393.

21. Delzell, "Allied Policy," pp. 29, 32–33. For an American account of the Darlan debacle, see Murphy, *Diplomat among Warriors*, pp. 156–65.

22. Eisenhower to CCS, September 30, 1943, in Coles and Weinberg, *Civil Affairs*, p. 236.

23. Macmillan, *The Blast of War*, pp. 329–30. See also Macmillan, *War Diaries*, pp. 412–20.

24. Murphy, *Diplomat among Warriors*, pp. 198–99. Harry Hopkins has also been credited with the "gaga" comment.

25. Edelman, "Incremental Involvement," pp. 10, 60, 134.

26. Mason-Macfarlane to Eisenhower, November 2, 1943, NARS ACC file 10000/100/4; Eisenhower to Mason-Macfarlane, n.d., in Coles and Weinberg, *Civil Affairs*, p. 432.

27. Stettinius to Roosevelt, February 14, 1944, NARS RG 59 865.01/1060a. The acting secretary of state wrote, "You may rest assured that we will take all action necessary to ensure that no effort is made by this government to effect any change in the existing government of Italy at the present time and until our military situation in the Italian campaign is sufficiently improved to warrant any possible risk in the implementation of our position."

28. Harris, *Allied Administration*, pp. 1–29, 105–25; Macmillan, *War Diaries*, pp. 366–67; Mercuri, *1943–1945*, pp. 145–47; Ellwood, *L'alleato nemico*, pp. 228–39.

29. Regarding the different approaches taken by the two powers toward Allied administration, see Mercuri, *1943–1945*, pp. 43–59, 145–47.

30. *New York Herald Tribune*, July 25, 1943; Poletti Papers 195 s45.

31. *Chicago Tribune,* July 25, 1943; Poletti Papers 195 s45.

32. Macmillan, *War Diaries,* pp. 397–98.

33. Directive, HQ, AMG to RCAOs Regions I and II, December 4, 1943, NARS CAD Files 319.1 AMG 8-17-43 Sec. 2; Directive, Region III, AMG to all SCAOs, December 20, 1943, ibid., Sec. 3. These materials can be found in Coles and Weinberg, *Civil Affairs,* pp. 385–86.

34. Neufeld, "The Failure of Allied Military Government in Italy." See also Neufeld's chapter in Friedrich, *American Experiences in Military Government in World War Two,* pp. 111–47.

35. Neufeld admired Poletti and felt that he was the most capable administrator among the Allies. He believed that Poletti's success was the result of his political and administrative experience in America. Neufeld, personal correspondence with author. C. F. R. Harris spoke for the regular military when he wrote that much confusion resulted from "indiscriminate zeal" of younger field security personnel and counterintelligence corps officers. Harris, *Allied Administration,* pp. 49, 112–14.

36. Headquarters AMG report, October 1943, NARS ACC files 10000/101/501, in Coles and Weinberg, *Civil Affairs,* p. 384.

37. Rennell Rodd to Allied Forces Headquarters (hereafter cited AFHQ), July 3, 1943, in Coles and Weinberg, *Civil Affairs,* p. 185.

38. Churchill, *The War Speeches,* 2:367–68. See also K. Duff in Toynbee and Toynbee, *Survey of International Relations, 1939–1946,* 6:410–11. On July 27, 1943, Churchill reiterated before the House of Commons that Germany was the enemy to be dealt with and that all decisions regarding Italy should be made with that in mind. Churchill, *Winston Spencer Churchill,* p. 6812.

39. Stimson to Hull, April 22, 1944, NARS RG59 865.01/2392; Solborg to Bissell, April 8, 1944, ibid.; Grandi to Stimson, March 1, 1944, ibid.; Hill to Dunn, April 25, 1944, NARS RG59 865.01/2393; Churchill to Orme Sargeant, January 21, 1947, PRO FO371 6780/A; Ennio Di Nolfo, "The Shaping of Italian Foreign Policy during the Formation of the East-West Blocs: Italy between the Superpowers," in Becker and Knipping, *Power in Europe,* pp. 488–89.

40. Stone to Bonomi, November 16, 1944, ACS PCM 1944–47 1/7 10124 s. 37, b. 117.

41. Harris, *Allied Administration,* p. 37.

42. NARS CAD files 461.01 4-7-43 (1) bulky package, in Coles and Weinberg, *Civil Affairs,* p. 192. See also Harris, *Allied Administration,* pp. 37–42.

43. Regarding the employment of "moderate Fascists," see Rossini, *Democrazia cristiana e costituente,* p. 733. See also Joseph Bonfiglio report, April 22, 1944, NARS RG226 E190 Box 99 f. 148.

44. Maj. F. W. Tooby to Domenico Boffito, Comitato di Liberazione Nazionale dell'Alta Italia (hereafter cited CLNAI), CCE, June 30, 1945, Merzagora Papers, b.1 f.1. See also Lewis, *Naples '44,* pp. 32–33.

45. Neufeld, "The Failure of Allied Military Government in Italy," p. 140.

46. Monthly report, February 1944, Poletti Papers 194 s32. The AMG's Col-

onel Hume noted that "great difficulty is experienced in finding suitable persons to replace former Fascist officials who are acceptable to the people." Hume report, January 28, 1944, in Coles and Weinberg, *Civil Affairs*, p. 386.

47. Coles and Weinberg, *Civil Affairs*, pp. 474–76; Mercuri, *L'Epurazione*, pp. 30–31. OSS report, May 14, 1944, NARS RG226/125/51 f. 439.

48. Poletti memorandum no. 4, October 30, 1944, Poletti Papers 194 s30.

49. Poletti to Murphy, December 10, 1943, ibid., 194 s4.

50. Poletti report, August 31, 1943, ibid., 194 s26.

51. Chief of Political Intelligence Section for Chiefs of Staff report, NARS CAD files 319.1 Foreign (1), November 1, 1943, in Coles and Weinberg, *Civil Affairs*, pp. 383–84. See also Bracci, "Come naque l'amnistia," pp. 1090–107. For an account of Germany's equivalent of the *scheda* that rings as cynical as the attitude of the Italians, see Salomon, *Fragebogen, The Questionnaire*.

52. "Z" to OSS, May 4, 1944, NARS RG226 70243.

53. De Antonellis, *Le quattro giornate di Napoli*, pp. 152–54. Hume report, September 9–December 15, 1943, NARS ACC 10000/129/167, in Coles and Weinberg, *Civil Affairs*, p. 281; Bertoldi, *Contro Salò*, pp. 223–24.

54. Hume report, September 9–December 15, 1943, NARS ACC 10000/129/167; NARS ACC 10000/100/1093, in Coles and Weinberg, *Civil Affairs*, p. 384; Klibansky to Percy Lorraine, December 23, 1943, PRO FO898 File 168. Klibansky indicated that Frignani was later arrested but the Vatican petitioned for his release.

55. Monthly report, May 10, 1944, Poletti Papers 194 s32.

56. Allied Commission in Italy, *Review of Allied Military Government*, p. 2.

57. Minutes of ACC meeting, April 14, 1944, PRO FO371 43285 R9487.

58. ACS Regio governo italiano, scatola 1 f.36 b.1. Regarding the situation on Sardinia, see Ugo Pirro's perceptive novel, *A Thousand Betrayals*.

59. PWB reports on liberated Italy, September 18, 1943, and November 16, 1944, PRO FO371 R43974 pp. 286, 325. For a somewhat different account see Harris, *Allied Administration*, pp. 102–3. Harris notes that much of the investigation was initiated by the British commanding officer on the island. It was discovered that much of the evidence had been duplicated, and Martini was brought to trial in 1944.

60. Fabris to Interior Ministry, February 5, 1944, ACS Regio governo italiano, scatola 1 f.36 b.1.

61. Hoover report, April 21, 1944, in Coles and Weinberg, *Civil Affairs*, p. 387.

62. Charles to Eden, April 28, 1944, PRO FO371 43857 1944 File 91 R7391; NARS CAD files 334 ACC 8-17-43 sec. 2, in Coles and Weinberg, *Civil Affairs*, p. 387. On the Advisory Commission, see Ellwood, *Italy, 1943–1945*, pp. 46, 83–85.

63. ACS Regio governo italiano, scatola 1 f.36 b.1.

64. Macmillan, *War Diaries*, pp. 329–37; Aga Rossi and Smith, *Operation Sunrise*, pp. 13–14.

65. Macmillan, *War Diaries*, p. 220; Mercuri, *1943–1945*, pp. 129–30.

66. Arangio-Ruiz to Badoglio, April 27, 1944, ACS PCM 1944–47 1/7 10124 b. 111 s.16; Casati to Badoglio, April 22, 1944, ibid. Marcello Flores considered Arangio-Ruiz to be one of the few in Badoglio's cabinet who truly advocated sanctions. Flores, "L'Epurazione," in Atti del convegno internazionale organizzato a Firenze il 26–28 Marzo 1976 con il concorso della regione Toscana/INSMLI, *L'Italia dalla liberazione alla repubblica*, pp. 418–19. However, in cabinet arguments it appears that Casati's calls went further than Arangio-Ruiz's, and disputes frequently raged between the two.

67. Badoglio's decision to broaden the complexion of his cabinet was due, again in part, to Allied pressure. Mercuri, *1943–1945*, pp. 47, 163–64, 168.

68. The meeting was originally to take place in Naples, but the Allies vetoed the location on account of an anti-Savoyard demonstration held there. Delzell, "Allied Policy," p. 38.

69. Regarding the formation of the first CLN in Rome, see Delzell, *Mussolini's Enemies*, pp. 271–73. For a summary of the coalescence of the CLN parties, see ibid., pp. 207–22.

70. A move, supported by the Socialist and Action parties, to declare the formation of a republic was scuttled by the Christian Democrats and the Communists. See also Croce, *Croce, the King, and the Allies*, pp. 70–74.

71. Harris, *Allied Administration*, pp. 147–49.

72. ACC Executive memo 67, "Guide for Initial Purge of Leading Fascists," April 7, 1945 (rev.), NARS ACC 10000/109/2110, in Coles and Weinberg, *Civil Affairs*, pp. 388–90. Casati to Badoglio, April 3, 1944, ACS PCM 1/7 10124 b. 111 s. 16.

73. The Zanardelli penal code of 1889 had abolished capital punishment in the Kingdom of Italy except in cases involving the military code. Mussolini reinstated it in 1926, and, already in March 1944, the Badoglio government had banned it in cases of common crimes.

74. "Z" to OSS, June 3, 1944, NARS RG226 74644; "Z" to OSS, June 15, 1944, ibid., RG226 76746; "Z" to OSS, June 20, 1944, ibid., RG226 80212; PWB report, Interview with Carlo Sforza, May 9, 1944, PRO FO371 43945; Rossini, *Democrazia cristiana e costituente*, pp. 778–95; Flores, "L'Epurazione," in Atti del convegno internazionale organizzato a Firenze il 26–28 Marzo 1976 con il concorso della regione Toscana/INSMLI, *L'Italia dalla liberazione alla repubblica*, pp. 414–19. On June 12, 1944, an enthusiastic OSS report indicated that the approval of the May 26 decree constituted "indisputable proof that the Italian people are determined to eradicate from their national life the evils of twenty-two years of Fascism." NARS RG226 E125 Box 51 f. 629. See also OSS report, May 13, 1944, ibid., f. 439.

75. "Z" to OSS, May 28, 1944, NARS RG226 77231.

76. Piovani and Contini to Omodeo, July 3, 1944, ACS PCM 1944–47 10124 1/7 s 3-1 b. 100. One vague reference to a sitting purge commission can be found in a memorandum from Lecce's Provincial Committee of Liberation to the Interior Ministry. In May 1944 the committee urged that the purge com-

mission be dissolved in anticipation of the new measures. The minister, however, vetoed that since the Anglo-Americans had been pestering him on its existence. ACS PCM 1944–47 1/7 10124 s16-1 bill.

CHAPTER 3

1. Piscitelli, *Storia della resistenza romana*, pp. 360–67. For accounts in English of the liberation, see Trevelyan, *Rome, 1944*, and Jackson, *The Battle for Rome*.

2. PWB report, part 2, "A PWB Officer's Impression on Liberated Rome," June 9, 1944, Poletti Papers 194 s8. This officer was entrusted with a specific task: to make contact with a future leader of Italy: "Two Swiss Guards welcomed us at the side [of St. Peter's] entrance. Then we asked for De Gasperi."

3. Regarding the Neapolitan uprising, see de Antonellis, *Le quattro giornate di Napoli*, pp. 109–40.

4. PRO FO371 43793 pp. 172–76.

5. An interesting first-hand account of life in the capital under the Nazi occupation can be found in deWyss, *Rome under the Terror*. It is also revealing that deWyss chose "Terror," a term so closely associated with the French Revolution, to describe the RSI administration of Rome. The word loses its political and historic specificity and becomes a generic concept emblematic of political excess.

6. *Il Corriere di Roma*, June 10, 1944.

7. The scramble for food looms throughout histories and accounts of wartime Italy. The example of Naples, for example, is poignantly described in Norman Lewis's *Naples '44*.

8. Monthly reports, August 9, 1944, and February 12, 1945, Poletti Papers 194 s32 and s34. Poletti felt that the food shortage cast the Allies in a bad light and that the Communists were exploiting the issue. Regarding the food crisis see Coakley and Leighton, *Global Logistics and Strategy*, pp. 773–79. Charles F. Delzell also discussed the low level of anti-Fascist reaction in Rome and posited that part of the reason must stem from the nature of the city as a bureaucratic and not an industrial place. Delzell, *Mussolini's Enemies*, pp. 385–89.

9. *Avanti!*, June 5–6, 1944.

10. Monthly report, part 1, February 12, 1945, Poletti Papers 194 s34.

11. *Risorgimento Liberale*, July 27, 1944.

12. *Italia Libera*, June 5, 1944.

13. Monthly report, July 9, 1944, Poletti Papers 194 s32.

14. PWB report, part 3, annex 22, June 9, 1944, ibid., 194 s8.

15. PWB interview with De Gasperi, June 7, 1944, ibid.

16. Churchill persisted in his support of the monarchy, but he could not ignore the rising prorepublicanist sentiment of the Roosevelt administration. In February 1944 Washington was ready to intervene unilaterally and end the monarchy but held off in order to maintain good relations with Britain. Roo-

sevelt wrote to Churchill, "I think . . . that you and I should regard this only as a reprieve for the two old gentlemen [Victor Emmanuel and Badoglio]. Churchill, *Closing the Ring*, pp. 501–5; Delzell, "Allied Policy," p. 39; Pinzani, "Gli Stati Uniti e la questione istituzionale in Italia."

17. Delzell, "Allied Policy," pp. 37, 39–40, 41.

18. Croce, *Croce, the King, and the Allies*, pp. 77, 106–10; Edelman, "Incremental Involvement," p. 167; Valiani, *Dall'antifascismo alla resistenza*, p. 124. See also Bertoldi, *Vittorio Emanuele III*.

19. Valiani, *Dall'antifascismo alla resistenza*, p. 137; Delzell, "Allied Policy," p. 42; Ennio Di Nolfo, "The Shaping of Italian Foreign Policy during the Formation of the East-West Blocs: Italy between the Superpowers," in Becker and Knipping, *Power in Europe*, p. 490.

20. Kogan, *Italy and the Allies*, pp. 76–79; Harris, *Allied Administration*, pp. 201–4; Edelman, "Incremental Involvement," pp. 131–32; Coles and Weinberg, *Civil Affairs*, p. 433.

21. Churchill to Charles, June 10 or 13, 1944, PRO FO371 43793 R9289.

22. Churchill to Roosevelt, March 13, 1944, C-618 21182/TOR 2255Z, in Kimball, *Churchill and Roosevelt*, 3:42; Churchill to Roosevelt, June 10, 1944, C-699 1943 Z, ibid., 3:176. See also Dilks, *The Diaries of Alexander Cadogan*. Churchill fumed to Cadogan, "This has been bungled . . . by that old woman Mason-Macfarlane" (ibid., p. 638). Nevertheless, the British did not exclude the possibility of an adequate substitute for Badoglio. See also Ellwood, *L'alleato nemico*, p. 280, and Delzell, *Mussolini's Enemies*, pp. 459–63. Regarding the pro-Bonomi OSS report, see OSS report, June 12, 1944, NARS RG226 E125 Box 51 f. 629.

23. Mercuri, *1943–1945*, pp. 229–40.

24. Bonomi wrote in 1948 that the primary goal of his administration was "the restoration of law and order." Pietro Barbieri, *Il Travaglio della democrazia cristiana 1943–1947*, Introduction (by Bonomi), p. 18. Bonomi to Roosevelt, July 2, 1944, NARS RG226 E125 Box 51 f. 629. See also Roberto Battaglia, *Storia della resistenza italiana*, pp. 240–41. Churchill's mollification over Bonomi has been mentioned in Delzell, *Mussolini's Enemies*, p. 392, and Kogan, *Italy and the Allies*, pp. 78–79.

25. PWB report, June 9, 1944, Poletti Papers 194 s8; Kirk to State Department, June 17, 1944, NARS RG59 865.01/2661.

26. Churchill, *Triumph and Tragedy*, pp. 115–16; Ellwood, *Italy, 1943–1945*, pp. 101–3; OSS report, October 6, 1944, NARS RG226 E190 Box 99 f. 148. Churchill undoubtedly enjoyed comparing the magnificence of Rome to the shabby look of CLN politicians, "the tiny and transient beings who flitted within its bounds." He noted his perfect agreement with Pope Pius XII on the subject of anticommunism and delighted in the "powerful and engaging personality" of the crown prince. "I certainly hoped," wrote Churchill, "he would play his part in building up a constitutional monarchy in a free, strong, united Italy." The irrepressible prime minister then added, "However, this was none of my business."

27. The sixth party in the CLN coalition was Bonomi's Labor Democrats. It was hardly a mass party and existed mainly as an association of some southern landowners and old-line northern liberals around the figure of Bonomi. His retirement from politics resulted in the party's demise. For a summary of its stance on sanctions, see Lucio D'Angelo, "I demolaburisti," in Bizzarri, *Epurazione e stampa di partito*, pp. 43–66.

28. Legnani, *L'Italia dal 1943 al 1948*, pp. 27–30.

29. Spriano, *Storia del Partito comunista italiano*, pp. 138–77; Roberto Battaglia, *Storia della resistenza italiana*, pp. 250–61; Delzell, "Allied Policy," pp. 40–41; Urban, *Moscow and the Italian Communist Party*, pp. 154–67, 172, 190–200.

30. *L'Unità*, June 29, 1944. Togliatti announced his *svolta* in an April 11 speech, "The Communist Policy on National Unity." See also Togliatti, *On Gramsci and Other Writings*, pp. 29–65. Regarding Togliatti's relations with Badoglio, see Pieri and Rochat, *Pietro Badoglio*, pp. 849–51; see also Tamburrano, *Palmiro Togliatti*. On Pietro Secchia, see Urban, *Moscow and the Italian Communist Party*, p. 171.

31. *L'Unità*, April 11, 1944, cited in Gambino, *Storia del dopoguerra*, p. 90.

32. On July 9 Togliatti reiterated his support for conservative elements within the CLN coalition. Before an audience at the Teatro Brancaccio he repeated, "here in Rome, capital of the Catholic world, this declaration: that we respect the Catholic faith, the traditional faith of the majority of the Italian people" (Mercuri, "Il primo governo De Gasperi," pp. 145–46).

33. Legnani, *L'Italia dal 1943 al 1948*, pp. 27–30; Lucio D'Angelo, "I socialisti," in Bizzarri, *Epurazione e stampa di partito*, pp. 67–130.

34. *Avanti!*, June 5–6, 1944.

35. Ibid., June 7, 1944.

36. *Italia Libera*, June 5, 1944; Legnani, *L'Italia dal 1943 al 1948*, pp. 24–26. See also Lamberto Mercuri, "Gli Azionisti," in Bizzarri, *Epurazione e stampa di partito*, pp. 157–214. Regarding the Action party, see also De Luna, *Storia del Partito d'Azione*; Federazione Italiana Associazioni Partigiane, *Il Partito d'Azione dalle origini all'inizio della resistenza armata*; and Mercuri, *L'Azionismo nella storia d'Italia*.

37. *Italia Libera*, June 13, 1944.

38. Monthly report, June 9, 1944, Poletti Papers 194 s8.

39. Benedetto Croce, "Chi è fascista?," reprinted in Legnani, *L'Italia dal 1943 al 1948*, pp. 48–50.

40. *Risorgimento Liberale*, June 14, 23, 30, 1944.

41. Eliza Bizzarri goes so far as to say that, before July 1944, the Christian Democrats had no policy at all. Bizzarri, *Epurazione e stampa di partito*, pp. 15–22.

42. Mantelli, "La democrazia cristiana," pp. 253, 254, 257. Among the best histories of the DC in this period are Baget-Bozzo, *Il Partito cristiano al potere*, and Scoppola, *La proposta politica di De Gasperi*.

43. Scoppola, *La proposta politica di De Gasperi*, pp. 70–71.

44. *Il Quotidiano,* June 21, 1944. See also Legnani, *L'Italia dal 1943 al 1948,* pp. 36–42.

45. Sandro Mercuri, "I democristiani," in Bizzarri, *Epurazione e stampa di partito,* pp. 245–63.

46. *Italia Nuova,* June 14, 1944.

47. Ibid.

48. Charles to FO, September 18, 1944, PRO FO371 43797 File 15R. See also Martuselli-Scoccimarro report, November 1944, ACS PCM 1944–47 10124 1/7, which stated that one-third of the Roman bureaucracy had fled north.

49. Macmillan, *War Diaries,* pp. 200, 352–53, 584; Mercuri, *1943–1945,* p. 203. David W. Ellwood has noted that Poletti "made the field of epuration a personal specialty." Ellwood, *Italy 1943–1945,* p. 145.

50. Neufeld, personal correspondence with author.

51. *Italia Libera,* June 28, 1944. The 3,750 figure may be misleading in that Poletti began to remove certain Fascists the moment he assumed command in Rome. In addition, it may have been inflated by some zealous Allied propagandist. Nevertheless, the very impressive figure cannot be the result of more than a few weeks of work.

52. PWB report, July 8, 1944, PRO FO371 43945 R11178. Ellwood, *Italy 1943–1945,* p. 145. Ellwood, *L'alleato nemico,* p. 258.

53. *Italia Nuova,* July 14, 1944; *L'Unità,* June 29, 1944; *Avanti!,* July 5, 1944.

54. *Risorgimento Liberale,* June 7, 1944; *Il Corriere di Roma,* June 22, 1944. See also Murgia, *Il Vento del Nord,* p. 130.

55. *Il Corriere di Roma,* July 5, 9, 26, 1944.

56. See, for example, *Risorgimento Liberale,* June 22, 1944. See also Gigli, *The Memoirs of Beniamino Gigli,* p. 213. I am indebted to a student at Upsala College, John Maolucci, for valuable insights into the Gigli case.

57. Because this news preceded the end of the Zaniboni Commission by only a few weeks, the trials were apparently lost in the bureaucratic shuffle. Trials against these Fascists were later held under different circumstances.

58. *Risorgimento Liberale,* June 11, 1944.

59. AAC meeting minutes, August 12, 1944, PRO FO371 43827 R15312.

60. Neufeld, "The Failure of Allied Military Government in Italy," p. 140. Salvemini, "Friends, Romans, Aristocrats."

61. Foreign Office report, Mr. Clutton, December 1, 1944, PRO FO371 43827 R19826.

62. Conti, "La RSI e l'attività del fascismo clandestino," pp. 942–43, 952–55. See also Bertoldi, *Contro Salò,* pp. 189–90.

63. Kirk to State Department, March 5, 1945, NARS RG59 865.00/3-1045. For an interesting personality sketch of Alexander Kirk, see Kennan, *Memoirs,* pp. 117–20. Allied ambivalence over the Italian military and police can be examined in Dovey, "The Unknown War."

CHAPTER 4

1. Mercuri, *L'Epurazione*, p. 63.

2. These agricultural colonies never materialized.

3. The term "High Commission" reflects the Anglo-American, particularly the British, input into the legislation. It is not typically an Italian title.

4. In February 1944 Omodeo's Ministry of National Education changed its name to the Ministry of Public Instruction.

5. G. M. Gancia to Poletti, August 4, 1944, Poletti Papers 194 sg. Lieutenant Gancia acted as liaison between Poletti and the Rome CLN.

6. Neufeld, personal correspondence with author. See also Sforza's September 8, 1944, circular to High Commission personnel, which was included in his *Fini e limiti dell'epurazione*, p. 17. Regarding Sforza's interference in the Foreign Ministry, see Mercuri, *L'Epurazione*, p. 66. On the British and Sforza, see Woodward, *British Foreign Policy in the Second World War*, 2:508–17.

7. General Mason-Macfarlane referred to Berlinguer as "an intelligent little lawyer who talks passable French and whose son was recently locked up as a Communist in Sardinia." This son, Enrico Berlinguer, was many years later to become the secretary of the Italian Communist party. NARS ACC 10000/136/327 Box 35. Regarding Cingolani's *commissariato aggiunto* for illegal profits, see Vassalli and Sabatini, *Il collaborazionismo e l'amnistia politica*, and Vassalli, *La confisca dei beni*. See also *Risorgimento Liberale*, September 30, 1945, which stated that if the organization was ever mobilized in law, it would be an organization "technically imperfect, absolutely useless, in fact dangerous . . . [merely serving] to create sinecures and bureaucracies." For a list of subordinate figures in the adjunct commissions, see Mercuri, *L'Epurazione*, pp. 58–59.

8. "Z" to State Department and OSS, August 1, 1944, NARS RG226 89256.

9. Flores, "L'Epurazione," in Atti del convegno internazionale organizzato a Firenze il 26–28 Marzo 1976 con il concorso della regione Toscana/INSMLI, *L'Italia dalla liberazione alla repubblica*, p. 422.

10. Coles and Weinberg, *Civil Affairs*, p. 473; NARS ACC 10000/105/819. For a list of purge commissions established in Rome, see Mercuri, *L'Epurazione*, p. 103.

11. Upjohn to Stone, September 3 or 4, 1944, NARS ACC 10000/136/327 Box 35; Upjohn report, October 6, 1944, NARS ACC 10000/136/228-231 Box 23.

12. Charles to Eden, April 12, 1945, regarding Upjohn report on "Epuration," PRO FO371 49756 ZM2293.

13. Upjohn to Stone, September 2 or 3, 1944, NARS ACC 10000/136/327 Box 35.

14. Justice Ministry to PCM Cabinet, November 20, 1944, ACS PCM 1944–46 10124 1/7 f8 s18.1.

15. Taddeo Orlando to Bonomi, September 16, 1944, ACS PCM 1944–46 10124 1/7 f4 sg.

16. See Scoccimarro's complaint to "Z" in "Z" to State Department and OSS, August 1, 1944, NARS RG226 89256.

17. Since the Advocate General's office was under the jurisdiction of the Council of Ministers, this would have been the proper channel for such affairs. On September 30 Flores sent the *schede* off to Scoccimarro and the High Commission. The Advocate General's stationery still displayed the Fascist letterhead of the Savoyard Cross embraced by fasces. Through 1944 most government offices still used the old Fascist paper either unchanged or, perhaps, modified by penciling out the fasces. By December the Advocate General's office had procured a stamp to cancel the old symbol entirely. Flores to Scoccimarro, September 30, 1944, ACS PCM 1944–47 10124 1/7 f29 s5.

18. Secretary, Purge Commission for Advocate General's office to Flores, December 5, 1944, ACS PCM 1944–47 10124 1/7 f29 s1.

19. Both purgers and Fascists used the term *antemarcia* to refer to those who were enrolled in the party (or movement) before the March on Rome in 1922. By 1944 this was no longer considered a compliment south of the battle front.

20. Briganti (for Scoccimarro) to Purge Commission (for Avvocatura dello Stato), December 13, 1944, ACS PCM 1944–47 10124 1/7 f29 s5. The Avvocatura Generale changed its name to the Avvocatura dello Stato at the end of 1944.

21. Purge Commission for Avvocatura dello Stato to Bonomi, August 21, 1945, ACS PCM 1944–47 10124 1/7 f29 s6.

22. Senerchia to Bonomi, December 19, 1944, ACS PCM 1944–47 10124 1/7 f29 s6.

23. Trillò to Scoccimarro, December 15, 1944, ACS PCM 1944–47 10124 1/7 f29 s6-D; Molinari to Flores, December 16, 1944, ibid., 1/7 f29 s6.

24. Molinari to Spataro, December 20, 1944, ACS PCM 1944–47 10124 1/7 f29 s6. The copy on file was also sent to Flores.

25. L. Boccia, F. Poce, E. Rienzi, and B. Roselli to Spataro, December 18, 1944, ACS PCM 1944–47 10124 1/7 f29 s6-D; L. Boccia, F. Poce, E. Rienzi, and B. Roselli to Senerchia, December 20, 1944, ibid., 10124 1/7 f29 s6; L. Boccia, F. Poce, E. Rienzi, and B. Roselli to Bonomi, December 28, 1944, ibid., 10124 1/7 f29 s6-C.

26. Molinari to Bonomi, December 18, 1944, ACS PCM 1944–47 10124 1/7 f29; Bonomi circular dated December 22, 1944, ibid., 10124 1/7 f29 s6-D.

27. Briganti (for Scoccimarro) to Bonomi, December 22, 1944, ACS PCM 1944–47 10124 1/7 f29 s6; Senerchia to Bonomi, January 8, 1945, ibid., 10124 1/7 f29 s6-D. Senerchia wrote to the prime minister, "given the turn-around [*mancata accettazione*] of Trillò's resignation, how can one reconcile the nomination of the new commissioner, Professor Battara?"

28. Among Morelli's predecessors at the helm of the CNR was no less a figure than Pietro Badoglio, who had taken the position for a couple of years after Mussolini made him a scapegoat for the disastrous 1940 campaign in Greece. Visco had apparently fled the city.

29. Verbale della seduta della Commissione interna de Consiglio Nazional delle Ricerche, October 2, 1944, ACS PCM 1944–47 10124 1/7 f29 s7; Promemoria riservatissima for Guido De Ruggiero, October 7, 1944, ibid.

30. *Ricostruzione*, October 4 and November 1, 1944, ACS PCM 1944–47 10124 1/7 f29. The November 8 *Ricostruzione* referred to yet another man heavily tainted by fascism. The accused, a *consigliere*, wrote to the review to refute everything. On November 24, he was purged anyway; perhaps the publicity worked against him. On Sabato Visca, see Renzo De Felice, *Storia degli ebrei*, pp. 325–26.

31. Scoccimarro to De Ruggiero, September 11, 1944, ACS PCM 1944–47 10124 1/7 f32 s1; Jemolo to Stangoni, September 13, 1944, ibid.; Bonomi to De Ruggiero, December 28, 1944, ibid. See also the Jemolo report contained in ibid.

32. On January 5 Sforza reported that 160 purge commissions were operating. Sforza, *Fini e limiti dell'epurazione*, p. 11. The High Commission acknowledged that the ministers themselves had seen fit to suspend employees. No numbers have come down to us regarding these suspensions, although they are probably smaller that those of the Alto Commissariato.

33. The *pubblica sicurezza* has traditionally taken responsibility for the more quotidian police duties in Italy, such as traffic control and investigation of minor crimes. The Carabinieri have a more elitist reputation and handle more serious crimes as well as being a paramilitary organization.

34. Scoccimarro report, December 5, 1944, ACS Alto Commissariato per le sanzioni contro il fascismo (hereafter ACSF) 1/20; Casati to Bonomi, October 4, 1944, PCM 1944–47 10124 1/7 f36.

35. Mengozzi, *L'Epurazione nella città del Duce*, p. 41.

36. High Commission report, December 5, 1944, ACS ACSF 1/20.

37. Terni listed 131 removals out of 241 investigations; Siena, 92 out of 394 (probably incomplete); and Pescara, 13 of 46.

38. Mercuri, *L'Epurazione*, pp. 72–73. The legal scholars published their manifesto in the political journal *Domenica*.

39. Villari, *The Liberation of Italy*, pp. 152–53. See also Tamaro, *Due anni di storia*, p. 342. Tamaro labeled Maroni a "hot Fascist." Mercuri, *L'Epurazione*, p. 124 n. 91.

40. Charles F. Delzell states that, all told, 7,000 people participated in the riot. Delzell, *Mussolini's Enemies*, p. 398. Among those in the camera crew was the noted director Luchino Visconti. Visconti's biographer, however, confused the Caruso execution with Pietro Koch's, which occurred about a year later. Servadio, *Luchino Visconti*, pp. 109–10.

41. Much of this information comes from a report on the riot compiled by a government commission headed by Emanuele Piga, a judge from the appellate court. Kirk to State Department, November 15, 1944, NARS RG59 865.00/11-1544. See also Algardi, *Il processo Caruso*, and Algardi, *Processi ai fascisti*, pp. 74–77. Some of those who participated in the Carretta lynching were put on trial in 1946.

42. Charles F. Delzell wrote that among the many anti-Fascists whom Carretta had helped to escape was the moderate Socialist and future president of Italy, Giuseppe Saragat. Delzell, *Mussolini's Enemies*, p. 398.

43. The Piga report (cited in note 41 above) concluded that Ricottini was a madwoman with a "psychopathological stigma." Mental illness evidently ran in her family. Her sister, who suffered from infantile paralysis, was a "certified lunatic." Ricottini's behavior on September 18 was interpreted by the learned men as a manifestation of "raptus freneticus." In submitting the Piga report to Washington, Ambassador Kirk reported that Carretta had demanded a bribe from Ricottini to secure her son's release from Regina Coeli.

44. *Italia Nuova*, September 20, 1944; *Avanti!*, September 19, 1944; *Italia Libera*, September 19, 1944. On September 21, *Italia Nuova* reported that the vice questore of Rome, Dr. Mario Lener, had been suspended. The Piga report of the Carretta incident concluded on November 3 that no political crimes had been committed. It was an act of an uncontrollable, hysterical mob and nothing more.

45. Kirk to State Department, September 18, 1944, NARS RG59 865.00/9-1844 OMM; Charles to Foreign Office, September 19, 1944, PRO FO371 43874 R14877.

46. Charles to Foreign Office, September 19, 1944, PRO FO371 43874 R14877.

47. *Avanti!*, September 21, 1944; *Italia Nuova*, September 21, 1944.

48. Algardi, *Processi ai fascisti*, p. 94.

49. *Italia Libera*, September 22, 1944. The double game took on an even more nefarious connection when Occhetto was discovered to have only begun to use it at the end of May, a few days before Rome was liberated.

50. Ibid., September 23, 1944.

51. *Avanti!*, September 22, 1944; *Risorgimento Liberale*, September 23, 1944. The article in *Italia Libera* was far more curt. Against the important headline space devoted to it in other papers, the *azionista* journal covered the execution in a small story in the lower right-hand corner of page 1.

52. *Italia Nuova*, September 24, 1944. This seems to have been Fascist propaganda.

53. *Avanti!*, October 10, 1944.

54. PWB reports, October 16 and 26, 1944, PRO FO371 File 1677, 43947 pp. 75-77, 162-63.

55. Ibid.

56. *Italia Nuova*, October 11, 1944.

57. Once again the trial locus was switched: to the Palazzo della Sapienza in the Corso Rinascimento. An architectural jewel, it was the site of the University of Rome before Mussolini built his modernist Città Universitaria in the 1930s. The building today houses some of the city's archives.

58. Kirk to State Department, December 20, 1944, NARS RG59 865.00 12-2044; Research and Analysis report, March 17, 1945, NARS RG59 Lot file

2688; PWB report, December 28, 1944, NARS RG 59 865.00/3-1345; PWB report, November 9, 1944, PRO FO371 43947 R19122. General Messe was the officer who surrendered all Axis forces in North Africa to the Allies in May 1943. He was briefly interned but returned to Italy to serve the Regno del Sud.

59. On April 20, 1945, *Italia Libera* reported that Del Tetto died in prison. Promemoria 44, listed as "Memoria OP 44—Promemoria 1 and 2," was reprinted in Zangrandi, *1943*, pp. 364–72.

60. Pietro Nenni in *Avanti!*, December 23, 1944, reprinted in Nenni, *Il Vento del Nord*, p. 249.

61. Upjohn report on Epuration, summarized in Charles to Eden, April 12, 1945, PRO FO371 49756 ZM2293. Regarding the collaborationist trials in France, see Novick, *The Resistance versus Vichy*, pp. 140–90.

62. Upjohn report on Epuration, summarized in Charles to Eden, April 12, 1945, PRO FO371 49756 ZM2293.

63. *Risorgimento Liberale*, October 19, 1944. Lauro eventually passed twenty-two months in jail.

64. Luisa Ferida, a very popular screen idol during the *ventennio*, was another female celebrity killed by anti-Fascists during the liberation. Servadio, *Luchino Visconti*, p. 72.

65. *Italia Nuova*, December 3, 22, 23, 24, 1944; *Risorgimento Liberale*, December 3, 23, 1944; *Italia Libera*, December 23, 1944; Kirk to State Department, December 28, 1944, NARS RG59 865.00/2.2844.

CHAPTER 5

1. Croce, *Croce, the King, and the Allies*, pp. 43–44.

2. Corrado Barbaglio, "Neofascismo," *Avanti!*, November 29, 1944.

3. Poletti report, October 9, 1944, Poletti Papers 194 s33. Regarding increased polarization in Italian politics, see, for example, OSS interview with Croce, July 27, 1944, NARS RG226 E125 Box 51 f. 622. Croce felt that Togliatti could no longer be trusted as a political partner. The Liberal commented that the Communist leader was "acquiring the reputation of being the greatest liar in Italy."

4. OSS report, October 16, 1944, NARS RG226 R100794.

5. Achille Corona, "Perchè l'epurazione non va avanti," *Avanti!*, November 10, 1944.

6. "I lupi e le volpi all'Istituto dei Cambi," *L'Unità*, November 10, 1944.

7. Poletti report, December 9, 1944, Poletti Papers 194 s33. Even Poletti expressed some second thoughts, labeling Scoccimarro's tactics "a curious procedure for a member of the Government."

8. Soleri to Bonomi, November 11, 1944, ACS PCM 1944–47 10124 1/7 f32 s12 b117.

9. Soleri to Scoccimarro, November 11, 1944, ACS PCM 1944–47 10124

1/7 f32 s12. Despite the animosity found in the letter, Soleri continued to use the familiar "tu" form of address with Scoccimarro.

10. Soleri to Bonomi, November 12, 1944, ACS PCM 1944–47 10124 1/7 f32 s12. Soleri was very ill, with less than a year to live. Regarding Allied opinion of Soleri, see OSS biographical sketch, NARS RG226 100924. See also Flores, "L'Epurazione," in Atti del convegno internazionale organizzato a Firenze il 26–28 Marzo 1976 con il concorso della regione Toscana/INSMLI, *L'Italia dalla liberazione alla repubblica*, p. 422.

11. De Courten was also angry over a fight among the purgers that resembled the situation at the Central Statistical Institute.

12. De Courten to Bonomi, November 24, 1944, ACS PCM 1944–47 10124 1/7 f32 s10.

13. Mercuri, "Il primo governo De Gasperi e il problema dell'epurazione," pp. 166–71. See also Mercuri, *L'Epurazione*, pp. 76–77, regarding Commodore Stone's opposition to a purge of the military.

14. OSS report, November 28, 1944, NARS RG226 R10592; OSS report, November 24, 1944, ibid., RG226 105835. The Liberals were also irritated by the failure of the Bonomi government to deliver an ambassadorial post in London for Manlio Brosio.

15. Giuseppe Mammarella, for example, considered that Bonomi's resignation to Umberto was a slap in the face for the CLN. Mammarella, *Italy after Fascism*, pp. 77–78.

16. Kirk to State Department, March 12, 1945, NARS RG59 865.00/3-1245. Regarding the New Deal for Italy, see Harris, *Allied Administration*, pp. 212, 231–52, and Mercuri, *1943–1945*, pp. 262–63. Regarding the British position, see Woodward, *British Foreign Policy in the Second World War*, 3:453–66. Regarding Stone, see Mercuri, *L'Epurazione*, p. 70. To emphasize America's new attitude, Secretary of State Stettinius and Roosevelt's aide, Harry Hopkins, toured Italy immediately after the cabinet crisis. Furthermore, on March 1, 1945, the Political Section of the Allied Commission was abolished as a sign of good will.

17. Aga Rossi and Smith, *Operation Sunrise*, p. 46; Macmillan, *War Diaries*, p. 701; Kogan, *Italy and the Allies*, pp. 108–9; Delzell, *Mussolini's Enemies*, p. 452–53; Churchill, *Triumph and Tragedy*, pp. 108–14, 283–325; Department of State, *Foreign Relations of the United States*, pp. 269–70.

18. Orme Sargent to Charles, June 20, 1944, PRO FO371 43793 57509.

19. W. A. B. Bowen-Buscarlet, Air Force subcommissioner, ACC Air report no. 21, October 9, 1944, PRO FO371 43951 R17941. Ross's comments on the paper are dated November 13. See also Mercuri, *1943–1945*, p. 213.

20. Charles to Foreign Office, December 6, 1944, PRO FO371 43801 R20124. The report also stated that Togliatti had proposed a new government to be headed by De Gasperi. See also Woodward, *British Foreign Policy in the Second World War*, 3:466–68. Macmillan noted that, during the November crisis, he and Charles attended "an immense and very pre-war party at the Em-

bassy." Even Macmillan, however, seemed somewhat embarrassed by the presence of Italian guests who had been prominent in the old regime and now appeared "more 'allied' than 'co-belligerent.'" He felt, nevertheless, that "on the whole [it was] right and certainly inevitable for anyone like Charles (who knew them all when he was here in 1940)." Macmillan, *War Diaries*, p. 583.

21. Charles to Foreign Office, December 6, 1944, PRO FO371 43801 10422.

22. Churchill to Eden, December 7, 1944, PRO FO371 43801 20423.

23. Eden to Lord Halifax, December 7, 1944, PRO FO371 43801 20424. Regarding the Allied failure to reinforce Italian forces against the Germans after the Armistice, see Davis, *Who Defends Rome?*, pp. 370–81, 437–68.

24. Sir B. Newton, D. O., to Commonwealth Governors General, October 1, 1945, PRO FO371 49777 ZM5021.

25. Broad to Macmillan, December 9, 1944, PRO FO371 43801 20425; Charles to Foreign Office, December 7, 1944, FO371 43801 20233. Harold Macmillan agreed with Badoglio and Charles, advocating British protection. He insisted, however, that the Americans act with the British as a united front on this matter. Macmillan, *War Diaries*, p. 597.

26. Churchill to Charles, December 8, 1944, PRO FO371 43801 20233.

27. Charles to Foreign Office, January 21, 1945, PRO FO371 49768 ZM525. On January 21 Berlinguer assured the British Ambassador that "all talk of action against Marshal Badoglio was nonsense." See also Charles to Macmillan, December 11, 1944, PRO FO371 R20577; Foreign Office to Halifax, December 10, 1944, PRO FO371 43802 pp. 54–55; and Halifax to Foreign Office, December 12, 1944, PRO FO371 43802 pp. 73–74. Regarding British animosity toward Sforza, see PRO FO371 43802 R20451–R20542.

28. Charles to Foreign Office, January 19, 1945, PRO FO371 49768 ZM525; Halifax to Foreign Office, March 6, 1945, PRO FO371 49754 ZM1401. Harold Macmillan was also very concerned over the upcoming Roatta trial. He believed that the defendant possessed a document proving that Neville Chamberlain had offered French colonies to Mussolini. Macmillan, *War Diaries*, pp. 645, 649–50. Berlinguer promised Commodore Stone that he would personally sit in through the entire trial to ensure that no sensitive information would be divulged.

29. Wiskeman to Charles, December 6, 1945, PRO FO371 60581 ZM56. See also Charles to Foreign Office, December 17, 1945, PRO FO371 60581 ZM.

30. Monthly report, November 9, 1944, Poletti Papers 194 s33.

31. *Avanti!*, November 28, 1944, December 9, 1944. Nenni's December 9 editorial is quoted in Gambino, *Storia del dopoguerra*, p. 21, and Nenni, *Il Vento del Nord*, p. 239.

32. Velio Spano, "Epurazione: problema da risolvere," *L'Unità*, January 3, 1945.

33. *Risorgimento Liberale*, November 10, 1944.

34. *Italia Nuova*, January 4, 1945; Enzo Selvaggi, "Dietro la facciata," *Italia Nuova*, November 19, 1944.

35. Bizzarri, "Mondo cattolica," in Bizzarri, *Epurazione e stampa di partito*, pp. 16, 21, 23, 33.

36. Sandro Mercuri also believes that De Gasperi's triumph at the party's Naples Congress in July triggered a move toward a "moderate" position. De Gasperi did not believe in a sweeping purge as he felt more disposed toward the Liberal notion of reeducation and a "moral reconstitution." Sandro Mercuri, "I democristiani," in ibid., p. 250–55.

37. Charles to Foreign Office, December 6, 1944, PRO FO371 R20124.

38. Report of conversation between Stone and Bonomi, September 11, 1944, NARS 10000/136/104 Box 10.

39. During the December 4 meeting of the Council of Ministers, Manlio Brosio of the PLI launched a blistering attack on Nenni. Togliatti intervened to support the conservative Bonomi-Liberal position. Cattani, "Dalla caduta del fascismo al primo governo De Gasperi," pp. 740–41.

40. Charles to Foreign Office, December 10, 1944, PRO FO371 43802 R20467.

41. Sforza to Eden, December 2, 1944, PRO FO371 43802 20744; Charles to Orme Sargeant, December 2, 1944, ibid.

42. Mercuri, *1943–1945*, p. 255; Mercuri, *L'Epurazione*, p. 85.

43. PWB report, December 28, 1944, PRO FO371 49869 ZM466. See also Kogan, *Italy and the Allies*, pp. 94–98.

44. Kirk to State Department, April 11, 1945, NARS RG59 865.00/4-1145; PWB report, April 12, 1945, PRO FO371 49871 ZM2339; PWB report, April 19, 1945, PRO FO371 49871 ZM2485; Kogan, *Italy and the Allies*, p. 94.

45. Setta, *L'Uomo Qualunque*, pp. 36–38. Regarding the *qualunquista* press, see Setta's contribution to Bizzarri, *Epurazione e stampa di partito*, pp. 305–28. Regarding the purge of film artists see Mercuri, *L'Epurazione*, p. 62. On competition between the *qualunquisti* and the Christian Democrats for middle-class support, see Scoppola, *La proposta politica di De Gasperi*, pp. 150–51.

46. Guglielmo Giannini, "Questi fascismi," *L'Uomo Qualunque*, January 10, 1945. Setta, *L'Uomo Qualunque*, pp. 120–21. Regarding Ministry of Popular Culture payoffs to Giannini, see OSS report, March 24, 1945, NARS RG226 127156.

47. *L'Uomo Qualunque*, December 27, 1944.

48. Setta, *L'Uomo Qualunque*, p. 310.

49. *Italia Nuova*, June 15, 1944. See also PWB reports on the Salvarezza case: January 26, 1945, NARS RG59 865.00/2-345; January 31, 1945, and February 8, 1945, NARS RG59 865.00/2-845.

50. *Avanti!*, April 1, 1945. OSS report, February 8, 1945, NARS RG226 117036. For a Catholic view of the Gobbo affair, see *Il Quotidiano*, January 18 and 20, 1945.

51. Mercuri, *L'Epurazione*, p. 79.

52. Sforza, *Le Sanzioni contro il fascismo*. See also Sforza to Bonomi, January 5, 1945, ACS PCM 1944–47 10124 1/7 f4 s1.3; and Flores, "L'Epurazione," in

Atti del convegno internazionale organizzato a Firenze il 26–28 Marzo 1976 con il concorso della regione Toscana/INSMLI, *L'Italia dalla liberazione alla repubblica*, p. 434.

53. Casati to territorial commanders, January 22, 1945, ACS Carteggi Casati Box 5 f21. Sardinia continued to be a center of military filofascism. On February 22 "a few hundred" troops on leave in Sassari marched up and down the Via Roma shouting "Duce, Duce!" Note to Casati dated March 8, 1945, ibid. See also PWB report, April 20, 1945, PRO FO371 4981 ZM2486; and Mercuri, *1943–1945*, p. 243. See also Casati circular, April 5, 1945, ACS PCM 10124 1/7 f. 15 b. 111.

54. Claudio Pavone, "La continuità dello stato," in Piscitelli, *Italia, 1945– 1948*, p. 177. See also Ellwood, *Italia, 1943–1945*, pp. 152–56.

55. The Communist representative to the CLN somewhat contradicted the notion of an angry Florence when he reported to a PWB agent that members of the Ciano family continued to walk the streets unmolested. PWB report, April 30, 1945, NARS RG226 E190 f. 206; AMG report, September 30, 1944, NARS RG331 10700/133/76.

56. Delzell, *Mussolini's Enemies*, p. 409; Lt. Col. Ralph Rolph report, October 7, 1944, RG331 10700/109/7.

57. PWB report, February 23, 1945, PRO FO371 49870 ZM1466; PWB report, March 9, 1945, PRO FO371 49871 ZM1685; NARS RG59 865.00/3.645; Mercuri, *1943–1945*, pp. 213–14. C. F. R. Harris emphasized the strained relations between the Tuscan CLN and the Allies. Harris, *Allied Administration*, pp. 185–90.

58. PWB report, January 26, 1945, PRO FO371 49870 ZM1200. An OSS report found that, at the end of 1944, out of thirty-seven liberated provinces, only one, Rome, had a fully functioning purge commission. Research and Analysis report 2688, March 17, 1945, NARS RG59 Lot files.

59. PWB report, February 22, 1945, PRO FO371 49870 ZM1467; PWB report, March 8, 1945, PRO FO371 49871 ZM1684. Regarding Sicily, see also Research and Analysis report 2688, March 17, 1945, NARS RG59 Lot files; OSS report, September 2, 1944, NARS RG226 E165 f. 428; Consul General —Palermo, Alfred Nester to State, April 11, 1945, NARS RG59 865.00/4-1145; Mercuri, *L'Epurazione*, p. 33 and, regarding Basilicata, p. 91.

60. For an excellent summary in English of the Salò regime, see Deakin, *The 600 Days of Mussolini*, which is essentially the last third of his *Brutal Friendship*.

61. Rossini, *Democrazia cristiana e costituente*, p. 743; Flores, "L'Epurazione," in Atti del convegno internazionale organizzato a Firenze il 26–28 Marzo 1976 con il concorso della regione Toscana/INSMLI, *L'Italia dalla liberazione alla repubblica*, pp. 443–45.

62. Scoccimarro's November report claimed 6,859. See chapter 3, above. The problem of numbers always plagues any analysis of sanctions. In January 1945 the Allied Commission obtained more statistics on the "progress" of the

"epuration program." No mention was made on how these figures were arrived at, and they correspond only roughly with others from Scoccimarro and Grieco. Of 10,063 names submitted by the central government to the purge commissions, about one-third had been judged serious enough for formal judgment. Of these, 587 had been dismissed, 1,461 had received "lesser sanctions," and 1,530 had been acquitted. Kirk to State, March 6, 1945, NARS RG59 865.00/3-645. Another OSS report, furthermore, stated that, beyond the "600" removed by the purge commissions, 2,910 had been dismissed in line with Allied regulations. Research and Analysis report 2688. March 17, 1945, NARS RG59 Lot files. The AC's March report, based on information submitted in January, is one of the clearest presentations of numbers regarding the purge to that point. The report to Washington did not dispute these figures, although they often conflict with other tallies and occasionally are incorrectly added. The figures have not been adjusted and remain here as they appeared on the document.

Ministry, Etc.	Commissions	Persons Submitted for Purge		
		Grades		Total
		1–4	lower	
Council of Ministers	6	86	148	234
Foreign Affairs	1	49	40	89
Ind. Comm. and Labor	3	14	205	219
Agriculture	2	7	58	65
Public Works	1	2	8	10
Justice and Grace	4	81	271	352
Finance	5	6	34	40
Treasury	2	1	79	80
War	3	71	93	114
Navy	3	24	32	56
Air Force	3	34	349	383
Public Instruction	4	121	104	225
Italian Africa	2	12	0	12
Interior	3	118	1,350	1,468
Communications	11	5	78	83
Undersec. Press	1	3	146	149
Dependent Bodies	71	13	925	938
Commune and Province				
of Rome	1	0	536	536
Professional Men	3	624	4,326	4,960
Carabinieri	2	0	0	0
Royal House	1	0	0	0
Total	124	1,281	8,782	10,063

Ministry Etc.	Suspensions			Total
	By High Commission		Ordered by Minister	
	Requested	Made		
Council of Ministers	34	6	1	41
Foreign Affairs	13	4	3	20
Ind. Comm. and Labor	111	84	0	195
Agriculture	11	6	57	74
Public Works	18	0	117	135
Justice and Grace	49	34	0	83
Finance	90	8	16	114
Treasury	11	5	62	78
War	105	65	29	199
Navy	17	2	0	19
Air Force	200	3	1	204
Public Instruction	83	74	79	236
Italian Africa	0	0	0	0
Interior	423	254	100	777
Communications	20	20	1,923	1,963
Undersec. Press	0	0	0	0
Dependent Bodies	0	0	0	0
Commune and Province of Rome	28	11	489	528
Professional Men	45	24	0	69
Carabinieri	0	0	0	0
Royal House	0	0	0	0
Bodies controlled by War			28	28
Bodies controlled by Communication			2	2
Total	1,258	600	2,907	4,765

Ministry Etc.	Decisions			
	Dismissed	Lesser Sanctions	Acquittals	Total
Council of Ministers	32	59	15	106
Foreign Affairs	1	3	11	15
Ind. Comm. and Labor	21	22	10	53
Agriculture	5	7	2	14
Public Works	29	48	59	136
Justice and Grace	29	16	26	71
Finance	2	0	1	3
Treasury	28	46	24	98
War	2	7	28	37
Navy	5	122	277	404
Air Force	28	16	58	102
Public Instruction	54	118	14	186
Italian Africa	0	0	0	0
Interior	27	97	50	174
Communications	94	643	915	1,652
Undersec. Press	10	10	3	23

Ministry Etc., *continued*		Decisions		
	Dismissed	Lesser Sanctions	Acquittals	Total
Dependent Bodies	0	0	0	0
Commune and Province				
of Rome	10	28	5	43
Professional Men		(14 removed from the lists)		
Royal House	0	50	0	50
Bodies controlled by War	19	57	1	77
Bodies controlled by				
Communications	0	0	0	0
Bodies controlled by				
Ind. Comm. and Labor	120	105	25	250
Bodies controlled by				
Public Works	21	57	6	84
Total	587	1,461	1,530	3,578

63. See above. See also PWB report, December 28, 1944, NARS RG59 865.00/3-1345. On American impressions of the trial, see PWB report, February 8, 1945, NARS RG59 865.00/2-945; Kirk to State, January 16, 1945, NARS RG59 865.00/1-1645; PWB report, January 9, 1945, NARS RG59 865.00/1-2045. Regarding British sensitivity on the publication of embarrassing information, see Memorandum of Conversation, January 23, 1945, NARS RG59 865.00/1-2345.

64. PWB report, March 8, 1945, PRO FO371 ZM1648. Roatta's whereabouts became a hot topic of speculation. London's *Daily Express* reported that the general's voice had been heard on a monitored radio broadcast from the RSI on the day after the escape. In Washington, popular columnist Drew Pearson wrote that the British secretly engineered the whole thing and held Roatta in protective custody somewhere in Benghazi. Pearson believed that the Fascist had been blackmailing Churchill regarding Britain's attempt to "sell [the moderate Yugoslav partisan leader] Mihailovic down the river." The truth was that Roatta had somehow made his way to Spain and remained there until he returned to private life in Rome during the 1960s.

65. Stone to AFHQ, March 6, 1945, NARS ACC 10000/136/119 Box 12; AC to AFHQ, March 6, 1945, ibid; Nicholas Piombino, Assistant adjutant of AC, to AFHQ, March 6, 1945, ibid.; Brigadier General Lush to AFHQ, March 7, 1945, ibid.; Stone to AFHQ, March 8, 1945, ibid.; Stone to Bonomi, April 11, 1945, ibid. In order to appease public suspicion that nothing much had changed in the SIM, Bonomi reported to Stone that more power had been given to the minister of war and some personnel had been eliminated. The Allies, furthermore, ordered the Left press to cease protests over the situation in the SIM. Regarding the SIM situation, see Kirk to State, March 7, 1945, NARS RG59 865.00/3-745; Research and Analysis report 2688, March 17, 1945, NARS RG59 Lot files.

66. Prefectural reports, February 4 and March 11, 1945, ACS Interior Ministry 1944–46 b31 f2446.

67. Kirk to State Department, March 20, 1945, NARS RG59 865.00/3-2045. A copy of this report was also sent to the American embassy in Moscow. Bonomi had already been arranging for Orlando's removal. Another PWB report intimated that the demonstration may have even had some Fascist input. PWB report, March 22, 1945, PRO FO371 49871 ZM1971.

68. Lamberto Mercuri has told the author that he interviewed an eyewitness from the Socialist party who insisted that the dead man's body was brought into Bonomi's office and spread out on his desk. Another PWB report and a Carabiniere report on the actions of March 6 are contained in a note from Ambassador Kirk to Washington, dated March 8, 1945. NARS RG59 865.00/3-845.

69. *Avanti!*, March 7, 1945; PWB report, March 15, 1945, NARS RG59 865.00/3.2445; PWB report, March 22, 1945, ibid., RG59 865.00/4.445. See also Bonomi to Stone, April 23, 1945, NARS ACC 10000/136/351 Box 37; Macmillan, *War Diaries*, p. 710.

70. Pietro Nenni, "Vigilia insurrezionale," *Avanti!*, April 17, 1945. In October 1945 *Avanti!* claimed that the explosion of revolutionary justice at the end of the war deprived the High Court of any justification. Mercuri, *L'Epurazione*, p. 124 n. 91.

71. *Avanti!*, April 17, 1945. OSS report, April 7, 1945, NARS RG226 E125 f. 622.

CHAPTER 6

1. On the organization and division within partisan groups, see Delzell, *Mussolini's Enemies*, pp. 413–15, 506; and Roberto Battaglia, *Storia della resistenza italiana*, pp. 133–46, 333–40.

2. Gobbi, "Note sulla commissione d'epurazione del CLN regionale piemontese nel caso Valletta," p. 57.

3. The RSI has been often referred to as the Salò Republic, a name stemming from the town that served as the locus of the government press office.

4. Lazzero, *Le Brigate nere*, pp. 291–96.

5. NARS, Mussolini Papers, T-586, reel 299, frame 113205.

6. Massobrio and Guglielmotti, *Storia della Repubblica Sociale Italiana*, pp. 938–39, 946, 952, 981. In early 1944 Mussolini wrote to a friend, "You are too intelligent a woman not to understand what has happened. I am sad and I feel very much alone. I would advise you to get away from this place." Benito Mussolini, *Opera Omnia*, 32:208.

7. Even one old Fascist *squadrista* wrote to his Duce and complained that, as a blackshirt of the first hour, he understood violence; but the Black Brigades had simply gone too far. NARS, Mussolini Papers, T-586, reel 316, frames 112413–14.

8. To offset leftist criticism of Italy's Royal armed forces, Churchill praised the army and air force before the House of Commons. However, their contribution to the war effort was marginal. Deliberately limited in terms of size and task, they operated mainly as support and rear-guard peace-keeping forces. On the other hand, thousands of regular Italian troops, caught in the Balkans on September 8, joined partisan forces there and made an important mark in the war against Hitler. Harris, *Allied Administration*, pp. 139–40, 220–21, 356–57. Marshal Badoglio devoted much of his apologia toward a vindication of the Royal armed forces' actions after the Armistice. Badoglio, *Italy in the Second World War*, pp. 176–91. The best bibliographical essay on works pertaining to the immensely complex Italian Resistance is Delzell, "The Italian Anti-Fascist Resistance in Retrospect."

9. Mercuri, *L'Epurazione*, pp. 95–96.

10. ACS CIAG PS Sez II b326 s88. As early as September 1944, Carlo Sforza recommended that the Anglo-Americans transmit an order to partisan units behind the lines to collect information for future prosecution against collaborationists. Commodore Stone denied the request on the excuse that it would upset the war effort. Mercuri, *L'Epurazione*, p. 132. On the sanctions, measures, and actions in the self-liberated northern republics before April 1945, see Delzell, *Mussolini's Enemies*, pp. 400–432.

11. Tamaro, *Due anni di storia*, 3:541; Gobbi, "Note sulla commissione d'epurazione del CLN regionale piemontese nel caso Valletta," pp. 59–63. Charles F. Delzell discussed the different tones of the Turin and Milan Resistance in *Mussolini's Enemies*, p. 486.

12. ACS ACSF 1/3. A Giustizia e Libertà brigade in Biella sentenced a Fascist to death on March 21, 1945. CLNAI, *Documenti ufficiali*, p. 3.

13. J. Klahr Huddle (for Harrison) to State Department, NARS RG59 865.00/11.1544. See also the CLNAI's "Decree for the Administration of Justice," in Leo Valiani, *Dall'antifascismo alla resistenza*, p. 172.

14. Macmillan, *War Diaries*, pp. 741–43.

15. CLNAI, *Documenti ufficiali*, pp. 24–38. See also Deakin, *The 600 Days of Mussolini*, pp. 310–14. An excellent account of events in Milan during the days of the insurrection can be found in Giobbio, "Milano all'indomani della Liberazione."

16. PWB report, May 19, 1945, PRO FO371 49872 ZM3134; PWB report, May 19, 1945, NARS RG226 E190 f. 206; Alfred Bowman report, June 23, 1945, RG331/10700/125/9. *Italia Libera*, May 3, 1945. Italians employed, nearly universally, the euphemistic *giustiziati* instead of *fucilati* or *uccisi* to describe the events of late April. See also Giobbio, "Milano all'indomani della Liberazione," p. 10.

17. Brunetti to PCM, May 17, 1945, ACS PS CIAG Sez II P185 s55-14.

18. Major Amedeo Jacch to AMG Padua, May 16, 1945, ACS PS CIAG Sez II P185 s55-53.

19. Oreste Tancini to Interior, May 19, 1945, ACS CIAG PS sez II P189 s55-35. A PWB report listed 300 deaths in Genoa and along the Ligurian coast in the first days after the liberation. PWB report, May 5, 1945, NARS RG226 E190 f. 206.

20. Schnare to State Department, June 23, 1945, NARS RG59. Schnare mentioned that many partisans rounded up Fascists, brought them into Genoa for internment at the Marassi Prison, then left the city to go home.

21. *Avanti!*, May 22, 1945.

22. Psychiatrists to De Gasperi, November 1947, ACS PCM 1944-47 10124 1/7 s18 b112.

23. As early as January 17, 1945, Bonomi's minister at Bern, Berio, complained to the Swiss government about Fascists who were allowed to enter that country. Among the most notable were Edda Ciano, Count Volpi di Misurata, and Dino Alfieri. CLNAI, *Documenti ufficiali*, p. 68. Among other major industrialists, the CLNAI issued orders for the arrest of Antonio Benni, Guido Donegani, Alberto Pirelli, Giovanni Treccani, and Franco Marinotti. Mercuri, *L'Epurazione*, p. 133.

24. Salvatore Vento, "Milano," in Rugafiori, *Il Triangolo industriale tra ricostruzione e lotta di classe*, p. 105; *La Volontà del Popolo*, May 31, 1945.

25. Piscitelli, *Da Parri a De Gasperi*, p. 47.

26. Kogan, *Italy and the Allies*, p. 110.

27. *Italia Libera*, May 1, 1945. Regarding the situation in France, see Novick, *The Resistance versus Vichy*, pp. 158-61; Larkin, *France since the Popular Government*, pp. 124-25; Roy Macridis, "France: From Vichy to Fourth Republic," in Herz, *From Dictatorship to Democracy*, pp. 171-72.

28. Antonio Repaci insisted that the northerners trusted Rome too much in this potentially revolutionary situation. Repaci, *Fascismo vecchio e nuovo*, pp. 141-42; Mercuri, *L'Epurazione*, pp. 135-36; Stone memorandum, April 27, 1945, NARS RG331 10700/109/7; 15 Army Group Operations Instruction no. 5, "Treatment of Partisans in Northern Italy," April 12, 1945, ibid., RG331 10700/109/2.

29. Mercuri, *1943-1945*, pp. 300-301; Mercuri, *L'Epurazione*, pp. 135-36; Hughes, *The United States and Italy*, pp. 134-35.

30. *Il Popolo*, May 2, 1945.

31. Cadorna, *La Riscossa*, pp. 273-75.

32. Alatri, *Il Triangolo di morte*.

33. Police reports: Prefect of Siena to director general of PS, June 8, 1945, ACS PS sez II CIAG P189 s55-75, 14, 30, and 61; Carabiniere commander of Bologna to Interior Ministry, July 10, 1945, ibid.; Carabiniere commander of Florence to questore of Florence, August 6, 1945, ibid.; Prefect of Pisa (Perluzzo) to Interior Ministry, September 18, 1945, ibid.

34. Foreign Ministry to Interior Ministry, June 21, 1945, ACS Interior Ministry 1944-46 b36 f2861; Bologna prefectural report to minister of the interior, October 26, 1945, ACS PS CIAG Sez II, P189 s55-14. See also *Risorgi-*

mento Liberale, June 19, 1945. Regarding the opinions of Milan's Cardinal Ildefonso Schuster and the popular violence, see PWB report, May 12, 1945, NARS RG226 E190 f. 206. Execution of priests had also become a regular occurrence in Croatia. Stella Alexander, "Croatia: The Catholic Church and Clergy, 1919–1945," in Wolff and Hoensch, *Catholics, the State, and the European Radical Right,* p. 58.

35. Alatri, *Il Triangolo di morte;* Brunetti to Interior Ministry, June 10, 1945, ACS PS CIAG sez III P189 s55-14; Kirk to State Department, June 25, 1945, NARS RG59 865.00/6-2345.

36. W. R. Hare to Brigadier General Dunlop, July 20, 1945, PRO FO371 49774 ZM4189.

37. Kirk to State Department, June 25, 1945, NARS RG59 865.00/6-2345. Captain Alfred Bowman of the AC also felt that most of the assaults were the acts of "the lawless elements of the population rather than the patriots." Bowman report, June 23, 1945, NARS RG331 10700/125/9.

38. Graziani, *Ho difeso la patria,* pp. 525–52. A similar example surrounds the case of Prince Valerio Borghese, head of the "Decima MAS" amphibious unit. Borghese maintained some contacts with the OSS, which took a "special interest" in his safety. Murgia, *Il Vento del Nord,* pp. 108, 188; Algardi, *Processi ai fascisti,* pp. 201, 230. Regarding the Allies' interest in the "Decima MAS," see NARS RG226 E143, Boxes 6 and 7, ff. 84 and 103.

39. Vassalli and Sabatini, *Il Collaborazionismo e l'amnistia politica,* pp. 56–57; Brigadier General Lush to General Sir Brian Robertson, June 20, 1945, NARS ACC 10000/136/304 Box 32.

40. Lombardi to Poletti, July 10 and August 2, 1945, CLNAI Papers b62 f1.

41. *Italia Libera,* May 24, 1945; Prefect (Bolzano) to Interior, July 3, 1946, ACS Interior Ministry 1946 P277 f26738; Questore (Rome) to head of police, May 30, 1945, ACS CIAG PS sez II P189 s55-70; Legal division, AMG, to AC HQ (Caserta), July 16, 1945, NARS ACC 10000/136/304 Box 32. The Italian and Allied reports cited here indicate a desire to protect the Fascists from popular violence. The AMG legal division report also reveals concern over the popular mood. It suggests that all Fascists not on trial be transported south for reasons of public safety.

42. *L'Unità,* May 13, 1945; *Italia Libera,* May 1, 1945; Pietro Nenni, "Questo primo maggio," *Avanti!,* May 1, 1945; *Il Popolo,* May 1, 1945.

43. *Avanti!,* May 1, 1945; Pavone, "La continuità dello stato," in Piscitelli, *Italia, 1945–1948,* p. 154; Falaschi, *Gli Ultimi giorni del fascismo,* p. 101.

44. *Risorgimento Liberal,* April 30, 1945; *Italia Libera,* May 1, 1945; *Il Popolo,* April 30, 1945. The May 1 *Il Quotidiano* urged that Italians become Christians again and that the "heroic beauty" of the liberation not be marred with "repugnant gestures, cruelty, and vendetta." Regarding the DC position, see also Mantelli, "La democrazia cristiana," p. 264.

45. PWB report, June 7, 1945, PRO FO371 49872 ZM3492.

46. Gambino, *Storia del dopoguerra,* pp. 52–59, 69, 70; Piscitelli, *Da Parri a De*

Gasperi, pp. 54–60. Regarding Togliatti and Nenni, see ibid., pp. 15–16, 54–55. Giuseppe Spataro wrote that Nenni's flirtations with the PCI, coupled with the Communist party's endorsement of Marshal Tito, rendered impossible DC support for the Socialist's candidacy. Spataro, *I democratici cristiani dalla dittatura alla repubblica*, pp. 300–305.

47. Mammarella, *Italy After Fascism*, p. 103; Piscitelli, *Da Parri a De Gasperi*, Introduction. A Neapolitan friend of Piscitelli unkindly described Parri as a clown (*pazzariello*).

48. Parri, *Scritti, 1915–1975*, pp. 139–41.

49. Piscitelli, *Da Parri a De Gasperi*, p. 64; Scoppola, *La proposta politica di De Gasperi*, pp. 173–74. The Liberal Leone Cattani has also written that many of his PLI associates maintained no great fear of a Parri government and, in fact, had felt that the liberation turned out to be more moderate than what they had expected. Cattani, "Dalla caduta del fascismo al primo governo De Gasperi," p. 746. See also Mercuri, *L'Epurazione*, p. 149; Hughes, *The United States and Italy*, 145–51; Delzell, *Mussolini's Enemies*, pp. 561–63; Harris, *Allied Administration*, pp. 352–55.

50. Gambino, *Storia del dopoguerra*, p. 100.

51. Charles to Foreign Office, June 30, 1945, PRO FO371 49773 pp. 40–43.

52. Kirk to State Department, June 18, 1945, NARS RG59 865.00/6.1845.

53. The Catholic *Il Quotidiano* published almost daily stories regarding Greece from 1944 until the spring of 1945. See especially the December 10, 1944, issue. Regarding Churchill and the Greek question, see Churchill, *Triumph and Tragedy*, pp. 108–14. Regarding Yugoslavia, Togliatti came out in support of Tito in March 1945. Delzell, *Mussolini's Enemies*, p. 330. In April 1945, Umberto told an OSS informant that "the main preoccupation of the Communists at present is to gain power and more power. . . . Their stand on the Trieste issue shows their dependence on the Russian foreign policy line." OSS report, April 17, 1945, NARS RG226 E125 f. 471. The Liberals were also particularly alarmed over Tito and suspected that Nenni too wanted to hand Trieste over to the Communist Yugoslavs. Cattani, "Dalla caduta del fascismo al primo governo De Gasperi," p. 745. Regarding the conservative positions on Yugoslavia and Greece, see *Risorgimento Liberale*, July 1, 1945. In this issue Domenico Bartoldi drew parallels between the civil war in Greece and the Italian partisan violence toward Fascists. Stories described mass arrests, torture, and murder of whole families, priests, and innocents. See also *L'Osservatore Romano*, November 23, 1945; and *Risorgimento Liberale*, May 10, 12, and 13, June 23, October 7 and 27, and November 4, 1945. On May 15 and 18, 1945, the *azionisti* declared in *Italia Libera* that Tito was the aggressor and that Venezia Giulia should remain Italian.

54. Delzell, "Catholics in the Armed Resistance," p. 65. See also Delzell, *Mussolini's Enemies*, pp. 381–84, 444–47. DC animosity had already been triggered by the murder in March, in Calabria, of a priest and a local Catholic party leader. Spataro, *I democratici cristiani dalla dittatura alla repubblica*, pp. 288–89.

55. Gambino, *Storia del dopoguerra*, p. 33; Piscitelli, *Da Parri a De Gasperi*, pp. 15-16.

56. Claudio Pavone, "La continuità dello stato," in Piscitelli, *Italia, 1945-1948*, pp. 155-88.

57. Gambino, *Storia del dopoguerra*, p. 103; David W. Ellwood, *L'alleato nemico*, p. 155; Andreotti, *Intervista su De Gasperi*, pp. 41-43.

58. Appunto: Epurazione del personale delle imprese private, n.d., ACS 10124 1/7 f6 s15 b105; Boeri to Bonomi, April 16, 1945, ibid., 10124 1/7 f6 s10-4 b104; Gronchi to PCM, Ufficio studi e legislazione, March 12, 1945, ibid., 10124 1/7 f6 s15 b104. Parri refers to the Allied prodding for DLL 472 in a letter to Nenni: Parri to Nenni, July 4, 1945, ACS PCM 1944-47, 10124 1/7 f6 s10 b104. Regarding Stone's objections, see Appunto gabinetto, n.d., Stone to Bonomi, June 8, 1945, ACS PCM 1944-47 10124 1/7 f6 s9 b120; Bonomi to Stone, June 13, 1945, ibid., 10124 1/7 f6 s19 b105; Parri to Stone, September 17, 1945, ibid.; Stone to Parri, September 26, 1945, ibid.; and Parri to Stone, December 1945, ibid., 10124 1/7 f6 s19 b104. See also Flores, "L'Epurazione," in Atti del convegno internazionale organizzato a Firenze il 26-28 Marzo 1976 con il concorso della regione Toscana/INSMLI, *L'Italia dalla liberazione alla repubblica*, pp. 446-48.

59. Parri, *Scritti*, p. 143. See also PWB report, June 23, 1945, PRO FO371 49772 3361-695, pp. 272-73.

60. Mercuri, *L'Epurazione*, p. 137; Franceschelli report, ACS ACSF 1/20.

61. Roberto Tremelloni to CCE, June 28, 1945, Merzagora Papers, b33 Cont. C; Peretti Griva to Parri, September 17, 1945, ACS PCM 1944-47 10124 1/7 f6 s10 b104.

62. Harris, *Allied Administration*, p. 120. See also Comitato di liberazione nazionale dell'Alta Italia, *Verso il governo del popolo*, pp. 15-16, 30.

63. Clifford J. Norton to Foreign Office, June 29, 1945, PRO FO371 49777 File 3 1945 p. 29.

64. Mercuri, *L'Epurazione*, p. 134.

65. OSS report, August 4, 1944, NARS RG226 E125 f. 622.

66. Webster, *The Cross and the Fasces*, p. 173; Aga Rossi and Smith, *Operation Sunrise*, pp. 56-57; Delzell, *Mussolini's Enemies*, pp. 369-70; Adler, "Italian Industrials and Radical Fascism." Regarding information on Perelli, see PWB report, May 12, 1945, NARS RG226 E190 f. 206.

67. Canosa, *Le Sanzioni contro il fascismo*, pp. 88-89.

68. Bairati, *Vittorio Valletta*, p. 139; Gobbi, "Note sulla commissione d'epurazione del CLN regionale piemontese nel caso Valletta," pp. 63-73. Regarding the hearings, see also NARS RG226 L67995 (A58966). See also Castronovo, *Giovanni Agnelli*, pp. 503, 506, 510-15. GL partisans took the gravely ill Agnelli under their protection during the liberation.

69. Bairati, *Vittorio Valletta*, pp. 125-55; "Valletta," Istituto Storico della Resistenza in Piemonte (hereafter cited ISRP) C56 CLNRP fF. On September 11, Charles wrote to London that Valletta was "a most practical man . . . very

able and resourceful," who always turned down Fascist offers of positions. "It is therefore a bad sign that the extremist elements in the FIAT works should wish to get rid of him." Charles to Foreign Ministry, September 11, 1945, PRO FO371 49777 ZM4943; see also Gobbi, "Note sulla commissione d'epurazione del CLN regionále piemontese nel caso Valletta," pp. 66, 68.

70. CLNAI Papers b46 f3.

71. Archivio Agostino Rocca, b60, 61.

72. CLNAI Papers b47 f4. See also INSMLI Fondo CLNA b6: O.M., and b12, b13: Pirelli.

73. The Brown Boveri plant presented a special problem since it formed part of a larger Swiss corporation.

74. Archivi della Resistenza, Sesto San Giovanni, Fondo TIBB and Fondo Breda. See also Rugafiori, *Il Triangolo industriale tra ricostruzione e lotta di classe*, particularly Salvatore Vento, "Milano," pp. 127-60.

75. ACS PCM 1944-47 10124 1/7 so.

76. Sindacato ferrovieri italiani to Bonomi, December 7, 1944, and April 13, 1945, ACS PCM 1944-47 10124 1/7 s57 b119.

77. Interior Ministry to Bonomi (Spataro), January 23, 1945, ACS PCM 1944-47 10124 1/7 s64; Spataro to Interior Ministry, February 13, 1945, ibid. Bonomi was the minister of the interior, as well as prime minister, during this period.

78. Massimo Legnani, "'L'Utopia grande-borghese': L'associazionalismo padronale tra ricostruzione e repubblica," in Flores, *Gli Anni della Costituente*, p. 139.

79. Alexander to War Office, July 7, 1945, PRO FO371 49773 1945 file 3 3705-978 p. 3-4.

80. Schnare to State Department, July 29, 1945, NARS RG59 865.00/6.2945; Ellwood, *L'alleato nemico*, pp. 375-76.

81. Charles to Foreign Office, July 14, 1945, PRO FO371 49773. See also Foreign Office notes in margins.

82. See, for example, Delzell, *Mussolini's Enemies*, p. 501.

83. Monthly report, May 1945, Poletti Papers 194 s35. The report uses the term *camere di lavoro* for organized labor. Kirk to State Department, June 14, 1945, NARS RG59 865.00/6.1445; Alexander to War Office, July 7, 1945, PRO FO371 49773 File 3 1945, p. 22; PWB report, May 19, 1945, NARS RG226 E190 f. 206.

84. Grieco to Nenni, July 20, 1945, ACS ACSF 1/20.

85. Dino Roberto to Allied Military Command, Lombard Region, May 25, 1945, ACS ACSF 1/10.

86. Tubb to CLNAI Milan, May 31, 1945, CLNAI Papers b49 f1. Kogan, *Italy and the Allies*, p. 122.

87. Marshall to Antonicelli, July 25, 1945, CLNAI Papers b49 f1.

88. C. F. R. Harris notes that anti-Fascist anger was channeled into these official institutions and away from revolutionary people's tribunals. Harris, *Allied*

NOTES TO PAGES 174-81

Administration, p. 358. See also Repaci, "Il Processo Graziani," p. 20. Mercuri, *L'Epurazione*, p. 142, and Canosa, *Le Sanzioni contro il fascismo*, pp. 10–12.

89. Carabiniere reports, ACS Interior Ministry 1944–46 f12413 b140. See also ibid., f22208 b209.

90. Pepe, *Fascismo Rosso*. This is a strange work written by a Fascist in Celinesque style drawn heavily from newspaper sources regarding the mood, or feel, of the trials. Regarding the 200-lire figure, see Harris, *Allied Administration*, pp. 358–61.

91. Canosa, *Le Sanzioni contro il fascismo*, pp. 18–20.

92. *L'Uomo Qualunque*, June 6, 1945; Canosa, *Le Sanzioni contro il fascismo*, p. 20.

93. Canosa, *Le Sanzioni contro il fascismo*, p. 20–22; Carabinieri reports: Genoa, June 16, 1945, and Milan, June 15, 1945, ACS Interior Ministry 1944–46 f12413 b140; Protests from prefects of LaSpezia, Savona, Genoa, and Imperia, ibid.; Prefect Borlandi (Pavia) to Interior Ministry, January 25, 1946, ibid., f22208 b209.

94. Canosa, *Le Sanzioni contro il fascismo*, p. 56.

95. Ibid., pp. 7–18.

96. Mario Berlinguer, "Appunti sulla punizione dei delitti fascisti," March 30, 1945, ACS ACSF 1/3; Carlo Visconti Prasca to Parri, n.d., ACS ACSF 1/2; Mason-Macfarlane to MGS AFHQ, May 13, 1944, NARS ACC 10000/136/108, in Coles and Weinberg, *Civil Affairs*, p. 381. See also Berlinguer's note to the appellate judges indicating the nation's complete faith in them, August 12, 1945, ACS ACSF 1/2. Murgia, *Il Vento del Nord*, pp. 113–14; Guido Neppi Modona, "La Magistratura e il fascismo," in Quazza, *Fascismo e società italiana*, p. 172; Achille Battaglia, *Dieci anni dopo*, p. 353; OSS report, March 17, 1945, NARS RG59 Lot file 2688. See also Galante Garrone, "La Magistratura italiana fra fascismo e resistenza," for an account of the problem with particular attention paid to Piedmont. An excellent bibliographical essay on the problem of the judiciary in modern Italy can be found in Ungari, "Studi sulla storia della magistratura." Regarding the German judges, see Herz, "The Fiasco of Denazification in Germany," pp. 590–91. Peter Novick has written that French jurists often expressed reluctance to prosecute when it was so clearly a violation of *nullem crimen sine legge*. Novick, *The Resistance versus Vichy*, pp. 140–56.

97. CLN Liguria report, "Inconvenienti delle attuali leggi circa la punizione dei reati fascisti," n.d., for Parri and Nenni, ACS ACSF 1/2. See also "Appunto" to minister of the interior, "Stralcio della relazione del Com. Gen. CCRR 11.9.45," ACS Interior Ministry 1944–46 f16005 b168.

98. Vinciguerra, "Epurazione e depurazione"; Friedmann, *Allied Military Government*, pp. 120–21; Delzell, *Mussolini's Enemies*, pp. 67–70.

99. Delzell, *Mussolini's Enemies*, p. 172.

100. Achille Battaglia, "Il Tarlo di una legge."

101. Jemolo felt that some of the Fascist legacy should be preserved. The

Lateran Accords, for example, had been a step forward in Italy's church/state relations. Jemolo, *Per la Pace religiosa in Italia.*

102. Jemolo, "Le Sanzioni contro il fascismo e la legalità," p. 277. See also V. E. Alfieri, "La Legge contro il fascismo," pp. 682–86.

103. Already in summer 1944, the Catholics had begun to criticize prison conditions. On July 16, *Il Quotidiano* claimed that Rome's Regina Coeli was dark and putrid. With five or six men to a cell, the place was "an affront to the noble Christian spirit."

104. Murgia, *Il Vento del Nord*, pp. 123–47; Perluzzo to Parri, September 8, 1945, ACS Interior Ministry 49 f1610 b29; President Semini of Treviso PLI to Parri, September 19, 1945, ibid.; Manifesto of twenty-five families from Bassano Grappa to Parri, September 15, 1945, ibid.

105. Jacini to Parri, September 25, 1945, ACS Interior Ministry 49 f1610 b29. Jacini had served Mussolini as press liaison with the Italian occupation forces in Albania.

106. Jacini to Spataro, October 2, 1945, ACS Interior Ministry 49 f1610 b29; Jacini to Parri, October 5, 1945, ibid.

107. Capo della polizia to Interior, October 31, 1945, ACS Interior Ministry 49 f1610 b29; Peruzzo to Interior Ministry, November 14, 1945, ibid. Rachele Mussolini and Edda Ciano ended up in the penal colony on Lipari after their arrests upon crossing the frontier from Switzerland. Smyth, *Secrets of the Fascist Era*, pp. 71–72.

108. Red Cross official Gaetano Casoni to Paternò, November 14, 1945, ACS Interior Ministry 1944–46 p166 f15646 (contains the November 14, 1945, *La Patria* article). Regarding the women's camp, see Paternò to Interno, November 16, 1945, ibid.

109. Kirk to State Department, July 23, 1945, NARS RG59 865.00/7.2345; Kirk to State Department, August 6, 1945, ibid., 865.00/8.645.

110. Kirk to State Department, November 16, 1945, NARS RG59 865.00/11-1345. See also *Risorgimento Liberale*, September 22, 1945. Another who escaped was the RSI's finance minister, Domenico Pellegrini Giampietro, who slipped out of San Vittore. Stories of that occurrence received much less coverage than Donegani's escape.

111. Velio Spano, "Sua maestà, Donegani," *L'Unità*, March 15, 1945.

112. Canosa, *Le Sanzioni contro il fascismo*, p. 77; Murgia, *Il Vento del Nord*, p. 113; *La Volontà del Popolo* (Milan), July 21, 1945; *L'Unità*, July 20, 1945. CLNAI Papers b42 f2 is a folder packed with letters to the CLNAI protesting the Donegani escape; see also Capo della polizia PS to Interior Ministry, February 18, 1946, ACS Interior Ministry 46 P203 f21887.

113. Novick, *The Resistance versus Vichy*, Appendix D, pp. 209–14. See also Aron, *Histoire de l'épuration*, and Rioux, "L'épuration en France," pp. 24–32.

114. Bach, *America's Germany*, p. 169. See also Jurgensen, "British Occupation Policy after 1945"; Smith, *The West German Economy*, pp. 12–14; and Fredericksen, *The American Military Occupation of Germany*, pp. 97–98.

115. Friedmann, *Allied Military Government*, p. 121. Gimbel, *The American Occupation of Germany*, pp. 88–91, 101–10, 158–62, 171–74; Herz, "The Fiasco of Denazification in Germany," p. 577.

116. Friedmann, *Allied Military Government*, p. 113. Regarding the Soviet influence in Eastern Europe, some scholars have taken note of the particularly harsh purge that took place in Bulgaria after the war. The role of "People's Courts" and the purge of the military are described in Oren, *Revolution Administered*, pp. 85–89. See also Marshall Lee Miller, *Bulgaria during the Second World War*, pp. 213–20.

117. See, for example, Zaborowski, *Dr. Hans Globke*. Regarding Nuremberg arguments, see Wright and Mejia, *An Age of Controversy*, pp. 364–88.

118. Bowers, *Blind Eye to Murder*, p. 127; Gimbel, *The American Occupation of Germany*, p. 106.

119. Friedmann, *Allied Government*, pp. 119–20.

120. Ibid., p. 119; Bowers, *Blind Eye to Murder*, p. 219; Grosser, *Germany in Our Time*, p. 23; Gimbel, *The Allied Occupation of Germany*, p. 174. Of 12.75 million Germans who gave sufficient cause for investigation, charges were not filed for over nine million. Of 836,000 tried, 4,768 received sentences of over five years. Herz, "The Fiasco of Denazification in Germany," pp. 577–78.

CHAPTER 7

1. Pareto, *The Rise and Fall of Elites*, p. 60.

2. An interesting discussion of the negation of the partisan heritage, with particular attention to Christian Democratic activity, can be found in Emilio Franzina, "L'Azione politica e giudiziaria contro la resistenza (1945–1950)," in Istituto Gramsci Veneto, *La Democrazia cristiana dal fascismo al 18 Aprile*, pp. 220–59.

3. *Avanti!*, September 18, 1945.

4. Ibid.

5. Ibid., October 11, 1945; Vinciguerra, "Sanzioni contro il fascismo," pp. 907–9; Piscitelli, *Da Parri a De Gasperi*, pp. 78–79.

6. Regarding the 393 names, see *Il Quotidiano*, January 1, 1946. "The 393" became a media symbol of defascistization during this period. On the CLNA preference for Allied directives, see Ministry of Labor report, May 9, 1946, ACS PCM 1944–47 10124 1/7 f6 s10-2-2.

7. Mercuri, *L'Epurazione*, pp. 150–52.

8. *Il Popolo*, November 4, 1945.

9. Mario Lener, "Diritto e politica nelle sanzioni contro il fascismo e nell'-epurazione dell'amministrazione," *Civiltà Cattolica* 18, no. 95 (December 15, 1945): 378–92. The earlier articles in this series were published in the following issues of *Civiltà Cattolica*: June 6, 1945, pp. 289–300; September 1, 1945, pp. 278–89; October 20, 1945, pp. 83–93; and November 17, 1945, pp. 220–32.

10. Ferruccio Parri, *L'Espresso*, December 12, 1965, cited in Piscitelli, *Da Parri a De Gasperi*, p. 129; Nenni, *Tempo di guerra fredda*, pp. 154–58.

11. Cattani, "Dalla caduta del fascismo al primo governo De Gasperi," p. 763.

12. *New York Times*, November 25, 1945.

13. Nenni, *Tempo di guerra fredda*, p. 155; Cattani, "Dalla caduta del fascismo al primo governo De Gasperi," pp. 759–65. Regarding DC and PLI moves against Parri and, at the same time, the *Uomo Qualunque*, see Gambino, *Storia del dopoguerra*, pp. 93–99, 113. See also Harris, *Allied Administration*, pp. 362–63; Kogan, *Italy and the Allies*, pp. 124–25; and Piscitelli, *Da Parri a De Gasperi*, pp. 129–30. Nenni's comment on the end of the "Wind from the North," cited in Mercuri, "Il Primo governo De Gasperi e il problema dell'epurazione," p. 140.

14. Scoppola, *La proposta politica di De Gasperi*, pp. 166–67; Cattani, "Dalla caduta del fascismo al primo governo De Gasperi," p. 766.

15. On De Gasperi's opposition to a purge after World War I and his arrest, see Carrillo, *Alcide De Gasperi*, pp. 51–52, 86–94. On his later political and social principles, see Scoppola, *La proposta politica di De Gasperi*, pp. 89–92.

16. Richard Webster has written in De Gasperi's defense that, as foreign minister under Bonomi and Parri, he shouldered none of the responsibility for "fumbling" defascistization. Webster, *The Cross and the Fasces*, p. 177.

17. Antonio Bevere, "Fascismo e antifascismo nella prassi dell'aparato statale," in Quazza, *Fascismo e antifascismo nell'Italia repubblicana*, p. 55.

18. Peretti Griva report to Provincial Purge Commissions, October 1, 1945, ACS PCM 1944–47 10124 1/7 so.

19. Peretti Griva report, "La Nuova legge sull'epurazione della pubblica amministrazione (DLL 9 Novembre 1945 n. 702). Cenni illustrativi dei criteri sostanziali e delle norme processuali," n.d., ACS PCM 1944–47 10124 1/7 so; Peretti Griva "circolare," October 1, 1945, ibid.; Peretti Griva to De Gasperi, December 12 and 19, 1945, ibid.; Nenni to Cannarsa, December 22, 1945, ACS PCM 1944–47 10124 1/7 f4 s14-1. See also Mercuri, *L'Epurazione*, p. 155.

20. The official decree that ended the High Commission was DLL 22, February 8, 1946. The other Commissariati aggiunti had already been phased out by this period. The last to go was the office for the confiscation of Fascist profits, which was merged into the Treasury (and into obscurity) through the February 8 decree. Criticism and lack of direction determined that *commissariato* would never be effective. It was opposed by the entire business community and by the Allies, who represented British and American commercial interests in Italy. Even the attempt to sequester property of those Fascists who had been ennobled by the regime was squelched by Antonio Pesenti at the Ministry of Finance. On September 30, 1945, *Risorgimento Liberale* declared that the law had been "technically imperfect, absolutely useless, in fact contrary to its purpose." Mercuri, *L'Epurazione*, pp. 89–92. Regarding Nenni's bitter opinions on those lesser *commissariati aggiunti*, see ibid., p. 151. See also

Mercuri, "Il primo governo De Gasperi e il problema dell'epurazione," pp. 129–44.

21. Nenni circular no. 1, December 29, 1945, ACS ACSF 1/2.

22. Nenni's speech before the Socialist Congress in Florence, April 11, 1946, in Nenni, *Una Battaglia vinta.*

23. Arpesani to De Courten, December 13, 1945, ACS PCM 1944–47 10124 1/7 f5 s9.

24. ACS PCM 1944–47 10124 1/7 S6-10-3, an entire *busta* with records of this commission.

25. British embassy in Rome to Ernst Bevin, April 26, 1946, PRO FO371 60547 ZM1406. The Allied Commission assembled, during the early months of 1946, a statistical compilation of the purge in grades 1 through 6. Each subcommission of the AC obtained the figures from their corresponding Italian ministries. This may have caused some problems. For example, the numbers from the Foreign Ministry, as such, are not listed; and its equivalent subcommission is not easily discerned. A copy of the document was forwarded to the British Foreign Office on April 26, 1946.

Subcommission	Employees		Epuration Proceedings	
	Number	Investigations	Initiated	Concluded
Education	7,168	7,099	613	462
Legal	3,228	3,077	517	431
Local Government	764	764	269	225
Public Safety	729	506	249	139
Agriculture	813	742	205	160
Finance	8,290	4,169	1,267	1,007
Industry and Commerce	4,620	2,387	708	591
Transportation	3,981	3,981	679	580
Communications	442	439	221	202
Public Relations	49	49	37	20
Totals	30,084	23,213	4,765	3,817

Subcommission	Appeals		Appeals	
	Lodged	Heard	Dismissed	Retired
Education	165	86	118	26
Legal	129	52	58	55
Local Government	102	55	13	15
Public Safety	48	16	22	2
Agriculture	49	14	22	26
Finance	367	111	113	23
Industry and Commerce	190	64	130	10
Transportation	192	56	205	479

Subcommission, *continued*	Appeals		Appeals	
	Lodged	Heard	Dismissed	Retired
Communications	85	24	33	4
Public Relations	16	5	14	0
Total	1,343	483	728	640

Regarding Germany, see Herz, "The Fiasco of Denazification in Germany," pp. 590–91.

26. Upjohn circular, June 29, 1945, ACS PCM 1944–47 10124 1/7 s87-b. To the very end, Allied misgivings and doubts over sanctions were evident. An illustration of this is revealed in C. F. R. Harris's claim that the purge was successful. "The chief collaborators and dangerous Fascists were now eliminated," he wrote, "and precautions had been taken to guard against any recrudescence of Fascism. One of the chief objectives of Allied policy, on which the three-power Moscow declaration had laid such stress, had thus been accomplished." Yet in a footnote on the same page he noted, "In the end, most of the 1,879 Civil Servants who had been dismissed [*sic*] and the 671 who had been compulsorily retired were reinstated." Harris, *Allied Administration*, p. 361. See also Toynbee and Toynbee, *Survey of International Affairs*, p. 435.

27. Persico to Parri, August 16, 1945, ACS PCM 1944–47 10124 1/7 s87-H. One OSS report claimed that the Treasury had begun to hire some "Fascists and neo-Fascists" at the end of 1944. OSS report, March 17, 1945, NARS RG59 Lot file 2688.

28. Persico to Parri, September 15 and 18, 1945, and "appunto" PCM, n.d., ibid.

29. Persico to PCM, September 15, 18, 20, 26, 28, 1945, ACS PCM 1944–47 10124 1/7 s87H; Ufficio studi to PCM January 24, 1946, ibid.; Petition to De Gasperi from twenty-five purged workers, April 16, 1947, ibid., 10124 1/7 s87-i-1. See also Ortona to Pella, November 29, 1948, ibid., 10124 1/7 s87-i-1, which illustrates that the Corte dei Conti was working to get RSI personnel back into its ranks. Giovanni Gronchi also advocated a measure to facilitate readmission for administrators into private business. Gronchi to De Gasperi, June 27, 1946, ACS 10124 1/7 s6-15. See also Prefect of Nuoro to Ufficio studi PCM, February 13, 1947, ibid., 10124 1/7 s21–3. See also Ellwood, *Italy 1943–1945*, p. 144.

30. Ministry of Labor to PCM, May 9, 1946, ACS PCM 1944–47 10124 1/7 s-10-2-2; Prefect Triolo to Gronchi, January 31, 1946, ACS Interior Ministry 46 p. 211 f22327. See also Gobbi, "Note sulla commissione d'epurazione del CLN regionale piemontese nel caso Valletta," p. 61. On the replacement of CLN prefects with "career" prefects, see Carlo Galante Garrone, "Vita, morte e miracoli di un prefetto politico," *Il Ponte*, October 1946, pp. 861–76; and Scoppola, *La proposta politica di De Gasperi*, pp. 211–12.

31. Salvemini, "Italy against the Monarchy," pp. 623–24.

32. Gambino, *Storia del dopoguerra*, pp. 207–9, 215–17; Piscitelli, *Da Parri a*

De Gasperi, pp. 152–53; Mureddu, *Il Quirinale del Re*, p. 231; Mantelli, "La democrazia cristiana," pp. 266–67.

33. PWB report, May 12, 1945, NARS RG226 Box 101 f. 206. The agent remarked that Milanese opinion ran "violently against the Crown Prince." He also found Bologna to be "extremely indifferent" to Umberto. The historian Denis Mack Smith considered Umberto's political views as "flat and conventional, but not reactionary." Denis Mack Smith, *Italy and Its Monarch*, pp. 330–42. On Umberto, see also Research and Analysis report 1891, February 17, 1944, NARS RG59 Lot file.

34. "Italy's Choice," *The Economist* (June 1, 1946): 886–87; "After the Referendum," *The Economist* (June 22, 1946): 1005–6. Alberto Moravia wrote to an American audience that "the aristocracy and the rich bourgeoisie have kept their hill-top villas and in them American and English travellers meet charming ladies and distinguished men who bemoan in good English the activity of left-wing parties and sigh for the restoration of the Monarchy." Moravia, "Letter from Rome," p. 10. Regarding the church and the referendum, see Settembrini, *La Chiesa nella politica italiana*, pp. 55–61.

35. Downs, "Cynicism Wins in Italy," pp. 12–13; Nenni, *Una battaglia vinta*, p. ix; "Fine di una classe politica," *Il Ponte* 2, no. 5 (May 1946): 385–86; "2 giugno 1946: La pace," *Il Ponte* 2, no. 5 (June 1946): 485–86.

36. Aristotle, *The Athenian Constitution* (40), in Crawford and Whitehead, *Archaic and Classical Greece*, p. 465.

37. Hearder, *Italy in the Age of the Risorgimento*, pp. 236–37. Since the end of World War II, Italy has had twenty-four amnesties. *Corriere della Sera*, March 6, 1986. Herz, "The Fiasco of Denazification in Germany," p. 573.

38. Ironically, in 1904 the draft-dodging Mussolini returned to Italy from Switzerland after Victor Emmanuel's honoring the birth of Crown Price Umberto. Denis Mack Smith, *Mussolini*, p. 9.

39. Gambino, *Storia del dopoguerra*, pp. 255–56.

40. Achille Battaglia, *Dieci anni dopo*, pp. 347–48; Vassalli and Sabatini, *Il collaborazionismo e l'amnistia politica*, pp. 529–31; Canosa, *La Magistratura in Italia*, pp. 138–40; Algardi, *Processi ai fascisti*, pp. 18–19.

41. Pietro Secchia and Luigi Longo were never satisfied with the sanctions program, and their resentment was no secret within the party. Eventually Togliatti censured the rebellious Secchia. Lamberto Mercuri notes that, while the amnesty was not entirely the personal creation of Togliatti, the Communist leader never denied its paternity. Mercuri, *L'Epurazione*, p. 185; Bocca, *Palmiro Togliatti*, 458–59; Bracci, "Come nacque l'amnistia," *Il Ponte*, no. 11 (November–December 1947); Gambino, *Storia del dopoguerra*, pp. 253–56.

42. Charles F. Delzell, citing Herbert Matthews, wrote that, in Naples, the Anglo-Americans initially estimated that four hundred Italians had participated in the anti-Fascist uprising. By a year later, however, they had issued

4,900 certificates that testified to participation in the partisan cause. In March 1945 the AC estimated that half of all certificates issued were false. Mercuri, *L'Epurazione*, p. 105 n. 27.

43. Mercuri, *L'Epurazione*, pp. 145–46.

44. Friedmann, *Allied Military Government*, p. 122; Herz, "The Fiasco of Denazification in Germany," p. 580; Herz, "Denazification and Related Policies," in Herz, *From Dictatorship to Democracy*, pp. 30–31; Michael Ficter, "Non-State Organizations and the Problems of Redemocratization," in ibid., pp. 66–67.

45. *L'Uomo Qualunque*, June 12, 1946. This article claimed that another Communist journalist, Mario Alicata, had participated in the Fascist "Littorio" competition.

46. OSS report, March 24, 1945, NARS RG226 127156.

47. Togliatti, *Discorsi alla Costituente*, p. 135; *L'Unità*, June 20 and 22, 1946.

48. *L'Unità*, July 22 and 23, 1946; Togliatti, *Discorsi alla Costituente*, p. 133.

49. Togliatti to Parri, September 19, 1945, ACS PCM 1944–47 10124 1/7 s92.

50. *Il Popolo*, November 15, 1945; Charles to Bevin, November 20, 1945, PRO FO371 49780 ZM5894.

51. Sir Francis D'Arcy Godolphin Osborne to Bevin, January 9, 1946, PRO FO371 60547 ZM7; Chadwick, *Britain and the Vatican*, p. 308.

52. Paupini to Varino, August 6, 1946, ACS PCM 1944–47 10124 1/7 f22 s8/1; Varino to Paupini, August 13, 1946, ibid.; Miraglia to Justice Ministry, August 26, 1946, ibid. See also Giordani and Taylor, *Who's Who in Italy*, s.v. "Azzolini, Vincenzo."

53. For the text of DLL 625, see Vassalli and Sabatini, *Il collaborazionismo e l'amnistia politica*, pp. 579–86. See also AC monthly report for October 1945, PRO FO371 606026-1946 ZM209; Algardi, *Processi ai fascisti*, p. 11.

54. Canosa, *Le Sanzioni contro il fascismo*, p. 14.

55. ISRP, DCSA 35 Turin. Two other verdicts have no data or are ambiguous.

56. Ibid., DCSA 52 Turin, DCSA 60 Ivrea.

57. Achille Battaglia, *Dieci anni dopo*, pp. 338–39, 355; Canosa, *La Magistratura in Italia*, pp. 140–41; Canosa, *Le Sanzioni contro il fascismo*, p. 41; Algardi, *I processi ai fascisti*, p. 53.

58. Achille Battaglia, "Giustizia e politica nella giurisprudenza," in Achille Battaglia, *Dieci anni dopo*, pp. 346–51. Regarding torture, Battaglia cites Second Section rulings on September 2, 1946, March 10, 1947, March 12, 1947, July 7, 1947, and September 17, 1947.

59. CLNAI Papers b41 f14. This *busta* is crammed with letters denouncing the Liberals for the destruction of Parri's government.

60. Prefectural reports: f28049 (Alessandria), f28050 (Bologna), f28051 (Cuneo), f28052 (Forlì), f28053 (Genoa), f28060 (Imperia), f28061 (Novara), f28062 (Parma), f28063 (Verona), f28064 (Vicenza), f28066 (Pesaro), all in ACS Interior Ministry 46 P294. From Bologna came the word that the

amnesty had produced an unfavorable reaction "due to its excessive indulgence."

61. Regarding the Asti rebellion and the persistent violence in general, see Piscitelli, *Da Parri a De Gasperi*, pp. 168–75. It was also heavily reported in the August and September 1946 issues of *Risorgimento Liberale*.

62. The Pesarini report was dated February 1946. There is a chronological problem here in that the CLN prefects were, as a rule, replaced on January 1, 1946. In this case it might be reasonable to assume that Pesarini had written of the Bolognese events prior to the New Year.

63. Pesarini report to the Interior Ministry, c. February 1946, ACS CIAG PS 1947–48 b322 s1. Pesarini noted that the Communists were insisting that the blame for the "Emilian crimes" lay with the political Right and not the Left. Regarding the Carabinieri, see AC report, May 1944, NARS AC 10000/143/320, in Coles and Weinberg, *Civil Affairs*, p. 283; and Allied Commission in Italy, *Review of Allied Military Government*, pp. 59, 79.

64. Brady to Kirk, December 7, 1945, NARS AC 10000/136/351 Box 37.

65. Hopkinson report to Foreign Office, July 7, 1945, PRO FO371 49773 1945 p. 8. Hopkinson replaced Harold Caccia as British political advisor to the Allied Commission.

66. Regarding Prime Minister De Gasperi's trip to Washington and allegiance to the Western Alliance, see James Edward Miller, *The United States and Italy*, pp. 216–19; Galante, "La genesi dell'impotenza," pp. 245–303;.Galante, "La scelta americana della dc," in Istituto Gramsci Veneto, *La Democrazia cristiana dal fascismo al 18 Aprile*, pp. 112–63; Scoppola, "De Gasperi e la svolta politica del Maggio 1947," pp. 41–42; and Di Nolfo, *Le Paure e le speranze degli italiani*, pp. 235–37.

67. Carabiniere reports for Reggio, Bologna, Emilia Romagna, Ravenna, Forlì, Piacenza, and Parma, December 1946 and January 1947, all in ACS CIAG PS 1944–47 b322 s3.

68. Nicola Giudice, *Milano Sera*, September 28 and 29, 1948, ACS PS 1944–48, b322 s7. The two articles were clipped by a police archivist, who described them as "article[s] on the organization of the police in Emilia in hostile tone [in senso ostile]."

69. Bowers, *Blind Eye to Murder*, p. 328.

70. Nicola Giudice, *Milano Sera*, September 29, 1948; Luigi Longo, *L'Unità*, November 11, 1948. On September 28 Longo complained that the partisans had been targeted as enemies of Italy. Piscitelli, *Da Parri a De Gasperi*, p. 71.

71. Paolo Taviani, "Emilia: Banco di prova della democrazia," *Il Popolo*, December 1, 1948. This article can also be found in ACS PS CIAG 1947–49 b322 s7.

72. Carabiniere commander Caruso to Brunetti, November 25, 1948, ACS PS CIAG 1947–48 b322 s7.

73. Murgia, *Il Vento del Nord*, pp. 263–66; Weinberg, *After Mussolini*, pp. 14–15. Regarding Mussolini's reburial, see *New York Times*, August 31, September 1 and 2, 1957.

74. Among the most important Fascist memoirs and apologias are Acerbo, *Fra due plotoni di esecuzione*; Almirante, *Autobiografia di un fucilatore*; Amicucci, *I 600 giorni di Mussolini*; Anfuso, *Dal Palazzo Venezia al Lago di Garda*; Borghese, *Decima Flottiglia MAS*; Cione, *Nazionalismo sociale*; Dolfin, *Con Mussolini nella tragèdia*; Evola, *Gli Uomini e le rovine*; Rachele Mussolini, *La mia vita con Benito*; Pepe, *Fascismo Rosso*; Ruinas, *Pioggia sulla repubblica*; Senise, *Quando ero capo della polizia*; Silvestri, *Contro la vendetta*; Simiani, *I "giustiziati fascisti"*; Spampanato, *El Ultimo Mussolini*. Also, Mussolini's collected works were edited and published. Benito Mussolini, *Opera Omnia*.

75. Murgia, *Ritorneremo!*, pp. 211–12, 229–30; Murgia, *Il Vento del Nord*, pp. 296–99, 328–30 n. 2. Murialdi, *La Stampa italiana del dopoguerra*, pp. 106–16.

76. Weinberg, *After Mussolini*, pp. 16–17; Murgia, *Il Vento del Nord*, pp. 312–13; Murgia, *Ritorneremo!*, pp. 87–100; Rosenbaum, *Il Nuovo fascismo*; Ferraresi, "The Radical Right in Postwar Italy," pp. 71–119.

77. Robert D. Putnam, "The Political Attitudes of Senior Civil Servants in Britain, Germany, and Italy," in Dogan, *The Mandarins of Western Europe*, pp. 89, 110–13; Dogan, "The Political Power of the Western Mandarins: Introduction," in ibid., p. 13; Sabino Cassese, *La Formazione dello stato amministrativo*, pp. 227–33; and Aberbach, Putnam, and Rockman, *Bureaucrats and Politicians in Western Democracies*, pp. 115–69.

78. The Socialists gained reentry into the cabinet in 1962.

79. Nilsson, "Italy's 'Opening to the Right,'" pp. 96–97, 103, 114, 208. See also *Civitas*, June–July 1960, pp. 119, 132–33, 139.

80. Regarding the De Lorenzo attempt, see Colin, *The De Lorenzo Gambit*; Weinberg, *After Mussolini*, pp. 41–42; and Zangrandi, *Inchiesta sul SIFAR*, pp. 70–83. Regarding Borghese's attempted coup, see Weinberg, *After Mussolini*, pp. 56–57; *L'Espresso*, February 8, 1976.

81. When Juan Perón returned to Argentina from Spain in 1974, he was accompanied on the flight by Licio Gelli. Twenty-six prominent Argentine names were included on the P-2 roster. *New York Times*, October 3, 1982.

82. In the United States, the best place to start for a survey of events is the *New York Times*, particularly May 28, 29, and 31, 1981, December 2, 1981, and August 20, 1982. See also the *Wall Street Journal*, May 27 and 28, 1981, and September 20, 1982; and Gino Bianco, "The Political Crisis of the Italian State," *Survey* 26 (Winter, 1982): 65–73.

83. De Grazia, *The Culture of Consent*, p. 237.

84. Claudio Pavone, "La continuità dello stato," in Piscitelli, *Italia 1945–1948*, pp. 144–46. See also Crisafulli, "La continuità dello stato."

85. Claudio Pavone, "La continuità dello stato," in Piscitelli, *Italia 1945–1948*, pp. 228–67.

BIBLIOGRAPHY

ARCHIVES AND NEWSPAPERS

Archives

GREAT BRITAIN
Surrey
  Public Record Office
London
  Imperial War Museum

ITALY
Mantua
  Archivio dello Stato
Milan
  Istituto Nazionale per la Storia del Movimento di Liberazione in Italia
    Cesare Merzagora Papers
    CLNAI Papers
Rome
  Archivio Centrale dello Stato
  Istituto Gramsci
Sesto San Giovanni
  Istituto Storico della Resistenza
Turin
  Istituto Storico della Resistenza in Piemonte
  Fondazione Luigi Einaudi
    Archivio Agostino Rocca

SWITZERLAND
Bern
  Bundesarchiv

UNITED STATES
Washington, D.C., and Suitland, Md.
  National Archives and Records Service
New York, N.Y.
  Columbia University
    Herbert H. Lehman Library
      Charles Poletti Papers

Newspapers

Avanti!
Chicago Tribune
Civiltà Cattolica
Civitas
Corriere della Sera
Il Corriere di Roma
The Economist
L'Espresso
Italia Libera
Italia Nuova
New York Herald Tribune
New York Times
L'Osservatore Romano
Il Ponte
Il Popolo
Il Quotidiano
Ricostruzione
Risorgimento Liberale
Survey
L'Unità
L'Uomo Qualunque
Wall Street Journal

OTHER WORKS

Aberbach, Joel D., Robert D. Putnam, and Bert A. Rockman. *Bureaucrats and Politicians in Western Democracies*. Cambridge, Mass., 1981.

Acerbo, Giacomo. *Fra due plotoni di esecuzione: Avvenimenti e problemi dell'epoca fascista*. Bologna, 1968.

Adler, Franklin. "Italian Industrialists and Radical Fascism." *Telos* 30 (Winter 1976–77).

Aga Rossi, Elena. "La politica degli alleati verso l'Italia." *Storia contemporanea* no. 4 (1972).

———. "La situazione politica ed economica dell'Italia nel periodo 1944–45: I governi Bonomi." *Quaderi dell'Istituto per la storia d'Itali dal Fascismo alla Resistenza* no. 11 (1971).

Aga Rossi, Elena, and Bradley F. Smith. *Operation Sunrise: The Secret Surrender*. New York, 1979.

Alatri, Paolo. *Il Triangolo della Morte*. N.p., 1947.

Alfieri, Vittorio Enzo. "La legge contro il fascismo." *Il Ponte* 1, no. 8 (November 1945).

Algardi, Zara. *Processi ai fascisti: Anfuso, Caruso, Graziani e Borghese di fronte alla giustizia.* Florence, 1958.
————. *Il processo Caruso.* Rome, 1945.
Allied Commission in Italy. *Review of Allied Military Government and of the Allied Commission in Italy, July 10, 1943, D-Day Sicily, to May 2, 1945, German Surrender in Italy.* Rome, 1945.
Almirante, Giorgio. *Autobiografia di un fucilatore.* Milan, 1974.
Amicucci, Ermanno. *I 600 giorni di Mussolini.* Rome, 1949.
Andreotti, Giulio. *Concerto a sei voci: Storia segreta di una crisi.* Rome, 1945.
————. *De Gasperi e il suo tempo.* Milan, 1964.
————. *Intervista su De Gasperi.* Edited by Antonio Gambino. Bari, 1977.
Andreucci, Franco, et al. "I Parlamentari in Italia dall'unità ad oggi." *Italia contemporanea* no. 153 (December 1983).
Anfuso, Filippo. *Dal Palazzo Venezia al Lago di Garda.* Bologna, 1957.
Aquarone, Alberto. *L'Organizzazione dello stato totalitario.* Turin, 1965.
Arendt, Hannah. *Eichmann in Jerusalem: A Report on the Banality of Evil.* New York, 1979.
Aron, Raymond. *Histoire de l'épuration.* Paris, 1967–75.
Atti del convegno internazionale organizzato a Firenze il 26–28 Marzo 1976 con il concorso della regione Toscana/INSMLI. *L'Italia dalla liberazione alla repubblica.* Milan, 1978.
Bach, Julian. *America's Germany: An Account of the Occupation.* New York, 1946.
Badoglio, Pietro. *Italy in the Second World War.* London, 1947.
Baget-Bozzo, Gianni. *Il Partito cristiano al potere: La DC di De Gasperi e di Dossetti, 1945–1954.* Florence, 1974.
Bairati, Piero. *Vittorio Valletta.* Turin, 1983.
Barbieri, Pietro. *Il Travaglio della democrazia cristiana 1943–1947.* Rome, 1948.
Basso, Lelio. *Due Totalitarismi: Fascismo e Democrazia Cristiana.* Milan, 1951.
Battaglia, Achille. "Atti rilevanti." *Realtà Politica* no. 11 (June 1, 1945).
————. *Dieci anni dopo: Saggi sulla vita democratica italiana.* Rome, 1955.
————. "Il Tarlo di una legge: Gli 'Atti Rilevanti.'" *Realtà Politica.* June 1, 1945.
Battaglia, Roberto. *Storia della resistenza italiana.* Turin, 1964.
————. *The Story of the Italian Resistance.* London, 1957.
Becker, Josef, and Franz Knipping. *Power in Europe.* Berlin, 1986.
Ben-David, Joseph, and Terry Nichols Clark, eds. *Culture and Its Creators: Essays in Honor of Edward Shils.* Chicago, 1977.
Berle, Beatrice Bishop, and Travis Beal Jacobs, eds., *Navigating the Rapids: From the Papers of Adolf Berle.* New York, 1973.
Berlinguer, Mario. *È possibile richiedere allo Stato Vaticano l'estradizione dei criminali fascisti?* Città di Castello, 1945.
————. *In assise: ricordi di vita giudiziaria sarda.* Rome, 1945.
————. "Incongruenze e iniquità dell'amnistia." *Giustizia Penale* ff. 7–8, II, col. 484 (1946).

Bertoldi, Silvio. *Contro Salò: vita e morte del Regno del Sud*. Milan, 1984.

————. *Vittorio Emanuele III*. Turin, 1970.

Binchy, D. A. *Church and State in Fascist Italy*. New York, 1941.

Bizzarri, Elisa, et al. *Epurazione e stampa di partito, 1943–1946*. Naples, 1982.

Bocca, Giorgio. *Palmiro Togliatti*. Bari, 1977.

————. *La Repubblica di Mussolini*. Bari, 1977.

Bolla, Nino. *Colloqui con Umberto II*. Rome, 1949.

————. *Dieci Mesi di governo Badoglio*. Rome, 1944.

————. *Il Segreto di due re*. Milan, 1951.

Bonomi, Ivanoe. *Diario di un anno*. Cernusco sul Navaglio, 1947.

Borghese, Valerio. *Decima Flottiglia MAS*. Milan, 1950.

Bottomore, T. S. *Classes in Society*. New York, 1962.

Bowers, Tom. *Blind Eye to Murder: Britain, America, and the Purging of Nazi Germany—The Pledge Betrayed*. New York, 1984.

Bracci, Mario. "Come nacque l'amnistia." *Il Ponte* (November/December 1947).

————. *The Historical Factors of Italian Fascism and Our Duty*. Siena, 1945.

Brosio, Manlio. *Vittorio Valletta*. Rome, 1968.

Cadorna, Raffaele. *La Riscossa: Dal 25 luglio alla liberazione*. Milan, 1948.

Calamandrei, Piero. "Restaurazione clandestina." *Il Ponte* (November/December 1947).

Canosa, Romano. *La Magistratura in Italia dal 1945 ad oggi*. Bologna, 1974.

————. *Le Sanzioni contro il fascismo: Processi ed epurazioni a Milano negli anni 1945–1947*. Milan, 1978.

Cappelletti, Mauro. *The Italian Legal System: An Introduction*. Stanford, 1967.

Carocci, Giampiero. *Storia d'Italia dall'Unità ad oggi*. Milan, 1975.

Carrillo, Elisa. *Alcide De Gasperi: The Long Apprenticeship*. South Bend, Ind., 1965.

Cassese, Sabino. *L'Amministrazione dello Stato*. Milan, 1976.

————. *L'Amministrazione Pubblica in Italia*. Bologna, 1974.

————. *La Formazione dello stato amministrativo*. Milan, 1974.

Castronovo, Valerio. *Giovanni Agnelli: La FIAT dal 1899 al 1945*. Turin, 1977.

Cattani, Leone. "Dalla caduta del fascismo al primo governo De Gasperi." *Storia contemporanea* 5 (March 1974).

Chadwick, Owen. *Britain and the Vatican during the Second World War*. Cambridge, England, 1986.

Churchill, Winston. *Closing the Ring*. Boston, 1951.

————. *The Second World War*. Cambridge, Mass., 1953.

————. *Triumph and Tragedy*. New York, 1953.

————. *The War Speeches of the Right Honorable Winston S. Churchill*. Edited by Charles Eade. Vol. 2. Boston, 1953.

————. *Winston Spencer Churchill: His Complete Speeches, 1897–1963*. Edited by Robert Rhodes James. New York, 1974.

Cianfarra, Camilla. *The Vatican and the War*. New York, 1945.

Cione, Edmondo. *Nazionalismo sociale*. Rome, 1950.

Coakley, Robert W., and Richard M. Leighton. *Global Logistics and Strategy, 1943–1945*. Washington, D.C., 1968.

Coles, Harry L., and Albert K. Weinberg, eds. *Civil Affairs: Soldiers Become Governors*. Washington, D.C., 1964.

Comitato di liberazione nazionale dell'Alta Italia. *Documenti ufficiali del Comitato di Liberazione dell'Alt'Italia*. Milan, 1945.

———. *Verso il governo del popolo. Primo congresso del CLN regionali dell'Alt'Italia. 6–7 Giugno 1945*. N.p., n.d.

Conti, Giuseppe. "Aspetti della riorganizzazione delle forze armate nel Regno del Sud (settembre 1943–giugno 1944)." *Rivista di storia contemporanea* 6 (March 1975).

———. "La RSI e L'Attività del fascismo clandestino nell'Italia liberata dal settembre 1943 all'aprile 1945." *Storia contemporanea* 10 (1979).

Corvo, Max. *The OSS in Italy, 1942–1945: A Personal Memoir*. New York, 1989.

Crawford, Michael, and David Whitehead. *Archaic and Classical Greece: A Selection of Ancient Sources and Translation*. Cambridge, England, 1983.

Crisafulli, Vezio. "La continuità dello stato." *Revista di diritto internazionale* 47 (1964): 365–408.

Croce, Benedetto. *Croce, the King, and the Allies: July 1943–June 1944*. New York, 1950.

———. *Per una nuova vita dell'Italia*. Naples, 1944.

———. *Scritti e discorsi politici, 1943–1947*. Bari, 1963.

Czudnowski, Moshe M. *Does Who Governs Matter?* DeKalb, Ill., 1982.

Davis, Melton S. *Who Defends Rome? The 45 Days, July 25–September 8, 1943*. New York, 1972.

Deakin, F. W. *The Brutal Friendship: Mussolini, Hitler and the Fall of Italian Fascism*. New York, 1962.

———. *The 600 Days of Mussolini*. Garden City, 1966.

———. *Storia della Repubblica di Salò*. Turin, 1968.

De Antonellis, Giacomo. *Le Quattro Giornate di Napoli*. Azzate, 1973.

De Felice, Franco. "La Storiografia delle Elites nel Secondo Dopoguerra." *Italia contemporanea* no. 153 (December 1983).

De Felice, Renzo. *Interpretations of Fascism*. Cambridge, 1977.

———. *Mussolini il Duce*. 2 vols. Turin, 1974–81.

———. *Mussolini il fascista*. Vol. 1, *La conquista del potere, 1921–1925*. Turin, 1966.

———. *Mussolini il fascista*. Vol. 2, *L'organizzazione dello stato fascista, 1925–1929*. Turin, 1968.

———. *Mussolini il rivoluzionario, 1883–1920*. Turin, 1965.

———. *Storia degli ebrei italiani sotto il fascismo*. Turin, 1962.

———, ed. *L'Italia fra tedeschi e alleati: La Politica estera fascista e la seconda guerra mondiale*. Bologna, 1973.

Degli Espinosa, Agostino. *Il Regno del Sud*. Rome, 1946.

De Grazia, Victoria. *The Culture of Consent: The Mass Organization of Leisure in Fascist Italy*. New York, 1981.

Del Boca, Angelo, and Giovana Mario. *Fascism Today: A World Survey*. New York, 1969.

De Leonardis, M. "La Gran Bretagna e la monarchia italiana (1943–1946)." *Storia contemporanea* 13 (February 1981).

De Luna, G. *Storia del Partito d'Azione, 1942–1947*. Milan, 1982.

Delzell, Charles F. "Allied Policy toward Liberated Italy, 1943–1944: Repetition of Darlanism or Renewal of Democracy?" *Conspectus of History* 1 (1975).

———. "Catholics in the Italian Armed Resistance (1943–1945)." *Italian Quarterly* (Winter 1983).

———. "The Italian Anti-Fascist Resistance in Retrospect: Three Decades of Historiography." *Journal of Modern History* 47, no. 1 (March 1975).

———. *Mussolini's Enemies: The Italian Anti-Fascist Resistance*. Princeton, N.J., 1961.

Department of State. *Foreign Relations of the United States: Conferences at Malta and Yalta*. Washington, D.C., 1945.

DeWyss, M. *Rome under the Terror*. London, 1945.

Diamandourous, P. Nikoforos, et al. *A Bibliographical Essay on Southern Europe and Its Recent Transition to Political Democracy*, Florence, 1986.

Diggins, John P. *Mussolini and Italian Fascism: The View from America*. Princeton, N.J., 1972.

Dilks, D., ed. *The Diaries of Sir Alexander Cadogan, O. M. 1938–1945*, London, 1971.

Di Nolfo, Ennio. *Le Paure e le speranze degli italiani, 1943–1953*. Milan, 1986.

———. "The United States and Italian Communism, 1942–1946." *Journal of Italian History* 1 (Spring 1978).

Dogan, Mattei, ed. *The Mandarins of Western Europe: The Political Role of Top Civil Servants*. New York, 1975.

Dolfin, Giovanni. *Con Mussolini nella tragedia*. Cernusco sul Navaglio, 1949.

Dovey, H. O. "The Unknown War: Security in Italy, 1943–45." *Intelligence and National Security* 3 (1988).

Downs, Donald. "Cynicism Wins in Italy." *Nation* 162, no. 1 (January 5, 1946).

Edelman, Eric. "Incremental Involvement: Italy and United States Foreign Policy." Ph.D. dissertation, Yale University, 1981.

Ediger, Lewis J. "Post-Totalitarian Leadership: Elites in the German Federal Republic." *American Political Science Review* 54 (March 1960).

Ehrmann, John. *Grand Strategy*. Vol. 6, *October 1944–August 1945*. Edited by J. R. M. Butler. London, 1956.

Ellwood, David W. *L'alleato nemico: La politica dell'occupazione anglo-americana in Italia, 1943–1946*. Milan, 1977.

———. *Italy, 1943–1945*. New York, 1985.

————. "Ricostruzione: classe operaia e occupazione alleata in Piemonte, 1943–1946." *Rivista di storia contemporanea* no. 3 (1974).

Enciclopedia dell'antifascismo e della Resistenza. Milan, 1968–89.

Encyclopedia of the Social Sciences. New York, 1937.

Evola, Giulio. *Gli Uomini e le rovine.* Rome, 1953.

Falaschi, Candiano. *Gli Ultimi giorni del fascismo.* Rome, 1973.

Federazione Italiana Associazioni Partigiane. *Il Partito d'Azione dalle origini all'inizio della resistenza armata: Atti del Convegno (Bologna, 23–25 Marzo 1984).* Rome, 1985.

Fernando, Isabella. *Napoli Dall'8 Settembre ad Achille Lauro.* Naples, 1980.

Ferraresi, Franco. "The Radical Right in Postwar Italy." *Politics and Society* 16, no. 1 (March 1988).

Fini, Marco, ed. *1945–1975 Italia: Fascismo, antifascismo, resistenza, rinnovamento. Conversazioni promosse al Consiglio regionale lombardo nel trentennale della Liberazione.* Milan, 1975.

Fisher, Thomas R. "Allied Military Government in Italy." *Annals of the American Academy* 267 (January 1950).

Fitzgibbon, Constance. *Denazification.* London, 1969.

Flores, Marcello, et al. *Gli Anni della Costituente, Strategie dei governi e delle classi sociali.* Milan, 1983.

Forgacs, David, ed. *Rethinking Italian Fascism: Capitalism, Populism, and Culture.* London, 1986.

Fortunio, Tommasso. *La legislazione definitiva sulle sanzioni contro il fascismo: Delitti fascisti, epurazioni, avocazioni. Commento, Dottrina, Giurisprudenza.* Rome, 1946.

Francovich, Carlo, and Leone Di Benedetto, eds. *I giorni della libertà: l'aprile del '45.* Florence, 1969.

Fredericksen, Oliver J. *The American Military Ocuupation of Germany, 1945–1953.* Headquarters, U.S. Army in Europe, 1953.

Friedmann, W. *Allied Military Government of Germany.* London, 1947.

Friedrich, Carl. *American Experiences in Military Government in World War Two.* New York, 1948.

Gabrieli, Francesco. "De Monarchia." *Il Ponte* a. 2, no. 2. (February 1946).

Galante, Severino. "La genesi dell'impotenza: La politica estera della democrazia cristiana tra grande alleanza e guerra fredda (1943–1949)." *Storia delle relazioni internazionali* 2, no. 2 (1986).

Galante Garrone, Alessandro. "La Magistratura italiana fra fascismo e resistenza." *Nuova Antologia* a. 121, f. 2159 (July/September 1986).

Galante Garrone, Carlo. "Vita, morte e miracoli di un prefetto politico." *Il Ponte* 2 (October 1946).

Galkin, Alexander. "Capitalist Society and Fascism." *Social Sciences* no. 2 (1972).

Gallerano, Nicola. "L'influenza dell'amministrazione militare alleata sulla riorganizzazione dello stato italiano, 1943–1945." *Italia contemporanea* (April/June 1974).

————, ed. *L'Altro dopoguerra: Roma e il Sud, 1943–1945*. Milan, 1985.

Gallerano, Nicola, et al. *L'Italia dei quarantacinque giorni*. Milan, 1969.

Gambino, Antonio. *Storia del dopoguerra dalla liberazione al potere DC*. Rome, 1978.

Ganapini, Luigi, and Massimo Legnani. *L'Italia dei quarantacinque giorni*. Milan, 1969.

Ganapini, Luigi, et al. *La Ricostruzione nella Grande Industria: Strategia padronale e organismi di fabbrica nel Triangolo, 1945–1948*. Bari, 1978.

Garland, Albert N., and Howard McGaw Smyth. *Sicily and the Surrender of Italy*. Washington, D.C., 1965.

Garosci, Aldo. "Croce e la politica." *Rivista Storica Italiana* 95, no. 2 (1983).

Gianturco, B. "L'Amnistia e interesse dell'imputato innocente." *Giustizia Penale* f. 7–8, II, col. 487 (1946).

Gigli, Beniamino. *The Memoirs of Beniamino Gigli*. New York, 1977.

Gimbel, John. *The American Occupation of Germany: Politics and the Military, 1945–1949*. Stanford, Calif., 1968.

————. *A German Community under American Occupation: Marburg, 1945–1952*. Stanford, Calif., 1961.

Giobbio, Aldo. "Milano all'indomani della Liberazione." *Il Movimento di Liberazione in Italia* (October/December 1962).

Giordani, Igino, and Stephen S. Taylor. *Who's Who in Italy, 1957–1958*. Milan, 1958.

Gobbi, Romolo. "Note sulla commissione d'epurazione del CLN regionale piemontese nel caso Valletta." *Il Movimento di Liberazione in Italia* 89 (October 1964).

Gramsci, Antonio. *Quaderni del carcere*. 4 vols. Turin, 1975.

Grassi, G., and P. Lombardi, eds. *Democrazia al Lavoro: I verbali del CLN Lombardo, 1945–1946*. Florence, 1981.

Gravelli, Asvero. *Mussolini anedottico*. Rome, 1951.

Graziani, Rodolfo. *Ho difeso la patria*. Milan, 1947.

Gregor, A. James. *Interpretations of Fascism*. Morristown, N.J., 1974.

————. *Italian Fascism and Developmental Dictatorship*. Princeton, N.J., 1975.

Grosser, Alfred. *Germany in Our Time: A Political History of the Postwar Years*. New York, 1971.

Halperin, S. William. *Mussolini and Italian Fascism*. New York, 1964.

Harris, C. R. S. *Allied Administration of Italy, 1943–1945*. London, 1957.

Hearder, Harry. *Italy in the Age of the Risorgimento, 1790–1870*. London, 1983.

Herz, John. "The Fiasco of Denazification in Germany." *Political Science Quarterly* 63 (1948).

————. "On Reestablishing Democracy after the Downfall of Authoritarian or Dictatorial Regimes." *Comparative Politics* 10, no. 4 (July 1978).

————, ed. *From Democracy to Dictatorship*. Westport, Conn., 1982.

Howard, Michael. *The Mediterranean Strategy in the Second World War*. New York, 1968.

Hughes, H. Stuart. *The United States and Italy.* Cambridge, Mass., 1953.

Ingraham, Barton L. *Political Crime in Europe: A Comparative Study of France, Germany, and England.* Berkeley, Calif., 1979.

International Encyclopedia of the Social Sciences. New York, 1968.

Istituto Gramsci Veneto. *La Democrazia cristiana dal fascismo al 18 Aprile.* Venice, 1978.

Istituto Poligrafico dello Stato. *Raccolta ufficiale delle leggi e dei decreti della Repubblica Italiana.* Rome, 1946–47.

———. *Raccolta ufficiale delle leggi e dei decreti del Regno d'Italia.* Rome, 1944, 1945, 1946.

Jackson, W. G. F. *The Battle for Rome.* New York, 1969.

Jemolo, Arturo Carlo. *Chiesa e Stato in Italia negli ultimi cento anni.* Turin, 1971.

———. *Italia Tormentata.* Bari, 1951.

———. *Per la Pace religiosa in Italia.* Rome, 1954.

———. "Le Sanzioni contro il fascismo e la legalità." *Il Ponte* 1, no. 4 (July 4, 1945).

Jurgensen, Kurt. "British Occupation Policy after 1945 and the Problem of Re-educating Germany." *History* 68, no. 223 (June 1983).

Keller, Suzanne. *Beyond the Ruling Class: Strategic Elites in Modern Society.* New York, 1963.

Kennan, George F. *Memoirs, 1925–1950.* New York, 1969.

Kent, Peter. *The Pope and the Duce.* New Brunswick, N.J., 1982.

Kimball, Warren, ed. *Churchill and Roosevelt: The Complete Correspondence.* 3 vols. Princeton, N.J., 1984.

Kirchheimer, Otto. *Political Justice: The Use of Legal Procedure for Political Ends.* Princeton, N.J., 1961.

Knox, James MacGregor. *Mussolini Unleashed, 1939–1941: Politics and Strategy in Fascist Italy's Last War.* New York, 1982.

Kogan, Norman. *Italy and the Allies.* Cambridge, Mass., 1956.

Krippendorff, Ekkehart, ed. *The Role of the United States in the Reconstruction of Italy and West Germany.* Berlin, 1981.

Laqueur, Walter, ed. *Fascism: A Reader's Guide, Analysis, Interpretations, Bibliography.* Berkeley, Calif., 1976.

Larkin, Maurice. *France since the Popular Government: Government and People, 1936–1986.* Oxford, 1988.

Lazzero, Ricciotti. *Le Brigate nere: Il partito armato della repubblica di Mussolini.* Milan, 1983.

Legnani, Massimo, ed. *L'Italia dal 1943 al 1948: Lotte politiche e sociali.* Turin, 1973.

———. *Politica e amministrazione nelle repubbliche partigiane: Studio e documenti.* Milan, 1968.

———. *Regioni e Stato dalla resistenza alla costituzione.* Bologna, 1975.

Levi, Riccardo. "L'Azione economica e sociale dei CLN dell'Alt'Italia." *Il Ponte* (November/December 1947).

Lewis, Norman. *Naples '44*. New York, 1978.

Lyttleton, Adrian. *The Seizure of Power: Fascism in Italy, 1919–1925*. London, 1973.

———, ed. *Italian Fascisms: From Pareto to Gentile*. New York, 1973.

Mack Smith, Denis. *Italy and Its Monarchy*. New Haven, Conn., 1989.

———. *Mussolini*. London, 1981.

———. *Mussolini: A Biography*. New York, 1983.

Macmillan, Harold. *The Blast of War, 1939–1945*. New York, 1968.

———. *War Diaries*. New York, 1984.

Magister, Sandro. *La Politica Vaticana e L'Italia*. Rome, 1979.

Maier, Charles. *Recasting Bourgeois Europe: Stabilization in France, Germany, and Italy in the Decade after World War I*. Princeton, N.J., 1975.

———. "The Two Postwar Eras and the Conditions for Stability in Twentieth-Century Europe." *American Historical Review* 86, no. 2 (April 1981): 327–67.

Mammarella, Giuseppe. *Italy after Fascism: A Political History, 1943–1965*. South Bend, Ind., 1966.

Mantelli, Brunello. "La democrazia cristiana, 1943–1948: La costruzione del partito borghese di massa." *Rivista di storia contemporanea* 5 (1976).

Maroni, Lorenzo. "Alta Corte e decadenza dalla carica di Senatore." *Giustizia Penale* 1 (1947).

Massobrio, Franco, and Umberto Guglielmotti. *Storia della Repubblica Sociale Italiana*. Rome, 1968.

Mayer, Arno. "The Lower Middle Class as Historical Problem." *Journal of Modern History* 47 (September 1975): 409–36.

———. *The Persistence of the Old Regime: Europe to the Great War*. New York, 1981.

Mengozzi, Dino. *L'Epurazione nella città del Duce*. Rome, 1982.

Mercuri, Lamberto. "Amministrazione alleata e vita politica nel 'Regno del Sud.'" *Rivista trimestrale di Scienza Politica e dell'Amministrazione* no. 3 (1972).

———. *L'Epurazione in Italia, 1943–1948*. Cuneo, 1988.

———. *1943–1945: Gli Alleati e l'Italia*. Naples, 1975.

———. "Il primo governo De Gasperi e il problema dell'epurazione." In *Le forze armate dalla liberazione all'adesione dell'Italia alla Nato*, edited by Ministero della Difesa. Rome, 1986.

———. "La Sicilia e gli Alleati." *Storia contemporanea* 4 (1972).

———, ed. *L'Azionismo nella storia d'Italia*. Ancona, 1988.

Merzagora, Cesare. *I Pavidi*. Milan, 1955.

Michels, Robert. *Political Parties*. Glencoe, 1958.

Miller, James Edward. "The Search for Stability: An Interpretation of American Foreign Policy in Italy, 1943–1946." *Journal of Italian History* 1 (Fall 1978).

———. "Taking Off the Gloves: The United States and the Italian Elections of 1948." *Journal of Diplomatic History* 7, no. 1 (Winter 1983).

———. *The United States and Italy, 1940–1950: The Politics and Diplomacy of Stabilization*. Chapel Hill, N.C., 1986.

Miller, Marshall Lee. *Bulgaria during the Second World War.* Stanford, Calif., 1975.

Mills, C. Wright. *The Power Elite.* New York, 1956.

Missori, Mario. *Governi, alti cariche dello stato e prefetti del Regno d'Italia.* Rome, 1978.

Moravia, Alberto. "Letter from Rome." *Nation* 162, no. 1 (January 5, 1946).

Mosca, Gaetano. *The Ruling Class.* New York, 1939.

Mureddu, Matteo. *Il Quirinale del Re.* Milan, 1978.

Murgia, Pier Giuseppe. *Ritorneremo! Storia e cronaca del fascismo dopo la Resistenza (1950–1953).* Milan, 1976.

———. *Il Vento del nord: Storia e cronaca del fascismo dopo la Resistenza (1945–1950).* Milan, 1975.

Murialdi, Paolo. *La Stampa italiana del dopoguerra.* Bari, 1978.

Murphy, Robert. *Diplomat among Warriors.* Garden City, N.Y., 1964.

Mussolini, Benito. *Opera Omnia.* Edited by Edoardo Susmel and Duilio Susmel. Florence, 1960.

Mussolini, Rachele. *La Mia Vita con Benito.* Milan, 1948.

Nenni, Pietro. *Tempo di guerra fredda: Diari 1943–1956.* Milan, 1981.

———. *Una Battaglia vinta.* Rome, 1946.

———. *Il Vento del Nord.* Turin, 1978.

Neufeld, Maurice F. "The Failure of Allied Military Government in Italy." *Public Administration Review* 6 (April 1946).

Nilsson, Karl Robert. "Italy's 'Opening to the Right': The Tambroni Experiment of 1960." Ph.D. dissertation, Columbia University, 1964.

Nolte, Ernst. *Three Faces of Fascism: Action Française, Italian Fascism, National Socialism.* New York, 1969.

Novick, Peter. *The Resistance versus Vichy.* New York, 1968.

Oren, Nissan. *Revolution Administered: Agrarianism and Communism in Bulgaria,* Baltimore, Md., 1973.

Orfei, Ruggero. *L'Occupazione del Potere: I democristiani, '45–'75.* Milan, 1976.

Palmer, R. R. *Twelve Who Ruled: The Committee of Public Safety during the Terror.* New York, 1965.

Pareto, Vilfredo. *The Mind and Society.* New York, 1935.

———. *The Rise and Fall of Elites.* New York, 1979.

———. *Sociological Writings.* London, 1966.

Parri, Ferruccio. *Scritti, 1915–1975.* Rome, 1976.

Parry, Geraint. *Political Elites.* London, 1971.

Pavone, Claudio. "Sulla continuità dello Stato nell'Italia 1943–1945." *Rivista di storia contemporanea* no. 2 (1974).

———. "Tre governi e due occupazioni." *Italia contemporanea* no. 160 (September 1985).

Pepe, Mario (Humanus). *Fascismo Rosso.* Rome, 1946.

Peretti-Griva, Domenico. "Il fallimento dell'epurazione." *Il Ponte* (1947).

Pettinato, Concetto. *Purgatorio.* Rome, 1949.

Pieri, Piero, and Giorgio Rochat. *Pietro Badoglio*. Turin, 1974.

Pinzani, Carlo. "Gli Stati Uniti e la questione istituzionale in Italia, 1943–1946." *Storia contemporanea* 134 (January 1979): 3–44.

Pirro, Ugo. *A Thousand Betrayals*. New York, 1963.

Piscitelli, Enzo. *Da Parri a De Gasperi: Storia del dopoguerra, 1945–1948*. Milan, 1975.

————. *Storia della resistenza romana*. Bari, 1965.

Piscitelli, Enzo, et al. *Italia, 1945–1948: Le origini della Repubblica*. Turin, 1974.

Plumb, J. H. *The Origins of Political Stability: England, 1675–1725*. Boston, 1967.

Poletti, Charles. "Poletti rivela." *Il Sud* a. 1, no. 25 (November 2, 1947).

Pollard, John R. *The Vatican and Italian Fascism: A Study in Conflict*. New York, 1985.

Poulantzas, Nicos. *Political Power and Social Classes*. Thetford, Norfolk, 1971.

Pugliese, Emanuele. *Io difendo l'esercito*. N.p., 1946.

Quazza, Guido, ed. *Fascismo e antifascismo nell'Italia repubblicana*. Turin, 1976.

————. *Fascismo e società italiana*. Turin, 1973.

Repaci, Antonio. *Fascismo vecchio e nuovo*. Turin, 1954.

————. "Il Processo Graziani." *Il Movimento di Liberazione in Italia* nos. 17–18 (1952).

Richard, Colin. *The De Lorenzo Gambit*. Beverly Hills, Calif., 1976.

Rioux, Jean-Pierre. "L'Epuration en France (1944–1945)." *L'Histoire* no. 5 (October 1978).

Rochat, Giorgio. "La crisi delle forze armate nel 1943–1945." *Rivista di storia contemporanea* 7 (1978).

Rosenbaum, Petra. *Il Nuovo fascismo*. Milan, 1975.

Rossi, Ernesto. *Padroni del vapore e fascismo*. Bari, 1966.

Rossini, Giuseppe, ed. *Democrazia cristiana e costituente nella società del dopoguerra*. Rome, 1980.

Rugafiori, Paride, Salvatore Vento, and Fabio Levi. *Il Triangolo industriale tra ricostruzione e lotta di classe, 1945–1948*. Milan, 1974.

Ruinas, Stanis. *Pioggia sulla repubblica*. Rome, 1946.

Sabatini, G. "Il sistema processuale per la repressione dei crimini fascisti." *Giustizia Penale* 3 (1946).

Salomon, Ernst von. *Fragebogen, The Questionnaire*. New York, 1955.

Salvadori, Max. *Brief History of the Patriot Movement in Italy, 1943–1945*. Chicago, 1954.

Salvati, M. "La Dirigenza dei ministri economici, 1945–1951." *Italia contemporanea* no. 153 (December 1983).

Salvemini, Gaetano. "Friends, Romans, Aristocrats." *Nation* (November 1944).

————. "Italy against the Monarchy." *Nation* 162, no. 22 (June 1, 1946).

————. *The Origin of Fascism in Italy*. New York, 1973.

Sarti, Roland. *Fascism and Industrial Leadership in Italy, 1919–1940.* Berkeley, Calif., 1971.

Sauer, Wolfgang. "National Socialism: Totalitarianism or Fascism?" *American Historical Review* 73, no. 2 (December 1967).

Schmid, R. "Denazification: A German Critique." *American Perspective* 2 (October 1948).

Schuster, Ildefonso. *Gli Ultimi tempi di un regime.* Milan, 1946.

Scoccimarro, Mauro. *Il Secondo Dopoguerra.* Rome, 1946.

Scoppola, Pietro. "De Gasperi e la svolta politica del Maggio 1947." *Il Mulino* no. 231 (January/February 1974).

————. *La proposta politica di De Gasperi.* Bologna, 1988.

Secchia, Pietro. *Lotta anti-fascista e giovani generazioni.* Milan, 1973.

Senise, Carmine. *Quando ero capo della polizia.* Rome, 1946.

Serant, Paul. *I Vinti della liberazione.* Milan, 1966.

Servadio, Gaia. *Luchino Visconti: A Biography.* London, 1982.

Setta, Sandro. *L'Uomo Qualunque 1944–1948.* Bari, 1975.

Settembrini, Domenico. *La Chiesa nella politica italiana, 1944–1963.* Pisa, 1964.

Sforza, Carlo. *Fini e limiti dell'epurazione.* Rome, 1945.

————. *L'Italia dal 1924 al 1944 quale io la vidi.* Rome 1945.

————. *Monarchia o Repubblica.* Milan, 1946.

————. *Le Sanzioni contro il fascismo: Quel che si è fatto e quel che deve farsi. Dichiarazioni e documenti inediti.* Rome, 1945.

Sheppard, G. A. *The Italian Campaign, 1943–1945.* New York, 1968.

Shils, Edward. "Charisma, Order, and Status." *American Sociological Review* 30 (1965): 199–213.

Silvestri, Carlo. *Contro la vendetta.* Milan, 1948.

————. *Mussolini: Graziani e l'antifascismo.* Milan, 1949.

Simiani, Carlo. *I "giustiziati fascisti" dell'aprile 1945.* Milan, 1949.

Simpson, Christopher. *Blowback: America's Recruitment of Nazis and Its Effects on the Cold War.* New York, 1988.

Smith, Eric Owen. *The West German Economy.* New York, 1983.

Smyth, Howard M. "Italy: From Fascism to the Republic." *Western Political Quarterly* 1 (1948).

————. *Secrets of the Fascist Era.* Carbondale, Ill., 1975.

Snyder, Louis L., ed. *National Socialist Germany: Twelve Years That Shook the World.* Malabar, Fla., 1984.

Soleri, Marcello. *Memorie.* Turin, 1949.

Spampanato, Bruno. *El Ultimo Mussolini.* Barcelona, 1950.

Spataro, Giuseppe. *I democratici cristiani dalla dittatura alla repubblica.* Milan, 1968.

Spriano, Paolo. *Storia del Partito comunista italiano.* Vol. 5, *La Resistenza: Togliatti e il partito nuovo.* Turin, 1976.

Sylos Labini, Paolo. *Saggio sulle classi sociali.* Bari, 1982.

Tamaro, Attilio. *Due Anni di storia.* 3 vols. Rome, 1948–50.

————. *Vent'Anni di storia, 1922–1943*. Rome, 1953–54.

Tamburrano, Giuseppe. *Palmiro Togliatti*. Bari, 1979.

Tannenbaum, Edward R. *The Fascist Experience: Italian Society and Culture, 1922–1945*. New York, 1972.

Taylor, Myron C. *Vaticano e Stati Uniti, 1939–1952: Dalle carte di Myron C. Taylor*. Edited by Ennio Di Nolfo. Milan, 1978.

Togliatti, Palmiro. *Discorsi alla Costituente*. Rome, 1973.

————. *Lectures on Fascism*. New York, 1976.

————. *Linea di una Politica*. Milan, 1948.

————. *On Gramsci and Other Writings*. Edited by Donald Sassoon. London, 1979.

Toynbee, Arnold, and V. M., Toynbee, eds. *Survey of International Affairs, 1939–1946: The Realignment of Europe*. London, 1955.

Trabucchi, A. *I vinti hanno sempre torto*. Turin, 1947.

Traniello, F. "La Formazione della dirigenza democristiana." *Italia contemporanea* no. 153 (December 1983).

Trevelyan, Raleigh. *Rome, 1944: The Battle for the Eternal City*. New York, 1982.

Ungari, Paolo. "Studi sulla storia della magistratura, 1948–1968." *Storia contemporanea* 1, no. 2 (1970).

Urban, Joan Barth. *Moscow and the Italian Communist Party: From Togliatti to Berlinguer*. Ithaca, N.Y., 1986.

Valiani, Leo. *Dall'antifascismo alla resistenza*. Milan, 1959.

Valiani, L., G. Bianchi, and E. Ragionieri. *Azionisti: cattolici e comunisti nella Resistenza*. Milan, 1971.

Vassalli, G. "La collaborazione col tedesco invasore nella giurisprudenza delle sezioni speciali della cassazione." *Giustizia Penale* (1945).

————. *La confisca dei beni: Storia recente e profili dommatici*. Padua, 1951.

————. "Guardia nazionale repubblicana e presunzione di collaborazione col tedesco invasore." *Giustizia Penale* 2 (1946).

————. "Il Processo alle responsabilità del fascismo." *Socialismo*. March 10, 1945.

Vassalli, G., and G. Sabatini. *Il collaborazionismo e l'amnistia politica*. Rome, 1946.

Villari, Luigi. *The Liberation of Italy, 1943–1947*. Appleton, Wis., 1959.

Vinciguerra, Mario. "Epurazione e depurazione." *La Nuova Europa*. January 7, 1945.

————. "Sanzioni contro il fascismo." *Enciclopedia del diritto* 16 (1967).

Warner, Geoffrey. *Pierre Laval and the Eclipse of France*. London, 1968.

Weber, Max. *From Max Weber*. London, 1957.

————. *Max Weber on Charisma and Institution Building: Selected Papers*. Edited by S. N. Eisenstadt. Chicago, 1977.

Webster, Richard K. *The Cross and the Fasces: Christian Democracy and Fascism in Italy*. Stanford, Calif., 1960.

Weinberg, Leonard. *After Mussolini: Italian Neo-Fascism and the Nature of Fascism*. Washington, D.C., 1979.

Wolff, Richard J., and Jorg Hoensch, eds. *Catholics, the State, and the European Radical Right, 1918–1945*. New York, 1987.

Woodward, Llewellyn. *British Foreign Policy in the Second World War*. 3 vols. London, 1962–71.

Woolf, S. J., ed. *The Rebirth of Italy, 1943–1950*. London, 1972.

Wright, Gordon, and Arthur Mejia, Jr., eds. *An Age of Controversy*. Alternate Edition. Chicago, 1981.

Zaborowski, Jan. *Dr. Hans Globke, The Good Clerk*. Poznan, 1962.

Zangrandi, Ruggero. *Inchiesta sul SIFAR*. Rome, 1970.

———. *L'Italia tradita: 8 Settembre, 1943*. Milan, 1971.

———. *1943 (i.e. Millenovecentoquarantatre) 25 Luglio–8 Settembre*. Milan, 1964.

INDEX

Acerbo, Giacomo, 67, 138, 143, 214, 222
Acquarone, Pietro, 15
Action Party. See *Partito d'Azione*
Administrative Order Number 1, 65–66
Advocate General's Office, 83
Agnelli, Giovanni, 166
Air Force, Ministry of the, 88, 113
Albani, Giuseppe "Gobbo," 126–27
Alessandria, 177–78
Alexander, Harold, 25, 170, 171
Alfieri, Dino, 214, 222
Allied Commission (AC), 12, 25–27, 36, 38, 41, 53, 69, 113, 158, 172–73, 209. *See also* Allies
Allied Control Commission (ACC). *See* Allied Commission (AC)
Allied Military Government (AMG), 12, 25–27, 36, 39, 44, 51, 93–95, 151, 196, 203. *See also* Allies
Allied Military Government of Occupied Italy (AMGOT). *See* Allied Military Government (AMG)
Allies, 12, 13, 21–34, 35, 36, 38–39, 45–46, 107, 111, 112–18; opinions of Italians, 28–29; and Caruso trial, 93–95; and November 1944 cabinet crisis, 113–18; on purge, 130, 170–72, 203; and Roatta trial, 134–37; and relations with CLNAI at liberation, 150–52; and northern violence, 153–55, 217–18; and Ferruccio Parri, 158–60, 196; and Left, 159–60, 171; and denazification in Germany, 187–89; and Victor Em-

manuel's abdication, 204–5
Almirante, Giorgio, 223
Alto commissariato per le sanzioni contro il fascismo. See High Commission for Sanctions against Fascism
Amendola, Giovanni, 157
Amicucci, Ermanno, 222–23
Amnesty, 190–91, 206–11; protests over, 215–16
Anfuso, Filippo, 134, 214, 224
Antonicelli, Franco, 167, 173
Aosta, Duke of, 124
Arangio-Ruiz, Vincenzo, 39, 42
Arpesani, Giustino, 201–2, 203
Assize Courts, 143, 173–79, 185, 194, 209, 210, 212–14
Associazione nazionale partigiani italiani, 215–16, 219
Azzarino, Ares, 167–68
Azzi, Armando, 137
Azzolini, Vincenzo: trial of, 97–99; press reaction to trial of, 98–99

Badoglio, Pietro, 11–24 passim, 29, 32, 34, 37–39, 42, 46, 47, 51, 58, 60, 75, 101, 142; and Bari Congress, 40, 41, 42; leaves office, 53–54; relations with Communists, 56–57; and Charles Poletti, 66; rumors of arrest, 115–17
Banca Commerciale Italiana, 165
Bari: Congress, 40–41
Barletta, Gesualdo, 67
Basile, Carlo Emanuele, 174–76
Battaglia, Achille, 180
Battaglia, Roberto, 142
Bencivenga, Roberto, 51